RADICAL CRIMINOLOGY

SAGE FOCUS EDITIONS

1. **POLICE AND SOCIETY,** edited by David H. Bayley

2. **WHY NATIONS ACT: Theoretical Perspectives for Comparative Foreign Policy Studies,** edited by Maurice A. East, Stephen A. Salmore, and Charles F. Hermann

3. **EVALUATION RESEARCH METHODS: A Basic Guide,** edited by Leonard Rutman

4. **SOCIAL SCIENTISTS AS ADVOCATES: Views from the Applied Disciplines,** edited by George H. Weber and George J. McCall

5. **DYNAMICS OF GROUP DECISIONS,** edited by Hermann Brandstatter, James H. Davis, and Heinz Schuler

6. **NATURAL ORDER: Historical Studies of Scientific Culture,** edited by Barry Barnes and Steven Shapin

7. **CONFLICT AND CONTROL: Challenge to Legitimacy of Modern Governments,** edited by Arthur J. Vidich and Ronald M. Glassman

8. **CONTROVERSY: Politics of Technical Decisions,** edited by Dorothy Nelkin

9. **BATTERED WOMEN,** edited by Donna M. Moore

10. **CRIMINOLOGY: New Concerns,** edited by Edward Sagarin

11. **TO AUGUR WELL: Early Warning Indicators in World Politics,** edited by J. David Singer and Michael D. Wallace

12. **IMPROVING EVALUATIONS,** edited by Lois-ellin Datta and Robert Perloff

13. **IMAGES OF INFORMATION: Still Photography in the Social Sciences,** edited by Jon Wagner

14. **CHURCHES AND POLITICS IN LATIN AMERICA,** edited by Daniel H. Levine

15. **EDUCATIONAL TESTING AND EVALUATION: Design, Analysis, and Policy,** edited by Eva L. Baker and Edys S. Quellmalz

16. **IMPROVING POLICY ANALYSIS,** edited by Stuart S. Nagel

17. **POWER STRUCTURE RESEARCH,** edited by G. William Domhoff

18. **AGING AND SOCIETY: Current Research and Policy Perspectives,** edited by Edgar F. Borgatta and Neil G. McCluskey

19. **CENTRE AND PERIPHERY: Spatial Variation in Politics,** edited by Jean Gottmann

20. **THE ELECTORATE RECONSIDERED,** edited by John C. Pierce and John L. Sullivan

21. **THE BLACK WOMAN,** edited by La Frances Rodgers-Rose

22. **MAKING BUREAUCRACIES WORK,** edited by Carol H. Weiss and Allen H. Barton

23. **RADICAL CRIMINOLOGY: The Coming Crises,** edited by James A. Inciardi

RADICAL CRIMINOLOGY

The Coming Crises

Edited by
JAMES A. INCIARDI

 SAGE PUBLICATIONS   Beverly Hills   London

Chapters 4, 5, 6, and 18 in this book originally appeared in a special issue of *Criminology: An Interdisciplinary Journal* (Volume 16, Number 4, February 1979).

For information address:

SAGE Publications, Inc.
275 South Beverly Drive
Beverly Hills, California 90212

SAGE Publications Ltd
28 Banner Street
London EC1Y 8QE, England

Printed in the United States of America

Library of Congress Cataloging in Publication Data

Main entry under title:

Radical criminology.

(Sage focus editions ; v. 23)
Includes bibliographical references and index.
1. Crime and criminals. I. Inciardi, James A.
II. Series.
HV6021.R3   364   80-14408
ISBN 0-8039-1489-X
ISBN 0-8039-1490-3 (pbk.)

FIRST PRINTING

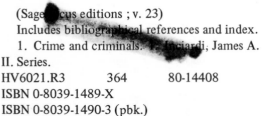

CONTENTS

Introduction
    James A. Inciardi   7

PART I. THE STATE OF THE PARADIGM

1. The Career of a Confusion: Radical Criminology in Britain
    Geoff Mungham   19

2. Radical Criminology in the United States:
An Interpretive Understanding
    David O. Friedrichs   35

3. Conflict Theory in Criminology
    C. Ronald Huff   61

PART II. DEBATE AND CONTROVERSY

4. Analyzing Official Deviance: For Nonpartisan
Conflict Analyses in Criminology
    Austin T. Turk   78

5. The Contemporary Crises of Marxist Criminology
    Carl B. Klockars   92

6. The New Criminology Is the Old Baloney
    Jackson Toby   124

7. Further Critical Thoughts on Marxist Criminology:
Comments on Turk, Toby, and Klockars
    Ronald L. Akers   133

8. A Tower of Babel: Marxist Criminologists and
Their Critics
    Milton Mankoff   139

9. Carl Klockars vs. the "Heavy Hitters":
   A Preliminary Critique
   David O. Friedrichs   149

10. Praxis and Radical Criminology in the United States
    Elmer H. Johnson   161

PART III. THE COMING CRISES

11. "Left-Wing" Criminology—An Infantile Disorder?
    Steven Spitzer   169

12. Some Problems of Credibility in Radical Criminology
    David Shichor   191

13. Conflict Theory and Differential Processing:
    An Analysis of the Research Literature
    Franklin P. Williams III   213

14. The New Criminology: Acceptance Within Academe
    William V. Pelfrey   233

15. Teaching Critical Criminology: The Ethical Issues
    Stephen J. Pfohl   245

PART IV. FUTURE CONCERNS AND DIRECTIONS

16. Radical Criminology as Functionalist Theory: The Nature
    and Implications of an Unacknowledged Identity
    Anne E. Pottieger   257

17. Can the "Old" and "New" Criminologies Be Reconciled?
    Edwin M. Schur   277

18. After Labeling and Conflict: An Aspect
    of Criminology's Next Chapter
    Laurin A. Wollan, Jr.   287

19. A Radical Alternative to "Radical" Criminology
    Harold E. Pepinsky   299

    About the Authors   316

INTRODUCTION

James A. Inciardi

During recent years a variety of writings have announced an alternative perspective for the field of criminology—the "new" criminology, "radical" criminology, "critical" criminology, "conflict" criminology, or "Marxist" criminology. The perspective is *new* and *radical* in that it departs somewhat from the mainstream or traditional criminological emphases on the nature and etiology of criminal behavior; it is *conflict* oriented and *critical* in that it focuses more fully on value and cultural differences, social conflicts, racism, and sexism as sources of crime and deviance in contemporary society; and it is *Marxist* in that a number of its representatives argue that law—and, by extension, crime—and the structure of individual and group interactions which support legal codes flow from the manner in which the relations of economic production are organized. Although there is noticeable variation among theorists whose perspectives have often alternatively been termed "new" or "critical," the vast majority of their numbers have been loosely grouped under the label of *radical criminology*.

To provide a clear and specific distinction between radical criminology and traditional criminology would be an impossible task, for the two schools of thought do have numerous converging lines of emphasis. Both radical and traditional thought focus to a great extent on etiology. In addition, the issues of value differences and social conflict as sources of crime and deviance can be found in earlier mainstream criminology. And to even further complicate any distinctions, the range in both theory and ideology of the radical perspective is significant. At one level, for example, it has been argued that there exists a closely knit "ruling class" which is bent upon the exploitation of the masses. By contrast, alternative lines of inquiry maintain the proposition that crime and exploitation are manifestations of the inherent contradictions of the political and economic organization of monopoly capitalism. Yet what unifies much of radical criminological thought, while at the same time separating it from mainstream criminology, is the emphasis on the notion that crime control cannot be ultimately realized within the prevailing socioeconomic order of modern society.

The emergence of radical criminology has elicited considerable debate in its challenge to traditional criminology. There are those who maintain that the radical perspective has little to say, suggesting that its entire contribution to the field of criminology might be summed up in the statement—"fascist imperialism and the political and economic order of monopoly capitalism are the handmaidens of repression, let me count the ways!" Others have indicated that the perspective is historically naive and empirically shallow. And its most damning criticism has come from those who argue that the radical perspective is quick to condemn mainstream liberal criminology for its intellectual domination of the field, while its own position advocates replacing one kind of domination with another. The validity of such claims will not be addressed in this introductory essay since they are explored at length throughout this volume by representatives from many sides of the debate. Nevertheless, since these criticisms do exist, and since radical thought suggests promise for liberating segments of mainstream criminology from what has been called its superficial reformism and correctionalizing trends, the *coming crises* have clearly emerged.

The coming crises, designated as the theme of this volume, are numerous indeed, for *both* radical and traditional criminology, and for the study of social problems in general. Among the crises for radical criminology are its credibility and acceptance. When such phrases as "historically naive," "empirically shallow," "emotionally based," "intellectually biased," and "scholastically bankrupt" are used to typify the works of radical theorists, and when such accusations appear repeatedly in the literature, uttered by both known and unknown traditionalists (and even some radicals), a crisis does indeed exist. In the absence of credibility and acceptance by the wider community of criminological scholars, the purpose of radical thought can never be achieved and its impact can never come to pass. And there are crises for mainstream criminology as well. The discipline of criminology has endured, now, for many generations, evolving a systematic body of knowledge which focuses on the study of crime from a position which is considered, by many, as almost sacred. The mere emergence of radical criminology represents a crisis within the mainstream of the field. The theoretical traditions which have been accepted for so long are being challenged; new paradigms are being pushed to the forefront; and alternative perspectives are competing for attention.

Perhaps the greatest crisis is one which exists within the study of crime, deviance, and social problems in general. Criminal behavior and the full range of phenomena which have long since been viewed as "social casualty statuses" have been traditionally approached as irritating and sometimes pervasive problems in an otherwise orderly social world. But the approaches to solving the problems of crime and "social disorganization" are clearly problematic. The social and behavioral sciences have yet to fully and effectively deal with the very issues they have targeted as of primary concern. And the crisis, then, circumscribes the need for a revolution in the mechanisms through which crime and social problems ought to be addressed. Both radical and traditional criminology have called for an intellectual revolution and a push for a new quest for knowledge. The nature of such a revolution, of course, has yet to be determined.

The texture of the *coming crises* and the debates between traditional and radical criminology were highlighted with the very decision of the American Society of Criminology to focus on the subject of radical thought. For years, the works of radical theorists have only infrequently appeared—for whatever reason, justifiable or otherwise—in the traditional criminology journals. Perhaps the material, because of its very subject matter, was summarily rejected; or perhaps, anticipating rejection, such work was never submitted for review. Most likely, at least a combination of both were operative. The end product was the emergence of a series of radically oriented professional journals which welcomed the products of this new perspective—*Crime and Social Justice, Contemporary Crises, The Insurgent Sociologist.* The outcome of this enterprise, however, was not only a greater number of publications from the radical perspective, but also the continued isolation of radical criminologists. This is not to say that the radicals themselves were unknown, for indeed, such figures as Richard Quinney, William J. Chambliss, and others were very widely published. But nevertheless, a significant portion of the radical work was not coming to the attention of those who were regular subscribers to the major journals in the field—*Journal of Criminal Law and Criminology, Crime and Delinquency, Criminology, Journal of Research in Crime and Delinquency.*

As the newly appointed editor of *Criminology* in 1978, I had hoped to make some preliminary inroads into this long-standing dilemma. Previous issues of the journal had little which could be construed as radical criminology, and during my term as editor-elect of the publication, in 1977, not a single paper of a "radical" nature was submitted for review.

When considerable discussion was generated by the plenary session papers presented by Richard Quinney and Austin T. Turk at the 29th Annual Meeting of the American Society in November 1977, I felt that it was timely to build an issue of *Criminology* around those thought-provoking essays. Quinney's paper certainly qualified as "Marxist," and Turk's was an expression of a conflict but nonpartisan position. Following these two "radical" papers, it was my decision to solicit two essays critical of those perspectives. Jackson Toby's critique of radical sentimentality, also presented at the 1977 conference, and an invited paper from Carl B. Klockars were selected to serve that role.

It was also announced at that annual meeting, although informally, that additional papers on the radical perspective were being sought for that special issue, but none was submitted. Therefore, and assuming that these four papers would mark strongly conflicting points of view, it seemed appropriate to solicit comments on them from both a "conventional" criminologist and a Marxist criminologist. Ronald L. Akers and William J. Chambliss, respectively, agreed to serve as such. And finally, Laurin A. Wollan, Jr.'s essay on criminology's next step beyond labeling and conflict, also from the 1977 conference, was chosen as the final essay.

As editor, it was clear to me that all perspectives on radical thought could not be expressed in a single journal issue, or even in a whole volume. For this reason, even prior to the publication of the special issue, I decided to expand the material into a more lengthy anthology, to be sponsored by the American Society of Criminology. What was not anticipated was the controversy and debate that were provoked relative to both the journal issue and the preparation of this very book.

The journal issue was indeed incomplete, as would be any short volume devoted to an entire field of inquiry. This was to be compounded by a lack of balance, further complicated by Chambliss's withdrawal as a commentator on the Quinney, Turk, Toby, and Klockars essays only days before the journal was scheduled to go to press. These contingencies, combined with the long-standing tenuous relationships between many radical and mainstream criminologists, led to a library of editorials and correspondence denouncing the papers, the journal, its editor, and its sponsoring society. Letters of both praise and condemnation were sent to *Criminology's* editorial offices from four continents which, in some measure, at least offered some testimony as to how wide the readership of the journal was. And too, both the journal issue and this volume became primary topics of discussion at the annual meeting of the East Coast Conference of Socialist Sociologists in May 1979 and at the business meeting of the American Society of Criminology during its annual convention in November 1979. The basic criticism was the contention that the special journal issue had been designed primarily to "infame radical criminology," that it was nothing more than "a thinly disguised excuse to attack radical and Marxist criminologists," and that it failed "to give even minimal presentation to the ideas of radical scholars."

The journal issue was indeed unbalanced, but it was never designed to bury radical criminology. Perhaps the greatest concern on the part of the radical scholars was Carl B. Klockars's essay "The Contemporary Crises of Marxist Criminology." While it was described by some as a "devastating critique," and as an essay that would be widely cited in the future and which Marxist criminologists would find difficult to answer, radical criminologists described it as "a misrepresentation of Marx," "preposterous," "one-sided villification," and "a tale told by an idiot."

In attempting to expand the special journal issue into this lengthier volume, the specter of the controversy loomed large. Within several quarters of the radical community, a decision was made to coordinate an informal boycott of the book. As such, assuming that the anthology would be designed as an "ad hominum attack on the critical perspective," many noted radical criminologists suggested to their colleagues that they not participate in any contributions to the volume. In fact, during the course of the preparation of the volume, a total of sixteen authors either withdrew their papers or reneged on their promised contributions. And to these can be added an additional ten authors who failed to show even the courtesy of responding when an invitation to contribute was offered.

In short, the enterprise was an eventful one, characterized by long-standing differences of intellectual opinion spirited into chaos by a misunderstanding that got out of control. But in the end, many of the hostilities have weakened, segments of radical and mainstream communities have developed closer intellectual relationships, and the book has come to pass. Further, what has evolved from the experience is perhaps the most controversial book in criminology in recent years.

ORGANIZATION OF THE VOLUME

In an attempt to present as many sides of the issues and debate over radical criminology as well as the varying perspectives of radical theorists and their critics, this volume has been divided into four distinct parts. In Part I, "The State of the Paradigm," three essays are offered which discuss the emergence of radical thought and the basic content of radical theory.

The opening essay, "The Condition of Criminology in Contemporary Britain" by Professor Geoff Mungham of University College, Cardiff, Wales, begins on the note that arguments have been made at various times in recent years claiming the emergence of a "radical criminology" in Britain. Professor Mungham responds to these claims by addressing the ideas that: (1) it is more accurate to speak of emerging radical *criminologies* in Britain, rather than a single criminology of dissent; (2) notions of what are taken as "radical" concepts, theories, and styles of action in this context are frequently confused and mystifying; (3) the idea of there being a substantial and distinctive "rupture" between the so-called "old" criminology and emergent "new" criminologies is seriously misleading, in part because "radical criminologists" in Britain often have only a weak grasp of the history of their own discipline; (4) the claims and critiques put forward by radicals have been subjected to criticism in turn (from both inside and outside of British criminology) and radical criminologists have yet to produce adequate replies; and (5) the case for a radical criminology which will represent not only a theoretical advance, but also the possibility of devising more concrete ways of transforming the present system of criminal justice in Britain.

By contrast, Professor David O. Friedrichs of the University of Scranton, in his "Radical Criminology in the United States," focuses on the nature of the presence of radical thought in the United States. He discusses the emergence of radical criminology in America over the last decade in terms of apparent linkages to developments in the larger society, to the discipline of criminology, to mainstream and interactional theory, and to Marxist and conflict theory. On an *objective* plane, Professor Friedrichs presents the basic themes of radical criminology through an application of the concept of legitimacy; on a *subjective* plane, he examines the career of Richard Quinney as a search for a radical humanism. And in conclusion, this essay targets a number of questions yet to be dealt with by radical criminology as well as the directions it is likely to take during the 1980s.

Professor C. Ronald Huff of Ohio State University argues in his "Conflict Theory in Criminology" that whatever label is to be applied—radical, conflict, critical, Marxist–radical criminology actually subsumes a number of somewhat different theoretical perspectives, all of which make use of the paradigm of social conflict. His essay attempts to provide an overview of some of the ways in which this paradigm has been utilized in criminological theory. Three dimensions of social conflict (socioeconomic class, culture and group conflict, and power and authority relationships) are discussed and for each of these dimensions the works of three scholars are briefly summarized. This presentation of exemplars illustrates both the historical continuity in conflict-oriented criminology and the differences which exist among these theoretical perspectives. Finally, the need to link conflict criminology with more general sociological theory is discussed, and it is suggested that one such linkage may exist in the area of social stratification. That is, it is conceivable that theories of crime, deviance, and delinquency may be systematically linked with conflict-oriented theories of social stratification and social mobility.

Part II of the volume, "Debate and Controversy," includes much of the material that was contained in the controversial February 1979 issue of *Criminology,* plus several new selections.

Initially, "Analyzing Official Deviance: For Nonpartisan Conflict in Criminology" by Professor Austin T. Turk of the University of Toronto, maintains that partisan criminological analysis is characterized by dogmatic theories whose validity is politically rather than scientifically determined. Methods of inquiry are used to demonstrate, instead of test theoretical propositions. Standard methodological tactics include assertion, anecdote, association, and analogy. In contrast, Professor Turk argues that nonpartisan conflict analysis treats as entirely problematic the processes by which conceptions of deviance are socially constructed and become the official concerns of those who wield state power. What, how, why, and by whom behavioral or nonbehavioral attributes are labeled deviant, he maintains, is viewed as a function of the relative power of parties in conflict over the distribution of life chances.

The heatedly debated essay, "The Contemporary Crises of Marxist Criminology" by Professor Carl B. Klockars of the University of Delaware, suggests that Marxist theory gains its critical capacity by presenting itself as in the process of being realized through class conflict; by locating its critical and empirical reality in an ideal, unrepressive, unoppressive, relatively crime-free future, it renders itself irresponsible for its own history and immune from empirical criticism. In order to sustain this vision in the absence of historical evidence, Professor Klockars argues that the chief promoters of a Marxist perspective in American criminology have found it necessary to invent untestable and irrefutable concepts whose principal function is to maintain a suspension of the relationship between history, social reality, and theory. Furthermore, Klockars maintains that because such work is more akin to religious prophecy than criminology, it presently appears to be irreconcilable with all heretofore accepted standards of academic scholarship.

Professor Jackson Toby of Rutgers University, also a critic of the radical perspective, suggests in his essay, "The New Criminology Is the Old Baloney," that the "new criminology" is neither *new* nor *criminology*, merely sentimental overidentification with the underdog masquerading as science. He argues that this sentimentality appeals to students of crime only because criminology has traditionally been sympathetic to the underdog; and that the hypotheses of discriminatory law enforcement and of white-collar immorality reflect such sympathy. Professor Toby maintains that the millenarian hopes of the new criminology are illusory; that justice is imperfect even in relatively decent societies is no excuse for embracing nihilism or for giving up the attempt to maintain social order.

Following these three essays, Professor Ronald L. Akers of the University of Iowa and Professor Milton Mankoff of Queens College, in separate essays, comment critically on the contributions of Turk, Toby, and Klockars. In addition, Professor David O. Friedrichs' "Carl Klockars vs. the 'Heavy Hitters' " focuses specifically on Professor Klockars's critique of Marxist criminology. Professor Friedrichs delineates four major positions on radical criminology; from a position identified as "soft" radical criminology a challenge is raised to Klockars's assessment of the theoretical inadequacies of the paradigm, to his interpretation of the viability of radical concepts, and to his distorted attribution of certain positions to radical criminology. Klockars's critique is countered with an appreciative interpretation of the basic contribution made by radical criminology to our understanding of crime and criminal justice. At the same time a qualified concession of the seriousness of many of Klockars's charges is offered, and the need for radical criminology to resolve some of its own contradictions is discussed.

Finally, to conclude Part II, Professor Elmer H. Johnson of Southern Illinois University offers a critique of the Marxist concept of *praxis*. Professor Johnson suggests that the concept unifies theory and practice in a particular sense, and that radical criminology in the United States has excessively diverted the potential of this concept into partisan strategic action.

Part III of the volume, "The Coming Crises," offers a view of some of the crisis issues both faced by and caused by radical criminological thought. Initially, Professor Steven Spitzer of the University of Northern Iowa, in his essay "Left-Wing Criminology—An Infantile Disorder?" points to the fact that radical criminology has been accused of a multitude of sins. Some of these criticisms are on target insofar as Marxist interpretations of crime and its control continue to be bound by an antithetical logic—a form of criticism through inversion which seeks to displace rather than transend traditional criminology. Starting with the assumption that a Marxist criminology can exist—an assumption not shared by all Marxists—Professor Spitzer attempts to outline and interpret some of the major problems which must be overcome if a truly critical criminology is to emerge. Among the most important of these problems are radical criminology's metafunctionalism, instrumentalism, and romaticism of illegality. To clarify why positivists so frequently misconstrue the Marxist approach to crime, the methodological presuppositions of both positivism and Marxism are also discussed. In general, it is argued that while "left-wing" criminology may be characterized as "infantile" in certain respects, it need only be a "disorder" if it remains committed to and limited by the conditions surrounding its birth.

From an alternative position, Professor David Shichor of California State College, examines some of the basic tenets, claims, and assumptions being made by radical criminologists. In his essay, "Some Problems of Credibility in Radical Criminology," Professor Shichor argues that radical theorists' handling of the nature of the law in capitalist societies, their neglect of analyzing crime in socialist countries, their deep political commitment and "praxis," their shunning of empirical research, their "religious" devotion to Marxist ideology and total belief in the "goodness" of socialist society, and their "overpoliticization" of crime, raise serious questions of credibility.

From an empirical posture, Professor Franklin P. Williams of Rochester Institute of Technology focuses on the fact that the conflict perspective in criminology has grown both in stature and in the number of its adherents during the past two decades, and that such growth seems to have emerged from the research "evidence" on differential processing within the criminal justice system. Professor Williams's essay, "Conflict Theory and Differential Processing: An Analysis of the Research Literature," argues that unfortunately much of this evidence seems to be drawn from a small number of familiar studies and that few substantive reviews are available. In an attempt to rectify this problem and gain a more comprehensive view

of the research literature, Professor Williams conducted a relatively
thorough search of the processing research. Some 89 studies, ranging from
1928 through 1977, were located and separated into 123 "separate"
examinations of racial and socioeconomic discrimination in six major areas
of interest: area of the criminal justice system, juvenile/adult system,
capital offense studies, region of study, median year of sample, and
method of analysis. Bivariate tabulation of the research generally indicated
a lack of evidence for the conflict position with the exception of studies
which used a southern data base and/or concentrated on postsentencing or
capital offense areas. A separate examination of the most methodologically rigorous research, however, revealed an overwhelming lack of
support for the existence of systematic processing differentials in every
area, with the possible exception of capital offense research. As a result,
Professor Williams suggests that conflict theorists might more appropriately concentrate their efforts on the creation of law.

Professor William V. Pelfrey of the University of Alabama offers a
rather unique analysis of what is viewed as a crisis question by exploring
the inclination of academic criminology and other crime-related disciplines
to accept or reject the new criminology as a viable alternative to the
traditional perspective. Professor Pelfrey's essay, "The New Criminology:
Acceptance Within Academe," suggests that mainstream criminology has
slipped its traditional bounds and the new criminology is gaining acceptance.

As a final item on "the coming crises," Professor Stephen J. Pfohl of
Boston College, in his "Teaching Critical Criminology: The Ethical Issues,"
argues that the successful teaching of a critical criminology poses a variety
of ethical dilemmas for the concerned student. Professor Pfohl examines
these dilemmas as well as the ethical responsibilities of the critical criminology instructor. In addition, in outlining ways in which the instructor
might address these responsibilities, he attempts to suggest avenues by
which a critical criminology can combine a serious program of theory and
research with an equally serious commitment to build a knowledgeable
community of persons accepting the historical responsibilities of present
structural arrangement and future structural change.

Part IV, "Future Concerns and Directions," examines some implica-
tions and alternatives for both radical and mainstream criminology. First,
Dr. Anne E. Pottieger of the University of Delaware offers an interesting
series of implications in her essay, "Radical Criminology as Functionalist
Theory: The Nature and Implications of an Unacknowledged Identity."
She argues that radical criminology as it currently exists displays a distinc-

tively structural-functionalist theoretic logic in both its general defining arguments and in the specific explanations offered by its proponents, Marxist and otherwise, throughout the range of topics they study. Consequently, both inadequate radical criminology and mainstream criminological objections to it often can be traced to the ease with which bad functionalism can be constructed. Professor Pottieger suggests, however, that future attention to its functionalist theoretical structure could—precisely because of, and not merely in spite of, its metatheoretical differences with functionalism—put radical criminology in a better position than conventional functionalism ever was to achieve comprehensive and logically adequate criminological explanations.

"Can the 'Old' and the 'New' Criminologies by Reconciled?" by Professor Edwin M. Schur of New York University comments on the notion that recent writings by radical criminologists have usefully contributed to a substantive reorienting of analysis in the sociology of crime, and have also served to alert us to the ever-present danger of cooptation. He points out, however, that often the declared radicals have exaggerated the extent to which sociologists have become "agents of the establishment"; that they have also tended to make excessively proprietary claims regarding key themes developed in their interpretations, and to dismiss peremptorily and without warrant so-called "traditional" approaches. Professor Schur maintains that, in fact, there now exist many important understandings about crime (partly grounded in "traditional" work) that cut across and are quite consistent with a variety of theoretical viewpoints. These common understandings are discussed in his essay, and the likely areas of persisting disagreement between "radicals" and "traditionalists" are considered. The penchant of some radical criminologists to adopt a "fetishism of rhetoric" and to engage in intramural name calling is deplored as counterproductive, and a greater acceptance of task pluralism within the sociology of crime is recommended.

Professor Laurin A. Wollin of Florida State University looks to criminology's next generation in his essay "After Labeling and Conflict: An Aspect of Criminology's Next Chapter." Professor Wollin's position is that criminology will become somewhat more concerned for values in the future, and hence, will shift slightly from the empirical, scientific end of the spectrum toward the normative, philosophical end. This will result, he suggests, from crises in criminal justice, from the "coming crisis in Western sociology," from the effects of "critical criminology," from changes in social science generally, and from the broader circumstances of criminology and criminal justice.

The concluding essay, "A Radical Alternative to Radical Criminology" by Professor Harold E. Pepinsky of Indiana University, provides us with a number of thought-provoking ideas. Professor Pepinsky argues that while radical criminology is usually equated with Marxist criminology, the equation is false because the Marxist point of view has already been synthesized into conventional criminology. The history of criminological thought can be depicted as a Hegelian dialectical process, of which Marxist criminology has been a part. The current radical antithesis of conventional criminology holds social structure rather than individuals responsible for crime, and may be called structural criminology. This antithesis, too, stands to be synthesized into conventional criminology—to become deradicalized. The next radical antithesis may consist of those proposing how to improve the quality of social justice within social structures in which crime is already well controlled. Not to be confused with political extremism, radical criminology has a vital role to play in the growth of criminological knowledge.

The essays in this volume clearly do not present all the issues, answer all the questions, resolve all the debates, or suggest all the implications. What is hoped, however, is that the material presented here will sharpen our insights into the concerns and perspectives of both radical and mainstream criminologists, as well as stimulate a level of discourse that will serve to reconcile some problems that these opposing schools of thought have placed before one another.

PART I THE STATE OF THE PARADIGM

1

THE CAREER OF A CONFUSION: RADICAL CRIMINOLOGY IN BRITAIN

Geoff Mungham

INTRODUCTION

This essay comes hard on the heels of four recent surveys of the condition of criminology in contemporary Britain. These reviews, written in turn by Cohen (1974), Hood (1974), Wiles (1976), and Downes (1978), all put down roughly the same markers and raised similar questions and issues. Each author attempted to sketch in the trajectory of criminology in postwar Britain by identifying a number of "stages" or "phases" in the evolution of the discipline. While some of their conclusions are incorporated into this essay (see next two sections), our main emphasis is upon what has come to be variously known as the "new," or "radical," or "critical" criminology. The character and claims of "radical criminology" went largely unrecorded in the earlier reviews of British criminology, in part because its very newness made analysis and evaluation difficult. Our intention is to pick up the story of British criminology at this point of previous departure and to try and assess the various claims of the "new," or "critical" criminology. But nothing we have said so far is meant to imply that the history of contemporary British criminology has followed some simple linear design, from "mainstream" to "radical." "Traditional" criminology, for instance, has pushed on with only a minimal acknowledgment of deviancy theory and radical criminology. (The reasons for the apparent obliviousness of the mainstream to external criticism and its continued influence on policy makers are important to grasp and come into our account later. For the moment we can note that certainly where policy is concerned the continued preeminence of the traditional approach in Britain owes less to its own strength and more to the weaknesses of the prescriptions offered by the new criminology.) On a related point, it is inevitable that any attempts to divide intellectual work into categories or phases does violence to the complexities of some writers' ideas, as well as leaving unresolved the problems posed by those authors who appear "out of their time." For example, the suggestions that before the emergence of deviancy theory in the 1960s criminology was somehow all encapsulated within a "traditional paradigm" is scarcely fair to the work of Mays (1954) and Morris (1957), whose criminological studies, as we shall see, took them along quite different lines of inquiry.

This said, our concern still remains with the anatomy and prescriptions of "radical" criminology. Various arguments have been advanced in recent years claiming to see the emergence of a distinctively "radical" criminology in Britain. Our response to these claims is first to suggest that it is more accurate to talk of emerging new criminologies in Britain, rather than a single dissenting criminology. It is also part of our position that many of what are regarded as "radical" concepts and ideas are often confused, confusing, and mystifying. We also wish to pursue the following points: that the idea of there being a clear "rupture" between the so-called "old" criminology and emergent "new" criminologies (whether these are self-consciously radical or not) is misleading, in part because radical criminologists in Britain tend to demonstrate only a weak grasp of the history of their own discipline. The problem of separatism has also been complicated, as we shall see, by the failure of radicals in the field to deal adequately with the issues of correction, sanction, and punishment, issues which traditional criminology has always been preoccupied with. Finally, we wish to consider some of the critiques of "radical" criminology, including those by mainstream criminologists, by Marxists, and by those who themselves once claimed a place in the ranks of the "new" criminologists.

"TRADITIONAL" OR "MAINSTREAM" CRIMINOLOGY

It has become a commonplace in reviews of trends in British criminological thought to point to the largely unchallenged sovereignty of what
Cohen (1974) called "mainstream British criminology" and Downes
(1978) "traditional criminology" in the 1940s and 1950s. The roots of
criminological orthodoxy are widely regarded as having been firmly
planted before World War II with the setting up of the Institute for the
Study and Treatment of Delinquency in 1931 (which in turn encouraged
the formation of the British Society of Criminology and its journal, the
British Journal of Criminology), and by the teaching of criminology at
London University by Herbert Mannheim. As Cohen (1974) points out,
the principal institutional framework for mainstream criminology after the
war was provided by the establishment of the Home Office Research Unit
in 1957 and the Institute of Criminology at Cambridge in 1958, under the
sponsorship of the Home Office. The style of inquiry favored by those in
the mainstream was pragmatic and atheoretical, with a strong correctional
bias and reformist interest. In this milieu criminology, argued Cohen
(1974), came to be regarded by those who dominated the field as an
interdisciplinary science, serving as a stamping ground for psychologists,
psychiatrists, and forensic scientists in particular, but giving little or no
ground to sociologists or even to legal theorists. According to Cohen, this
eclectic grouping produced a criminology that was, and still is, dominated
by a "clinical positivism," something which is still handsomely reflected in
the contents of the *British Journal of Criminology*.

As we hinted before, the criminological mainstream, while dominant in
this period, never had the field entirely to itself. The implication in the
work of the "new" criminologists who came later that all preceding British
criminology was blind to and innocent of anything that smacked of
structure, power, and class relations, and could not ever bring itself to peer
over the ramparts of correctionalism, is a highly misleading one. To insist
on holding to this position ignores, among other work, the pioneering
studies by Mays (1954) and Morris (1957). Mays's study of delinquency,
as in part the outcome of a confrontation between working-class values
and the structure of middle-class authority, managed, in Downes's (1978:
485) words, to anticipate "much that was to come." Again, Morris's
investigation of the social ecology of crime produced work that was
difficult to dismiss as "traditional" or as "correctionally oriented." Perhaps a related point here is Cohen's (1979: 18) acute observation that so
often exercises in the history of ideas end up making "us sound dumber in

the past than we really were in order to give the illusion of continual
cerebral progression." This preference of many of the "new" criminologists for casting "mainstream" criminology into a "dumb" mold has
obscured what was of value in this tradition. We can illustrate this point
best by indicating some of the *contemporary* reactions to the founding of
the Cambridge Institute in 1958. One orchestrator of conservative opinion
described the Institute's emergence in the following terms:

> It ... may provide agreeable summer schools. ... But because the
> causes of crime are always so much what they have always been that
> they are unlikely to be removed by giving them a different name. ...
> All need to inspire a detestation spreading from the very top
> throughout society of the shoddiness of mind from which crime
> springs [lead article in *Daily Telegraph,* quoted by Lord Butler,
> 1974: 8-9].

The former sponsor of the Institute also referred to "other views" which
simply favored heavier deterrents as a superior remedy to more research
(Butler, 1974: 9). In other words, even the orientation and predilections
of mainstream criminology—which have always been anathema to those
who came later and claimed a radical mandate for criminology—
represented an advance upon conventional posturings about crime causation and the necessary requirements for law and order. The sentiments
Butler pointed to provided more than a hint of the tensions and clashing
interests that come into play whenever criminology touches the garment
of public policy. Viewed from this perspective, even the most orthodox
criminological work and prescriptions opened up possibilities for fresh
thinking about causal and correctional questions. The point has been made
before, but can be profitably restated in this context, that good empirical
work in social science can be as "subversive" (in the sense of forcing a
redefinition of the commonplace and the taken-for-granted) as any piece
of research conducted in a self-consciously radical style.

THE "LIBERAL" SOCIOLOGY OF DEVIANCE

The term is borrowed from Downes (1979: 3-5) and refers to the
emergence after the mid-1960s of a sociology of deviance which leaned
heavily upon a labeling or interactionist approach and owed much of its
inspiration to the work of Americans like Becker, Cicourel, Goffman,
Lemert, and Matza. Although the hold of clinical positivism and its main

policy expression (correctionalism) had never been total, the sense of any formal opposition only really came in 1968, with the founding of the National Deviancy Conference (NDC). The place of its emergence—in the middle of a Home Office-sponsored conference at the Institute of Criminology at Cambridge, convened to discuss the teaching of criminology in British universities and opened by the Home Secretary—revealed where some of the incipient tensions lay in British criminology at the time. The founder members of the NDC all had assorted left-radical backgrounds and, as Cohen described it, a growing disenchantment with left politics as well as with mainstream criminology. Perhaps the best manifesto of the NDC in its early years is to be found in Cohen's (1971) introduction to the first collection of papers which came out of one of the group's conferences, when the defining essence of the new interest in deviant behavior was presented as "skepticism." A skepticism, that is, which typically found its expression in such questions as *who* makes the law, *who* settles policies of enforcement, and *whose* interests are best presented and advanced by the existing apparatus of crime control and sanctions against deviant behavior? In a later review of this phase, Taylor et al. (1975: 6) summarized their differences with liberal deviancy theory in this way. First, there was the need—as they saw it—to go beyond the mere "demystification" of "traditional correctionally oriented criminology" (1975: 6), though it was not clear if the break with correctionalism was to be total, or merely a point in favor of a radical criminology that would redefine the notion of "correction," or emphasize it less as a focus of concern. The "formal features" of the earlier approach were held to include: (1) the defense of the authenticity of the deviant, (2) a denial of absolutism, (3) a revolt against correctionalism (and the "scientificity" that underwrote it—namely positivism), and (4) the attempt to develop a more fully fledged sociological explanation of crime creation, but drawing especially from transactionist analysis.

The first of these "formal features" listed by Taylor et al. meant a frequent leaning toward an "appreciative stance" in the analysis of various deviant groups. "Appreciation," of course, carried its own implicit message of political relativism; the call was for "hands off the deviant" and an interest in policies of "decriminalization" and "nonintervention." This celebration of liberal pluralism maintained a certain credibility all the while the new deviancy theorists concentrated upon the study of sexual deviance, drug cultures, and mental illness. But the new constructs proved to be quite unable to cope with the harder issues of violent crime and crimes against property. Thus not only did the new deviancy theory fail to solve the problem of correctionalism, it also came dangerously close to preaching its own kind of amorality. If the new criteria of "rationality" were to be defined according to the (deviant) actor's standpoint, a moral and political atrophy seemed bound to result. The new fashion was not a comfortable fit for those who wanted a criminology and a sociology of deviance that could be *for* the furtherance of a radical politics.

But like traditional criminology, a sociology of deviance built upon interactionist foundations has not faded away in the face of criticism by radical criminologists. It is still firmly a part of the mosaic of criminological work in Britain and its usefulness and value have recently been restated in articles by Rock (1979) and by Plummer (1979). In particular, some of the policy implications deriving from deviancy theory have still to be properly explored and there seems to be no reason why experiments with the notion of, say, decriminalization need mean a complete capitulation to liberal pluralism and idealism. More than this, if notions of decriminalization are linked with the idea—increasingly popular with some of those grappling with the problem of policy prescriptions in this area, as we shall see—of the *decentralization* of control systems, then such innovations would mean not some mindless assertion of "diversity," but an attempt to reorder and reshape moral contours and sanctions.

THE "NEW" OR "RADICAL" OR "CRITICAL" CRIMINOLOGY

The obvious starting point for the delineation of a radical criminology in Britain was the appearance of Taylor et al.'s book *The New Criminology*, in 1973. The book has proved to be contentious. One reviewer greeted it as a "truly comprehensive critique ... an important study" (Gouldner, 1973. ix), only for another (Austin Turk) to dismiss it as a "perversion" of scholarship. Equally interesting, the response by Marxist writers was also profoundly ambivalent though, in the end, largely hostile (Hirst, 1975; Bankowski et al., 1977; Sumner, 1979). This kaleidoscope of opinion provided some important initial clues about the shape of the debate about radical criminology that followed the appearance of Taylor et al.'s (1973) book. Briefly, these critiques indicated there was to be no monolithic "radical" criminology, or anything like it, capable of commanding a general allegiance. At best, *The New Criminology* provoked several attempts to rethink the basis of what a "radical" criminology might look like. At worst, the political and policy thrusts of the book were rejected not only by the mainstream, but also by the liberal left and the Marxist left.

There is little value in "naming the parts" of *The New Criminology*. The book has been exhaustively reviewed elsewhere and readers who seek a guided tour of the contents are advised to go there. Our specific concern is with the claims of the book's authors to have produced a text that was both "new" and "radical." Our point of departure is the closing pages of the book, where Taylor et al. restate the essence of their critique of—as Marx might have put it—all hitherto existing criminology, and declare their own vision of the sort of society that lay at the end of the construction of a "fully social theory of deviance." As we shall try and demonstrate, that which was "new" was not necessarily "radical"—or even "new" in some certain, key respects. Efforts to move toward the creation of a "new" or "critical" criminology were in part a left-radical reaction against what were seen as the failures of deviancy theory to disengage itself from the snares of relativism and idealism. Clearly, if the new commitment was to be in a radical criminology that was going to say something about the nature of state power, crime, law, class, and property relations, then "liberal" deviancy theory had very little to offer, while the mainliners still remained hopelessly hooked on intellectual eclecticism and the idea of piecemeal reforms.

What then were the defining characteristics of the new criminology, according to Taylor et al.? First, and rather confusingly, "This 'new' criminology will in fact be an *old* criminology, in that it will face the same problems that were faced by the classical social theorists" (1973: 278). It was to be a criminology with the politics brought back in (1973: 278) and a criminology which held to the belief that "the abolition of crime *is* possible under certain social arrangements" (1973: 281). In its most powerful expression, the new criminology was to throw in its lot unambiguously with "anticorrectionalism" and with the glorification of the idea of "human diversity." As Taylor et al. (1973: 281-282) put it:

A criminology which is not normatively committed to the abolition of inequalities of wealth and power, and in particular of inequalities in property and life-chances, is inevitably bound to fall into correctionalism. And all correctionalism is irreducibly bound up with the identification of deviance with pathology. A fully social theory of deviance must, by its nature, break entirely with correctionalism. . . . The task is to create a society in which the facts of human diversity, whether personal, organic or social, are not subject to the power to criminalise.

There was a sense in which *The New Criminology* served as a kind of prologomena to the appearance of *Critical Criminology* in 1975, a series of essays edited by Taylor et al. which they described as "posing fundamental and consistent challenges to the everyday political assumptions, practices and implications of one of the most influential and State-dominated branches of applied social 'science'–the 'science' of criminology" (1975: 5). The only problem with the grand sweep of this formulation lay in the fact that one of the book's contributors (Hirst) set out to challenge not just the science of orthodox criminology, but the basic tenets of the "new" criminology as well, a sentiment endorsed by other Marxists and left critics (see section below).

In their long introductory essay in *Critical Criminology*, Taylor et al. (1975: 44) restated the radical manifesto for a new criminology. The only approach to the study of crime and law "which does not degenerate into mere moralising is a materialist one." The new advocacy of a "materialist criminology" represented Taylor *et al.*'s version of "transcendence" in relation to what they called "the troublesome question of alternatives" (1975: 28) and the absence of any clear account of what a "socialist penology" or a "socialist legality" might look like. The defining characteristics of the new approach were to be: (1) a criminology normatively committed to the abolition of inequalities in wealth and power, (2) a criminology that would "build a proper 'sociology' of law and crime alongside a social explanation of their roles in particular societies with particular modes of production" (1975: 54), and (3) using Marxism as its *method* (1975: 49) the task of "materialist criminology" was ultimately to expose the "mystification" of social conflict and social control in capitalist societies. Thus materialist criminology, like the earlier plea for a "fully social theory of deviance" was not concerned with criminal behavior in the narrow sense, but with the central institutional arrangements of society instead.

There was a sense in which the attempts by Taylor et al. to "toughen" their view of an agenda for radical criminology, in *Critical Criminology*, reflected developments in British society at large. The 1970s saw increasing unemployment, labor unrest, falling standards of living, and the orchestration of several "law-and-order" campaigns as a response to the general uncertainty and sense of deepening crisis. Many features of this crisis and its consequences for "law and order" were brilliantly captured in a recent book by Hall et al. (1978). It would have been strange indeed if any radical criminology failed to acknowledge these new configurations, and the new interest in law, class, and state power mirrored society where inequalities and class tensions were becoming ever more apparent. But all this forces consideration of some important questions. To what extent did (and does) the arguments for a new materialist criminology have something politically useful to say about the crisis in British society, particularly with reference to trends in the direction of more repressive legislation and the operation of the criminal justice system (Hall et al., 1978)? The answer has to be "little" or "none," although some of the ways in which the claims of the new criminology were responded to—even when these claims were rejected—opened up fresh intellectual and political discourses and possibilities. This is a point we now take up in the final section of the essay.

"RADICAL" CRIMINOLOGY:
CRITIQUE, COMMENT, AND REACTION

We begin with the issue of strategies and agendas. With the publication of *The New Criminology* and *Critical Criminology*, Taylor et al. appeared to throw out all "nonmaterialist" criminology. The call for a "fully social theory of deviance" in the former text surfaced in the latter in the guise of an argument for a materialist methodology. At the same time, the persistence of anticorrectionalism in their work (which they consistently linked up with the identification of deviance with pathology), their interest in "appreciation" (defending the "authenticity" of the deviant), and their celebration of the idea of "human" and "socialist diversity" was not a package that many on the political left would ever be likely to find persuasive. The problem of correctionalism and the inability or unwillingness of Taylor et al. to confront or resolve it at anything other than a rhetorical or metaphysical level created the sort of difficulty which Ainlay (1975-1976: 217) has captured well:

> The [new criminology's] critique of the social reaction approach marked an important turning point in the evolution of radical criminology. . . . The critique of social reactionism gave birth to *strategic anti-correctionalism*; henceforth . . . developments in radical criminology would . . . be considerably shaped and *constrained* by an overweening concern to formulate and adhere to strategies for avoiding correctionalism.

Their advocacy of "diversity" as a way of deflecting the correctional problem has returned to haunt them again and again. As Currie (1974: 139) put it:

> Where traditional criminology regarded deviance as innately pathological, Taylor, Walton and Young regard it as innately healthy. Neither approach seriously attempts to analyze the sources and consequences and political significance of particular kinds of deviance within the framework of an articulate set of political and moral values. ... The inadequacy of this cheerful perspective is most apparent if we look at the deviance of the powerful, rather than that of the powerless. When police "overreact" and kill innocent people, they're often considered deviant and treated as such: but is this an example of healthy "diversity" that should be "decriminalised"? An approach to deviance that can't distinguish between politically progressive and politically retrogressive forms of deviance doesn't provide much of a basis for real understanding or political action.

What Ainlay (1975-1976) called their "strategic anti-correctionalism," also has had profound consequences for their particular vision of what a socialist society might look like, and of the character of "socialist legality." To talk blandly of striving for a social order "in which the facts of human diversity, whether personal, organic or social are not subject to the power to criminalise' (Taylor et al., 1973: 282) is of little help or comfort. To turn to Currie (1974: 141) again:

> If they mean that in socialist society there will be less 'crime' of the conventional kind, and therefore less need for the conventional (class-based) apparatus of the state, then there's no quarrels every socialist has said this for centuries. But they seem to be saying something else—that in socialist society nothing human will be considered criminal; and this seems ... to dodge most of the important issues about crime and justice in revolutionary societies. It would be more reasonable to argue that what has happened in contemporary revolutionary societies and ought to happen in future ones, is not that 'the power to criminalise' disappears, but that the definition of crime loses its class character; crime becomes defined and treated on the basis of principles that are egalitarian and cooperative rather than hierarchical and exploitative. Here, once again, the authors' vision seems closer to the more extreme forms of interactionism than to Marxism.

Turning aside from the more grandiose calls for some sort of socialist reconstruction by largely unspecified means, the radical criminology of

Taylor *et al.* seems to have almost nothing of policy or prescriptive value to contribute toward the more immediate and urgent debates about the nature of criminal justice policy in Britain and, more generally, about the possibility of developing, as Cohen (1979: 49) puts it, "middle-range policy alternatives which do not compromise any overall design for fundamental social change." Their silence on these issues is more than deafening, it is also dangerous. To do nothing, or merely to brush off these concerns as "reformist" or as dragging us into yet more correctionalist traps, is only to give over the field to the Right and to general reaction. If we follow the drift of Cohen's argument about the need to discover routes back to the moral dimensions of criminal politics (1979: 23), then radical criminologists—just like anybody else doing criminological work—must face the issues of sentencing, sanctioning, and punishing. As Cohen (1979: 24) correctly states it, "it is punishment—in both its dimensions of ban and enforcement—which is at the core of criminal politics and always has been. It is fatal that, until recently, radicals have ignored or fudged the issue." What Cohen is pointing to here, like other critics of the programmatics of Taylor et al.—such as Brown (1978) or Downes (1979)—is that after the dust raised by the new criminologists has settled, we still find quite undisturbed the presence of some very old policy questions. Questions, that is, which turn upon the vexing and vexatious issues of blame, responsibility and corrections, and the prospects for and the constraints upon new thinking about these problems.

The reluctance of Taylor et al. to come out and debate these matters has been characterized by Rock (1979: 80) as part of "the drift into otherworldliness" by the new criminologists. Perhaps more serious still is Rock's important point that the conceptions held by Taylor et al. of what is socially possible and socially desirable has cut them off from other discourses to produce what is, in effect, a self-imposed excommunication. In Rock's (1979: 81) view, "There is now little left to bind radical criminology to the everyday world of ordinary people and the intellectual world of other sociologists." While there is much substance to this claim, in fairness it should also be pointed out that at least some of the new criminologists had already begun to sense their work was, at best, only of marginal relevance to contemporary debates about criminal justice, corrections, and for "law and order" more generally. Indeed, there was a certain irony in the fact that Young (himself one of the principal architects of the new criminology) had, in an article on "Working Class Criminology" (which was carried in *Critical Criminology*), went some way toward acknowledging the bankruptcy of radical thought on issues of public policy. In this article he recognized the gap between radical theories and prescriptions on the nature of order, control, and their alternatives in contemporary British society on the one hand, and social realities and working-class fears and aspirations on the other.

There can be no doubt that the question of what is to be done, as this applies to the criminal justice system and to the area of formal social control more broadly, still waits for an answer or answers. Traditional criminology has its program which, in its own terms, is coherent and plausible, facts which go a long way toward explaining its long preeminence as an influential force in the sphere of public policy on issues of control and corrections. Beyond the academy, the language of "law and order" and the frame of the debates are almost entirely monopolies of the Right. The "deep-rooted crisis" of British society, to which Taylor et al. constantly and properly refer, has produced no concrete responses from them. An even more severe indictment of this strand of radical criminology has come from Rock (1979: 83-84):

> More minutely, there are stresses and instabilities in the social organisation of radical criminology as an enterprise. The coalition of Marxists, anarchists, populists, conflict theorists and libertarians is prone to some internal dissension. The emergence of that coalition was made possible by a common group of adversaries, the liberal criminologists. Its future hinges on the resolution of internal contradictions. Anarchism and Marxism are not entirely complementary. Neither are libertarianism and structuralism. It is conceivable that radical criminology will shatter into a host of subordinate criminologies, each veering towards a parent world view. But the new criminology does not only associate itself with writers and thinkers. It depends upon an advocacy of praxis, joining with groups who represent, or claim to represent, prisoners, mental patients, welfare claimants and the like. Organizations which champion the dispossessed and the incarcerated are somewhat volatile. Their fate is often determined by the work of a few men, and those man tend to be changeable. Lacking a firm bureaucratic base, substantial finance and a powerful membership, these groups are also threatened by the politics of disrepute. There are taxing problems of legitimacy and political consequentiality. Confronting established and powerful agencies, they are strategically and tactically weak. In the main, the principal parties of the Left are unreceptive to their vision. As a result, the politics of the marginal politics, drifting into inaction or expressive displays.

It may be, of course, that radical criminology is being asked to carry an unfair burden. If there is no clear thinking from left-radicals in Britain about the problem of criminal justice or social order, it also needs to be said that there is equally no useful currency in circulation which might help get some purchase on the task of social reform and social recon-struction more generally. In this respect, the failures of radical criminology can be seen as part of a broader failure; namely the inability of the political left in Britain to produce *any* convincing or persuasive solutions to the country's problems. Thus if radical criminologists are to be indicted, others may have to look to their laurels as well.

All we have said so far by no means exhausts the analysis of trends in criminological thought in Britain. Our concentration on the work of Taylor et al. was for two main reasons. First, although the radical move-ment in criminology in Britain is of some complexity, the work of Taylor et al. has—until recently—been the most prodigious and the most theo-retically advanced. Hence it seemed sensible to examine the assumptions upon which their work is based and to examine the status their work gives to radical criminology. And second, their work raises, in the most acute form, the relationship between criminology and public policy. Since the major thrust of this essay has been directed toward trying to clarify the claims of the new criminology as a radical *enterprise,* it seemed only logical that most of our attention should have been given to that who, in Ainlay's (1975-1976: 215) words, produced what was "widely regarded as radical criminology's . . . manifesto."

There still remains, though, two final points to be made, to help fill out the picture of the character of the new criminology in Britain. To begin with, our preoccupation with the work of Taylor et al. has meant we have neglected the extent to which it is most accurate now to talk of the emergence in Britain not of a single new criminology, but of several new *criminologies.* This point has been forcibly argued by Wiles (1976: 33) who has made the claim that the new criminologies "are mutually exclu-sive, and therefore criminology today presents a more confusing picture than was the case with traditional criminology." Under Wiles's umbrella are collected not just the labors of Taylor et al., but their critics like Rock (1979) and Sumner (1976, 1979), as well as those like Damer (1974) and Parker (1974) whose work, if we follow Downes (1978: 493), has "the capacity . . . to transcend (and refute) simple labelling theory." Not all of those new criminologies were "radical," though the work of some of the new practitioners (Parker, 1974) was "subversive" in its own way, forcing many people (academics, law enforcers, welfare workers) to question some old certainties about youthful offenders and the structure and process of gang life.

Next, and briefly, there is that tradition which is not part of the criminological enterprise but instead has criticized and attempted to *deny* it, from a Marxist standpoint. We are referring now, as examples, to the arguments of Hirst (1975) and Bankowski et al. (1977) which sought to refute the very basis of Taylor et al.'s claims to produce a critical criminology grounded in a Marxist methodology. As Bankowski et al. (1977: 37-38) put it at the beginning of their article:

> We will argue that: (1) criminology and crime are not areas or resources worthy of study for a radical analysis of present (capitalistic) social arrangements; (2) that as the social scientist does become concerned with the objects (mode of production, etc.) that will allow a radical analysis, then crime and criminology become peripheral and marginal; (3) that our position is *logically entailed* by the adoption of the theoretical structure (Marxism) upon which Taylor, Walton and Young actually posit their radicalism. Their failure to reach this conclusion is due we contend to a tendency to conflate the ideological reasons for studying an empirical area (crime) with the rigour and epistemological protocols needed to provide a radical analysis. This conflation is made manifest in their lack of distinction between the *purposes* of study and the *objects* of study. Indeed it is overriding concentration upon purposes that finally makes their work epistemologically reductionist in nature and muted in potential for radicalism. Thus their work finally becomes victim to the epistemological and moral relativism they so rightly castigate in previous criminologies. Consequently the theoretical implications of their conception of radical criminology are restricted to a reification of personal moral outrage at the manifest inequalities of capitalist societies. Their work is capable only of producing a radical criminologist not a radical criminology.

We introduce their arguments not with a view to pursuing them any further here, but to give some idea of the complex range of responses and reactions to the assertions of radical criminologists. It should be clear from even this brief sketch that British criminology is no monolith. There exists a plurality of perspectives and tendencies, though all do not enjoy equal influence or standing. Radical criminology has, so far, made almost no impact on policy formulations nor does it seem inclined to try. We have tried to indicate the particulars of this attitude of disengagement. To end, though, on a more positive—or perhaps exhortatory—note, we can do no better than endorse Cohen (1979: 48, 50):

> There is a need for more 'Utopian' theory construction. All the loose talk about legality, morality, justice and tolerance needs to be related to classic and current attempts . . . to specify the abstract properties of a just system. . . . But these tasks must be performed with at least one eye open on the day-to-day world of crime and criminal justice politics. When this world goes out of the frame—as it has tended to in the past—we lose the chance of influencing it.

The errors of radical criminology are possibly that it falls sadly short of the two main objectives set down for a critical criminology by Cohen. There is, in this tradition, no ideal sketch of the society that might be "fully human" or which may be said to carry the stamp of "socialist diversity." And, more immediately, there is a silence on those everyday troubles which, whether we like it or not, help shape most people's perceptions of the "crime problem" and its management and control. Thus while we have never been more in need of the sort of critical criminology Cohen advocates, all we have had so far is a radical criminology that has mostly led us into a series of dead-ends.

REFERENCES

AINLAY, J. (1975-1976) "Review of the new criminology and critical criminology." Telos 25-26: 213-225.

BANKOWSKI, Z., G. MUNGHAM, and P. YOUNG (1977) "Radical criminology or radical criminologist?" Contemporary Crises 1, 1: 37-52.

BROWN, R. (1978) "The new criminology," pp. 81-107 in E. Kamenka et al. (eds.) Law and Society. London: Edward Arnold.

BUTLER, Lord (1974) "The foundation of the Institute of Criminology in Cambridge," pp. 1-10 in R. Hood (ed.) Crime, Criminology and Public Policy. London: Heinemann.

COHEN, S. (1979) "Guilt, justice and tolerance: some old concepts for a new criminology," pp. 17-51 in D. Downes and P. Rock (eds.) Deviance and Social Control. London: Martin Robertson.

——— (1974) "Criminology and the sociology of deviance in Britain; a recent history and current report," pp. 1-40 in P. Rock and M. McIntosh (eds.) Deviance and Social Control. London: Tavistock.

——— [ed.] (1971) Images of Deviance. Harmondsworth: Penguin.

CURRIE, E. (1974) "Beyond criminology—a review of the new criminology." Issues in Criminology 9, 1: 139-145.

DAMER, S. (1974) "Wine Alley: the sociology of a dreadful enclosure." Sociological Review 22, 2.

DOWNES, D. (1979) "Praxis makes perfect," pp. 1-16 in D. Downes and P. Rock (eds.) Deviance and Social Control. London: Martin Robertson.

——— (1978) "Promise and performance in British criminology." British Journal of Sociology 29, 4: 483-505.

GOULDNOR, A. (1973) "Foreword," pp. ix-xiv in I. Taylor et al. (eds.) The New Criminology. London: Routledge & Kegan Paul.

HALL, S., C. CRITCHER, T. JEFFERSON, J. CLARKE, and B. ROBERTS (1978) Policing the Crisis: Mugging, the State, and Law and Order. London. Macmillan.

HIRST, P. Q. (1975) "Marx and Engels on law, crime and morality," pp. 203-232 in I. Taylor et al. (eds.) Critical Criminology. London: Routledge & Kegan Paul.

HOOD, R. [ed.] (1974) Crime, Criminology and Public Policy. London: Heinemann.

MAYS, J. (1954) Growing Up in the City. Liverpool: University of Liverpool Press.

MORRIS, T. (1957) The Criminal Area: A Study in Social Ecology. London: Routledge & Kegan Paul.

PARKER, H. (1974) Views from the Boys. Newton Abbot: David & Charles.

PLUMMER, K. (1979) "Misunderstanding labelling perspectives," pp. 85-121 in D. Downes and P. Rock (eds.) Deviance and Social Control. London: Martin Robertson.

ROCK, P. (1979) "The sociology of crime, symbolic interactionism and some problematic qualities of radical criminology," pp. 52-84 in D. Downes and P. Rock (eds.) Deviance and Social Control. London: Martin Robertson.

SUMNER, C. (1979) Reading Ideologies. London: Academic.

——— (1976) "Marxism and deviancy theory," pp. 159-174 in P. Wiles (ed.) The Sociology of Crime and Delinquency in Britain, Vol. 2: The New Criminologies. London: Martin Robertson.

TAYLOR, I., P. WALTON, and J. YOUNG [eds.] (1975) Critical Criminology. London: Routledge & Kegan Paul.

——— (1973) The New Criminology. London: Routledge & Kegan Paul.

WILES, P. (1976) The Sociology of Crime and Delinquency in Britain, Vol. 2: The New Criminologies. London: Martin Robertson.

YOUNG, J. (1975) "Working class criminology," pp. 63-94 in I. Taylor et al. (eds.) Critical Criminology. London: Routledge & Kegan Paul.

2

RADICAL CRIMINOLOGY IN THE UNITED STATES: AN INTERPRETIVE UNDERSTANDING

David O. Friedrichs

THE EMERGENCE OF RADICAL CRIMINOLOGY

Radical criminology may be considered the most recent paradigm in this area of study to establish a separate generalized identity, emerging only in the early 1970s as something more than an isolated set of critiques.[1] It has been variously described as "conflict," "Marxist," "social-ist," "new," "left-wing," or "critical" criminology![2] Still very much in the emergent stage, radical criminology may be said to involve a two-pronged attack upon not only the social, economic, and political establishment of a capitalist society, but also upon the establishment of the sociological and criminological disciplines. It may be seen as a product (in part, at the very least) of the radicalizing events of the 1960s, including in particular the civil rights struggle, the Vietnam war and the resulting protest movement,

AUTHOR'S NOTE: This work is principally derived from two papers presented at meetings of the American Society of Criminology and the Association for Humanist Sociology (1979). Earlier versions of the ASC paper were presented at the AKD Sociological Research Symposium, Virginia Commonwealth University, February 1979, and the East Coast Conference of Socialist Sociologists, University of Delaware, May 1979.

the growing awareness of exploitative and illegal activity committed by economic and political elites, and the general emergence of a "liberated" consciousness and literature, both domestically and internationally (see Platt, 1974; Gibbons, 1979a: 166).[3] For some criminologists it was no longer possible to maintain a "neutral" perspective with regard to the responses of the state and the police to a rising crime rate and considerable political unrest, or to be a part of research sponsored by a government involved in oppressive policies.

THE PARADIGMATIC CONFLICT:
BREAKING WITH MAINSTREAM THEORY

The developments in the larger society noted above were reflected by an ongoing paradigmatic conflict within sociology and criminology (as well as related disciplines) which gained considerable momentum in the late 1960s and early 1970s.[4] The radicals' break with the traditional, positivistic paradigm—especially in its functionalist and pathological form (see Gibbons, 1979a)—is quite distinct and obvious: The incorporation of a consensus model of law and society, the claim of objectivity and neutrality by scientists uncovering valid causal relationships based upon reliable quantitative data, and the tendency to regard lawbreakers as fundamentally different (both sociologically and psychologically) from respectable citizens are all elements of the traditional approach wholly or largely rejected by radical criminologists (but see Meier, 1977).

The emerging radical perception that law is not really a reflection of the common interest, and that crime itself must be best understood in terms of the structure of the economy, has roots in earlier American thought.[5] As early as 1822 we have Edward Livingston, scion of a prominent American Family—and himself the holder of a number of high offices— writing in the preliminary report of his model penal code:

> Everywhere, with but few exceptions, the interest of the many has, from the earliest ages, been sacrificed to the power of the few. Everywhere penal laws have been framed to support this power (1822: 45).[6]

Eighty years later we find Clarence Darrow, the most celebrated American lawyer of his time, observing in his "Address to the Prisoners in the Cook County Jail" in 1902 that "it's easy to see how to do away with what we call crime. ... It can be done by giving the people a chance to live—by destroying special privileges" (1979: 465).

Despite the social prestige of Livingston and Darrow, their ideas, and similar themes advanced by others, were not really adopted by mainstream

American criminological thought, or American legal culture.[7] Although sociologists of the "progressive" school and various other criminological theorists (e.g., Merton with his "anomie" theory) had either decried the misery of the masses and crimes of the rich *or* had attempted to indicate the relationship between the cultural values and the opportunity structure of the economic system and criminal behavior, they had not (with isolated exceptions) challenged that system as such (see Vold, 1979; Gibbons, 1979a; Quinney, 1979d). Prior to the late 1960s it is true that individual criminologists began to recognize fundamental deficiencies in mainstream conceptions of crime and justice: for example, Sutherland's attention to white-collar crime (1940), Jeffery's call for closer study of criminal law (1978), and Vold's recognition of the role of conflict (1979).[8] But by the early 1970s a significant number of criminologists began to conclude, usually quite gradually, that the *entire framework* and *basic premises* of traditional and mainstream criminological theory were inappropriate for a proper understanding of crime and criminal justic in a capitalist society.

If the break with the mainstream consensus model and positivist paradigm has been especially obvious and clear-cut, the relationship of radical criminology to interactionist and constructionist perspectives which had also challenged mainstream criminology is more complex. It would seem to be quite evident that many radical criminologists were influenced by this school of thought's rejection of the consensus model, focus upon the problematic meaning of crime, and shift of attention from individual or social pathology to the formulation, implementation, and consequences of a stigmatizing "labeling" process (see Gibbons, 1979a: 143-155; but also Beirne, 1979). Nevertheless radical criminologists have *also* generally rejected the alleged subjectivity, the focus upon traditional criminal classes, the failure to deal with the power structure and to recognize the uses of power for consciousness control, and the unwillingness to provide guidelines for transformation into a more humane world which it associates with this paradigm (see Quinney, 1974b: 7-13; Liazos, 1972; Taylor et al., 1973: 220-221; Manders, 1975).

MARXIST AND CONFLICT THEORY

Radical criminology is most closely identified with Marxist and conflict theory, but it can be argued that in a strict sense it is synonymous with neither.

With regard to Marx and Engels it is generally conceded that they did not develop a systematic criminological theory (see Taylor et al., 1973: 217). But it is possible to extrapolate a generalized Marxist perspective on crime and criminal law, following the analysis of Bonger (1916; see also Taylor et al., 1973: 222-236) and others.

Briefly stated, in this Marxist perspective it is not human nature itself but capitalism which produces egocentric, greedy, and predatory human behavior; the ownership class is guilty of the worst crime—the brutal exploitation (even unto death) of the working class; revolution is effectively a form of counterviolence, and is generally both necessary and morally justifiable; the state and the law itself are ultimately tools of the ownership class, and they reflect mainly the economic interests of that class; conventional crime is essentially a product of extreme poverty and economic disenfranchisement, of "false needs" and the dehumanizing and demoralizing effects of the capitalist system. But conventional crime is neither an admirable nor an effective means of revolutionary action, and is in some respects reactionary; conventional crime pits the poor against the poor. Crime is also observed, perhaps ironically, to be productive, providing employment and business for many. In a truly communist society the state and the law will "wither away," with the formal law being replaced by a form of communal justice.[9]

The above is an outline, necessarily somewhat simplified, of some of the main elements of a Marxist theory of crime, such as it is. Despite the widespread eruption of radical activity, consciousness, and thought in the United States in the late 1960s, Marx has had relatively little *direct* influence here (see Gibbons, 1979a: 137). One suspects that most radical criminologists were "radicalized" by the historical events and circumstances referred to earlier, and only *then* turned to Marx for a theoretical framework through which their radicalism could be expressed; accounts given by Platt and Quinney of their movement toward a radical perspective would seem to support this interpretation (see Currie, 1973; Goldwyn, 1971).

It might be argued, then, that Marx's general theory, his conceptualizations, and the critical dimension of his analytical approach, rather than the full content of his work, has been inspirational and significant to radical criminologists. Objections have been raised by a number of commentators to the effect that many radical criminologists who profess to be Marxists differ significantly from Marx's own views on positivistic methods and the role of the *Lumpenproletariat*, as two examples (see Denisoff and MacQuarie, 1975: 108-112; MacDonald, 1976: 257-272; Hirst, 1972: 28-43). The basic radical rejoinder to this has been that Marxism is not a closed system (see Quinney, 1973a: 66; Chambliss, 1975: 150-169); insofar as American radical criminologists have a Marxist orientation, it is to refer to this orientation as *neo*-Marxist. Furthermore, significant distinctions have been made between some of the varieties of neo-Marxist orientation: for example, *instrumental* and *structural* Marxian analysis (see Beirne, 1979: 379-380). More generally it is necessary to distinguish between a "Marx's" criminology which adheres strictly to his own clearly identifiable views,[10] a contemporary American (and European) radical criminology broadly based upon Marxist theory, and criminology as presently practiced in the USSR and other socialistic countries, which draws upon Marxist theory but in many respects has a closer relationship to American mainstream criminology in its focus upon personal and social pathology (see Buchholz et al., 1974).

Finally, American radical criminology has obviously been influenced by conflict theory, and in a strict evolutionary sense this theoretical orientation has probably been the most common antecedent to the development of a radical criminological perspective (for example, in the cases of Quinney and Chambliss).[11] It continues to be common for criminology text authors to confuse conflict and radical theory (see Vold, 1979: 315-322), and this confusion may be virtually inevitable given the classification of "early" Quinney (1970a, 1970b) and Chambliss (and Seidman, 1971) with non-Marxist conflict theory.[12] Although some of Marx's insights have been utilized by conflict theorists, their conceptual orientation may be said to have a greater affinity with the tradition of Simmel (see Collins, 1975). In the field of criminology it has been most commonly associated with works such as Vold (1979; originally 1958), Turk (1979; and this volume), and Hills (1971), in addition to the aforementioned work of Chambliss and Quinney. For present purposes a few limited, general observations can be made: Conflict criminologists tend to recognize a *plurality* of interests and power, and do not put a singular emphasis on capitalism as do radicals; they tend to favor "nonpartisan" academic research (see Turk, this volume) and they do not reject the legal order as such, or the use of legalistic definitions of crime; insofar as conflict criminologists concern themselves with policy it is in the direction of reform as opposed to revolution (see Michalowski, 1977a; Chambliss, 1976a: 1-28; Keller, 1976: 227-243; Denisoff and MacQuarie, 1975: 110-113). There has been a considerable exchange of critiques between conflict and radical criminologists, although it must be conceded that the differences in terms of either perspective or specific personalities is not always entirely clear, and the designation "radical" is not uncommonly applied to individuals who might not be so identified by criminologists who lay claim to a Marxist orientation.[13]

RADICAL CRIMINOLOGY IN THE UNITED STATES TODAY

Radical criminology in the United States today is made up of a relatively fluid group of academics, for the most part, the more conspicuous including R. Quinney, W. Chambliss, H. Schwendinger, J. Schwendinger, T. Platt, P. Takagi, H. Pepinsky, R. Michalowski, B. Krisberg, J. Reiman, and D. Humphries. It has become a conspicuous presence at professional conferences; radical criminologists have met together under the auspices of the Union of Radical Criminologists, the East Coast Conference of Socialist Sociologists, and other caucuses and affiliations; journals such as *Crime and Social Justice* (edited by Takagi and Platt) and *Contemporary Crises* (edited by Chambliss) have provided a forum for the publication of radical criminological work; radical criminological texts and readers have been published, especially by Quinney (1979d, 1975, 1974a), Chambliss (and Mankoff, 1976), and Krisberg (1975); provocative and frequently cited radical critiques have been produced (e.g., Quinney, 1977, 1974b). Perhaps exemplifying an ideal in radical criminological productions would be the Center for Research on Criminal Justice's *The Iron Fist and the Velvet Glove* (1977), insofar as it is an essentially Marxist analysis of the police, collectively written, and oriented toward *praxis,* with a section on "Implications for Organizing"; this volume is a product of Berkeley-based radical criminologists who were subjected during the 1970s to a concerted conservative effort to purge them from the University of California.

While self-identified radical criminologists may remain relatively few in number, their influence on the discipline has been not inconsiderable (see Pelfrey, this volume), with the book in hand but one more indication of continuing interest in the radical criminology controversy. That the impact of radical criminology has extended beyond the academy is, to date, less clear. Whether or not it is fair to say that the paradigm is experiencing a crisis, as Klockars (this volume) suggests, it has rather undeniably been in a state of flux.[14]

Radical criminologists tend, of course, to share certain general premises, perceptions, and principles; the intellectual careers, and specific elements of their thought, differ between individual radical criminologists. In what follows, radical criminology will be interpreted on the "objective" plane, utilizing the concept of legitimacy to critically identify some of its basic tenets, and on a "subjective" plane, through an examination of the career of an especially prominent radical criminologist, Richard Quinney.

THE OBJECTIVE DIMENSION:
A QUESTION OF LEGITIMACY

In his controversial critique of radical criminology, Klockars (this volume) argues that the concepts of *class* and *interest* are basic to the analysis of that paradigm. In this section the argument is advanced that the concept of *legitimacy* is explicitly or implicitly central to an understanding of the principal themes of radical criminology.

The question of the legitimacy of the legal order, and the consequences of challenges to legitimacy claims—especially in the form of a "legitimacy crisis"—is widely recognized to be a central concern for contemporary American society.[15] Legitimacy, following Weber, is generally regarded as an orientation toward an order;[16] this implicitly suggests the presence of legitimating attributes of the order itself. Such legitimating attributes may be inherent, fundamental, and long-standing features of the order ("taken-for-granted" legitimacy) or they may be deliberately advanced by the governing elite of the order to help generate popular legitimacy (i.e., they are "claims"). The evaluation of legitimacy may focus on legitimacy orientations and ascriptions (i.e., the nature of popular perceptions of an order) *or* it may focus upon either the inherent attributes of the order or the specific legitimacy claims of the governing elite. This distinction is frequently not made (see Friedman, 1977: 138-139). "Legitimacy" itself may then describe both a state of affairs and a process, and is generally considered to be at least a wholly desirable and at most an absolutely necessary element of a stable and effective political order (see Friedrichs, 1979a; Vidich and Glassman, 1979; but also Useem and Useem, 1979). Ultimately it involves explicit or implicit justifications for the authority of an order on the one hand, and the development of a concomitant sense of obligation on the part of subjects or citizens of that order on the other hand. On another level we may say that legitimacy involves the generation of expectations relating to the political order and the generation of support necessary for their successful fulfillment. Within the present context we can distinguish between what we might call *inherent* (universal and natural) legitimacy and *perceptual* (relative and positive) legitimacy.[17]

When we refer to inherent legitimacy we are focusing on the order itself, applying some type of criteria or indices of evaluation; such an evaluation assesses whether the order *ought* to exist, whether it *ought* to be complied with, and whether it corresponds to inherently justifiable principles upon which an order should be based. Such an evaluation is critical, and is inevitably expressed within the context of an ideological posture. This conception differs from perceptual legitimacy, which refers to citizen acceptance of, and the development of a sense of obligation toward, an order.

The above distinctions have been made as a preface to an examination of the explicit or implicit invocation of the question of legitimacy by radical criminologists.

ON THE INHERENT LEGITIMACY OF THE LAW

With regard to law radical criminology very directly challenges traditional conceptions. In the traditional view law secures and enhances civilization; law is based upon the universal good and democratic consensus. Law settles disputes, defines relationships, educates, promotes desirable behavior, and protects the idea of justice. Law is both desirable and absolutely necessary; a "lawless society" is a contradiction in terms. There are bad laws, but law itself is good (see Friedrichs, 1979a; Friedman, 1977: 10-19).[18]

In the radical conception law, as well as the legal order itself, is inherently *il*legitimate. It is oppressive and generally supportive of elitist interests, and is developed mainly through coercion and the accumulation of power, not through an expression of common will (see Cloke, 1971; Quinney, 1972a, 1973a, 1974b, 1977; Chambliss, 1976b).[19] The legal definition of crime is not a reflection of objective standards of harm, and in fact the most harmful actions—imperialism, racism, and so on—are not legally criminal (see Schwendinger and Schwendinger, 1970, 1977). The criminal justice system and its various agencies are mainly directed toward the maintenance of the capitalist system, not the protection of the people (see especially Michalowski, 1979; Center for Research on Criminal Justice, 1977; Reiman, 1979). It has been suggested that law itself may be neither inevitable nor necessary; since it is in fact oppressive it should be abandoned and replaced by "popular justice" (see Quinney, 1974b: 20-26; 1977: 27, 45, 162; Pepinsky, 1978; Tifft, 1979).[20] Bankowski and Mungham (1976) specifically argue that "liberalized" law is no real improvement, as it is the *form* of law which is the problem. Poverty law is said to   benefit lawyers more than the poor.

ON PERCEPTUAL LEGITIMACY

We may then turn to the matter of *perceptual* legitimacy. Quinney and other radical criminologists have generally conceded that the forces of law and order *are* largely supported by the public (see Quinney, 1974b: 151). The reason given for this is that the government and the elite manipulate public consciousness (see Quinney, 1974b: 137, 153; 1977: 47; 1979d: 35).[21] The truly repressive state does not rely upon directly coercive measures, but indoctrinates through the media, LEAA programs, police community relations departments, and other state workers (Quinney, 1977: 12, 133; 1979c; 1979d: 36, 52, 404; Pepinsky, 1978: 325). The criminal law itself contributes to the legitimation process by promoting street crime images and drawing attention away from capitalist crime, and by promoting the myth of legality and evenhanded justice (see Humphries, 1975; Michalowski and Bohlander, 1976: 104; Reiman, 1979). But it is also noted that the capitalist state is faced with the contradiction of maintaining the "rule of law" for long-term legitimacy versus the short-term goal of maintaining order (see Balbus, 1973: 3; Denisoff & MacQuarie, 1975: 116; Beirne, 1979; Reiman, 1979). Thus laws and legal acts protecting rights and serving broad public interests and the powerless may be seen as contributing to the enduring survival of the capitalist system.

Insofar as mainstream criminologists are concerned, they are seen as accepting and helping to maintain the official ideology; thus Quinney claims that the purpose of traditional criminology as a discipline is to maintain the legitimation of the legal order (1973a: 75-82; 1974b: 19-26; 1979c: 278-283). Too much mainstream criminological research is carried out with government funding, and is too directly responsive to governmental needs, with a resulting "purchased virtue" (see Galliher, 1979).[22] The chosen role of radical criminologists themselves is to demystify and expose the inherent illegitimacy of the legal order (see Quinney, 1979d: 36-37). The new criminology, Krisberg (1975: 4) tells us, addresses itself to the basic questions of justice and humanity. Insofar as radical criminologists are able to contribute to the development of perceptual illegitimation, this should help produce class consciousness, which should in turn lead to active class struggle and revolution. Radical criminologists themselves must develop a working-class consciousness, and an active commitment beyond intellectual activity (Quinney, 1979c: 284-290).

The potential for the development just outlined is seen in the form of the "legitimation crisis" identified by Habermas (1973; see also Friedrichs, 1979a; Quinney, 1977: 85-87), indicated by widespread discontent, the emergence of libertarian movements, the growth of critical imagination, and various everyday class struggles (Quinney and Wildeman, 1977: 172). One notes the failure of the state to solve problems created by a capitalist economy, and the increasing difficulty of maintaining the false ideology that capitalism benefits the workers (see Quinney, 1977: 52-60, 85). An increasing tension develops through the state's effort to maintain legitimacy *and* elitist efforts to uphold a capitalist economy; increasingly larger resources must be utilized to fulfill the legitimation function (see Quinney, 1977: 108, 122, 157). The eventual withdrawal of perceptual legitimation is a precondition—although not a sufficient condition in and of itself—for the development of revolutionary *praxis,* which should lead to the emergence of a socialistic state with popular justice (see Quinney, 1974b: 196; 1979d: 45). All of this will take time.

ON COMPLIANCE WITH THE LAW

Two remaining questions pertinent to the radical criminological treatment of legitimacy issues are: First, *if* law is inherently *il*legitimate, is there an obligation to comply with it? Second, are conventional lawbreakers to be regarded as engaging in a valid form of delegitimation?

The first question has been little dealt with by mainstream criminology, either because the answer is taken for granted, or the question itself is regarded as lying beyond the disciplinary jurisdiction. In Friedman's (1975: 117) formulation our obligation to comply is related to the general soundness of the law, and the unacceptable consequences of noncompliance (i.e., violence and anarchy). Radical criminologists have also tended to evade this issue, either because the answer is regarded as implicit or awkward. Quinney (1970a) has suggested that an illegitimate system need not be obeyed, and Davis (1974) has spoken of a "justification for no obligation" on the part of black Americans, on the basis of historical inequality and disenfranchisement. Insofar as the radical criminologist complies with the law, it must be because it coincides with independent moral and pragmatic choices.

With regard to the second question, concerning conventional criminality, it must first be noted that some radical criminologists have disputed the legalistic conception of crime—as observed earlier—as well as the mainstream disregard for elitist crimes (see Schwendinger and Schwendinger, 1970, 1977; Hepburn, 1977; Reiman, 1979). Quinney (1979d: 228) and Gordon (1973: 163), among others, have suggested that illegal and criminal acts *may* be viewed as rational responses to a capitalist system. In an earlier work Quinney suggested that criminals and deviants could be regarded as rationalistic, voluntaristic, and creative; he rejected the traditional conception of causation (1965a: 119-122; 1970a: 5-7; 1979d: 228-230). Criminal behavior must be understood in the context of an artificially created reality. Recently Quinney (1977: 54, 93-99) has viewed conventional criminality as reproducing capitalist behavior and victimizing the oppressed; but at least *some* criminality may be considered in terms of conscious, political choice. Within a Marxist framework the voluntaristic dimension is compromised by recognition of capitalist controls (see Quinney, 1979c: 445; 1979d: 229), with human beings as creators *and* products of their culture.

Ultimately it must be said that the radical criminological perspective on conventional criminality is characterized by some ambivalence, with the following three tendencies evident: It is largely disregarded as *relatively* insignificant activity; it is regarded as an inevitable product of a capitalist system; it is regarded as political, with a potential for radicalizing and forming a coalition with the proletariat (see Platt, 1978; Krisberg, 1975: 20-79). It should be stressed that a radical orientation does not necessarily condone conventional illegality, nor does it preclude support for programs which attempt to limit or produce relief from the immediate problem of street crime (see Humphries, 1979: 237; Reiman, 1979: 18-34).

THE SUBJECTIVE DIMENSION:
A SEARCH FOR A RADICAL HUMANISM?

Richard Quinney is probably the most prolific, the most frequently cited, and the most controversial contemporary radical criminologist. The thesis advanced here is that his career is better understood within the broader framework of a search for a radical humanism than simply as the evolution of a Marxist criminologist.[23]

A product of the American heartland, Quinney attended a small midwestern college before taking his Ph.D. at the University of Wisconsin in 1962.[24] He has said that he came to criminology through social theory and circumstance, after working for the late social theorist Howard Becker (Goldwyn, 1971); his dissertation on prescription violations by pharmacists was indicative of an early interest in the illegal activities of respectable elements of society (1962, 1963). Some of his first published work included essays on conceptualizations of deviance and human nature (1964b, 1964c, 1965a, 1965b) and thus indicated a reflective and philosophical orientation as opposed to the dominant positivistic and functionalist tenor of the time. Other work of his, however, on demographic and ecological analysis (1964a; 1966), differential association (with DeFleur, 1966) and criminal behavior typologies (with Clinard, 1967) fitted more naturally within the framework of mainstream criminological concerns.

By the late 1960s Quinney's orientation had shifted quite clearly into the realm of conflict theory, exemplified by publication of a reader in the sociology of criminal law (1969), which outlined a sociological theory of criminal law advancing propositions focusing upon the relevance of power, conflict and interests in the law, with readings stressing these themes. His text, *The Social Reality of Crime* (1970a), published the following year, amplified upon this theory. The format of this text represented a fairly clear break with conventional criminological texts in its special attention to philosophical premises and its emphasis upon the social *meaning* of crime and criminal justice. Quinney advanced a conception of social action which is specifically humanistic, insofar as "man's actions are purposive and meaningful . . . man engages in voluntary behavior . . . we may see him as changing and becoming, rather than merely being" (1970a: 13). Upon these premises Quinney formulated his six oft-cited propositions concerning the interrelationship of definitions of crime, conflict of interest, the differential application of power, criminal behavior and the diffusion of conceptions of crime (1970a: 15-23). A softcover text published the same year (1970b) applied a conflict perspective to an interpretation of the historical and philosophical evolution of crime.

In a 1971 interview Quinney asserted that a scientist must not only ask what is, but what ought to be as well; his own thinking was being influenced more by what was happening "outside" than by fellow criminologists, and he referred to a wide variety of these influences among exposé journalists, revisionist historians, leftist activists, and poets (Goldwyn, 1971: 43-49). His stated premise was that "basically man is good and given his chance to build decent institutions so he can live his life with others man does not need formal authority over him" (1970b: 52). At this stage Quinney disavowed a specifically Marxist character to his ideas, attributing this to the non-Marxist character of his training (1970b: 48). But his productions of the early 1970s on the violence commission (1971), the ideology of law (1972a), the question of victimization (1972b), and the issue of repression (1972c; 1973a) reflected an increasingly critical orientation toward the larger legal order. Quinney's affinity for "transcendental" thought was also clearly emerging during this period (1973d).

In a remarkable essay entitled "There's a Lot of Us Folks Grateful to the Lone Ranger" (1973b), published two years after the interview cited above, Quinney's leftward shift became even more evident. In a classically reflective examination the author traces his movement away from the "Lone Ranger" mentality of frontier individualism—a myth that had to be repudiated, a dialectic which had to be exposed, a threat to our very existence—to reveal the true meaning of law and order in capitalist society. In response to the adoption of a critical and ultimately a neo-Marxist theoretical perspective, Quinney undertook significant revisions of his earlier books. Even the second edition of *Criminal Behavior Systems* (Clinard & Quinney, 1973) adds "corporate crime" and reflects a more politicized stress in its interpretation of crime. A new reader, *Criminal Justice in America: A Critical Understanding* (1974a) is directly acknowledged to be organized upon Marxist premises, and has the avowedly humanistic objective of providing "the understanding necessary for the creation of an authentic human existence" and serving "the advancement of human possibilities" (1974a: v, 2). A second edition of *The Problem of Crime* (with Wildeman, 1977: 6, 11) states as its objective a critical analysis of commonplace assumptions regarding crime and criminal justice, rooted in Marxist analysis. A capitalist society cannot be responsive to authentic human needs; the emergence of a critical public imagination—"one capable of unmasking the contradictions spawned by existing political and economic structures" (1977: 170)—must eventually lead to transformation into a new socialist society, "a world freed from the dehumanizing conditions and contradictions of capitalism, freed from the brutality of class oppression, hierarchy and domination" (1977: 172). A complete revision of *The Social Reality of Crime* (1970d) took the form of a new text, *Criminology: Analysis and Critique of Crime in America* (1975), itself subsequently revised in a second edition simply entitled *Criminology* (1979d). In these texts Quinney advances, elaborates upon, and illustrates extensively the "critical-Marxist" theoretical perspective on crime and criminal justice which increasingly characterized his thought during the decade. The ultimate objective was to work toward the elimination of exploitative conditions and repressive relationships, and to demystify capitalist ideology (1979d: 26, 69).

In two shorter, more narrowly focused works published during these years the critical and Marxist analysis of law and criminal justice are explored in more depth. In *Critique of Legal Order* (1974b) Quinney pays special attention to what he calls "scholarship in the service of social control" and the inherently conservative character of criminal code bills and crime control bureaucracies such as the LEAA. In this book the tactics of criminal justice system reform are quite specifically rejected because liberal reform does not abolish the oppression inherent in a capitalist state (1974b: 170). Quinney adopts Marx's position that through socialist revolution a transformation of humans into "authentic species-beings" occurs (1974b: 188), and the alienated nature characteristic of those living in a capitalist society disappears: "The socialist vision is one of human liberation" (1974b: 188). In *Class, State and Crime* (1977) Quinney reexplores these themes and reaffirms his Marxist analysis. Rejecting the prevailing conception of justice in a capitalist society, he notes the "idea of justice as distribution according to *need*" (1974b: 22). Following a Marxist analysis of the oppressive nature of criminal justice in a capitalist society, and the manipulation of popular consciousness within such a society, Quinney calls for combining theory and practice and for fostering a political, revolutionary consciousness among the oppressed (1974b: 104-105, 159-161). We are told that critical social theory aids people in understanding their objective conditions (1974b: 161-164); in a socialist society *popular justice* will replace capitalistic criminal justice (1974b: 162-163). And in a subsequent essay (1979c) Quinney elaborates on the theme of human beings and criminology itself as products of a capitalist structure capable of creating change through the development of socialist consciousness.

In his most recent work (1979a, 1979b; 1980) Quinney for the first time shifts his focus on capitalist society beyond the framework of crime and criminal justice. The most remarkable feature of these new products of Quinney's fertile mind lies in their attempt to integrate sociology, Marxism, *and* theology, the material and the spiritual, the sacred and the secular. The crisis of advanced capitalism is seen as both material *and* spiritual, the transition to socialism is both political and religious, and "A socialism without the sacred would become a system as materialist and alienating as that of capitalism" (1979a: 127). For Quinney, now:

> The task at hand is that of uniting these two universal forms of thought and belief (the philosophy of Marxism and the theology of Tillich) into a framework for both understanding our human history and acting in fulfillment of our personal and collective being [1979a: 211].

The specific implications of this extraordinary new direction in Quinney's thought for his understanding of crime and criminal justice have apparently not yet been worked out. That he has made an existential "leap," so to speak, into a perspective from which most of those who identified with the specifically sociological, secular, and Marxist elements of his work in criminology would disaffiliate themselves is a reasonable conjecture. For Quinney's adoption of a prophetic social critical mode of thought casts him in the position of advocating the most extreme of all possible dissents from conventional, positivistic social science, but it is consistent with his ongoing search for a radical humanism.

Quinney's contributions to criminology to date might be classified, thoretically and chronologically, as conventional, conflict oriented, critical, neo-Marxist, and most recently prophetic. This singular intellectual career over a period of approximately two decades may be virtually without parallel in the discipline. But whatever direction his work now takes Quinney has undeniably made a fundamental contribution to the development of radical criminology.

CONCLUDING REMARKS: OF THINGS YET TO COME

In future histories of the discipline of criminology the emergence of a radical paradigm during the decade of the 1970s will be regarded as one of the more striking developments of the period. Although the argument has been made (Meier, 1977) that this radical paradigm has simply coopted and politicized important elements of mainstream criminology, or is simply the "old baloney"—of false sentimentality—in new garb (see Toby, this volume), the basic thesis advanced here is that radical criminology has provided us with an authentic alternative to traditional conceptions of crime and criminal justice. While some of its sentiments are indeed of old vintage, and it undeniably evolved out of more conventional criminological perspectives, it can also be submitted that radical criminology establishes a new framework and set of fundamental assumptions. While closely related to the theory of Marx, and conflict theory, it is here distinguished from both. The establishment of radical criminology as a visible—if controversial—presence within the discipline is beyond dispute.

On the objective plane the question of legitimacy is critical. A deeper understanding of law, crime, and justice requires a fuller realization of the concept of legitimacy.

In the foregoing analysis an explication of the radical understanding of the legitimacy question was presented. In sum, radical criminology challenges the "taken-for-granted" inherent legitimacy and legitimacy claims which mainstream criminology has tended to implicitly or explicitly accord to the legal order and the criminal justice system. The principal task remaining here is the elaboration of an understanding of what a viable social order devoid of law, or law as we know it, would look like. This will require further theoretical explorations of an anarchic conception of law (see Tifft, 1979) as well as a more systematic analysis of existing socialistic and communist states in terms of the success or failure of their law or system of social control to conform to the criteria for an inherently legitimate order (see Pepinsky, 1975).

With regard to what we have called perceptual legitimacy, radical criminology has provided us with the following: an explanation for diffuse public ascription of legitimacy to the legal order; an interpretation of the role played—wittingly or unwittingly—by mainstream criminologists in the maintenance of legitimacy; a chosen role for radical criminologists in contributing to the *de*legitimation of the legal order (by exposing its structurally oppressive nature) and thereby promoting the development of class consciousness; and an analysis suggesting that the contradictions of the capitalist legal order are catching up with it and are leading to an emerging "legitimacy crisis." Radical criminology also raises questions about moral obligation to comply with an inherently illegitimate order and compels us to consider conventional criminal behavior not only as a product of an economically inequitable and oppressive system, but also at least potentially as conscious political choice. While radical criminology does not condone "street crime"—most directed against the poor—it challenges a legal conception and criminal justice system response which does not deal with the most harmful crimes effectively—namely those committed in the name of the state or by an economic elite.

Much work remains to be done in terms of arriving at a better understanding of the complex process of legitimation, delegitimation, and the development of class consciousness. (Radicals might more positively draw upon KOL studies of attitudes toward law, the political socialization literature, and theories of moral reasoning toward this end.) While mainstream criminologists are likely to continue to reject the radical interpretation of their role as well as the perceived unilateral explanation for crime and criminal justice, radical criminology must address itself to the problem of its own perceived legitimacy as a viable paradigm if it wishes to reach and be taken seriously by a larger audience.[25]

With regard to the legitimacy crisis, a more extensive examination of its nature and dynamics is required, especially in terms of the role of illegal behavior and conceptions of law. A legitimacy crisis may be seen as a failure of the legal order to meet demands or expectations, *or* as a product of the diffuse recognition of the inherent illegitimacy of the order (see Friedrichs, 1979a). American society is not simply "late capitalist" but is also a quasi-democratic, modern mass society with a Judeo-Christian heritage. Specifically, how do these different elements interact insofar as a legitimacy crisis is concerned?

The ethical implications of the radical criminological position have not been entirely worked out. Why comply with law at all? What is the nature of the normative order toward which radical criminologists are oriented?

Insofar as conventional criminality is concerned, an ambivalent stance has been noted. Metaphysical and typological ambiguities and contradictions require more attention; radical criminology must more successfully disassociate itself from a perceived direct identification with predatory conventional offenders.

The career of the most visible radical criminologist of the 1970s, Richard Quinney, was reviewed and interpreted in the final analysis as a search for a radical humanism.[26] The argument here is that an authentic understanding of radical criminology requires attention to the subjective dimension, to individual intellectual careers. The American socialization experience and the character of our higher education produces individuals generally unwilling to adhere in large numbers to a narrow, rigid "party line"; for this reason American radical criminology will probably always be characterized by an idiosyncratic aspect. Readers of Quinney's various texts cannot help but be aware of his vast reading in the criminological literature, and much of his writing in these books is firmly rooted in that literature and its findings. On another level, however, principally in his critiques and papers, Quinney has sought to go beyond what *is* into the realm of what *could be.* Not only has Quinney obviously and persistently been attacked by mainstream criminologists (e.g., see Klockars, this volume) but he has also been criticized by those more sympathetic to his political orientation for being a poor "role model" (Mankoff, this volume), writing in places more of a religious tract than a scientific analysis (Greenberg, 1979) and for not dealing systematically with important issues (Humphries, 1975). Quinney himself has chosen to devote his not inconsiderable energies to moving on with his own work rather than simply responding to his critics. But it is quite obvious that Quinney's orientation is *ultimately* toward the critical, transcendental, and prophetic, and is best read as providing us with alternatives to the framework and metaphors which have dominated our intellectual universe. Quinney himself has always exemplified the spirit of personal tolerance toward those with whom one disagrees (see Akers, this volume); he deserves not only greater tolerance but the lasting gratitude as well of all American criminologists for compelling them to confront their major premises, for provoking productive controversy (this volume being but one obvious outcome), and for providing a *basic* framework for the radical understanding of crime and criminal justice. With rare intellectual courage, immense scholarly erudition, awesome imagination, and remarkable productiveness Quinney has explored the outer reaches of the criminological frontier. Even if Quinney is "wrong" or "one-sided" in many instances, the conviction remains that his work and thought will continue to be discussed, will continue to inspire and provoke, long after his more timid if technically more "correct" criminological brethren are forgotten or relegated to obscure footnotes.

What can we expect of radical criminology as it enters its second decade? I have elsewhere (this volume) suggested that we can distinguish between "hard" and "soft" versions of radical criminology. Going beyond that basic distinction, it is projected here that the paradigm will be moving in several directions.

First, an *orthodox neo-Marxist* analysis will undoubtedly continue to characterize the work of many radical criminologists, although the division between those with a *structural* and those with an *instrumental* orientation (noted earlier, see Beirne, 1979) may become more pronounced. Relatedly, tensions may increase between *praxis* or action-oriented radical criminologists and those who will maintain a more conventionally academic and intellectual orientation. But elaboration upon the application of Marxian categories and concepts to an interpretation of crime and justice is certainly likely to continue.

Second, reconciliation with *humanistic* orientations in their many varieties will probably increase. We have noted Quinney's unorthodox movement toward the prophetic; elsewhere I have explored the possible reconciliation of radical criminology with more conventional strains of humanistic sociology (Friedrichs, 1979c).[27] This effort may also include more attention on the part of radical criminologists to the tradition of socialist or Marxist humanism.

Third, still other radical criminologists may move toward a reconciliation with *sociological positivism,* with increasing application of conventional methodology to a more systematic testing of radical propositions, with a search for viable explanations for nonverification, and toward an integration of relevant mainstream theory and research with a generalized radical framework. The recent work of Carter and Clelland (1979) might be cited as a possible illustration of this direction.

Whatever direction they move in, radical criminologists will remain united in their belief of the central role of capitalism in explaining problems of crime and criminal justice and in their commitment to fundamental societal transformation. But it is obvious that the projection outlined above may be interpreted negatively by radical criminologists as suggestive of splintering and the ever-present dangers of cooptation. A more positive assessment considers the possibility that the emerging varieties of radical criminology will complement and strengthen each other and that by 1990 the radical framework—being the most responsive to the likely economic chaos of the 1980s—will have become the dominant criminological paradigm.[28]

Will radical criminology enhance its own legitimacy and effectiveness by addressing itself to its remaining contradictions and inadequacies *within* the framework of tolerance for the very different styles presently emerging, or will it attempt to insist upon maintaining a "pure" application of Marxist analysis in a comprehensive way to the interpretation of crime and criminal justice, at the cost of its own potency and persuasiveness?

This is the question we may attempt to answer ten years hence.

NOTES

1. The use of "paradigm" with reference to radical criminology is controversial (see Geis and Meier, 1978: 280), but I follow Michalowski (1977a: 20, 33-37) on this point.

2. The title of this volume coincides with my own preference for the term "radical criminology" as opposed to the alternatives. My reasoning parallels Garofalo (1978: 18) and is, very briefly stated: "conflict" (nonradical identity, misleading); "Marxist" (problematic connotations dealt with in essay); "socialist" (too easily confused with Soviet/Eastern European criminology); "new" (silly; in a few years "old new" criminology; also associated with conservative "new realists," Humphries, 1979); "left-wing" (overly political contra analytical); and "critical" (Frankfort School connotations). "Radical" is suggestive of a fundamental break with mainstream criminology with a leftist orientation.

3. For a more general discussion of the emergence of the New Left, see Lader (1979), Bouchier (1978), and Clecak (1973).

4. The paradigm crisis in sociology which led to the emergence of a radical sociology may be understood by reference to Kuhn's (1970) formulation of paradigm, and then Mills (1959) and Gouldner (1970). The perspective of radical sociology in its "heyday" is found in Colfax and Roach (1972); a recent radical text is Szymanski and Goertzel (1979).

5. As Schafer (1969: 256) reminds us, the seminal insight linking crime to economic conditions or the structure of the economy can be traced back to classical Greeks and Romans.

6. Karl Marx was four years old at this time!

7. Livingston's penal code was specifically rejected by his state's legislative body; Darrow's remarks were rejected as "too radical" by one of the inmates who heard them (1979: n 466).

8. Ironically, Jeffery (1978) is now interested in biosocial theory.

9. Primary source material for Marx's analysis of crime and criminal law has been compiled by Chambliss (1975).

10. Engels's observations are encompassed by this statement.

11. Platt, on the other hand, seems to have come to radical criminology via labeling theory (see Currie, 1973).

12. Marx is in fact barely mentioned in these two books.

13. Turk would be one example.

14. A fully realized assessment of the many-hued, evolving character of radical criminology would be premature. Certainly there is no pretense here of speaking for the radical position (see Friedrichs, this volume, for a clarification) and no more than an indication of the present work of radical criminologists is given. Space limitations necessarily require some simplifications.

15. Citation of the large number of sources upon which the discussion of legitimacy is based is precluded by space limitations; however, see Friedrichs (1979a, 1979b), and for recent discussions Vidich and Glassman (1979).

16. Bensman (1979: 42-43) has recently shown us that Weber utilized the concept of legitimacy in a variety of "extremely complex and often contradictory" ways: as belief, claim, justification, promise, and self-justification.

17. But see Weber (1954: 6), Friedman (1977: 79-80), and Yankelovich (1972: 520-526) for other conceptual categories.

18. The interpretive paradigm has a more problematic conception of law, but does not challenge the basic legitimacy of the law.

19. Again, it is useful in this context to distinguish between instrumental and structural Marxist conceptions of law, as Beirne (1979) does, with the instrumental perspective perceiving all laws as directly reflecting capitalist interests, and the structural perspective seeing the overall thrust of the law, but not each specific law or legal act, as directed toward maintaining the economic status quo. For another dissenting radical perspective on law, see Fraser (1978).

20. Turk (1979) reviews the different conceptions of "the demise of law," and finds them all wanting.

21. Sinden (1979) reports on empirical research which challenges the manipulation-of-consciousness thesis.

22. Mainstream responses to these charges, as well as their critical examinations of various dimensions of the radical criminological analysis, are largely neglected here, although they were dealt with quite extensively in my original paper (1979b). The reasons are obvious: limitations of space, as well as the generous representation of mainstream critiques in this volume. However, readers are referred especially to Klockars (this volume), Gibbons (1979a), and Garofalo (1978) for relatively recent such critiques.

23. Space limitations preclude any examination of the meaning of humanism here, and the relationship of radical criminology to humanistic sociology (but see Lee, 1978; Friedrichs, 1979c). Quinney (1979e) has disaffiliated himself from the "sole reliance on the individual" which he takes to be a fundamental tenet of humanism, but conceives of his more recent work as a contribution to the need for "new symbols and metaphors to express our humanity in relation to the universe." This objective, in my view, is not inconsistent with the interpretation of his career advanced here.

24. After eighteen years of teaching at such institutions as New York University, City University of New York, and Brown, Quinney has returned to his native state as Professor of Sociology and Director of the Urban Social Institution's Interdisciplinary Ph.D. program at the University of Wisconsin–Milwaukee.

25. For a discussion of problems and prospects for teaching radical analysis to not entirely receptive audiences of students and workers, see Faith (1977) and Michalowski (1977b).

26. The substantial reliance of this essay on the work of Quinney—and the focus on his career—can be expected to displease some radical criminologists, as a number (Platt and Takagi, 1979) have been especially critical of him. But the fact remains that Quinney alone has produced a full-scale radical text (1979d), a radical reader (1974a), and two basic critiques of the American legal order from a neo-Marxist viewpoint (1974b, 1977). If Quinney's more recent work in particular has been controversial among his fellow radicals it is contended that the basic themes of radical criminological analysis can be validly extracted from his work, especially that of the mid-1970s. These books are likely to serve as a primary basis for understanding radical criminology for some time. If we look at recent discussions of radical criminology in books about criminological theory, we find, *inevitably*, that the largest block of space by far is devoted to Quinney (Gibbons, 1979a; Vold, 1979). Chambliss, Platt, and the Schwendingers, for example, tend to be more often cited for narrower contributions (e.g., vagrancy laws, child-saving, and humanistic definitions of crime).

27. Schwendinger and Schwendinger (1977: 10) seem to specifically reject this possibility.

28. Gibbons (1979b) at least alludes to the possibility.

REFERENCES

AKERS, R. (1979) "Theory and ideology in Marxist criminology: comments on Turk, Quinney, Toby, and Klockars." Criminology 16 (February): 527-544.

BALBUS, I. (1973) The Dialectics of Legal Repression. New York: Russell Sage.

BANKOWSKI, Z. and G. MUNGHAM (1976) Images of Law. London: Routledge & Kegan Paul.

BEIRNE, P. (1979) "Empiricism and the critique of Marxism on law and crime." Social Problems 26 (April): 373-385.

BENSMAN, J. (1979) "Max Weber's concept of legitimacy: an evaluation," pp. 17-48 in A. Vidich and R. Glassman (eds.) Conflict and Control. Beverly Hills, CA: Sage.

BONGER, W. (1916) Criminality and Economic Conditions. Boston: Little, Brown.

BOUCHIER, D. (1978) Idealism and Revolution. New York: St. Martin's.

BUCHHOLZ, E., R. HARTMANN, J. LEKSCHAS, and G. STILLER (1974) Socialist Criminology. Lexington, MA: D. C. Heath.

CARTER, T. and D. CLELLAND (1979) "A Neo-Marxian critique, formulation and test of juvenile dispositions as a function of social class." Social Problems 27 (October): 96-108.

Center for Research on Criminal Justice (1977) The Iron Fist and the Velvet Glove. Berkeley, CA: Author.

CHAMBLISS, W. J. (1976a) "Functional and conflict theories of crime," in W. J. Chambliss and M. Mankoff (eds.) Whose Law? What Order? New York: John Wiley.

——— (1976b) "The state and the criminal law," in W. J. Chambliss and M. Mankoff (eds.) Whose Law? What Order? New York: John Wiley.

——— (1975) "Toward a political economy of crime." Theory & Society 2 (Summer): 150-170.

CHAMBLISS, W. J. and M. MANKOFF (1976) Whose Law? What Order? New York: John Wiley.

CHAMBLISS, W. J. and R. B. SEIDMAN (1971) Law, Order & Power. Reading, MA: Addison-Wesley.

CLECAK, P. (1973) Radical Paradoxes: Dilemmas of the American Left, 1945-1970. New York: Harper & Row.

CLOKE, K. (1971) "The economic basis of law and state," in R. Lefcourt (ed.) Law Against the People. New York: Vintage.

CLINARD, M. and R. QUINNEY (1973) Criminal Behavior Systems: A Typology. New York: Holt, Rinehart & Winston.

——— (1967) Criminal Behavior Systems: A Typology. New York: Holt, Rinehart & Winston.

COLFAX, J. D. and J. ROACH [eds.] (1972) Radical Sociology. New York: Basic Books.

COLLINS, R. (1975) Conflict Sociology: Toward An Explanatory Science. New York: Academic.

CURRIE, E. (1973) "Dialogue with Anthony M. Platt." Issues in Criminology 8 (Spring): 21-33.

DARROW, C. (1979) "Address to the prisoners in the Cook County Jail," in J. J. Bonsignore et. al. (eds.) Before the Law—An Introduction to the Legal Process. Boston: Houghton-Mifflin.

DAVIS, J. (1974) "Justification for no obligation." Issues in Criminology 9 (Fall): 70-75.

DENISOFF, R. S. and D. MACQUARIE (1975) "Crime control in capitalist society: a reply to Quinney." Issues in Criminology 10 (Spring): 109-112.

FAITH, K. (1977) "Learning to teach: radical education and criminal justice system workers." Crime and Social Justice 7 (Spring/Summer): 63-68.

FRASER, A. (1978) "The legal theory we need now." Socialist Review 40/41 (July/October): 147-178.

FRIEDMAN, L. (1977) Law and Society. Englewood Cliffs, NJ: Prentice-Hall.

——— (1975) The Legal System: A Social Science Perspective. New York: Russell Sage.

FRIEDRICHS, D. O. (1980) "The legitimacy crisis in the U.S.: a conceptual analysis." Social Problems 27 (June).

——— (1979a) "The law and the legitimacy crisis," pp. 290-311 in R. G. Iacovetta and D. H. Chang (eds.) Critical Issues in Criminal Justice. Durham, NC: Carolina Academic.

——— (1979b) "Inherent and perceptual legitimacy: a critique of radical criminology." Presented at the American Society of Criminology annual meeting, November 7-10, Philadelphia.

——— (1979c) "Criminology: a radical-humanist perspective." Presented at the Association for Humanist Sociology annual meeting, October 21-23, University of Pittsburgh at Johnstown.

GALLIHER, J. F. (1979) "Government research funding and purchased virtue: some examples from criminology." Crime and Social Justice 11 (Spring/Summer): 44-50.

GAROFALO, J. (1978) "Radical criminology and criminal justice: points of divergence and contact." Crime and Social Justice 10 (Fall/Winter): 17-26.

GEIS, G. and R. F. MEIER (1978) "Looking backward and forward: criminologists on criminology as a career." Criminology 16 (August): 273-288.

GIBBONS, D. C. (1979a) The Criminological Enterprise–Theories and Perspectives. Englewood Cliffs, NJ: Prentice-Hall.

––– (1979b) "The criminological enterprise: where do we go from here?" Presented at the American Society of Criminology annual meeting, November 7-10, Philadelphia.

GOLDWYN, E. (1971) "Dialogue with Richard Quinney." Issues in Criminology 6 (Summer): 44-54.

GORDON, D. (1973) "Capitalism, class and crime in America." Crime and Delinquency (April): 163-187.

GOULDNER, A. W. (1970) The Coming Crisis in Western Sociology. New York: Basic Books.

GREENBERG, D. (1979) "Book review: class, state and crime." Crime and Delinquency 25 (January): 110-113.

HABERMAS, J. (1973) Legitimation Crisis. Boston: Beacon.

HEPBURN, J. (1977) "Social control and the legal order: legitimate repression in a capitalist state." Contemporary Crises 1 (January): 77-90.

HILLS, S. (1971) Crime, Power and Morality. New York: ITT.

HIRST, P. Q. (1972) "Marx and Engels on law, crime and morality." Economy & Society 1 (February): 39-43.

HUMPHRIES, D. (1979) "Crime and the state," pp. 224-241 in A. J. Szymanski and T. G. Goertzel (eds.) Sociology–Class, Consciousness and Contradictions. New York: Litton.

––– (1975) "Review of R. Quinney, *Criminal Justice in America.*" Crime and Social Justice 3 (Spring/Summer): 78-80.

JEFFERY, C. R. (1978) "Criminology as an interdisciplinary behavioral science." Criminology 16 (August): 149-169.

KELLER, R. L. (1976) "A sociological analysis of the conflict and critical criminologies," Ph.D. dissertation, University of Montana.

KLOCKARS, C. (1979) "The Contemporary Crises of Marxist Criminology." Criminology 16 (February): 477-515.

KRISBERG, B. (1975) Crime and Privilege–Toward A New Criminology. Englewood Cliffs, NJ: Prentice-Hall.

KUHN, T. (1970) The Structure of Scientific Revolutions. Chicago: University of Chicago Press.

LADER, L. (1979) Power on the Left. New York: Norton.

LEE, A. M. (1978) Sociology for Whom? New York: Oxford.

LIAZOS, A. (1972) "The poverty of the sociology of deviance: nuts, sluts and perverts." Social Problems 20 (Summer): 103-120.

LIVINGSTON, E. (1822) The Complete Works . . . On Criminal Jurisprudence. Montclair, NJ: Patterson Smith (Reprint, 1968).

MANDERS, D. (1975) "Labeling theory and social reality: a Marxist critique." Insurgent Sociologist 6 (Fall).

MANKOFF, M. (1980) "Comments on Turk, Toby, and Klockars." This volume.

McDONALD, L. (1976) The Sociology of Law and Order. Boulder, CO: Westview.

MEIER, R. F. (1977) "The new criminology: continuity in criminological theory." Journal of Criminal Law and Criminology 67: 461-469.

MICHALOWSKI, R. J. (1979) "Criminal justice for whom? A critical appraisal," pp. 3-21 in R. G. Iacovetta and D. H. Chang (eds.) Critical Issues in Criminal Justice. Durham, NC: Carolina Academic.

——— (1977a) "Perspective and paradigm: structuring criminological thought," pp. 7-39 in R. F. Meier (ed.) Theory in Criminology—Contemporary Views. Beverly Hills, CA: Sage.

——— (1977b) "A gentle pedagogy: teaching critical criminology in the South." Crime and Social Justice (Spring/Summer): 69-73.

——— and E. W. BOHLANDER (1976) "Repression and criminal justice in capitalist America." Sociological Inquiry 46: 95-106.

MILLS, C. W. (1959) The Sociological Imagination. New York: Grove.

PEPINSKY, H. (1978) "Communist anarchism as an alternative to the rule of criminal law." Contemporary Crises 2: 315-334.

——— (1975) "Reliance on formal written law, and freedom and social control in the United States and the People's Republic of China." British Journal of Sociology 26 (September): 330-342.

PLATT, A. M. (1978) "Street crime: a view from the left." Crime and Social Justice (Spring/Summer).

——— (1974) "Prospects for a radical criminology in the United States." Crime and Social Justice 1 (Spring/Summer): 2-6.

——— and P. TAKAGI (1979) "Letter." Crime and Social Justice (Spring/Summer): 4.

QUINNEY, R. (1980) Providence: The Development of Social and Moral Order. New York: Longman.

——— (1979a) "The theology of culture: Marx, Tillich and the prophetic tradition in the reconstruction of social and moral order." Union Seminary Quarterly Review 34 (Summer): 203-214.

——— (1979b) Capitalist Society: Readings for a Critical Sociology. Homewood, IL: Irwin.

——— (1979c) "The production of criminology." Criminology 16 (February): 445-457.

——— (1979d) Criminology. Boston: Little, Brown.

——— (1979e) Personal communication.

——— (1977) Class, State & Crime. New York: David McKay.

——— (1975) Criminology: Analysis and Critique of Crime in America. Boston: Little, Brown.

——— (1974a) Criminal Justice in America: A Critical Understanding. Boston: Little, Brown.

——— (1974b) Critique of Legal Order: Crime Control in Capitalist Society. Boston: Little, Brown.

——— (1973a) "Crime control in capitalist society: a critical philosophy of legal order." Issues in Criminology 8 (Spring): 75-95.

——— (1973b) "There's a lot of us folks grateful to the Lone Ranger: some notes on the rise and fall of American criminology." Insurgent Sociologist 4 (Fall): 56-64.

——— (1973c) "Feature review symposium: the new criminology." Sociological Review (Autumn): 591-592.

——— (1973d) "A transcendental way of knowing," pp. 168-177 in N. M. Regush (ed.) Visibles and Invisibles—A Primer for a New Sociological Imagination. Boston: Little, Brown.

——— (1972a) "The ideology of law: notes for a radical alternative to legal oppression." Issues in Criminology 7 (Winter): 1-12.

——— (1972b) "Who is the victim?" Criminology 10 (November): 314-323.

——— (1972c) "From repression to liberation: social theory in a radical age," pp. 317-341 in R. A. Scott and J. D. Douglas (eds.) Theoretical Perspectives on Deviance. New York: Basic Books.

——— (1971) Review of the National Commission on the Causes and Prevention of Violence Reports." American Sociological Review 36 (August): 724-727.

——— (1970a) The Social Reality of Crime. Boston: Little, Brown.

——— (1970b) The Problem of Crime. New York: Dodd Mead.

——— (1969) Crime and Justice in Society. Boston: Little, Brown.

——— (1966) "Structural characteristics, population areas and crime rates in the United States." Journal of Criminal Law, Criminology and Police Science 57 (March): 45-52.

——— (1965a) "A conception of man and society for criminology." Sociological Quarterly 6 (Spring): 119-127.

——— (1965b) "Is criminal behaviour deviant behavior?" British Journal of Criminology 5 (April): 132-142.

——— (1964a) "Crime, delinquency and social areas." Journal of Research in Crime & Delinquency 1 (July): 149-154.

——— (1964b) "The study of white collar crime: toward a reorientation in theory and research." Journal of Criminal Law, Criminology and Police Science 55 (June): 208-214.

——— (1964c) "Crime in political perspective." American Behavioral Scientist 8 (December): 19-22.

——— (1963) "Occupational structures and criminal behavior: prescription violation by retail pharmacists," Social Problems 11 (Fall): 179-183.

——— (1962) "Retail pharmacy as a marginal occupation: prescription violation." Ph.D. dissertation, University of Wisconsin.

——— and M. DeFLEUR (1966) "A reformulation of Sutherland's differential association theory and a strategy for empirical verification." Journal of Research in Crime & Delinquency 3 (January): 1-22.

——— and J. WILDEMAN (1977) The Problem of Crime: A Critical Introduction to Criminology. New York: Harper & Row.

REASONS, C. E. (1975) "Social thought and social structure: competing paradigms in criminology," Criminology 13 (November): 333-365.

REIMAN, J. H. (1979) The Rich Get Richer, and the Poor Get Prison. New York: John Wiley.

SCHAFER, S. (1969) Theories in Criminology. New York: Random House.

SCHWENDINGER, H. and J. SCHWENDINGER (1977) "Social class and the definition of crime." Crime and Social Justice 7 (Spring/Summer): 4-13.

——— (1970) "Defenders of order or guardians of human rights?" Issues in Criminology 5 (Summer): 123-157.

SINDEN, P. G. (1979) "Perceptions of crime in capitalist America: the question of consciousness manipulation." Sociological Focus 17, 4.

SUTHERLAND, E. H. (1940) "White-collar criminality." American Sociological Review 5: 1-12.

SZYMANSKI, A. J. and T. G. GOERTZEL (1979) Sociology—Class, Consciousness and Contradictions. New York: Litton.

TAYLOR, I., P. WALTON, and J. YOUNG (1973) The New Criminology. London: Routledge & Kegan Paul.

TIFFT, L. (1979) "The coming redefinitions of crime: an anarchist perspective." Social Problems 26 (April): 392-402.

TOBY, J. (1980) "The new criminology is the old baloney." This volume.

TURK, A. (1979) "Analyzing official deviance: for nonpartisan conflict analyses in criminology." Criminology 16 (February): 459-476.

——— (1979) "Conceptions of the demise of law," pp. 12-26 in P. J. Brantingham and J. M. Kress (eds.) Structure, Law and Power—Essays in the Sociology of Law. Beverly Hills, CA: Sage.

——— (1969) Criminality and Legal Order. Chicago: Rand McNally.

USEEM, B. and M. USEEM (1979) "Government legitimacy and political stability." Social Forces 57 (March): 840-852.

VIDICH, A. J. and R. M. GLASSMAN [eds.] (1979) Conflict and Control. Beverly Hills, CA: Sage.

VOLD, G. (1979) Theoretical Criminology. (Prepared by T. J. Bernard). New York: Oxford.

WEBER, M. (1954) On Law in Economy and Society. (Edited by M. Rheinstein). New York: Simon & Schuster.

YANKELOVICH, D. (1972) "A crisis of moral legitimacy." Dissent (Fall): 520-526.

3

CONFLICT THEORY IN CRIMINOLOGY

C. Ronald Huff

Debates among academic criminologists and sociologists often revolve around competing theoretical perspectives concerning the nature of crime, the evolution and functions of criminal law, and the state's role in administering penal sanctions. None of these debates is particularly recent, but one phenomenon which has become increasingly apparent in these debates is the politicization of ideas and the use of labels in classifying scholarship (and scholars) as "radical," "liberal," "conservative," "fascist," "reactionary," "critical," "Marxist," or some other designation designed to place their work along ideological and political lines. Like all labels, these tend to reduce complexity to simplicity and to promote numerous distortions and misrepresentations of scholarly work. Not surprisingly, some of the "debates" which have been generated along these lines have degenerated into *ad hominem* arguments, as the focus of discussion has shifted from the ideas themselves to the perceived political implications of those ideas.

One of the central issues in these debates comprises the substance of this book: i.e., radical criminology. Whatever the label which is to be attached, the term "radical criminology" actually subsumes a number of somewhat diverse theoretical perspectives, all of which incorporate, in various ways, the paradigm of social conflict. For this reason, and to sort

61

out some of the important theoretical differences, it may be useful to review some of the historical uses of conflict theory in criminology and to demonstrate the historical continuity which exists between early conflict theorists and their contemporary counterparts.

THE PARADIGM OF SOCIAL CONFLICT

As a point of departure, it should be noted that while there exist two major paradigmatic approaches to the analysis of criminology (deriving from more general analyses of social structure), perhaps too much has been made of the differences between these two perspectives. As Coser (1968: 235-236) notes:

> Conflict and order are correlative. Both the cementing and the breaking of the cake of custom constitute part of the dialectic of social life. One is hence ill-advised to distinguish sharply a sociology of order from a sociology of conflict, or a harmony model of society from a conflict model. Such attempts can only result in artificial distinctions. The analysis of social conflicts brings to awareness aspects of social reality that may be obscured if analytical attention focuses too exclusively on . . . social order; but an exclusive attention to conflict . . . may obscure the central importance of social order and needs to be corrected by a correlative concern with the ordered aspects of social life.

With this admonition in mind, one can begin to make distinctions between these two models without losing sight of the fact that both the functionalist perspective, based on social order, and the conflict model represent "phases of one process which always involves something of both" (Cooley, 1918: 39).

The functionalist model, which rests on the theories of Durkheim, incorporates the view that crime is a normal social phenomenon and represents the violation of societal norms based on consensus and social order. Criminal law evolves, from this perspective, as an expression of social consensus concerning values. Crime is functional for society in that it illustrates the boundaries between acceptable and unacceptable behavior. Criminal behavior, as a challenge to dominant social values, helps to reinforce these values among the citizens. Likewise, the state's punishment of criminal behavior serves to dramatize the importance of boundary maintenance and provides a method for symbolically expressing the group's moral indignation against the transgressor.

Advocates of a conflict perspective, however, challenge these views and assert that criminal law does not reflect group consensus. Instead, conflict theorists argue that criminal law evolves as a consequence of differential values in conflict with one another. In this struggle among competing sets of values, some values (those of the more powerful groups) predominate and are reflected in the laws. Law becomes an oppressive tool of the powerful, rather than a legitimate method of conflict resolution necessitated by norm-violating behavior. Criminal behavior may be viewed as an expression of social conflict, rather than a result of defective socialization or differential life chances.

What is social conflict? How has the concept been incorporated into criminological theory? Coser (1968: 232) has defined social conflict as

> a struggle over values or claims to status, power, and scarce resources, in which the aims of the conflicting parties are not only to gain the desired values but also to neutralize, injure, or eliminate their rivals. Such conflicts may take place between individuals, between collectivities, or between individuals and collectivities. Intergroup as well as intragroup conflicts are perennial features of social life.

The conflict perspective, like the functionalist perspective, has a lengthy intellectual tradition. Although many contemporary discussions of conflict theory emphasize the catalytic importance of the social upheaval of the 1960s and trace conflict theory back to Karl Marx, the importance of social disorder and conflict was recognized at least as early as the fourth century B.C., when Plato and Aristotle were deeply influenced by the turmoil of Greek political life (Eisenstadt, 1968: 24). Perhaps the first systematic application of a conflict perspective to the analysis of society was that made by Ibn Khaldun, a fourteenth-century Islamic social philosopher and historian (Steinmetz and Straus, 1974: 5). The early theoretical contributions of Machiavelli and Hobbes also were of critical importance in the development of this perspective (Collins, 1975: 56-57). However, the elaboration of conflict-oriented analyses into systematic thought in social philosophy, sociology, and criminology has not been especially well documented, and its importance has been overshadowed by the dominance of the functionalist model. Recently, however, the conflict paradigm in criminology and sociology has received renewed attention, and scholarly work in this intellectual tradition has increased significantly.

DIMENSIONS OF CONFLICT

There is no single, monolithic conflict theory in criminology, just as there is no single "radical criminology." A number of theorists have made use of the conflict paradigm in various ways, and in discussing these contributions to conflict criminology, one method of organizing this body of theoretical knowledge is to analyze the dimensions of conflict which assume central importance in these writings. The dimensions of social conflict which have attracted the most attention on the part of these theorists have included (1) socioeconomic class, (2) group and cultural conflict, and (3) power and authority relationships. The following discussion explicates the works of three major figures associated with each dimension of conflict, thereby demonstrating the intellectual continuity attributable to these conflict perspectives. The selection of three theorists as exemplars of each dimension of conflict is not intended to represent an exhaustive presentation of conflict theory in criminology; rather, the works of these nine theorists can be used to illustrate both (1) continuity in theoretical development and (2) theoretical diversity among multiple conflict-based perspectives.

SOCIOECONOMIC CLASS: MARX, BONGER, AND QUINNEY

It is somewhat ironic that Karl Marx should be widely credited with playing such an important role in the field of criminology, since he devoted relatively little attention to the subject of crime (Taylor et al., 1973: 209). Nevertheless, Marx's writings on political economy provided a broad intellectual framework which has served as a sensitizing perspective utilized by subsequent generations of scholars, some of whom have focused their attention on crime and social deviance.

Collins (1975: 57) has summarized the principal tenets of Marx's sociology as follows:

> 1. Historically, particular forms of property (slavery, feudal landholding, capital) are upheld by the coercive power of the state; hence classes formed by property divisions (slaves and slave-owners, serfs and lords, capitalists and workers) are the opposing agents in the struggle for political power—the underpinning of their means of livelihood.

2. Material contributions determine the extent to which social classes can organize effectively to fight for their interests; such conditions of mobilization are a set of intervening variables between class and political power.

3. Other material conditions—the means of mental production— determine which interests will be able to articulate their ideas and hence to dominate the ideological realm.

Marx's sociology, when applied to the subject of crime, suggests a strongly deterministic view; i.e., that crime is a result of class conflict based on economic inequality. The political economy was, for Marx, the critical explanatory variable. Furthermore, there is in Marx's writings, and in the writings of subsequent Marxist scholars, a strong social reform emphasis, oriented toward the construction of another kind of society:

> At a certain stage of their development, the material forces of production in society come in conflict with the existing relations of production, or what is but a legal expression of the same thing—with the property relations within which they had been at work before. From forms of development of the forces of production these relations turn into their fetters. Then comes the period of social revolution. With the change of the economic foundation the entire immense superstructure is more or less rapidly transformed [Marx, 1859; as quoted in Vold, 1958: 161].

This view is in marked contrast to the views of Durkheim and other functionalists, who posit that crime is a necessary part of society. Indeed, one of the characteristics of Marxist thought on crime has been this insistence that crime is a manifestation of class conflict and economic inequality, and, therefore, that crime can be eliminated with the development of a classless society. The connection between Marxist theory and an action orientation (radical reform of capitalist society), known as "praxis," is one which remains quite prevalent in contemporary Marxist thought. The emphasis on radical restructuring of the political economy is often contrasted with what Marxists refer to as the incrementalism of liberal criminology and the status quo protectionism of conservative criminology.

In assessing Marx's contributions to sociological thought, Eisenstadt (1968) argued that Marx's use of conflict as an important sociological concept represented both his greatest contribution and the most serious weakness in his theory. While recognizing the widespread existence of social conflict and its possible relationship to social change, Marx made the assumption that conflict was a transitory phenomenon—a feature of class society which would disappear with the evolution of the classless society. Critiques of the Marxist model, even by those who advocate a conflict perspective, cite the erroneous empirical predictions generated by Marxian theory and argue that the monocausal nature of Marxist theory, along with its classical view of labor, greatly impede its development and its applicability in contemporary society (Collins, 1975: 427-430). Nevertheless, it is certainly true that Marx's innovative use of conflict, along with his realism, contributed greatly to the development of social thought. Insofar as the application of Marxian thought to the field of criminology, most of the significant work has actually been accomplished by subsequent scholars.

Willem Adriaan Bonger (1876-1940), a Dutch criminologist, probably has been the most important continuator of the Marxist tradition in criminological scholarship, although one would not necessarily appreciate the significance of his contributions by reading most criminology texts. Austin Turk has done much to revive interest in the importance of Bonger's scholarship, especially by providing an abridged version of Bonger's (1916) classic work, along with an excellent introduction (Bonger, 1969).

The issue of praxis comes through clearly in Bonger's works, consistent with the Marxist tradition. Bonger's defense of minority and oppressed groups permeates his writings. He staunchly opposed any form of oppression and did so, physically as well as in his writings, until his death by suicide. Bonger was regarded by the Nazis as an archenemy of their ideology, and this denunciation of him was broadcast by the Nazis via radio. Although he was aware that a Nazi invasion of Holland would mean certain death for him, he refused to emigrate to the United States. On May 10, 1940, the Germans invaded Holland and Bonger wrote to his son: "I don't see any future for myself and I cannot bow to this scum which will now overmaster us." Five days later, Bonger committed suicide, a form of death which Bonger had referred to as "the only one in which the human will plays a role" (van Bemmelen, 1972: 455).

Bonger's (1916) central argument concerning criminality was that in any system of exchange, the economic interests of men are necessarily in opposition; capitalism, however, is characterized by the control of the means of production by relatively few, with most men being totally deprived of those means. Therefore, the masses come under the economic control of the few in order to survive. Bonger argued that this situation stifles men's "social instincts" and leads to unlimited egoism and a spirit of domination on the part of the powerful. The powerful become insensitive to the plight of the powerless who, in turn, develop jealousy and servility. It is important to note that for Bonger, the gap between the "haves" and the "have nots" serves to dehumanize both.

From Bonger's perspective, then, crimes committed by the dispossessed masses are related to their economic subjugation, while crimes committed by the bourgeoisie (such as fraudulent bankruptcy) may be related to the economy as well, both directly (declining business fortunes) and indirectly (the insensitivity fostered by inequality of wealth). Bonger believed that a wide variety of crimes could be directly attributable to the economy: vagrancy, theft, robbery, fraudulent bankruptcy, crimes of vengeance, infanticide, political crimes, and even sexual crimes such as adultery (related to the difficulty in obtaining a legal divorce at that time), prostitution (related to the inferior economic status of women and their demoralization as a result of such economic subjugation), and rape (attributable in part to the prevalent belief that women, who occupied an inferior "class" position, should be expected to submit to the sexual desires of men). Interestingly, Bonger was far ahead of the rest of criminology in predicting that the socioeconomic liberation of women, which he favored, would temporarily lead to an increase in their crime rate, relative to men, during that "transition period" (Bonger, 1916). Recent crime statistics tend to confirm this prediction, although there is much debate concerning whether the rise in female crime is attributable to the socioeconomic "liberation" of women.

In summary, it must be said that Bonger's theory of crime causation was basically a global, unidimensional one based on classical Marxist theory. Although Bonger did not deny the influence of other factors such as hereditary traits, he attributed no causal power to them in the absence of criminogenic environmental conditions. Most of his writings stressed this socioeconomic basis of crime and attacked the views of Lombroso and others of a biological persuasion. However, despite the fact that Bonger's arguments centered around economic determinism, he frequently used terms which certainly could be interpreted as implying some individual, idiosyncratic influence on events, and his comments concerning suicide certainly reflected an existential theme which may be contrasted with the heavy determinism prevalent in the corpus of his scholarship. Nevertheless, insofar as his theory of crime, Bonger clearly elaborated the Marxist doctrine of economic determinism and enhanced the Marxist tradition in criminology.

Among contemporary continuators of the Marxist tradition, Richard Quinney has enjoyed a preeminent status in the field of criminology, and he certainly has been the most prolific contributor of Marxist thought on criminology during the past decade. Permeating Quinney's writings, especially in the past six years (Quinney, 1974a, 1974b, 1974c, 1977), has been the simultaneous critique of capitalist society as a criminogenic state and the call for the establishment of a socialist alternative. In one of his books, for example, Quinney, (1974a: v) states:

> In my opinion, Karl Marx proposed the strongest alternative to the juridical concept of justice. Since the state and its legal order are an expression of the prevailing mode of production, and given that capitalist production is destructive of a human existence, the legal system supporting this kind of social and economic order is not capable of promoting justice.

Further, in addressing the issue of crime control, Quinney (1974b: 16) outlined what he called "a critical theory of crime control in American society":

1. American society is based on an advanced capitalist economy.

2. The state is organized to serve the interests of the dominant economic class, the capitalist ruling class.

3. Criminal law is an instrument of the state and ruling class to maintain and perpetuate the existing social and economic order.

4. Crime control in capitalist society is accomplished through a variety of institutions and agencies established and administered by a governmental elite, representing ruling class interests, for the purpose of establishing domestic order.

5. The contradictions of advanced capitalism—the disjunction between existence and essence—require that the subordinate classes remain oppressed by whatever means necessary, especially through the coercion and violence of the legal system.

6. Only with the collapse of capitalist society and the creation of a new society, based on socialist principles, will there be a solution to the crime problem.

Perhaps Quinney's most unique contribution to criminological scholarship has been his attempt to develop a theoretical perspective which brings together orthodox Marxism, phenomenology, and what he calls "critical philosophy," in analyzing the crime problem. As might be expected, this approach has been met with considerable controversy, reflected elsewhere in this book.

GROUP AND CULTURAL CONFLICT:
SELLIN, MILLER, AND VOLD

Another important tradition in conflict criminology has been the analysis of conflict between groups, subcultures, and entire cultures. What Sellin (1938) termed the "conflict of conduct norms" may occur in a number of situations, ranging from the micro level (small group conflict) to the macro level (conflict among cultures and nation-states), and some of these conflicts may involve behavior which becomes defined as criminal. While the theme of group conflict may be found in the writings of Simmel, Park, and Burgess, and was developed in a number of ways by the early Chicago School, its specific application to criminology is best exemplified by three scholars whose work built upon these earlier contributions. These three, Thorsten Sellin, Walter Miller, and George Vold, serve to illustrate the application of conflict theory on the cultural level (Sellin), subcultural level (Miller), and the interest group level (Vold).

Sellin's (1938) theory of culture conflict is based on the idea that "conduct norms" are defined differently by different groups and that the processes of socialization serve to instill differential definitions of proper versus improper conduct, depending on which group serves as one's primary reference group. The normal processes of social differentiation bring these group conduct norms into a conflict that Sellin termed "culture conflict." Sellin posited that culture conflict could occur in any of the following ways:

(1) when these codes clash on the border of contiguous culture areas
(2) when, as may be the case with legal norms, the law of one cultural territory is extended to cover the territory of another
(3) when members of one cultural group migrate to another.

The "primary conflict" (conflict between two cultures) of which Sellin wrote has often been applied in analyzing the problems associated with immigration. The large waves of European immigrants who settled in the United States confronted a number of social problems (inadequate housing, poverty, crime) and were perceived as socially deviant by the dominant, native American groups. The interests of early American sociologists often centered on these social problems and have had a profound historical effect on the development of American sociology. Many of the early American sociologists were former ministers and had a reformist orientation. Partly because of this fact, criminology and social deviance as fields of academic inquiry in the United States have been strongly associated with sociology, while in some European nations, for example, criminology is subsumed under law or medicine.

The use of the primary conflict model in American society lost much of its utility with the cessation of massive in-migration, but the recent arrival of Southeast Asian refugees may provide an occasion for renewed utilization of this perspective. The problems of South Vietnamese refugees who have been resettled in Texas, for example, already have included violent disputes over fishing practices. The socially deviant status accorded such groups often places the "burden of proof" on them during the process of cultural adaptation and accommodation. In addition to this recent example in American society, primary conflict remains an important explanatory framework in other societies where large-scale in-migration has been an important sociological variable (e.g., Israel).

Following the cessation of large-scale European in-migration to the United States, Sellin's concept of "secondary conflict" (conflict within one culture) assumed paramount importance. With so many different groups located within one emerging culture, the focus obviously shifted to intergroup relations and the development of subcultures. Functionalist analysis of subcultures, based on Durkheim's (1947) and Merton's (1968) development of the concept of anomie, provides a rich tradition in criminology. From the functionalist perspective, the social structure includes culturally prescribed goals and culturally prescribed means to attain those goals. There is, in this perspective, an assumption that groups are socialized to value the culturally prescribed goals (such as monetary success), but that they have differential success in attaining these goals and they utilize different methods of adaptation in their quest for goal attainment (or, in some cases, subsequent rejection of culturally prescribed goals). The picture which emerges from this perspective is one of a society which is characterized by one dominant set of culturally prescribed goals and means to attain those goals; groups seeking to attain these goals use different means, some of which are regarded as criminal or otherwise deviant. Important elaborations of this basic theme have been made by Cohen (1955) and by Cloward and Ohlin (1960), but the essence of the functionalist position on subcultures has remained intact.

By way of contrast, the conflict tradition in the analysis of subcultures is illustrated by the work of anthropologist Walter Miller. Miller's (1958) influential publication on subcultural delinquency challenged the traditional functionalist perspective by suggesting that lower-class subcultures in American society were neither disorganized nor striving to attain any universal American dream. Rather, he argued that the socialization processes which occur in such subcultures emphasize *different* values. Miller asserted that this differential socialization reflected a heterogeneous culture which has emerged in a stratified, highly complex society following massive in-migration by groups from a variety of cultural traditions. Rather than a "melting pot" which would turn out essentially homogeneous versions of American culture, American society was viewed by Miller as a pluralistic society. In this sense, the similarity between Miller's position and Sellin's concept of "secondary conflict" is evident. Miller argued that delinquency evolved as a result of differential conduct norms and differential socialization. Miller viewed delinquency neither as a pathological behavioral problem nor as a reaction against middle-class norms, but rather as the result of normative conflict. This meant that one could be socialized within a subculture whose values and/or behavior *conflicted* with more dominant groups in society; this situation could, in turn, lead to behavior which, while consistent with in-group norms and values, was regarded as criminal in the larger society. The distinctive subcultural values and traditions of the lower class, then, bring its members into conflict with the conduct norms of more dominant classes in society.

Finally, one of the most influential of the group conflict theorists in criminology has been George Vold, whose excellent textbook on criminological theory (Vold, 1958) was the first to treat conflict in a systematic way, emphasizing its importance as a theoretical perspective for the analysis of crime, although making no claim that it was (or could be) a grand theory to explain all criminal behavior.

Drawing on the earlier writings of Simmel (1950) and Park and Burgess (1924), Vold's theory was more social psychological in nature than were the theories of either Sellin or Miller. Vold's units of analysis were interest groups within the same culture, and he was especially interested in the processes by which in-group loyalties could bring one into conflict with external groups in a politically organized society. Vold rejected the concept of abnormality as an explanation for this kind of intergroup conflict, arguing instead that

> there are many situations in which criminality is the normal, natural response of normal, natural human beings struggling in understandably normal and natural situations for the maintenance of the way of life to which they stand committed [Vold, 1958: 218].

As illustrations of these kinds of conflict, Vold (1958: 214-217) cited crimes which result from: (1) political conflict (e.g., "A successful revolution makes criminals out of the government officials previously in power, and an unsuccessful revolution makes its leaders into traitors subject to immediate execution."); (2) labor-management conflict (e.g., violent behavior which accompanies strikes and strike-breaking attempts); (3) jurisdictional disputes between labor unions (e.g., violent behavior which is an expression of loyalty to one labor union involved in conflict with a competing union); and (4) racial conflict (e.g., violence associated with efforts to challenge racial segregation in the United States and South Africa). Vold's analysis, then, focused on interest groups within one politically organized society and, as such, differed somewhat from the cultural and subcultural foci of Sellin and Miller. The commonality, however, is the use of the conflict paradigm in understanding group conflict behavior which may be defined as criminal.

POWER AND AUTHORITY RELATIONSHIPS:
WEBER, DAHRENDORF, AND TURK

One other important dimension of conflict analysis has been the focus on power and authority relationships. This body of scholarship is exemplified in the works of Max Weber, Ralf Dahrendorf, and Austin Turk. Essentially, Weberian theory, like the Marxist perspective, represents a theory of social stratification which has been applied to the study of crime. Dahrendorf and Turk have made especially valuable contributions to the continuation and elaboration of Weberian theory in this important area of inquiry.

Max Weber was a German social historian, economist, and sociologist whose views on social stratification both agreed with and diverged from Marxist thought. Weber recognized the importance of the economy in the analysis of social stratification, but he did not believe that such a unidimensional approach could satisfactorily explain the phenomenon of social stratification. He added two additional dimensions, power and prestige, to the Marxist emphasis on property, and he believed that these three variables were responsible for the development of hierarchies in society. Weber held that property differences led to the development of classes, differences in power created political parties, and prestige differences led to the development of status groupings or strata (Tumin, 1967: 6).

Weber discussed the implications of stratification and introduced the concept of "life chances" into sociological analysis (Weber, 1953). Weber argued that one's life chances were differentially related to his social class.

It is in his analysis of legal evolution (Rheinstein, 1954) and his discussion of the implications of social stratification that criminologists have found the most useful material concerning a general model of crime. In addition, Weber's writings on social organization are regarded as classics and are extensively utilized by contemporary criminologists in the analysis of criminal justice agencies. Weber's legacy in criminology, and in sociology more generally, is indeed profound.

Like Marx, Weber provided a general theoretical framework which has served as the basis for later application to the study of crime. Weber's emphasis on power and prestige as explanatory variables greatly broadened Marxist theory and provided a perspective which may be applied in analyzing *any* society, whether it be capitalist, state socialist, or some other type of political/economic system. Instead of an exclusive concern with the economic variable, Weberian criminologists pursue the differential distribution of power (defined by Weber as the ability to secure compliance against someone's will to do otherwise) and prestige as critical variables in the analysis of crime and crime control. The Weberian approach emphasized the implications of social stratification based on these dimensions as determinants of criminality.

From this perspective, criminality and other forms of social deviance exist in *all* societies and are the result of the political struggle among different groups attempting to promote or enhance their own life chances. Thus, it might be expected that in an "egalitarian," socialist society (if one could be created), crime and social deviance would still exist (a functionalist theme articulated by Durkheim) and would be defined by "elites" (perhaps the intellectual or political leaders), since the society must be politically organized. Many forms of criminal or deviant behavior which occur in "socialist" societies have not been adequately addressed or explained by Marxist scholars, but can be successfully analyzed from the Weberian perspective, since the units of analysis and the critical variables remain the same, independent of the economic or political system. Thus, the criminality of a Soviet factory manager who falsifies an inventory report in order to comply with a state-imposed production quota can be analyzed from the Weberian perspective, along with the white-collar criminality of his American counterpart whose behavior may be motivated by capitalist greed. Marxists, on the other hand, have been much more at ease with the latter case than with the former.

Both Dahrendorf and Turk have extended the Weberian tradition in the field of criminology by emphasizing the relationships between authorities and their subjects. For Dahrendorf (1958, 1959), power is the critical explanatory variable. He argued that Marx had built his theory on only one form of power (property ownership) and that a more useful theoretical perspective could be constructed by incorporating broader conceptions of power. Thus, Dahrendorf (1959: 139) essentially substitutes "authority" for "class":

> If we define classes by relations of authority, it is *ipso facto* evident that "economic classes," i.e., classes within economic organizations, are but a special case of the phenomenon of class. Furthermore, even within the sphere of industrial production it is not really economic factors that give rise to class formation, but a certain type of social relations which we have tried to comprehend in the notion of authority.

Drawing on both Weber and Dahrendorf, Turk (1966, 1969) posits that every society is characterized by norms of deference and norms of domination associated with the authority structure. Criminality reflects the instability in these relationships. The task for criminology

> becomes the study of relations between the statuses and roles of legal *authorities*—creators, interpreters, and enforcers of right-wrong standards for individuals in the political collectivity—and those of *subjects*—acceptors or resisters but not makers of such law creating, interpreting, and enforcing decisions [Turk, 1969: 35].

Turk's theoretical perspective is one in which crime is conceptualized as a social status which is assigned to some of those who resist norms and which reflects the existence of social conflict between authorities and their subjects. As such, this perspective may be applied to a wide range of "criminal behavior" occurring in various types of social structures and diverse political and economic systems:

> For Weberians, criminality is coming to be seen as a category of phenomena defined solely by the actions of the authorities of *any* politically organized society. The "meaning" of criminality is that it refers to those persons, acts, or non-behavioral attributes officially defined as punishable. . . . In short, criminality is a political concept, not strictly a legal and certainly not a behavioral one. Where the Marxians use an "absolute morality" (i.e., their own sense of social justice) in defining criminality as exploitation, Weberians use a "relativistic amorality" in defining criminality as whatever is made punishable by the actions of whoever exercises the power of the state [Turk, 1977: 217].

CONFLICT CRIMINOLOGY:
PROBLEMS AND PROSPECTS

It is possible to view theories of deviance and criminality essentially as theories of social stratification, rather than (or in addition to) the traditional "social problem" or "individual pathology" perspectives which have dominated criminological literature for so long. In the quest to tie social deviance theory with broader sociological theory, one important linkage is social stratification. The process of identifying and processing deviants, criminals, and delinquents may be viewed as a sort of "ranking" or social stratification based on status and prestige. Also, from the conflict perspective, those who are in positions of power have the ability to determine *what* shall be deviant, criminal, or delinquent and have a great deal of discretion in determining *who* shall be identified and processed as deviant, criminal, or delinquent. These theoretical considerations are especially consistent with a Weberian approach to conflict sociology.

Collins, in his excellent and comprehensive treatment of conflict sociology, has proposed just such a linkage between general conflict sociology and the specialized area of social deviance. Collins's argument (1975: 460-461) is as follows:

> When removed from the sphere of value judgments within which it is usually handled, the study of "deviance" is essentially a matter of explaining careers. A good deal of it emphasizes particular kinds of failures (i.e., downward mobility), particularly processes of cumulative failure produced by being labeled by official agencies. . . . The connection between the materials of deviance and conflict theory is obvious. A conflict theory of social mobility may be applied toward explaining various types of "deviance." Conversely, this area of study helps us to understand the complexity of some of the phenomenon of stratification.

Collins (1975: 461), in attempting to construct a systematic, explanatory theory based on social conflict, contends that the three levels of analysis which have been utilized in the study of social mobility (structural relationships, individual careers, and statistical rates of mobility) are easily adaptable to the special field of deviance:

> Applied to deviance, this helps us reconcile various types of theorizing about deviance. Labeling theory and related approaches emphasizing the social construction of deviance operate on a structural level and are a subcategory of the historical organization of stratification. The social-psychological models which have been so promi-

nent in explaining individual deviance are like explanations of individual mobility. Finally, rates of deviance are quite analogous to rates of social mobility.

While the admonitions of Coser, Vold, and Dahrendorf caution us against the belief that the conflict perspective can evolve into a grand theory of criminality or deviance, it nevertheless seems apparent that the conflict perspective can be much more systematically linked with general sociological theory. Whether this occurs at the macro level, as Collins has suggested, or at the micro level (utilizing general social-psychological theory or continuing to develop the phenomenological perspective), the attempt to integrate deviance theory with broader theoretical frameworks seems essential. The current theoretical eclecticism (or, in some cases, agnosticism) certainly is understandable and in many respects defensible, but it also has impeded serious efforts in the direction of theory construction and verification.

Finally, critical analyses of conflict theory in criminology, such as those provided by Taylor et al. (1973) and Turk (1977) are indispensable catalysts to this kind of theoretical development of the conflict perspective. The debates which are taking place, and which are reflected in this book, demonstrate not only the salience of the issue but also the vitality which currently exists in the field of criminology. These debates and controversies are interpreted by many as indicating a crisis in criminology, and there is, among some, great despair over the failure to settle on a dominant paradigm. Advocates of a conflict perspective, however, recognize this sort of conflict as not only inevitable, but also desirable.

REFERENCES

BONGER, W. A. (1969) Criminality and Economic Conditions. Bloomington: Indiana University Press.

――― (1916) Criminality and Economic Conditions (trans. by H. P. Horton). Boston: Little, Brown.

COHEN, A. K. (1955) Delinquent Boys: The Culture of the Gang. New York: Macmillan.

CLOWARD, R. A. and L. E. OHLIN (1960) Delinquency and Opportunity: A Theory of Delinquent Gangs. New York: Macmillan.

COLLINS, R. (1975) Conflict Sociology: Toward an Explanatory Science. New York: Academic.

COOLEY, C. H. (1918) Social Process. New York: Scribner.

COSER, L. (1968) "Conflict: sociological aspects," pp. 232-236 in D. L. Sills (ed.) International Encyclopedia of the Social Sciences (vol. 3). New York: Macmillan.

DAHRENDORF, R. (1959) Class and Class Conflict in Industrial Society. London: Routledge & Kegan Paul.

——— (1958) "Out of utopia: toward a reconstruction of sociological analysis." American Journal of Sociology 67 (September): 115-127.

DURKHEIM, E. (1947) The Division of Labor in Society. New York: Macmillan (originally published in 1893).

EISENSTADT, S. N. (1968) "Development of sociological thought," pp. 23-35 in D. L. Sills (ed.) International Encyclopedia of the Social Sciences (vol. 15). New York: Macmillan.

MARX, K. (1904) Critique of Political Economy. New York: International Library (originally published in 1859).

MERTON, R. K. (1968) Social Theory and Social Structure. New York: Macmillan.

MILLER, W. B. (1958) "Lower-class culture as a generating milieu of gang delinquency." Journal of Social Issues 15: 5-19.

PARK, R. E. and E. W. BURGESS (1924) Introduction to the Science of Sociology. Chicago: University of Chicago Press.

QUINNEY, R. (1977) Class, State, and Crime: On the Theory and Practice of Criminal Justice. New York: David McKay.

——— (1974a) Criminal Justice in America: A Critical Understanding. Boston: Little, Brown.

——— (1974b) Critique of Legal Order: Crime Control in Capitalist Society. Boston: Little, Brown.

——— (1974c) Criminology: Analysis and Critique of Crime in the United States. Boston: Little, Brown.

RHEINSTEIN, M. [ed.] (1954) Max Weber on Law in Economy and Society (trans. by E. Shils and M. Rheinstein). Cambridge. MA: Harvard University Press.

SELLIN, T. (1938) Culture Conflict and Crime. New York: Social Science Research Council.

SIMMEL, G. (1950) The Sociology of Georg Simmel (trans. by K. Wolf). New York: Macmillan.

STEINMETZ, S. K. and M. A. STRAUS (1974) Violence in the Family. New York: Dodd, Mead.

TAYLOR, I., P. WALTON, and J. YOUNG (1973) The New Criminology: For a Social Theory of Deviance. London: Routledge & Kegan Paul.

TUMIN, M. M. (1967) Social Stratification: The Forms and Functions of Inequality. Englewood Cliffs, NJ: Prentice-Hall.

TURK, A. T. (1977) "Class, conflict, and criminalization." Sociological Focus 10 (August): 209-220.

——— (1969) Criminality and Legal Order. Chicago: Rand McNally.

——— (1966) "Conflict and criminality." American Sociological Review 31 (June): 338-352.

van BEMMELEN, J. M. (1972) "Willem Adriaan Bonger," pp. 443-457 in H. Mannheim (ed.) Pioneers in Criminology. Montclair, NJ: Patterson Smith.

VOLD, G. B. (1958) Theoretical Criminology. New York: Oxford University Press.

WEBER, M. (1953) "Class, status, party," pp. 63-75 in R. Bendix and S. M. Lipset (eds.) Class, Status, and Power. New York: Macmillan.

4

ANALYZING OFFICIAL DEVIANCE: FOR NONPARTISAN CONFLICT ANALYSES IN CRIMINOLOGY

Austin T. Turk

A preoccupation with programmatics (often ideologically loaded debates over what is to be investigated, why, and how) has been unfortunately prominent in recent discussions of criminological theory. Instead of increasing the sophistication of our thinking and our research projects, too often our argumentation has generated far more confusion than enlightenment about the nature of scientific inquiry and about the difficult conceptual and methodological problems confronting criminologists. There is, of course, no way to state or illustrate alternative theoretical perspectives without implying (or, more accurately, connoting) ideological differences. Theoretical and methodological differences are inevitably associated with differences in ideological and political inclinations. That such associations are not *logically* inevitable, but only subjectively or polemically so, is a proposition consistent with my understanding of conflict theory and analysis. My tasks in this essay are (1) to specify that understanding, (2) to outline my conception of the criminological enterprise as the analysis of official deviance, and (3) to indicate how I am using that conception in studying political criminality.

FOR NONPARTISAN CONFLICT ANALYSIS

Conflict *theory* as a set of ideas about the subject matter of criminology, and conflict *analysis* as a research strategy, have been frequently misrepresented and misunderstood by both proponents and critics of the conflict perspective. The most pernicious notion has been that such work is synonymous with partisan ideological treatises on behalf of less powerful collections of people against more powerful collections.

The conflict theorist invariably questions the legitimacy of existing practices and values [and promotes the values of] freedom as autonomy, change, action, qualitative growth [Horton, 1966].

Increasingly, it is becoming clear that . . . contemplation and suspension . . . are not enough. . . . The new criminology must therefore be a normative theory: it must hold out the possibilities of a [radical political] resolution to the fundamental questions [Taylor et al. 1973: 280].

A radical criminology . . . defines crime as a violation of politically defined human rights: the truly egalitarian rights to decent food and shelter, to human dignity and self-determination, rather than the so-called right to compete for an unequal share of wealth and power [Platt, 1974].

The conflict perspective [depicts criminal law as] a set of rules laid down by the state in the interests of the ruling class and resulting from the conflicts inherent in class-structured societies; some criminal behavior is no more than the "rightful" behavior of persons exploited by the extant economic relations [Chambliss, 1976: 6].

In understanding criminal justice—its theory and practice under capitalism—we provide a theory and a practice that has as its objective changing the world. The importance of criminal justice is that it moves us dialectically to reject the capitalist order and to struggle for a new society. We are engaged in socialist revolution [Quinney, 1977: 165].

Enthusiasts of the idea that conflict theory is and should be a partisan critique generally go on to advance the self-defeating thesis that *any* theory is nothing more than an ideology. Truth becomes merely a function of one's subjective commitments as these are, in turn, determined by one's position in some class or other social structure. Objectivity is dismissed as illusion that serves only to mask political inclinations and intentions. The "correct" theory, then, is that set of factual assertions and explanatory accounts which is shared by all "progressive" people—i.e., all those who are in agreement (with the proponents) regarding the virtues of some kinds of people and social arrangements and the evils of other kinds.

Instead of being a *variable* feature of a possibly inadequate line of reasoning, truth is construed as a *categorical* attribute of a certainly adequate revelation. Rather than a *supposition* offered for testing by methods of controlled observation designed to minimize the biasing impact of the observer's hopes and fears, a theory thus becomes a *presupposition* to be elaborated and demonstrated so as to produce the desired political effects. Methodology becomes a matter of *tactics* more than of techniques; even though techniques of data collection and analysis cannot be entirely dispensed with, their power as checks on individual fallibility is subverted. Standard tactics in partisan criminological research (both the "left" and the "right" variants) include the following.

Assertion. Propositions are either deductions or imputations from abstract principles of faith, or else generalizations grounded more in obsolete or methodologically dubious information than in systematic research. Example: "The prosecutor's influence is great, as he determines whom the police arrest, the volume of cases in the courts, and whether convicted offenders are imprisoned" (Lefcourt, 1971: 28):

Anecdote. Propositions are supported by illustrations, examples, and cases selected to *fit* rather than to test them. Example: "From this case [two detectives slapping a driver who was slow to produce his registration] it is apparent that, from the officer's point of view, the essence of the offense that provokes punishment is defiance, and the justifiability of that defiance has little to do with his reaction. It is easy to imagine that in many cases an assertion of right may be seen as more of a threat even than an out-and-out insult" (Chevigny, 1969: 69).

Association. Propositions are generated from convenient juxtapositions, conjunctions, and sequences without either sampling or (at least logical) experimental controls; negative cases are not recognized as such, but are defined away as inappropriate comparisons. Example: Evidence suggesting that some police agencies continued to expand during periods of (temporarily) declining official crime rates is interpreted to mean that crime "may be virtually unrelated to the development of the police institution" (Harring, 1976: 55). However, Harring's conclusion is unwarranted in the absence of systematic attention to the at least apparent facts (a) that such cases are extremely rare, and (b) that such factors as erroneous beliefs about the crime problem, careerism and empire-building, and local political patronage may well have more to do with police budgets than do *either* an immediate reaction to crime rates *or* a deliberate policy of class oppression.

Analogy. Propositions invoke evidence regarding one class of phenomena to sustain descriptive accounts and causal imputations regarding a different class. Example: "The earliest form of the modern American police lies in the [pre-Civil War] Southern slave patrols" (Center for Research on Criminal Justice, 1977: 20). The emphasis of this study on the irremediable brutal repressiveness of policing in contemporary America is further amplified by discussions and imagery associating it with atrocities and oppression elsewhere, especially in Latin America, Asia, and Africa. Differences in the historical and social contexts of policing, as well as in the frequency and form of violence employed, are considered only as variations in the problem and tactics of working-class control under capitalism. Systematic comparative case analyses are not offered—e.g., comparing the repressiveness of policing in early capitalist, advanced capitalist, state socialist, and premodern societies.

The validity of specific propositions resting on assertion, anecdote, association, or analogy is not at issue here. That their validity cannot be assessed without sharing or rejecting their authors' ideological assumptions *is* the issue. Even if true, such propositions are "demonstrated" only to the converted or naive. Worse, true or at least promising ideas can easily be discredited by ideological opponents who have merely to point out the gross biases of the methodological tactics used to promote those ideas. Propositions: (a) Partisan conflict analysis may well be counterproductive even for wakening and encouraging political faith; (b) Nonpartisan conflict analysis is more likely to produce knowledge that is demonstrably valid, and therefore usable for more than hortatory purposes (Turk, 1977).

Regardless of political victories or defeats, the intellectual prospects for partisan conflict criminology are indeed bleak. If the never fully attainable *ideal* of objectively valid and reliable knowledge is abandoned, issues of understanding can only be resolved by force—the ultimate arbiter always so attractive to the impatient and impassioned. Yet, as Mao well understood, it is not *truth* but *power* that comes out of the muzzle of a gun. Contrary to some currently fashionable sophistry, power and truth do not constitute an identity.

Nonpartisan conflict theory and analysis assumes that the ideological bent of theorists or the political utilities of theories are irrelevant for assessing the validity of knowledge claims. Ideological assumptions, implications, and uses cannot be inferred from a theory as such (*pace* Schwendinger and Schwendinger, 1970 and 1974, who are engaged in an ideological "war of position," 1977: 11). Recognizing that values can never be totally excluded from the research process, nonpartisan conflict analysts also recognize that approximations to value-neutral procedures and knowledge are possible. It is further understood that knowledge is always partial and probabilistic, never complete and certain: The knowledge-seeking process is endless.

Because inquiry can never provide final, unquestionable knowledge, there is always a point at which human beings must make a "leap of faith" beyond the limits of their knowledge in order to act at all. Political and other value commitments cannot be *fully* justified by any body of knowledge, no matter how convincing. Equally well-informed people can and do arrive at different and often conflicting positions of commitment. Nonpartisan conflict analysts recognize this simply as a social fact: Relative degrees of knowledge (and of power) can in principle be estimated, but the moral worth of any position is considered beyond empirical assessment. Thus, while the analyst as a *person* may prefer, and even join, one side instead of another, as an analyst he or she must value demonstrable truth above any political or other moral commitment.

THE CRIMINOLOGICAL ENTERPRISE

My conception of criminology is that it is part of the effort to develop and use a general model of social *deviance,* which in this discipline becomes the task of developing a specific model of *criminality*. That is, in criminological inquiry the focus moves from deviance in all its manifestations, unofficial as well as official, to *official* deviance. The perspective which I bring to the criminological enterprise is a developing combination of substantive "conflict sociology" (Collins, 1975) and conflict systems analysis (Boulding, 1962; Rapoport, 1960, 1974; Schelling, 1960). Informally, my working premises are as follows:

(1) Individuals diverge in their understandings and commitments.
(2) Divergence leads, under specifiable conditions, to conflict.
(3) Each conflicting party tries to promote his or her own understandings and commitments.
(4) The result is a more or less conscious struggle over the distribution of available resources, and therefore of life chances.
(5) People with similar understandings and commitments tend to join forces, and people who stay together tend to develop similar understandings and commitments.

(6) Continuing conflicts tend to become routinized in the form of stratification systems.

(7) Such systems (at least at the intergroup level) are characterized by economic exploitation sustained by political domination in all forms, from the most clearly violent to the most subtly ideological.

(8) The relative power of conflicting parties determines their hierarchical position; changes in position reflect only changes in the distribution of power.

(9) Convergence in understandings and commitments is generated by the (not necessarily voluntary) sharing of experiences in dealing with "insiders," "outsiders," and the natural environment.

(10) The relationship between divergence and convergence in human understandings and commitments is a dialectical one, ergo the *basic* social process or dynamic is one of conflict.

There are at least three major implications for developing the general model of social deviance. First, every human encounter involves both deviating and correcting behavior. Each person and each set or group of persons (i.e., each *party*) behaves in such a way as to communicate approval, tolerance, disapproval, or rejection of other parties' behavior and/or nonbehavioral attributes. Disapproval or rejection indicates that the offending party must change, or else that the relationship must either change or terminate. In any encounter there is a stake—i.e., what happens directly or potentially affects the enhancement/reduction of life chances. For this reason, parties encountering one another try to correct the other's deviations *as these are perceived and understood in terms of an overriding concern with increasing or ensuring the welfare of self or one's own kind.* Deviations are whatever is felt, consciously or not, to be threatening. Thus, merely being *different* becomes *deviant* insofar as the difference is one that elicits the sense of threat, in ways from the most subtle to the most obvious (cf. Lofland, 1969: 14).

Second, there is *no* absolute standard of rightness/wrongness which can be articulated and applied at the empirical level. In research, therefore, the criterion of deviance is always relative to the normative expectations and demands of some particular interested party dealing with some other party. Even if universal agreement should be found with respect to, say, some survey questionnaire proposition about the absolute or relative seriousness of some act (cf. Rossi et al., 1974; Newman, 1976), conflict theory leads one to ask *how* such a fascinating unanimity (of perception *and* interpretation *and* behavior?) has been arrived at in a world of diversity, *what* or *who* sustains it, and *what* or *who* could or will alter it. No empirical basis for moral absolutism is to be found.

And third, conflict is implicit in social interaction, and especially salient in hierarchical relationships. The assumption here is that there are limits to the human capacity to include other humans as "we." That there *are* limits is so far well attested (LeVine and Campbell, 1972), regardless of any metaphysical hopes for some tremendous breakthrough to a utopian state of universal love, or at least comradeliness! Human diversity, ethnocentrism, and insecurity generate conflicts or perception and interest which, for each party, may be reduced but cannot be eliminated by increasing power in a relationship. It follows that the political organization of social life does not *end* conflict, including inter*group, structured* antagonisms. "The ceaseless emergence and ceaseless resolution of contradictions is the dialectical law of the development of things" (Mao Tsetung, 1968: 95). Rather, political organization involves the creation and *imposition* (to some degree or other) of procedures for containing, redirecting, deescalating, transforming, or otherwise handling conflicts so as to benefit and protect *some* party or parties caught up in the process. Perhaps sometimes and happily *all* involved parties may in some measure be benefited and protected; but no perfectly egalitarian, universally satisfactory, and permanent solution is humanly attainable.

The general model of social deviance, as it is beginning to look from the above perspective, may be briefly sketched as a set of dichotomous relations symbolizing complex *variables* in relation to one another. These are suggested as the major problematics with which conflict criminology is concerned. In the form of questions:

- Is the deviance in question behavioral, or is it a matter of nonbehavioral attributes?

- Is the deviance demonstrably present, or is it merely imputed to exist (be present, have occurred)?

- Has the behavior or attribute in question been treated as deviance (labeled) by the relevant others (e.g., the legal authorities), or is it either unknown or ignored (denied)?

- Is the deviance defined by the sanctioning behavior of a polity's agents, or by that of some other party? *(I.e., is the deviance official?)*

- Is the labeler personally concerned about the deviance in question (i.e., morally indignant, acting "authentically"), or impersonally performing an institutional role?

- Is the actual or potential labelee deliberately resisting the labeler's normative expectations or demands, or resistant only because of ignorance, indifference, or incapacity?

- Is the primary objective of labeling the control of actually or potentially deviant individuals (*person* control), or the maintenance of a generalized structure of authority relationships (*population* control)?

- Is the normative context of labeling *cultural* (articulated in a legal or other language) *or social* (implicit in the sanctioning pattern, i.e., the labeling behavior itself)? *(And why are there congruencies and discrepancies between cultural and social normative contexts? And why are there changes in cultural and social normative contexts and in their relationship?)*

The main features of a nonpartisan conflict criminology having now been presented, the remainder of this essay is devoted to indicating how I am using these ideas in research on political criminality, possibly the least ambiguous form of *official* deviance—at least in theory.

ILLUSTRATION: ANALYZING POLITICAL CRIMINALITY[1]

The labeling of political criminality is itself a tactical move in conflicts between those who are committed to preserving a political structure and those committed to its subversion. When the authorities wish to emphasize the subversion threat in order to rally popular support, they are quick to designate even limited civil disobedience as political crime. If the public is not considered sufficiently loyal, the threat may be ideologically minimized by denying the politicality of even major challenges by stressing the irrationality and ordinary criminality of challengers. For instance, organized demonstrators against war policies or racial discrimination may be characterized as merely freaks, fools, troublemakers, or hustlers.

Serious political challengers play the same game. Confronted by efficient repression and a populace unhelpful because of "false consciousness," resisters tend to prefer a low profile and encourage the perception of them as ordinary lawbreakers or, best of all, conventional political contenders or lobbyists. If the will or ability of the authorities to stop them is doubted, and the general population appears sympathetic or at least indifferent, resisters to political dominance are much more likely to emphasize their prominence and strength as the radical alternative.

Given that the designation of political criminality and criminals is a function of the conflict over who shall control, it is impossible to take either the law or the assertions of participants at face value. One finds that laws explicitly dealing with treason, sedition, and other presumptively political offenses are characteristically vague in regard to the authorization of enforcement. Moreover, conventional criminal and other ostensibly nonpolitical laws may be invoked to justify the coercive treatment of politically troublesome persons and collectivities.

Because the overriding aim of political policing is to secure the polity against radical change, the legality of procedures is necessarily secondary to their effectiveness in suppressing actual subversion and deterring potential challenges. Accordingly, political criminality may be imputed to more as well as less innocent persons, with an eye less for their individual innocence/guilt than for the probable general deterrent impact. A political criminal is, then, anyone who is subjected to any form of deprivation justified by the authorities (at least to themselves if not publicly) on the grounds of "polity security"—and who may or may not have committed acts of political resistance.

What kinds of people become political criminals? Or more specifically, who becomes eligible for political criminalization? The problematic linkage between the *behavioral* realities of political resistance and the *definitional* realities of criminalization by authorities makes such questions extremely difficult to answer, or to ask, without also asking about the political, economic, and other environmental conditions in which resistance and criminalization occur. People may (1) resist without being criminalized, (2) be criminalized without having resisted, or (3) resist and be criminalized. The research strategy adopted in this study is to consider "kinds of people," "resistance," and "political criminalization" as *variables* that may interact in causally significant ways. Even though the quality of available evidence is generally poor, the *model* or *analogy* of quantitative analysis should at least help in suggesting when and how behavioral and definitional realities coincide.

Kinds of people includes all those attributes of social advantage or disadvantage, learning experiences, situational pressures or inducements, and mental capacities or states which have been considered in studies of persons believed to have engaged in political resistance or to be prone to do so.

Resistance refers to any form and degree of dissent, evasion, disobedience, or violence in challenging authorities. Acts of resistance may be instrumental or expressive, calculated or spontaneous, and organized or unorganized.

Political criminalization encompasses all forms and degrees of punitive attention given to actual or putative resisters by authorities, with reference to whether such attention is direct or indirect, legal or extralegal, and mild or severe. In seeking to relate political criminalization to kinds of people and resistance, one must be especially alert to the fact that authorities are concerned not only with resistance per se but also with population control in the broadest sense. Individualized guilt or innocence is subordinated to control strategies aimed at maintaining the current structure of power and privilege—strategies that may at times dictate the sacrifice of innocents.

Political resisters and nonresisters have been compared in regard to various indicators of status, class, and power, as well as social attitudes and psychological states or inclinations. There has generally been a presumption that the social, attitudinal, and psychological measures are interrelated, or else that their relationships should be a primary research concern. Investigation has typically centered on status, class, or power differences, then moved toward consideration of attitudinal and/or psychological characteristics as correlates of such differences. Thus, *kinds of people* as a variable becomes "social class" in terms of the bulk of available research. The evidence so far suggests that political offenders may be higher or lower class (though more likely to be higher class, contrary to the "riffraff" theory), politically sophisticated or merely resentful, and broader or narrower in their focal concerns and objectives. However, there is more evidence that lower-class people are more likely to be joiners than initiators and to be more focused on immediate problems of economic well-being and security. Both lower- and higher-class resisters seem likely to combine cultural and political alienation with political sensitivity and a sense of personal efficacy. In addition, age and social class appear to have some relation to the form which political resistance takes.

There appear to be four basic forms of political resistance. *Dissent* includes any mode of speaking out against the personages, actions, or structures of authority. *Evasion* refers to any attempt to avoid being constrained by the expectations and demands of authorities, as in hiding or fleeing to avoid military conscription. *Disobedience* is any explicit nonviolent rejection of such expectations and demands. *Violence* is any rejection involving physical threats or injuries to persons or objects.

Among the generalizations suggested by the literature are the following.

Dissent is a characteristically higher-class form of resistance, especially insofar as it is an articulate elaboration of a reasoned political philosophy. Lower-class resisters seem more likely to favor nonverbal over verbal resistance, and to trust emotional commitments undertaken in faith more than reasoned commitments derived from theoretical analyses.

Evasion has been a characteristically lower-class form of resistance, for those experienced in powerlessness learn to avoid rather than seek confrontations as far as possible. When physical withdrawal is impossible, subtle and ingenious tactics may be adopted to withhold conformity (e.g., feigning stupidity, working below one's abilities, flattering the masters).

Disobedience is characteristically higher class insofar as it involves what are perceived to be high risks of failure and punishment. Though lower-class resistance may erupt in spontaneous disobedience, deliberately to set oneself up as a target for official displeasure goes against the lessons painfully learned by the powerless (who do *not* readily follow Gandhi or Martin Luther King).

Violence has been associated with lower classness; and though the association has been exaggerated, there is some support for the traditional view. Spontaneous, unorganized collective violence expressing resentment of the fact or the consequences of political subjugation is characteristically lower class. Planned, tactical violence—whether small scale or large scale—is quite likely to be the work (directly or indirectly) of organized, politically sophisticated higher-class resisters.

Political criminalization occurs as authorities react to their perception of what actions are required to forestall or neutralize resistance. *Direct* reaction is by officials without involving nonofficial sources of pressure or restraint; *indirect* reaction involves the use of such sources (e.g., employers, creditors, news media). *Legal* reaction utilizes legal norms and procedures to deal with resisters; *extralegal* reaction refers to any form or degree of punitive response that is beyond legal review and whose legality is clearly dubious even by the criteria of political crime laws. *Severe* reaction is any degree of punitive response that involves physical assault, imprisonment beyond a few days, and/or the loss of material resources for either the resister or persons emotionally significant to the resister; *mild* reaction is anything less. Some generalizations:

(1) If resistance is believed to be spontaneous, unorganized, and limited to a few politically resentful individuals, the severity of reaction will probably be greatest for violence, less for disobedience, somewhat less for dissent, and least for evasion. The more public and explicit the challenge, the more the authorities will feel constrained to act.

(2) Irrespective of the form and degree of resistance, lower-class resisters are likely to receive more severe treatment than are higher-class resisters.

(3) The use of legal methods alone will be more likely where the form of resistance is dissent or disobedience instead of evasion or violence, given that the scale of resistance is viewed as unthreatening.

(4) Direct methods are more likely to be used against lower-class individuals to the extent that indirect methods are more costly or cumbersome. Legal methods alone are more likely to be used against higher-class resisters.

(5) Given calculated and organized resistance, reaction will probably be relatively severe for each form and degree of resistance. Where social discontent is widespread, deliberate resistance will be especially threatening and met with marked severity. With political stability, some class variation seems likely: lower-class resisters can be expected to receive harsher treatment than higher-class ones.

(6) The greater the threat, the greater the range of controls the authorities will mobilize: indirect as well as direct, extralegal as well as legal.

Generalizations about political criminality and policing presuppose a hierarchical, politically organized society in which established dominant parties try to preserve the structure against efforts to change it, and thereby end their dominance. The aim of inquiry is to develop a predictively useful theory of political criminality applicable to *any* such society, regardless of the ideological claims and beliefs of rulers or ruled. Seeming exceptions (e.g., the eradication of millions of "higher-class" Russian *kulaks*) are, it now seems clear, found where revolutionary change is under way—i.e., where the (apparently inevitable) transition from one hierarchical structure to another is being made. When such upheavals will occur, and how long the transition will take, are questions for studies of revolutionary social change. Until some relatively settled distribution of power is fought out, the concepts of political criminality and policing simply have no utility. People at war do not criminalize one another; they merely destroy or conquer.

CONCLUSION

Debates over the "correct" *goals* of inquiry cannot be resolved, except by the logic of force. However, debates over the most fruitful *strategies* for inquiry (e.g., partisan versus nonpartisan analytical methods) can be resolved, *if* the criterion of explicable predictive power is accepted. If it is not, then again there is no possible resolution in intellectual terms—only in political ones. We may assume either that truth is independent of anyone's political intentions and demands, or that it is not. If we assume that it is not, logically our research can amount to nothing more than partisan propaganda.

NOTES

1. This section is mainly adapted from portions of a volume now under revision for publication. As the purpose here is solely to illustrate nonpartisan conflict analysis in criminology, no effort has been made to do more than sketch some substantive ideas. Form, not content, is the matter at hand. Readers interested in political criminality and policing are asked to hold their fire until they have had a chance to see the book.

REFERENCES

BOULDING, K. E. (1962) Conflict and Defense: A General Theory. New York: Harper & Row.

Center for Research on Criminal Justice (1977) The Iron Fist and the Velvet Glove: An Analysis of the U.S. Police. Berkeley, CA: Author.

CHAMBLISS, W. J. (1976) "Functional and conflict theories of crime: the heritage of Emile Durkheim and Karl Marx," pp. 1-28 in W. J. Chambliss and M. Mankoff (eds.) Whose Law, What Order? A Conflict Approach to Criminology. New York: John Wiley.

CHEVIGNY, P. (1969) Police Power: Police Abuses in New York City. New York: Random House.

COLLINS, R. (1975) Conflict Sociology: Toward an Explanatory Science. New York: Academic.

HARRING, S. L. (1976) "The development of the police institution in the United States." Crime and Social Justice 5 (Spring/Summer): 54-59.

HORTON, J. (1966) "Order and conflict theories of social problems as competing ideologies." American Journal of Sociology 71 (May): 701-713.

LEFCOURT, R. (1971) "Law against the people," pp. 21-37 in R. Lefcourt (ed.) Law Against the People: Essays to Demystify Law, Order and the Courts. New York: Vintage.

LeVINE, R. A. and D. T. CAMPBELL (1972) Ethnocentrism: Theories of Conflict, Ethnic Attitudes, and Group Behavior. New York: John Wiley.

LOFLAND, J. (1969) Deviance and Identity. Englewood Cliffs, NJ: Prentice-Hall.

MAO TSE-TUNG (1968) Four Essays on Philosophy. Peking: Foreign Languages Press.

NEWMAN, G. (1976) Comparative Deviance: Perception and Law in Six Cultures. New York: Elsevier North-Hollaland.

PLATT, T. (1974) "Prospects for a radical criminology in the United States." Crime and Social Justice 1 (Spring/Summer): 2-10.

QUINNEY, R. (1977) Class, State, and Crime. New York: David McKay.

RAPOPORT, A. (1974) Conflict in Man-Made Environment. Markham, Ontario: Penguin.

——— (1960) Fights, Games, and Debates. Ann Arbor: University of Michigan Press.

ROSSI, P., E. WAITE, C. E. BOSE, and R. BERK (1974) "The seriousness of crimes: normative structure and individual differences." American Sociological Review 39 (April): 224-237.

SCHELLING, T. C. (1960) The Strategy of Conflict. Cambridge, MA: Harvard University Press.

SCHWENDINGER, H. and J. R. SCHWENDINGER (1977) "Social class and the definition of crime." Crime and Social Justice 9 (Spring/Summer): 4-13.

——— (1974) Sociologists of the Chair. New York: Basic Books.

——— (1970) "Defenders of order or guardians of human rights?" Issues in Criminology 5 (Summer): 123-157.

TAYLOR, I., P. WALTON, and J. YOUNG [eds] (1973) The New Criminology: For a Social Theory of Deviance. London: Routledge & Kegan Paul.

TURK, A. T. (1977) "Class, conflict, and criminalization." Sociological Focus 10 (August): 209-220.

5

THE CONTEMPORARY CRISES OF MARXIST CRIMINOLOGY

Carl B. Klockars

History does nothing, possesses no enormous wealth, fights no battles. It is rather man, the real, living man, who does everything, possesses, fights. It is not "History," as if she were a person apart, who uses men as means to work out her purposes, but history itself is nothing but the activity of men pursuing their purposes.

—Karl Marx

The task of framing a critique of radical criminology is formidable. During the past decade a number of new criminologies have appeared. Some of the best (Lofland, 1969, for example) fall well within the tradition of conventional criminology, though are profoundly critical of it. Others have taken up the helpful cultivation of sophisticated methodological, cross-cultural, and historical studies, and still others have brought to criminology needed exchange with the disciplines of economics, psychology, philosophy, and political science. Such work, I am relatively certain, will benefit, broaden, and be welcomed by conventional criminology.

But while I am relatively certain that conventional criminology will welcome and accommodate these varieties of radical criminology, I do not believe that the most visible and celebrated variety, drawing its inspiration from Marx, will survive the rigors of scholarly scrutiny. Although it sought to revolutionize conventional criminology and even heralded itself as signaling a "paradigm shift," it never managed to create the theoretical or empirical dialogue that would make that shift possible. Although it found conventional criminology "unimaginative," "bankrupt," "bourgeois," "positivistic," and "without passion," one leader of the movement still maintained as late as 1974 that "the most imaginative criminology has been written by 'criminals'—Brendan Behan, Claude Brown, Eldridge Cleaver, Angela Davis, George Jackson, and Sam Melville to name a few" (Platt, 1974a: 3).

Imagination is one thing; criminology, another. But given this collection of characters, their revolutionary zeal, and their contempt for conventional criminology, neither their poor scholarship, embarrassing empirical failures, nor their strident moral and political imperialism were surprising. Even though, in the tradition of Sutherland, one can learn a great deal from prisoners and criminals, I believe it would be unfair, Platt's endorsement notwithstanding, to frame a critique of radical criminology about the work of these "criminologists." However, among the ranks are a few scholars whose work in earnest has been and ought to be taken seriously. The contribution of Turk (1980) to this book is precisely such a labor, but must be read as an attempt to rescue some portion of the radical perspective before its total bankruptcy is declared and all its resources are divided up among the growing ranks of its discreditors.[1] Whether or not Turk will be successful in his salvage remains to be seen.

We are, I believe, in the late phase of Marxist criminology, a point at which its capacity for contribution is exhausted, and where it must confront the reality of its own theoretical and empirical poverty or wither and die. In offering an account of this contemporary crisis in Marxist criminology, I have made four assumptions. The first is that this crisis is *not* due to personal inadequacies of Marxist criminologists. The crisis, as I see it, is theoretical. Platt (1974a: 6), however, has suggested that the poverty of radical criminology is at least partially due to the "repression of Marxist scholarship in universities and the liberal emphasis on pragmatism and social enginering," thus making the possibility that Marxist criminology has attracted the more heroic or less talented among us worth considering. Nevertheless, I do not know how to judge a church except by its preachers, no matter how humble or heroic they may be.

My second assumption is that the crisis is best represented in the American version of Marxist criminology. I not only believe that American

Marxist criminology is a few years ahead of things on the other side of the Atlantic, but that its theoretical and empirical poverty is most visible when juxtaposed with certain undeniable elements in American culture. For this reason, I have chosen to focus on the Marxist themes in the theoretical core of a few of American Marxist criminology's most influential and most productive scholars: William Chambliss, Anthony Platt, Herman and Julia Schwendinger, and Richard Quinney. Although there are differences between them and some of their work follows the best traditions of liberally pragmatic conventional criminology, they seem to have converged rather tightly around a Marxist strain and constitute, to use a metaphor from baseball, the "heavy hitters in the lineup." So while there are some worthy players outside the American League, on the bench and in the minors, their talents will have to be left to other innings.

The third assumption framing the critique of certain portions of the work of the "heavy hitters" of American Marxist criminology is that they share a certain moral consensus with criminologists of vastly different theoretical, methodological, and political persuasions. Along with criminologists—left, right, and center—they find repugnant and abhorrent the racism, sexism, brutality, crime, and corruption that are to be found in many parts of the American criminal justice system. In fact, Chambliss, Platt, and the others have all been among the most passionate and articulate spokesmen in the fight against these injustices. Consequently, this critique does not raise the question of whether or not criminology ought to serve to eliminate such abuses, but of the adequacy of the accounts offered by the leading figures of American Marxist criminology in explaining them.

Finally, it is appropriate to assume and declare in any critique of Marxist or Neo-Marxist analyses that there are many "Marxs" and many versions of "Neo-Marxism," a few of which would undoubtedly have the old master spinning in his grave. Thus, while I undertake to criticize the interpretive line taken by those I regard to be the best representatives of American Marxist criminology, I certainly would not wish to suggest that Marx is dead, but only that the particular interpretive line these criminologists have taken is at a dead end.

THE CORE OF THE PROBLEM: THE DOGMA OF CLASS

If there is a single concept around which the heavy hitters of American Marxist criminology have been willing to rally, it is *class*. We could find similar expressions in the work of Quinney (1970, 1974a, 1974b, 1975, 1977, and 1979), Platt (1969, 1971, 1973, and 1974), and the Schwendingers (1964, 1970, 1972, 1973, 1974, 1976a, and 1976b), but Chambliss is as good a guide to the centrality of class as any of the others:

> Criminal behavior is explained by the forces of class interests and class struggles, and most fundamentally by the contradictions inherent in the social relations created by the society's particular modes of production. In capitalist society crime and criminal law are the result of the social relations created by a system which expropriates labor for the benefit of a capitalist class [1976: 5].

The single most important feature of the radical criminologist's understanding of class may be discerned from this quote from Chambliss: Class is bad. Chambliss claims it to be the generator of criminal behavior and, as if that were not, bad enough, criminal behavior generated at the cost of labor "expropriated [exploited?] for the benefit of a capitalist class." I suspect Chambliss would agree with the Schwendingers, who find class to be the source of "imperialistic war, racism, sexism, and poverty" (1970), and possibly even with Quinney, who, in his contribution to the February 1979 issue of *Criminology* finds it to be the inspiration of bad art, "the ideological reproduction of capitalism." Although I find evidence for these relations unconvincing for reasons I will explain below, the assumption of the evil of class unites the radical criminologists.

It is, however, an assumption that is intellectually and historically questionable. The evidence for the role of class in periods of great cultural production in art, music, literature, and scholarship is overwhelming. Class hierarchy has served as protector and cultivator of artistic and intellectual pursuits, defending them from both the power of the state and the jealousy and envy of the masses. More than one student of intellectual history has made the point that determined egalitarianism, with its reverence for the talents and opinions of the celebrated man in the street is, to say the least, not particularly hospitable to the life of the mind.[2]

Furthermore, for much of English history and for a time in the American experience, social class performed the important functions of creating, maintaining, and perpetuating a set of standards which carried authority and inspired the rest of society. James Baldwin, not easily dismissible as a victim of false consciousness, may serve as a source for the importance of this function of social class at one time in this country's history:

> I suppose it can be said that there was a time in this country when an entity existed which could be called a majority, let us say a class,

for the lack of a better word, which created the standards to which the country aspired. I am referring to or have in mind, perhaps somewhat arbitrarily, the aristocracies of Virginia and New England. These were mainly of Anglo-Saxon stock and they created what Henry James was to refer to, not very much later, as our Anglo-American heritage, or Anglo-American connections. Now at no time did these men ever form anything resembling a popular majority. Their importance was that they kept alive and they bore witness to two elements of a man's life which are not greatly respected among us now: (1) the social forms, called manners, which prevent us from rubbing too abrasively against one another, and (2) the interior life, or the life of the mind. These things are important; these things were realities for them and no matter how rough-hewn or dark the country was then it is important to remember that this was also the time when people sat up in log cabins studying very hard by lamplight or candlelight [1962: 124].

Finally, if class is to be credited with full responsibility for all the ills of modern American society, it would seem only fair to credit to it as an economic phenomenon the threefold increase in the real wage of American workers since 1900; the fact that the "typical *poverty* family today can buy as much food as the *average* U.S. worker could buy in our grandparents' time—plus better housing, more clothing, furniture, heat, and medical care" (Lebergott, 1976: 4); the accomplishment of a standard of "poverty" such that 99% of families beneath it have electricity, flush toilets, and mechanical refrigeration, 96% live in housing with one or fewer persons per room, 90% own televisions, and 41% own at least one car. As Harrington (1969: 178) states: "the American poor are not poor . . . in the sixteenth century, they are poor here and now in the United States. They are dispossessed in terms of what the rest of the nation enjoys. . . . They watch the movies and read the magazines of affluent Americans and these tell them they are internal exiles." In what might be the single greatest testimony to the hegemony of the U.S. advertising profession, two American Marxist economists, Baran and Sweezy (1966: 288-289), classified as "poor" those American families which could not regularly purchase cans of "room air freshener."[3]

While I am not convinced that an economically and socially classless society would be a "good" society and my reasoning generally follows Baltzell (1958, 1964), Popper (1945), Djilas (1957, 1969), Ellul (1964, 1975), Solzhenitsyn (1975), Young (1961), and the frightening promises of Lenin (1932) and Skinner (1971), the chief purpose of this essay is neither to defend class nor to restore some appreciation for the functions it once served to its credit. The truly critical question to be derived from the quote from Chambliss and echoed in the writings of the other radical criminologists concerns the ability of class to "explain" crime: Namely, in contemporary American society, does class as understood by the leading figures of American Marxist criminology actually explain crime, criminal law, and criminal behavior as they claim it can? And, if so, what is the nature of the explanation it offers?

To answer this question, we need a working definition of class. Quinney offers this one:

> On the *abstract* level, class structure is an expression of the struggle of classes, the antagonistic relation between those who own *and* control the means of production and those who do not [1977: 67-68; *italics added*].

In the above quotation, which defines class in the dichotomous distinction between owners and nonowners of the means of production, *abstract* and the presumed unity of ownership *and* control are emphasized because they conceal the bases for the most devastating critiques of the dogma of class. The first is that class, however useful it may have been to understand earlier periods in American history, and still may be for the analysis of underdeveloped countries, is little more than an abstraction for the analysis of contemporary American society.[4] This argument, which Quinney knows very well, is that in modern society class is ideology, not social reality. This does not mean, of course, that there are not owners and nonowners of the means of production. What it does mean is that the empirical social reality of classes of the kind that Marx could behold in nineteenth-century England, that Baldwin speaks of in an earlier quotation, and even into the early part of this century Fitzgerald's great Gatsby could strain to imitate, exists in America's past rather than in its present.

In attempting to contend with the social unreality of class in modern America, but without raising it directly, Quinney quotes the following gymnastic explanation of the failure of class to correspond to empirical social reality:

> A concrete historically given society cannot correspond directly to abstract categories. As we have said, Marxism does not use abstraction formally. After it has elaborated the concept abstractedly, it later denies it, showing the limitation of this level of concept. Hence the need for passing to more concrete levels of abstraction [Dos Santos, 1970: 177 quoted in Quinney, 1977: 68].

Quinney follows this quotation with the line, "in the analysis of a given society at a specific time, then, a description of class structure may be quite elaborate" (p. 68). Indeed, it would certainly have to be quite elaborate to force empirical social realities into concepts which do not take abstraction formally, which admit a lack of correspondence empirically and which are constantly being elaborated and denied. To muscle the complexities of contemporary American society, with its interest groups, occupational, political, economic, racial, ethnic, technological, cultural, status, kinship, party, familial, and institutional complexities, into a single procrustean bed of social class—owners and nonowners—necessitates exactly the kind of grotesque mystification that Dos Santos provides and Quinney accepts.

As we shall see, the opportunities which empirically contentless concepts offer American Marxist criminologists are manifold, but the most immediate brings us to the second critique concealed in Quinney's abstract elaboration of class: the assumed unity between ownership and control of the means of production. Conceptually, of course, the relationship between ownership and control is not logically necessary, as anyone who has owned a recalcitrant puppy can attest. On a somewhat higher plane of analysis, ownership need not imply control of the organizational level either. The only way to get a "Piece of the Rock," my insurance man tells me, is to buy a policy, but neither any other Prudential owner nor I exercise any control over our company. What we realize is that our company and many other corporate bodies have driven a wedge between ownership and control, and that our organizations are not controlled by owners but by bureaucrats and managers (Berle, 1954; Berle and Means, 1967; Hindley, 1970; Larner, 1970; Monson et al., 1968; Williamson, 1963, 1970). At the highest levels of analysis the relationship between ownership and control is still not guaranteed: Authority relations are obviously a broader category of relations on control than are property relations (Weber, 1946: 180-195; Dahrendorf, 1959: 136-138), although property relations may be counted as one important type of them. For example, most Soviet Jews find their life chances controlled by parties with whom they have no property relations whatsoever.

Given the fact that the theoretical and conceptual relationship between ownership and control of *anything* is not *automatic,* the following questions are empirical: (1) whether or not those who technically own the means of production in contemporary American society actually control them; or (2) whether other relations of control are more compelling explanations. That is, the questions must be demonstrated to exist in a way that satisfies some reasonable epistemological standards. My own perceptions based on both empirical and theoretical studies in the literature of political science, community power, and general stratification is that contemporary American and Soviet society *both* suffer from control by managers, technocrats, bureaucrats, well- and sometimes not-so-well-meaning "professionals" and officials, and that the problems of those relations of control exist irrespective of the private ownership of the means of production. That Soviet citizens or citizens of any other modern industrial state governed under a Marxist-Leninist ideology suffer more than U.S. citizens at the hands of such bureaucrats, managers, technocrats, and officials is beyond question (Barghoorn, 1966; Barry and Barner-Barry, 1978; Beichman, 1972; Cocks, 1976; Conquest, 1968; Gastil, 1976; Kaiser, 1976; Salisbury, 1974; Schapiro, 1967; Shub, 1969; H. Smith, 1976; Solzhenitsyn, 1975; Wesson, 1972).

THE RADICAL CRIMINOLOGISTS
AND ALLOPLASTIC INTEREST

None of the leading figures of American Marxist criminology would find convincing any work demonstrating the pluralistic nature of American society, its multiple interest groups, its varied levels of social prestige and occupational status, or its considerable distribution of power and income, any more than they would be moved by the observation that neither legislatures, the courts, the police, nor any part of the criminal justice system is owned by the owners of the means of production. Their claim is that, although the criminal justice system is not owned by the owners, it is, by and large, their "agent" acting out their "interests."[5]

The concept of "interest" is as critical to American Marxist criminology as it is to Marxist theory generally. Without it, and more precisely without a very special concept of it, Marxist analysis of contemporary American society would be relegated to the well-known dustbin of history. Given the empirical disappearance of the great owning and nonowning classes of bygone days, the failure of American workers to "proletarianize" or "pauperize" as Marx had prophesied, and the bourgeoisie behaving like the vanguard of the proletariat in massive interest groups like the Consumer Movement and Common Cause, it must be argued that the *concept of "interest" is the central concept with which Marxist theory must tie the actual operation and organization of contemporary American society to the owners of the means of production.*

With respect to the concept of interest, the history of some of the leading figures of American Marxist criminology is most interesting. Platt in *The Child Savers* (1969) employed a theoretical perspective on interests quite amenable to a pluralist interest-group model. "Child-saving may be understood as a crusade which served symbolic and ceremonial functions for native, middle-class Americans" (p. 98). The child-saving movement, Platt wrote originally, produced the Illinois Juvenile Court Act of 1899 whose "success was due in large measure to the fact that it was *widely* sponsored and in turn satisfied *diverse interest groups*" (p. 134; italics added). That was the Platt of 1969. In 1973 (p. 26) we find Platt criticizing his own treatment of interests in *The Child Savers:* "The problem with *The Child Savers* is that . . . [it] focuses too much attention on middle class reformers . . ." A year later, Platt "reasons anew that the impetus for delinquency legislation flowed from close and compromising links between members of the middle and upper classes (1974b: 369) and that 'the juvenile court system was part of a general movement directed towards developing a specialized labor market and industrial discipline under corporate capitalism by creating new programs of adjudication and control . . .' (1974: 377)" (Hagan and Leon, 1977).

Chambliss is more interesting still. In 1964 his little classic, "A Sociological Analysis of the Law of Vagrancy" appeared in *Social Problems*. It appeared in its original form in Chambliss's 1969 reader, *Crime and the Legal Process,* a volume Chambliss dedicated to Chief Justice Earl Warren. Six years later, Chambliss published a reader which began as an attempt to revise *Crime and the Legal Process,* but ended as a quite different reader, *Criminal Law in Action* (1975). In the preface, Chambliss confesses that his own orientation has changed considerably since 1969 and hopes that the articles reprinted in his new reader "will stimulate inquiring minds to benefit from the mistakes as well as the truths contained in this volume" (Chambliss, 1975: viii). However, lest his own law of vagrancy article be understood to fall in the "mistakes" rather than "truths" category, he not only removes parts of it which might soften a radical Marxist perspective on criminal law, but also rewrites his own earlier analytical passages without mentioning any revisions to his readers.

The credit to the "Law of Vagrancy" article in *Criminal Law in Action* reads: " 'Source: A Sociological Analysis of the Law of Vagrancy,' *Social Problems,* Vol. 12, Summer, 1964, pp. 46-47. By permission of the author and publisher." The substantive changes revolve around the concept of interest and are summarized in Table 1. To see what was left out in addition to what was rewritten, inquiring minds are invited to compare the

TABLE 1   A Change of Interest

William J. Chambliss, "A Sociological Analysis of the Law of Vagrancy," in *Social Problems*, Summer *1964*, Volume 12, #1, pp. 46–67.	"The Law of Vagrancy," in William J. Chambliss (ed.) *Criminal Law in Action*, Hamilton; Santa Barbara, *1975*. "Source: A Sociological Analysis of the Law of Vagrancy, Social Problems, Summer 1964, Volume 12, #1, pp. 46–47."

The innovation in the law, then, was a direct result of the afore-mentioned changes which had occurred in the social setting. *In this case these changes were located for the most part in the economic institution of the society.* The vagrancy laws were designed to alleviate a condition defined by the lawmakers as undesirable. (Page 70)	The innovation in the law, then, was a direct result of the afore-mentioned changes in the social setting. *The law was clearly and consciously designed to serve the interests of the ruling class of feudal landlords at the expense of the serfs or working classes.* The vagrancy laws were designed to alleviate a condition defined by the lawmakers as undesirable. (Page 11)
Beginning with the lessening of punishment in the statute of 1563 we find these changes. However, instead of remaining dormant (or becoming more so) or being negated altogether the vagrancy statutes experienced a shift in focal concern. With this shift the statutes served a new and equally important function for the *social order of England*. (Page 71)	Beginning with the lessening of punishment in the statute of 1530 [sic], we find these changes. Instead of remaining dormant (or becoming more so) or being negated altogether the vagrancy statutes experienced a shift in focal concern. With this shift the statutes served a new and equally important function for the *ruling class of England*. (Page 11)
This analysis of the vagrancy statutes (and Hall's analysis of theft as well) has demonstrated *the importance of "vested interest" groups in the emergence and/or alteration of laws*. The vagrancy laws emerged in order to provide the powerful landowners with a ready supply of cheap labor. When this was no longer seen as necessary and particularly when the landowners were no longer dependent upon cheap labor *nor were they a powerful interest group in society* the laws became dormant. *Finally a new interest group emerged and was seen as being of great importance to the society and the laws were then altered so as to afford some protection to this group*. These findings are in agreement with Weber's contention that "status groups" determine the content of the law. (Page 77)	This analysis of the vagrancy statutes (and Hall's analysis of theft as well) has demonstrated *the important emergence and role of ruling classes in the alteration of laws.* The vagrancy laws emerged in order to provide the powerful landowners with a ready supply of cheap labor. When this no longer seemed necessary and particularly when the landowners were neither dependent upon cheap labor *nor so powerful* the laws became dormant. *Finally a new ruling class emerged and the laws were then altered so as to provide some protection to them.* These findings are thus in agreement with Weber's contention that "status groups" determine the content of the law. (Page 15)

entire original *Social Problems* article with the quietly revised version in *Criminal Law in Action.*

Quinney's history is less dramatic. In 1970 in the *Social Reality of Crime* he offers a tentative critique of Pluralist interest analysis, but identifies a variety of normative orders from which interests emanate. In addition to political and economic institutions he adds religious, kinship, educational, and public interests. To demonstrate these various sources, in his third chapter, "Interests in the Formulation of Criminal Laws," he takes his students through Erikson's *Wayward Puritans* (1966), various studies of Sabbath Law, Hall (1952) on the law of theft, an interesting argument that "antitrust legislation has been inspired and led by the business interest itself" (p. 77), a similar case for pure food and drug legislation, Sutherland (1950) and Tappan (1950) on sex offender laws, Schur's (1965) and the original Chambliss (1964) on vagrancy.

Chambliss (1974: 38) in fact chides Quinney's treatment of interests in the *Social Reality of Crime* as a bit too liberal. Not to worry! Quinney's ideological evolution had already caught up with Chambliss, and in 1974 he specified in *Critique of the Legal Order* the proper Marxist pose on "interest":

> In a radical critique of American society we are able, in addition, to get at objective interests that are external to the consciousness of individuals. We are able, furthermore, to suggest no motive evaluations of those interests. Pluralists on the other hand are bound by subjective interests of individuals. [Here Quinney cites Balbus (1971).] The critical perspective allows us to understand the actual and potential interests of classes, of the ruling class as well as those who are ruled. What this means for a critique of legal order is that we can break with the official dominant ideology which proclaims the diversity of interests among competing groups. We are able to determine the interests of those who make and use law for their own advantage [1974a: 54].

Quinney explains in the above passage the two concepts of interest which the Marxist analyst employs. The first is subjective; Quinney says the Pluralist analysts are "bound by" this concept. Simply stated, "subjective" interest is what people believe they want, what they organize to get, and what they sometimes attempt to influence the political process in behalf of. Thus Platt's child savers, as they understood themselves and as Platt understood them while he was writing *The Child Savers,* were a "good ol' American" interest group acting out their "subjective interests." Sensible sociology, not to mention political science and history, is full of such accounts of the activities of crusaders, interest groups, and associations of one type or another.

It is very clear, however, that if American Marxist criminologists had been armed only with a concept of subjective interests, they would have never got off the ground. At least since Sellin and Wolfgang's *Measurement of Delinquency* (1964), there has been strong evidence to show that the American bourgeoisie and proletariat (no matter how you slice it) share an overwhelming consensus on the relative seriousness of most common crimes. Since 1964, replications of Seriousness Index studies in Canada (Normandeau, 1966; Akman et al., 1967) and England (Akman and Normandeau, 1970) have confirmed the *Measurement*'s scale of relative seriousness as has a more recent study based on samples of incarcerated *lumpenproletariat* (Figlio, 1975). To these studies we can add the work of Thomas (1976) based on surveys of 3,334 households in Norfolk, Virginia which found that rankings of gravity of 17 offenses and the punishments they merited were not affected in any substantial way (the lowest between-group correlation was .917) by respondents' age, sex, race, education, income, or occupational prestige. Furthermore, Newman's (1976) study of nine acts of varying seriousness evaluated by respondents from India, Indonesia, Iran, Sardinia, Yugoslavia, and the United States found not only a cross-cultural consensus as to the wrongness of the offenses, but a strong similarity in the intensity with which respondents from these various countries wished to sanction traditional criminal behavior.

In light of such evidence one might think that Platt, the Schwendingers, Quinney, or Chambliss, who in 1974 (p. 37) decreed, "in any complex, modern society there is no value consensus relevant to the law," might be moved to reconsider. However, the concept of objective interest gives American Marxist criminologists the vehicle they believe they need to "transcend" the social reality of this research. To understand objective interest let us turn to Balbus whom Quinney cites in his earlier quote. Objective interest, says Balbus (1971: 53) is "objective because it refers to an effect by something on the individual which can be observed and measured by standards external to the individual's consciousness." This concept makes possible the contention "that an individual may be unaware of or mistaken about, his interests, i.e., that he may be unaware of, or may misjudge the effect that something has on him" (p. 153). Balbus goes on to assert that the poverty of Pluralist analysis of society and social order is that it "consistently refuses to recognize any but subjective interests" (p. 154). It is the concept of objective interest that enables Marxists to speak of people being "falsely conscious."[6]

Is some concept of "objective interest" necessary for political, socio-logical, or criminological analysis? The answer is, of course, yes. People do, in fact, form false notions, make decisions whose consequences they do not anticipate, and are affected by processes they do not understand. But that is true of everyone and is neither beyond nor new to Pluralist political analysis, any variety of sociological theory, nor any tradition in crimino-logical thought. Such work commonly demonstrates that people are falsely conscious of their interests, do things which come back to haunt them, or affect their own lives or the lives of others in ways they do not anticipate. Could it be that after all these years the Marxists somehow missed hearing about latent functions?

The answer is, of course, no. But when the leading figures of American Marxist criminology employ a concept of objective interest—that is, when they actually use it in their work as an analytical device—they clearly have something very different in mind than the old standard, the latent func-tion. However, neither Quinney nor his source (Balbus, 1971) clearly explicates the concept of objective interest, though the former uses it constantly and the latter mystifies it for more than twenty-five pages in the article cited by Quinney. I submit that whatever abstract mystification Marxist criminologists may summon to define objective interest, it is nothing more than *the faith that private ownership of the means of production is so profoundly and thoroughly evil that nothing which it produces can be anything but evil as well.*

The nature of the passionate assumption of evil makes it immune to refutation as well as the mechanism through which evil is discovered and identified. Before analyzing the somewhat more complex use of objective interest as the pursuit of evil by Marxist criminologists, a simple example may help as a guide to both these properties of its passionate assumption. Let us suppose that I am coming up for tenure and my department chair, who is also my good friend, is having a birthday the week before I do. Let us further assume, solely for the purposes of this example, mind you, that I am a thoroughly evil person. Suppose I buy her a birthday present. Ahha! Clearly an attempt at bribery. Suppose, however, I do not. Given that I am so thoroughly and profoundly evil, is that not also an example of deceit and treachery, demonstrating that I am a real Iago feigning the *appearance* of integrity? The point is not only that *nothing* I can do will refute the assumption of my evilness, but also that the ideology of evil can direct attention to *anything* I do as evidence for its confirmation.

Let us now turn to a few examples of the pursuit of evil/objective interest in the canons of the heavy hitters of American Marxist crimi-nology.

First, consider Quinney's "critique" of first amendment freedoms in his *Critique of the Legal Order* (1974a: 145).

> Contrary to the legal ideology, civil liberties are not a safeguard of human rights. Those liberties that are abstractly guaranteed are the province of the ruling class. That is, those from whom we are to be protected dispense our civil liberties. There is a one-way allocation of civil liberties, from the top down, from those with power to those without. Civil liberties are thus parceled out to us at the discretion of the authority that we wish to dissent from, alter or destroy. All is on their terms, according to their rules and their application of the rules. The expectation that we should get a fair hearing stretches even the most optimistic liberal imagination. Yet the legal ideology would have us believe the official guarantees.

In this passage, Quinney "transcends" the "official dominant ideology" with a characteristic application of the ideology of objective interest as evil. It is important to emphasize that Quinney is not simply remaking the point, often made by liberals and conservatives alike, that first amendment freedoms have been abused, denied, or otherwise seriously tampered with at many times in American history. Quinney's *Critique of the Legal Order* charges that civil liberties *themselves* are not safeguards of human rights, but merely one more part of the legal ideology that legitimates repression. For this reason it will not refute Quinney's contention to make an empirical case that denials of civil liberties in China, Cuba, or Soviet bloc countries are far more extensive than they are in the United States; nor the historical argument that in repeated cases of the most violent denials of human rights, tyrannies, dictatorships, and totalitarian regimes of all sorts have thought enough of the capacity of civil liberties to protect human rights to abolish them.

The only way out of this maze of mystification is to recognize that it rests upon a special sorting of civil liberties into those enjoyed in capitalist societies which seem to work against their destruction, and those which are denied in Marxist-Leninist states that serve to preserve them. If one removes that Manichean division, and maintains that civil liberties—the freedom of speech, press, publication, association, and religion—*are* human rights, Quinney's critique is absurd.[7]

Of course, it does not follow that getting a fair hearing will result in getting one's way, a situation which often disturbs people who hold passionate beliefs. But, fortunately, few would go so far as to claim with Quinney that "Only by the most extreme and, by definition, the most illegal of means can the opposition be assured of a voice and possible effective action"[8] (1974a: 145).

Chambliss is more subtle. Although he does not employ the official Marxist terminology of "objective interests," he uses extensively (1974, 1975, 1977) a functionally equivalent concept, "the mobilization of bias." This concept, borrowed from Schattschneider (1960: 71), Chambliss claims to be the key to understanding a "whole world of criminal law information which reflects the interest of economic elites *not* consciously but nonetheless effectively" (Chambliss, 1974: 21; emphasis in original). It does so, Chambliss explains, because it not only calls our attention to the class consequences of decisions which courts and legislatures *do* make, but also to their "non-decision-making."

As an example of the power of the "mobilization of bias" to take us into this world of non-conscious, non-decision-making, Chambliss offers the following illustrations:

> For example, neither legislature nor appellate court in the United States would consider the question of whether it is criminal for a motion picture magnate to spend $20 thousand on a birthday party for his daughter while people are starving a few blocks from the night club he rented for the occasion, or whether it should be a crime for the wife of the Attorney General of the United States to have 200 pair of shoes while people in the Appalachian Mountains cannot afford shoes to send their children to school. It is simply assumed as part of the prevailing definition of reality that such an issue is "beyond the pale" of law-making constitutions [1974: 21].

Of course, the list of non-decisions "beyond the pale" of the prevailing definition of reality is infinite. "Neither legislature nor appellate court in the Unites States would consider the questions" of whether it should be criminal for clocks to turn clockwise, policemen to smile, or toads to have wings. Moreover, no empirical method exists for identifying any one of the infinite number of possible non-conscious, non-decisions that is any more a non-decision than any other. Clearly, the only bias that is being mobilized in the above quoted examples of non-decision-making is Chambliss's, but let us take it somewhat seriously for a moment.

Suppose some well-intentioned legislature were to consider the criminalization of lavish birthday parties and excessive shoe purchasing by filthy rich people. What should they criminalize? Any Marxist lawmaker with the best interest of the poor at heart and a rudimentary knowledge of economics would, I suspect, be obliged to criminalize spending of *less* than $20,000 on birthday parties and purchasing of *fewer* than 200 pairs of shoes. In fact, our Marxist lawmaker would be well advised to raise both minimums, for, with every catered potlatch and every new Gucci buckle, wealth is distributed and jobs are maintained or created. The sin of capitalism, at least as far as the poor and unemployed are concerned, is accumulation, *criminal saving* not spending.

But let us not forget that it is Chambliss's bias, and not the bias of the poor and unemployed, that is being mobilized in his example. He could have chosen to speak of the failure of legislatures to criminalize the purchase of great works of classical art and sculpture by the filthy rich, a type of spending which typically does not redound to the economic interests of the poor and unemployed. He does not because the real thrust of the examples he mobilizes is not to be found in the affluence of the spenders, but in their bad taste. So while in tasteful academe we love our Guggenheims and deplore Miami Beaches, I suggest as a reasonable compromise between our interests and those of the poor and unemployed that we not criminalize either.

It should also be remembered, however, that Chambliss's promise for the concept of mobilization of bias was twofold, and even if its ability to identify non-conscious, non-decisions is visionary, we must also contend with its twin capacity, the identification of the connections between economic interests and law-making decisions which actually are made. Chambliss applies the concept of mobilization of bias to the Bill of Rights:

> The Founding Fathers, having just rebelled against precisely the same aristocratic government against which the new English industrialist class was still struggling, demanded legal-rational legitimacy. They wrote into the new Constitution most of the significant reforms that were still being incubated in England: due process of law, the independence of the judiciary, the right to a jury, *habeas corpus*, the right to counsel, the right to summon witnesses in defense, the right to bail, indictment by grand jury, the privilege against self-incrimination. *In short, due process ensured the institution of the adversary system and resolved a major conflict between competing elites without redistributing power or privilege to the lower classes.* Significantly, all this came about in England and the United States through the mobilization of bias in the criminal law process as the perspective and needs of those who control societies' economic resources get translated into law [Chambliss, 1974: 25; emphasis added].

One could dismiss this analysis on the ground that it is simply another case of invoking the alloplastic category of non-decision-making (the Bill of Rights, due process, and the adversary system were created, but redistributing power and privilege to the lower classes was a non-decision), but to do so in peremptory fashion one would fail to recognize that Chambliss's claim goes much further. In particular, he asserts that due process, the Bill of Rights, the adversary system, and other constitutional guarantees failed to redistribute power or privilege to the lower classes and merely reflected the needs and perspectives of the controllers of the society's economic resources.

Under any known concept of power or privilege, Chambliss is simply wrong. People are more powerful with the right to a jury than without it. The constitutional privilege against self-incrimination clearly extended privilege where it did not exist before. The rights of free speech, free press, free association, public trial, *habeas corpus,* and governmental petition extended substantial power to colonials who, to one degree or another, had previously been denied them. Even if one adopts the silly concept of power, shared by Maoists and the National Rifle Association, that it is something which flows out the barrel of a gun, one is obliged to admit that the second amendment effected a redistribution of power. Only under the sacred canopy of an assumption of the profound, calculating evil of the Founding Fathers could it be imagined that the increases in power and privilege they constituted did not exist.

One additional and fascinating property of the dogma of objective interest as evil must be mentioned—its capacity to reverse itself and find "goodness" in the most remarkable places. Because the concept of objective interest can uncover and "explain" the evil of anything preceeding from the American state, its law and its economy, the leading figures of American Marxist criminology have generally restricted its application to the creation of criminal law and legal administration. They tend to find the question of criminal behavior a political preoccupation of bourgeois criminology, whose single purpose, Quinney declares, has been "the legitimation of the existing social order" (1974a: 26). Nevertheless, some minor incursions into the explanation of individual etiology have occurred, largely to account for the fact that certain members of the proletariat sometimes do some very nasty things. When they do them to their employers, the bourgeoisie, people who look like the bourgeoisie, or the state, their acts emerge as political or protopolitical crimes. In such cases the dogma of objective interest bares its bright side and permits the explanation and legitimation of such acts as forms of resistance to evil, though protocriminals of this type need not know that they are behaving politically.

What is, however, more problematic to American Marxist criminology is the rather extensive nastiness involving the victimization of one *prole* by another in acts such as rape, murder, drug dealing, assault, theft, mugging, etc. Marx, it is well known, had little patience or appreciation for the *"lumpenproletariat,"* and on this issue Quinney and the Schwendingers are, so to speak, somewhat holier than the Pope.[9]

Quinney, for instance, offers the explanation that murder, assault, and rape, *personal crimes,* are "pursued by those who are already brutalized by the conditions of capitalism. These actions occur in immediate situations that are themselves the result of more basic accommodations to capitalism." *Predatory crimes,* including burglary, robbery, drug dealing of various sorts, "although pursued out of a need to survive, are *a reproduction of the capitalist system.* The crimes are nevertheless antagonistic to the capitalist order" (Quinney, 1975: 54; italics added).

A similar explanation for rape is given by the Schwendingers:

> *Crimes of violence as we know them today have been produced by capitalism;* and the contradictions of capitalism will continue to feed the hatred of certain men toward women. To resolve the contradictions and *the expression in rape of the social psychological effect of these contradictions,* is to change a class system of oppression in America today to a socialist political economy and a relatively crime free tomorrow. [1974: 25; italics added]

What can one say of an explanation of predatory crime that finds it to be the "reproduction of capitalism" or an interpretation of rape as the social-psychological effect of the contradictions of capitalism? How can one respond to the declaration that "crimes of violence as we know them today have been produced by capitalism"? Stalin's purge of the thirties is not, after all, today. Are the Gulags (Solzhenitsyn, 1975) close enough? Does the rape and carnage described in chapter eight of *Gulag Archipelago Two,* "Women in Camp," somehow not matter? Or is it dismissible as some kind of evil atavism of capitalism thrown up within the darker reaches of a "relatively crime free" socialist political economy?

Is Cuba close enough? Since 1959 the reduction in many crimes, homicide, prostitution, drug dealing, and gambling is relatively certain. But is that change due to the new political economy, the charisma of Fidel, the increases in the severity of penal sanctions (including the death penalty), the law requiring that every citizen has an affirmative duty to act as a police informer, or the policy of rounding up and publicly shaving the heads of "the bands of schizophrenics" who "hang about listening to imperialist juke boxes"? Is it to be explained by the Cuban variety of child saving, begun in 1973, of arresting youths not working and not in school and forcing them to do productive labor? Possibly the key to understanding the change is to be found in Cuba's vagrancy laws. In 1971 the Anti-Loafing Law made failure to work or excessive absenteeism from work a crime and penalties of up to two years imprisonment were imposed. The Act brought approximately 100,000 "parasitical" loafers into the labor force. Perhaps the reduction in crime is at least in part attributable to Cuba's Worker's Dossier Law of the late 1960s. It created a work force control card containing information on each worker's employment history, work habits, and job performance, which may have created an investigative omnipresence of significant deterrent impact. Could it be that the more violent Cubans were selected from the population and given the opportunity to vent their aggressions in Zaire, Angola, Somalia, and Yemen? Perhaps the torture Amnesty International (1975) found in Cuban prisons is the answer.

Whether or not these questions hold the answers to the problems of crime, criminal law, and criminal justice in modern America, they have *not* been raised by American Marxist criminologists nor, for that matter, by the "bourgeois" conventional criminologists of whom the heavy hitters have been so contemptuously critical. Conventional criminologists have not raised the questions of *gulags, stalags,* and the variety of Cuban solutions at least in part because Quinney is half right when he claims that the sole purpose of American criminology has been "the legitimation of the existing social order." American criminology remains largely *corrective* in its approach and seeks to describe, criticize, explain, and reform what in the United States is understood as bad news, bad practices, bad policies, and bad people. At times, American criminology has been in the forefront of such realizations, but more often far behind. Given the nature of "bourgeois" scholarship, sometimes it is found that the policies and procedures are worse than had been imagined, or those people once thought so bad, are not so bad after all. Be that as it may, American criminology's preoccupation with such concerns has given it a somewhat domestic and parochial cast. Furthermore, it should be added that such "solutions," though they may work, are not considered relevant by conventional American criminologists because they are morally reprehensible and constitute intolerable abridgments of civil rights.

THE CONTEMPORARY CRISES
OF MARXIST CRIMINOLOGY

The leading figures of American Marxist criminology have not raised the details of Gulag or Cuban solutions to the problems of crime in America, nor have they seriously examined such solutions in states which legitimate them. They have not done so for reasons which are, I think, very different from the domestic, parochial, and morally self-imposed limitations in the imaginations of conventional criminologists. Their reasons are, I find, profoundly theoretical. They reflect a unique understanding of the relationship between history and theory, a relationship that is radically different from that of conventional criminology and fundamentally irreconcilable with it. It is this understanding which gives Marxist criminology its great imagination, its grand passion, and its critical capacity. Alas, it is also the source of its theoretical and empirical poverty and its contemporary crisis.

For the Marxist theorist, the object of theory is to change history. For the conventional criminologist, history—past, present, and future—is a test of theory. For the Marxist, *The Theory* is sacred; for the conventional criminologist, history and theory both must be. If one suspends that critical relationship between history and theory, theory takes on the character of religious prophesy and cannot legitimately present itself or produce as an academic discipline, though for a time it may appear to be doing so. This enchanted relationship between history and theory is at the source of the nine most critical contemporary crises in Marxist criminology.

1. Marxist Criminology as a Social Movement I—Untrustworthiness. The most obvious reason the Marxist criminologists have not engaged in detailed considerations of Gulag or Cuban solutions is because doing so would discredit their false promise of a relatively crime free future. Furthermore, it would subject to some form of comparative test the explanations they offer for the class origins of crime, law, and criminal behavior. Third, it would raise the enormous problem of the *costs,* in freedom, lives, and liberties which, in the People's Republic of China for instance, the efforts at eradicating crime and deviance have involved. Although these are not inconsequential issues, they are, I believe, merely practical political considerations for the leading figures of American Marxist criminology. No social movement can be expected to lead with its dirty linen.

The problem with social movements which claim to be academic disciplines is that the goals of one may not be compatible with the obligations of the other. If one gives the movement a higher priority than the academic mandate, then the trust a scholar must have from his readers and students is seriously eroded.

2. Marxist Criminology as a Social Movement II—Predictability. The character of social movements is such that once they pass from the frantic enthusiasm of a small sect, they take on certain orthodox lines and positions. This process, which Weber analyzed under the theme of the "routinization of charisma," gives coherence and stability to the movement and allows its members to act together and sustain themselves in collective endeavors. But while this process is necessary and desirable in the development of social movements, in intellectual enterprise it produces an orthodoxy and predictability that is fatal. After class explains *everything,* after the whole legal order is critiqued, after *all* predatory and personal crime is attributed to the conditions and reproduction of capitalism, there is nothing more to say—except more of the same.

3. Marxist Criminology and Objective Interest I. Beyond the problem of the politics of social movements lies a more serious theoretical problem that is reflected in the failure of Marxist criminologists to consider the details of Maoist, Gulag, or Cuban solutions to the problem of crime. It is that their central theoretical tool, the concept of objective interest, gains all of its explanatory energy from the dogmatic assumption of the evil of class. And while such a concept can be used to discover all that is evil in contemporary American society, from its bad art to its bad taste, its racism, sexism, and imperialism, its conspiratorial illusion of civil liberties, and its ideological reproduction in robbery and rape, it is powerless to explain the criminality which exists in states where the private ownership of the means of production has been abolished. This applies not only to the criminality of such states in the past and as they presently exist, but to the criminality of any such state in the future. Consequently, while the leading figures of American Marxist criminology look to such states with willing hearts, they do so with empty hands.

4. Marxist Criminology and Objective Interest II. It might be argued that the third contemporary crisis of Marxist criminology is merely transitional. Once the objective of destroying the present evil order is served, a newer criminology will rise to replace the one that was necessary to effect the transition to the new society. Although a reconciliation may be possible at some presently incalculable level, the leading figures of American Marxist criminology may well have destroyed the basis for doing so. Convinced that an ideal, unoppressive, unrepressive, relatively crime-free future will be brought about through class conflict, they have given legitimacy to types of scholarly work that the less convinced would find morally and academically dangerous. Out of their faith in that future and the class dialectic that leads to it, they have maintained the dogma of class long after its empirical erosion, reduced history to a predictable formula, tampered with it when it suited their purposes, ignored substantial portions of it altogether, translated wide varieties of social, legal, and cultural conflict into class conflict, and strained to find class conflict in situations of overwhelming consensus. In order to accomplish these feats, they have invented grotesque devices of mystification that not only permit the discovery of evil in everything proceeding from the American state, its law, and its economy, but also obliterate the distinction between laws which are good and promote justice, and those which are bad and do not.

Such tactics are undoubtedly useful in gaining power and prominence and signaling academic and social revolution. But the legitimation of such cavalier transcendence of reality would appear to destroy the foundation upon which any subsequent criminology could be created once power, prominence, and revolution is achieved. If the suspension of the relationship between theory and history is given legitimacy, nothing short of a Second Coming can demand its return.

5. Marxist Criminology and Objective Interest III. In accepting the dogma of objective interest as evil, leading figures of American Marxist criminology have *not,* contrary to frequent claims, enabled themselves to "demystify" the "myth" of the American state. Except for a few big children who write civics texts for little ones, it is a myth which no 'one believes. There is a fairly widespread and quite healthy belief in American society that no politician can be trusted, though on rare occasions American will make exceptions, particularly if the politician lived a long time ago and is now safely dead. Consensus on this position, developed through two centuries of *praxis* under the same constitution, embodies a rustic reading of Durkheim and an inversion of Cloward and Ohlin. That is, crime is normal and politicians get more opportunities than most.

This widespread belief has given Americans a healthy resistance to political theories which require, even as a temporary "phase" in moving to a promised land, giving politicians any more power than they already have.

In this context, such attempts to demystify the myth of the American state, degenerate to attempts to "remystify" it for transparent political purposes.

6. *Marxist Criminology and Objective Interest IV.* The chief advantages of the dogma of objective interest as it is currently used, are: (1) the derivation of moral ideas from locations in the class structure; (2) the "demystification" of those moral ideas as class based (class conscious or falsely conscious); and (3) the collapse of all the knotty problems of justice into the economic interests of (real or potential) classes. Possessed with such a concept, Marx himself was able to dismiss non-Marxist talk of "justice" as "twaddle" and transcend it (Marx, n.d.). In extending the thesis of objective interest to crime and other wrongs, the leading figures of American Marxist criminology reveal the error of the original, but far more limited, formulation.

Giving priority to "interests" over "justice" suffers (first) because the capacity for individuals and groups at all levels of the social structure to *want* is limitless, and (second) because once one gets beyond what humans need to survive, what they have a *right* to have and what others *ought* to share with them is no longer a question of what they have an "interest" in getting, but of what they "justly" deserve. In short, "objective interests" derive from morals and not the other way round.

7. *Marxist Criminology and Moral Revitalization.* If the contemporary crises of Marxist criminology went no further, it might still be possible to maintain a tentative reconciliation between it and conventional criminology. The relationship might be invigorating, inspiring, and occasional, rather like going to church on Sundays to hear a bit about good and evil. Is there not, after all, some evil to the jury and the right to *habeas corpus,* to Norman Rockwell and Andrew Wyeth, to the Sabbath Jew and the Everyday Jew, to movie moguls and attorney generals' wives with bad taste? Is there not evil to James F. Short and Marvin E. Wolfgang and the dozens of other criminologists who, Quinney claims, became handmaidens of violence by serving on and granting legitimacy to "the existence and conception of the [1968] Violence Commission" (1972: 725)?

There is, but the problem with the type of evil that the best representatives of American Marxist criminology consistently discover and dramatize is that it is only visible from a moral ground set so high and so far removed from any extant social reality that it loses all perspective. The only thing more evil than the jury, and *habeas corpus,* the freedoms of religion, bad art and bad taste, and the 1968 Violence Commission would be *not* having them. The real evils of crime, discrimination, sexism, racism, corruption, and injustice are fully visible with the concepts of conventional criminology. Neither the passionate enthusiasm for their discovery nor the addition of superficial diagnoses of "evil" are necessary, helpful, or edifying. In these difficult and dangerous times when merely doing good is so demanding, the choice of a plane of perfection from which to level one's critical guns is the height of irresponsibility.

8. Marxist Criminology and Critical Irresponsibility. This irresponsibility is a common perversion of Marxist theory, though one which Marx himself, particularly in his early writings, seemed to have encouraged. It is found in the works of all those Neo-Marxists who would elevate Marx from the status of time-bound social analyst to that of prophetic saint. By presenting itself as ideal and as inevitable, of inexorably moving toward a relatively crime-free, unexploitive, unrepressive, unoppressive future, Marxist theory relieves itself of all responsibility for the exploitation, corruption, crime, and human abuse which has been and continues to be perpetrated in its name. By locating its realization in a utopian and inevitable future, it enjoys the twin privileges of the right to be passionately critical of all that exists and the escape of responsibility for its own history. No other sociological or political theory enjoys such divine immunity from its own past or present historical consequences. Consider what would and should happen if some Neo-Nazi or Neo-Fascist "criminology" were advanced with a plea for the same immunity. To be critical without the obligation of being responsible for the past, present, and future of one's critical theory reduces the act of criticism from an active, involved, vital, and dangerous game to nothing more than a spectator sport.

9. Academic Prophesy. For conventional criminologists, who from time to time may look with envy upon the leading figures of American Marxist criminology for the passion and evil they seem to have found, the game of theory must be slower, cooler, less daring, and more painful. Leaps of faith, when they are necessary, must be tentative and small. Such is the fate of having to contend with history and working with theories that can be refuted by it. Grounded by history and trained in the skills of evaluating what is and what has been done and testing in small and controlled increments what might be, conventional criminologists are best suited to say what has *not* worked, what ought *not* to be done.

The gift of prophesy, of "providing us with a new set of moral imperatives" (Chambliss, 1975: 477), of promising a "relatively crime free future" and guaranteeing that such a promise is "not utopian" (Schwendingers, 1974: 25); is not given to conventional criminologists. It may be that "Only with the collapse of capitalist society and the erection of a new society, based on socialist principles will there be a solution to the crime problem" (Quinney, 1974a: 16). But the history of millennial promises and final solutions is not a happy one. Those of us without the gift of vision are not only doomed to wait and see, but to marshall all the tools of responsible criticism which might reveal the errors of *the way*. This foot dragging, liberally pragmatic, halting attitude comes from having to live with history. It ought not to be mistaken for a lack of passion or unwillingness to change. This is, after all, the country of beaten paths to better mousetraps. But, it is also the land of Billy Graham and Billy Sunday, of Rabbi Korff and Reverend Ike. For us nonbelievers in a world that Weber taught was disenchanted, it is no easier to bring a genuine intellectual sacrifice to the new churches than to the old ones.

NOTES

1. I have made no attempt to collect all the literature empirically or theoretically expressly critical of radical criminology. My sampling does include Chiricos and Waldo (1975), Cohen (1973), Coulter (1974), Hagan and Leon (1977), Hopkins (1975), Horwitz (1977), Meier (1977), Miller (1973), Mugsford (1974), Sykes (1974), Nettler (1978), Skolnick (1972), Thomas (1976), Thompson (1975), and Wolfgang (1973).

2. Tocqueville's seminal analysis of the relations between social class and culture in many areas of American life are adumbrated in Hofstadter (1962). I suspect of particular interest to radical criminologists, especially those who find the universities repressive of Marxist scholarship, would be the illuminating essay by Samuels (1969) on the protection of radical intellectuals in those bastions of class, Oxford and Cambridge, and Feuer (1969: 237-271) on intellectual freedom among the classless elites in Soviet universities. The orthodox line on the proper relation between common men and those who would march to a different drummer may be drawn from Lenin:

> When *all* have learned to manage, and independently are actually managing by themselves social production, keeping accounts, controlling the idlers, the gentlefolk, the swindlers and similar "guardians of capitalist traditions" then the escape from this national accounting and control will inevitably become so difficult, such a rare exception and will probably be accompanied by such swift and severe punishment (for the armed workers are men of practical life, not sentimental intellectuals, and they will scarcely allow anyone to trifle with them) that very soon the necessity of observing the simple, fundamental rules

of everyday social life in common will have become a *habit*. The door will then be wide open for the transition from the first phase of Communist society to its higher phase, and along with it to the complete withering away of state [1932: 84].

I suspect the door will *then* be wide open for *anything*.

3. The above observations are taken from Lebergott (1976: 3-20). We ought not to take poverty lightly, especially the crippling and blinding kind rampant in modern Mexico. One way to do something about this devastating and destructive poverty would be to allow free and open U.S. immigration to the thousands of desperately poor unemployed workers of Mexico. Countless lives would be saved, as Lebergott points out (p. 4). But both Harrington (1969: 50) and American agricultural labor unions are violently opposed to such a measure.

4. In this section I follow the lead of Robert Nisbet's essay "The Decline and Fall of Social Class" (1968). I am willing to admit for genuine colonials the utility of class analyses of violence like that of Fanon (1968), but with the conceptual reservations registered in Arendt's "On Violence" (1972b) and the obvious theoretical and empirical inadequacies Zolberg and Zolberg (1967) and Killian (1968) have identified in attempts to Americanize it. Similarly, the brilliant and beautiful work of Thompson, *Whigs and Hunters: The Origin of the Black Act* (1975), employs a class analysis to study crime and punishment in the eighteenth-century, a totally appropriate concept for that classical period of English history. Even in such periods, as Manning's recent work on the formation of the English police (1977: 38-81) has shown, class may not be a very important variable.

5. Actually there are arguments other than the "interest" argument which intend to show that the criminal justice and legal systems are the agents of the owners of the means of production. One type repeatedly discovers that powerful people have power and then searches their biographies for acquaintances or associations they may have had in big business or the military. Hence we find Quinney (1974a: 76) publishing mini-biographies of everyone on the Senate Subcommittee on Criminal Laws and Procedures and assuming we will learn something from the fact that the simple country lawyer, Sam Ervin, was "twice wounded in battle, twice cited for gallantry in action, and awarded the French Fourragere, Purple Heart with Oak Leaf Cluster" etc. Were this analytical approach pursued with scholarly seriousness it might be justified under the theoretical guidance of differential association theory, notwithstanding the curious contradiction such an approach would imply for conflict theorists. However, as a tool in the political arena of radical criminology it is a variety of conspiracy theory in dogged pursuit of what logicians call the genetic fallacy— arguing that a statement is wrong because of its source. Such *ad hominem* arguments are, obviously, out of place in academic discourse.

6. It is also no doubt why the heavy hitters do not appear to be particularly concerned about using their core concept of "class" consistently. When mixed into the phrase "ruling class" they use it to refer to elites, bureaucracies, and politically, socially, or economically influential individuals or organizations. When combined with "middle," "upper," or "lower" it generally refers to income level irrespective of social origins, status honor, political persuasion, or whether or not such people work at their own or others' means of production. Other times it is used unmodified as the equivalent of "group," "category," "caste," "estate," "union," or "political party."

Such conceptual flexibility is enormously helpful in demonstrating the importance of "class" in contemporary society.

7. Although absurd, it is still profoundly orthodox. Marx, in endorsing the denial of civil liberties, except trading, to Jews in nineteenth-century Germany, employed precisely the same Manichean distinction:

> Let us consider the real Jew: not the Sabbath Jew, but the *Everyday Jew*.

> Let us not seek the secret of the Jew in his religion, but let us seek the secret of the religion in the real Jew.

> What is the profane basis of Judaism? *Practical* need, *self-interest*. What is the worldly cult of the Jew? *Huckstering*. What is his worldly god? *Money*.

> Very well: then in emancipating itself from *huckstering* and *money*, and thus from real and practical Judaism, our age would emancipate itself.

> An organization of society which would abolish the preconditions and thus the very possibility of huckstering, would make the Jew impossible. His religious consciousness would evaporate like some insipid vapour in the real, life-giving air of society. On the other hand, when the Jew recognizes his *practical* nature as invalid and endeavors to abolish it, he begins to deviate from his former path of development, works for general *human emancipation* and turns against the *supreme practical* expression of human self-estrangement.

> We discern in Judaism, therefore, a universal *antisocial* element of the *present time*, those historical development, zealously aided in its harmful aspects by the Jews, has not attained its culminating point, a point at which it must necessarily begin to disintegrate.

> In the final analysis, the *emancipation* of the Jews is the emancipation of mankind from *Judaism* [Marx, 1964: 34].

In his foreword to Bottomore's collection of Marx's early writing, in which *Die Judenfrage* appears, Erich Fromm, who is to Marxism what Pat Boone is to adolescence, finds in words such as these evidence that "Marx was a humanist, for whom man's freedom, dignity, and activity were the basic premises of a "good society" (Fromm, 1964: iii).

8. The next volume in the history of the repression of Marxist scholarship must surely be written around the following snippet from *Publisher's Weekly* (October 30, 1972: 36; quoted in Reiff, 1972: 195n):

> Angela Davis has signed a contract with Bantam Books and Bernard Geis Associates to write a book entitled, "The Education of a Revolutionary." According to Mr. Geis, Bantam is paying the former member of the faculty of the University of California a "high six-figure" advance against royalties. While there have been numerous books about Angela Davis, Mr. Geis points out that this will be the first book by her.

> In cooperating with Bantam on the Davis book, Mr. Geis, whose company recently has been experiencing financial difficulties, said his firm was embarking on a new program of originating, editing and promoting books although his company last year had filed . . . under the Federal Bankruptcy Act.

Let us hope that the perfect marriage of Miss Davis's bankruptcy and Mr. Geis's turns out well for both parties. Indeed, Mr. Platt, some of the most imaginative criminology has been written by 'criminals.'

9. In the *Communist Manifesto* Marx (and Engels, 1948: 20) declare:

The 'dangerous class,' the social scum (lumpenproletariat), that passively rotting mass thrown off by the lowest layers of the old society, may here and there be swept into the movement by a proletarian revolution; its conditions of life, however, prepare it far more for the part of a bribed tool of reactionary intrigue.

In this passage Marx and Engels were prescient enough to realize that the frivolous application of the label "political criminal" would encourage the creation of an opportunistic body of criminal politicians whose new-found faith in class oppression might appear to some a bit self-serving. American "Marxists," having failed to find any substantial support among American workers, cannot afford to be so choosy.

10. I have no data on the proportion of Americans who would agree to the proposition that all politicians are crooks, but I suspect it is very high. With important qualifications it is a proposition shared by Machiavelli, Weber, and Camus, each of whom wrestled with what had come to be known in political philosophy as "the dirty hands problem." See the brilliant essay by Walzer (1973) and the *realpolitik* efforts by Arendt (1968, 1972a) dealing with it.

REFERENCES

AKMAN, D. D. and A. NORMANDEAU (1970) "The crime index for England and ten other countries." Criminologist 5 (May-August): 63-71.

––– and S. TURNER (1967) "The measurement of delinquency in Canada." Journal of Criminal Law, Criminology and Police Science 58 (September): 330-337.

Amnesty International (1975) Report on Torture. New York: Farrar, Strauss & Giroux.

ARENDT, H. (1972a) "Lying in politics," pp. 9-43 in Crises of the Republic. Hammondsworth, England: Penquin.

––– (1972b) "On violence," pp. 83-163 in Crises of the Republic. Hammondsworth, England: Penquin.

––– (1968) "Truth and politics," pp. 227-264 in Between Past and Future. New York: Viking.

BALBUS, I. D. (1971) "The concept of interest in pluralist and Marxian analysis." Politics and Society 1 (February): 151-177.

BALDWIN, J. (1962) Nobody Knows My Name. New York: Random House.

BALTZELL, D. (1964) The Protestant Establishment. New York: Random House.

––– (1958) The Philadelphia Gentlemen: The Making of a National Upper Class. New York: Macmillan.

BARAN, P. and P. SWEEZY (1966) Monopoly Capital: An Essay on the American Economic and Social Order. New York: Monthly Review.

BAGHOORN, F. C. (1966) Politics in the U.S.S.R. Boston: Little, Brown.

BARRY, D. D. and C. BARNER-BARRY (1978) Contemporary Soviet Politics. Englewood Cliffs, NJ: Prentice-Hall.

BECKER, H. S. (1963) Outsiders: Studies in the Sociology of Deviance. New York: Macmillan.

BEICHMAN, Al (1972) Nine Lies About America. New York: Library.

BERLE, A. (1954) The 20th Century Capitalist Revolution. New York: Harcourt Brace Jovanovich.

––– and G. C. MEANS (1967) The Modern Corporation and Private Property. New York: Harcourt Brace Jovanovich.

CHAMBLISS, W. J. (1976) "Functional and conflict theories of crime," in W. J. Chambliss and M. Mankoff (eds.) Whose Law What Order? New York: John Wiley.

––– (1975) Criminal Law in Action. Santa Barbara, CA: Hamilton.

––– (1974) "The state, the law, and the definition of behavior as criminal or delinquent," in D. Glaser (ed.) Handbook of Criminology. Chicago: Rand McNally.

––– (1969) [ed.] Crime and the Legal Process. New York: McGraw-Hill.

––– (1964) "A sociological analysis of the Law of Vagrancy." Social Problems 12 (Summer): 46-67.

CHIRICOS, T. G. and G. P. WALDO (1975) "Socioeconomic status and criminal sentencing: an empirical assessment of a conflict proposition." American Sociological Review 40 (December): 753-772.

COCKS, P. (1976) "The policy process and bureaucratic politics," pp. 156-178 in P. Cocks et al. (eds.) The Dynamics of Soviet Politics. Cambridge, MA: Harvard University Press.

COHEN, A. K. (1973) "Political and ideological implications of the new deviancy theory." Presented at the National Deviancy Conference, York, England, January.

CONQUEST, R. (1968) The Great Terror: Stalin's Purge of the Thirties. New York: Macmillan.

COULTER, J. (1974) "What's wrong with the new criminology?" Sociological Review 22 (February): 119-135.

DAHRENDORF, R. (1959) Class and Class Conflict in Industrial Society. Palo Alto, CA: Stanford University Press.

DJILAS, M. (1969) The Unperfect Society: Beyond the New Class. New York: Harcourt Brace Jovanovich.

––– (1957) The New Class. New York: Praeger.

DOS SANTOS, T. (1970) "The concept of social class." Science and Society 34 (Summer): 166-193.

ELLUL, J. (1975) The New Demons. New York: Seabury.

––– (1964) The Technological Society. New York: Knopf.

ERIKSON, K. T. (1966) Wayward Puritans. New York: John Wiley.

FANON, F. (1968) The Wretched of the Earth. New York: Grove.

FIGLIO, R. M. (1975) "The seriousness of offenses: an evaluation by offenders and non-offenders." Journal of Criminal Law & Criminology 66 (June): 189-200.

FOOTE, C. (1956) "Vagrancy type law and its administration." University of Pennsylvania Law Review 104 (March): 603-650.

FEUER, L. S. (1969) Marx and the Intellectuals. New York: Doubleday.

FROMM, E. (1964) "Foreword," pp. i-vi in T. B. Bottomore (trans. and ed.) Karl Marx: Early Writings. New York: McGraw-Hill.

GASTIL, R. D. (1976) "The comparative survey of freedom: VI." Freedom at Issue 34 (January/February): 11-20.

HAGAN, J. and J. LEON (1977) "Rediscovering delinquency: social history, political ideology and the sociology of law." American Sociological Review 42 (August): 587-598.

HALL, J. (1952) Theft, Law and Society. Indianapolis: Bobbs-Merrill.

HARRINGTON, M. (1969) The Other America. New York: Macmillan.

HINDLEY, B. (1970) "Separation of ownership and control in the modern corporation." Journal of Law and Economics 13 (April): 185-221.

HOFSTADTER, R. (1962) Anti-Intellectualism in American Life. New York: Vintage.

HOPKINS, A. (1975) "On the sociology of criminal law." Social Problems 22 (June): 608-619.

HORWITZ, A. (1977) "An exchange on Marxian theories of deviance and social control: a critique of Spitzer." Social Problems 24 (February): 362-369.

KAISER, R. G. (1976) Russia: The People and the Power. New York: Atheneum.

KILLIAN, L. M. (1968) The Impossible Revolution? Black Power and the American Dream. New York: Random House.

LARNER, R. J. (1970) Management Control and the Large Corporation. Cambridge, MA: University Press Dunellen.

LEBERGOTT, S. (1976) Wealth and Want. Princeton, NJ: Princeton University Press.

LENIN, N. (1932) State and Revolution. New York: International Publishers.

LINDESMITH, A. R. (1965) The Addict and the Law. Bloomington, IN: Indiana University Press.

LOFLAND, J. (1969) Deviance and Identity. Englewood Cliffs, NJ: Prentice-Hall.

MANNING, P. K. (1977) Police Work. Cambridge, MA: MIT Press.

MARX, K. (1964) "On the Jewish question," pp. 1-41 in T. B. Bottomore (ed.) Karl Marx: Early Writings. New York: McGraw-Hill.

––– and F. ENGELS (1948) The Communist Manifesto. New York: International Publishers.

––– (n.d.) [Marx to Engels, July 20, 1870] Correspondence, 1846-1895. New York: International Publishers.

MEIER, R. F. (1976) "The New Criminology: continuity in criminological theory." Journal of Criminal Law & Criminology 67 (December): 461-469.

MILLER, W. (1973) "Ideology and criminal justice policy: some current issues." Journal of Criminal Law & Criminology 64 (June): 141-161.

MONSON, J. R., J. S. CHIU, and D. F. COOLEY (1968) "The effect of separation of ownership and control on the performance of the large firm." Quarterly Journal of Economics 82 (August): 435-451.

MUGSFORD, S. K. (1974) "Marxism and criminology: a comment on the Symposium Review of 'The New Criminology'." Sociological Quarterly 15 (Autumn): 591-596.

NETTLER, G. (1978) Explaining Crime. New York: McGraw-Hill.

NEWMAN, G. (1976) Comparative Deviance. New York: Elsevier, North-Holland.

NISBET, R. (1968) "The decline and fall of social class," pp. 105-128 in R. Nisbet (ed.) Transition and Revolt. New York: Random House.

NORMANDEAU, A. (1966) "The measurement of delinquency in Montreal." Journal of Criminal Law, Criminology and Police Science 57 (June): 172-179.

PLATT, A. (1974a) "Prospects for a radical criminology in the United States." Crime and Social Justice 1 (Spring/Summer): 2-10.

——— (1974b) "The triumph of benevolence: the origins of the juvenile justice system in the United States," pp. 356-389 in R. Quinney (ed.) Criminal Justice in America. Boston: Little, Brown.

——— (1973) "Dialogue with Anthony Platt." Issues in Criminology 8 (Spring): 19-33.

——— (1969) The Child Savers. Chicago: University of Chicago Press.

POPPER, K. (1945) The High Tide of Prophecy: Hegel, Marx and the Aftermath, Vol. II of The Open Society and its Enemies. Princeton, NJ: Princeton University Press.

QUINNEY, R. (1979) "The production of criminology." Criminology 14 (February): 445-457.

——— (1977) Class, State, and Crime. New York: David McKay.

——— (1975) Criminology: Analysis and Critique of Crime in America. Boston: Little, Brown.

——— (1974a) Critique of the Legal Order: Crime Control in Capitalist Society. Boston: Little, Brown.

——— (1974b) "The ideology of law: notes for a radical alternative to legal oppression," in J. Sussman (ed.) Crime and Justice: 1971-1972. New York: AMS.

——— (1971) Review of "National Commission of the Causes and Prevention of Violence: Reports." American Sociological Review 36 (August): 724-727.

——— (1970) The Social Reality of Crime. Boston: Little, Brown.

REIFF, P. (1972) Fellow Teachers. New York: Harper & Row.

SALISBURY, C. Y. (1974) Russian Diary. New York: Walker.

SAMUELS, S. (1969) "English intellectuals and politics in the 1930's," pp. 213-268 in P. Reiff (ed.) On Intellectuals. New York: Doubleday.

SCHAPIRO, L. (1967) The Government and Politics of the Soviet Union. New York: Random House.

SCHATTSCHNEIDER, E. E. (1960) The Semi-Sovereign People. New York: Holt, Rinehart & Winston.

SCHUR, E. (1965) Crimes Without Victims. Englewood Cliffs, NJ: Prentice-Hall.

SCHWENDINGER, H. and J. SCHWENDINGER (1976a) "The collective varieties of youth." Crime and Social Justice 5 (Spring/Summer): 7-25.

——— (1976b) "Marginal youth and social policy." Social Problems 24 (December): 184-191.

——— (1974) "Rape myths in legal, theoretical and everyday practice." Crime and Social Justice 1 (Spring/Summer): 18-26.

——— (1973) "Sociologists of the chair and the natural law tradition." Insurgent Sociologist 3 (Winter): 2-18.

——— (1972) "Continuing debate on the legalistic approach to the definition of crime." Issues in Criminology 7 (Winter): 72-81.

——— (1970) "Defenders of order or guardians of human rights?" Issues in Criminology 7 (Winter): 123-157.

——— (1964) "The swinging set, delinquent stereotypes of probable victims," in J. Lohman (ed.) The Handling of Juveniles from Offense to Disposition. Berkeley: University of California School of Criminology.

SELLIN, T. and M. WOLFGANG (1964) The Measurement of Delinquency. New York: John Wiley.

SHUB, A. (1969) The New Russian Tragedy. New York: W. W. Norton.

SKINNER, B. F. (1971) Beyond Freedom and Dignity. New York: Knopf.

SKOLNICK, J. (1972) "Perspectives on law and order." Presented at the Inter-American Congress of the American Society of Criminology, Caracas, Venezuela, November.

SMITH, H. (1976) The Russians. New York: Quadrangle.

SOLZHENITSYN, A. I. (1975) The Gulag Archipelago Two 1918-1956. New York: Harper & Row.

SUTHERLAND, E. H. (1950) "The diffusion of sexual psychopath laws." American Journal of Sociology 56 (September): 142-148.

SYKES, G. (1974) "Critical criminology." Journal of Criminal Law & Criminology 65 (June): 206-213.

TAPPAN, P. W. (1950) "Sex offender laws and their administration." Federal Probation 14 (September): 32-37.

THOMAS, C. W. (1976) "Public opinion of criminal law and legal sanctions: an examination of two conceptual models." Journal of Criminal Law & Criminology 67 (March): 110-116.

THOMPSON, E. P. (1975) Whigs and Hunters: The Origin of the Black Act. New York: Pantheon.

TURK, A. (1980) "Analyzing official deviance." This volume.

WALZER, M. (1973) "Political action: the problem of dirty hands." Philosophy and Public Affairs 2 (Winter): 160-180.

WEBER, M. (1946) From Max Weber. H. Gerth and C. Wright Mills (eds. and trans.). London: Routledge & Kegan Paul.

WESSON, R. C. (1972) The Soviet State: An Aging Revolution. New York: John Wiley.

WILLIAMSON, O. E. (1970) Corporate Control and Business Behavior. Englewood Cliffs, NJ: Prentice-Hall.

――― (1963) "Managerial discretion and business behavior." American Economic Review 53 (December): 1032-1057.

WOLFGANG, M. E. and J. F. SHORT [eds.] (1972) Collective Violence. Chicago: AVC.

WOLFGANG, M. (1973) "Developments in criminology in the United States with some comments on the future." Presented at the Fifth National Conference at the Institute of Criminology, University of Cambridge, July.

YOUNG, M. (1961) The Rise of the Meritocracy, 1870-2033: An Essay on Education and Equality. New York: Viking.

ZOLBERG, A. and V. ZOLBERG (1967) "The Americanization of Franz Fanon." Public Interest 9 (Fall): 49-63.

6

THE NEW CRIMINOLOGY IS THE OLD BALONEY

Jackson Toby

The New Criminology is not new. It draws upon an old tradition of
sentimentality toward those who break social rules. The stereotype of the
prostitute "with a heart of gold" is frequent in literature and in the
theater, e.g., "Camille," "Irma, La Douce," if not in the real world. This
same tradition portrays thieves who steal from the rich and give to the
poor, the implicit notion being that a Robin Hood is motivated to violate
the laws against theft by a higher morality. But the most important
manifestation of traditional sentimentality—important, that is, as a fore-
runner of radical criminology—is the notion that the poor are *compelled* to
steal by the unbearable misery of their lives, by hunger, cold, and other
biological deprivations. Jean Valjean, the long-suffering hero of *Les Misérables* (Hugo, 1862) stole a loaf of bread because he was hungry. In point
of fact, one thief in a thousand in urban industrial societies steals because
he is hungry or cold; color television sets and automobiles are stolen more
often than food or blankets.[1] Thieves may be envious of those who have
more than they, and opportunities to be envious are endemic in affluent
modern societies. But envy is not equivalent to biological deprivation.

The notion that the poor are compelled to steal by the unbearable
misery of their lives reflects overidentification with the underdog. The
same overidentification characterizes radical criminology. But traditional
sentimentality does not deny that the poor engage in theft to a greater
extent than more affluent population segments. It simply justifies lower-

class criminality in terms of deprivation. In this respect Victor Hugo, Anatole France, and conventional criminologists are agreed. Radical criminology goes further; it regards the question of comparative crime rates as meaningless. How did this come about? Within conventional criminology itself, two lines of criticism were directed at the finding, replicated in many countries, that persons from lower socioeconomic strata were arrested and convicted disproportionately for crime. The obvious inference was that crime occurred more frequently in low than in high places, but this inference was challenged by the charge of discriminatory law enforcement against the underprivileged and by the doctrine of white-collar crime. I propose to examine these two challenges to a straightforward interpretation of official data because they made possible the more radical challenge of "the new criminology."

THE HYPOTHESIS OF
DISCRIMINATORY LAW ENFORCEMENT

Official bias was invoked as a *possible* explanation of the disproportionate contribution to arrest statistics of socioeconomically disadvantaged and minority persons. However, empirical studies showed that, while the police may be somewhat more prone to arrest persons in certain social and ethnic categories, the major factor in police response is the seriousness of the act alleged to have been committed by the accused and, to a lesser extent, the pressure of a complainant (Reiss, 1971). Nevertheless, when anonymous self-report studies of delinquency and crime showed no relationship between social origins and criminality (Nye et al., 1958; Christie et al., 1965), the hypothesis of discriminatory law enforcement was widely regarded as confirmed. Surprisingly, the possibility that respondents from *lower* socioeconomic backgrounds might have responded less fully or less accurately was not considered seriously. Many criminologists proved more skeptical of the impartiality of the police than of the truthfulness of low-status respondents in self-report studies. From a *logical* point of view, there are no firmer grounds for believing one hypothesis than the other. There is negligible *empirical* evidence for believing that official bias is sufficient to account for observed differences in arrest rates—although there is little evidence about response bias of self-reports either. One notable study that attempted to assess the response bias of self-reports (by checking them against polygraph examinations of the respondents) dealt exclusively with college students (Clark and Tifft, 1966); response bias may be atypical in a college population—or at least different from the response bias in a poorly educated group.

On *theoretical* grounds, the higher arrest and conviction rates of persons from lower socioeconomic levels are plausibly explained in terms of the sociological meaning of social stratification. Higher social status means better life chances; lower social status means poorer life chances. Life chances for what? Among the nonmaterial advantages children from higher social strata enjoy is the greater likelihood of being socialized in a stable family that inculcates the same cultural values embodied in the criminal law. That is, the theory of social stratification provides a basis for expecting that children from middle-class backgrounds are more likely to *want* to conform to the prohibitions of the crimininal law (Toby, 1971: 483-484). Furthermore, those middle-class children whose atypical family experiences tend to produce alienated or rebellious personalities are exposed more frequently than children from lower social levels to peer groups, educational organizations, and informal neighborhood interaction that reward conformity and disapprove of deviance. Thus, the theory of social stratification suggests also that *informal social control* reinforces socialization more effectively on more advantaged socioeconomic levels. Apart from discriminatory law enforcement, then, the anticipation should be that, motivationally, middle-class persons are less oriented to criminality (Toby, 1974: 90-91). In the face of these theoretical considerations, how can we explain the credulity with which some criminologists responded to the finding of no relationship between self-reported crime and socioeconomic status? One possible explanation is a sentimental desire to deny the uncomplimentary characterization of disadvantaged persons suggested by arrest and conviction statistics.

WHITE-COLLAR CRIME: AN ASSUMPTION OF MIDDLE-CLASS IMMORALITY

Like the theory of discriminatory law enforcement, the theory of white-collar crime seeks to correct the complacent assumption by middle-class persons that crime lurks mainly in low places. The theory of white-collar crime does not accuse the individual law enforcement officer of bias; it accuses the law itself. According to Sutherland (1949) blue-collar persons commit the "garden variety" of crimes and white-collar persons commit crimes in the course of their business and professional activities.

Since criminal statistics emphasize ordinary crimes rather than white-collar crimes, the *apparent* higher incidence of criminality in the lower class may be an illusion. If white-collar crimes were recorded as diligently and prosecuted as successfully as blue-collar crimes, the public might perceive as much crime in high places as in low. The white-collar-crime concept denies the traditional equation of "crime" with "immorality" and makes a direct judgment of "immorality." This shift is intellectually useful for counterbalancing high lower-class arrest and conviction rates with middle-class behavior that Sutherland suggested was morally worse. As he pointed out (1949), some shady business and professional practices are either not technically illegal or are extremely difficult to detect and punish. Those who consider white-collar crime at least as socially destructive as ordinary crime are therefore tempted to classify these borderline activities on the part of middle-class persons as the moral equivalent of larceny and assault. It is, of course, impossible to compare the relative prevalence of white-collar and blue-collar crime once white-collar criminality is defined so vaguely. Consequently, there is no way to refute the assertion that white-collar crime is more prevalent among middle-class persons than ordinary crime is among blue-collar persons. Furthermore, it is theoretically sloppy to assume that only white-collar persons commit crimes in the course of their occupational activities (what about the dishonest garage mechanic?) and that middle-class persons do not engage in "ordinary" crime (don't middle-class persons commit murder, rape, and assault?).

Surely the enthusiasm with which the concept of white-collar crime was embraced by criminologists had less to do with its intellectual power than with its usefulness for challenging the moral complacency of "the establishment." The possibility that middle-class persons are as antisocial as lower-class persons was appreciated before Watergate, but the Watergate scandal seemed to provide concrete evidence that crime and corruption in high places is widespread. The anti-middle-class bias implicit in the white-collar-crime argument was made more explicit by labeling theorists (Kitsuse, 1975; Schur, 1975), who maintain that the criminal law criminalizes the transgressions of the weak and powerless and does not criminalize the transgressions of the affluent and powerful.

THE ULTIMATE RELATIVISM:
RADICAL CRIMINOLOGY

Radical criminology has built an attack on the finding of disproportionate arrests and convictions of underdogs more sweeping than the

charge of discriminatory law enforcement or even of discriminatory legislation (white-collar crime). Consider the concluding paragraph from *The
New Criminology*, which asserts that no behavior should be evaluated as
reprehensible and therefore be punishable:

> It has often been argued, rather misleadingly, that for Durkheim
> *crime* was a normal social fact (that it was a fundamental feature of
> human ontology). For us, as for Marx and other new criminologists,
> *deviance* is normal—in the sense that men are now consciously
> involved (in the prisons that are contemporary society and in the
> real prisons) in asserting their human diversity. The task is not
> merely to "penetrate" these problems, not merely to question the
> stereotypes, or to act as carriers of "alternative phenomenological
> realities." The task is to create a society in which the facts of human
> diversity, whether personal, organic or social, are not subject to the
> power to criminalize [Taylor et al., 1973: 282].

What proponents of this view are asserting—some more explicitly than
others—is that organized society has no business incarcerating *anybody* for
so-called criminality or mental illness, that we should recognize incarceration as political oppression of powerless people, and that we should allow
"deviants" to "do their own thing" in the name of freedom and pluralism.

Doing away with authority holds attractions for many people of good
will, especially young people, partly because *some* contemporary societies
are oppressive to powerless persons. The systems of criminal justice and of
mental health in the Soviet Union are used to stifle what would be
considered permissible dissent in Sweden, Great Britain, or the United
States. The South African government uses its police powers to prevent
the Afrikaner minority from losing its dominant positive vis-à-vis a black
majority. But *The New Criminology* was not published in the Soviet Union
or in South Africa—it could not have been, of course—but in England.
Philosophical anarchism fails to distinguish between societies where governments are customarily oppressive and societies where governments
generally are not. Ignoring this distinction leads to descriptions of
Swedish, British, and American societies that make them sound like Nazi
Germany or contemporary South Africa.

The notion of complete decriminalization is appealing also because,
even in the handful of Western democracies with traditions of minority
rights, the tendency exists to use the criminal law more than is necessary
for social defense. Antiabortion laws, which have recently been declared
unconstitutional by the United States Supreme Court, are an example of
such efforts to legislate morality. But excessive use of the criminal sanc-

tion does not mean that the criminal sanction can never be used appropriately—any more than occasional instances of injustice to minority-group members mean that a convicted minority-group criminal is necessarily an oppressed political prisoner. Recall Eldridge Cleaver, who declared (1968: 14) that he raped white women as a form of social protest against racial oppression in the United States. Many of his readers lionized him because they were not willing or able to make the distinction between dissent (against which the criminal sanction is inappropriate in a democracy) and rape, the punishment of which is not usually considered to raise serious civil-liberty questions.

THE ANSWER TO RADICAL CRIMINOLOGY: IMPERFECT JUSTICE IN AN IMPERFECT WORLD

The punishment of rape is not a denial of civil liberty to the rapist merely because rape is politically defined; all crimes are defined in the course of a political process in all societies. What the radical criminologists refuse to recognize is that the political process in a reasonably open society is responsive to public opinion. Not perfectly responsive. Certainly the opinions of lower-class youths about rape are considered less seriously than the opinions of middle-class adults. It is the nature of a political process that all constituencies do not participate to the same extent. But recognizing unequal influence in specifying the punishment for rape is not equivalent to affirming that rapists are oppressed. In only a trivial sense are persons imprisoned for rape political prisoners: the definition of their offense, the penalty established for it, and the process of adjudication are products of collective decisions, which necessarily means compromises and "horse-trading." It is a trivial sense, however, because the differential influence of various constituencies in the political process does not necessarily mean oppression, only imperfection.

The inevitability of imperfection in any political process recalls the unfashionable message of theologian Reinhold Niebuhr. Believing as he did in universal sin, which meant for him a chronic tendency to egocentric self-concern, Niebuhr did not assume that law violators are virtuous and that only police, judges, and assorted politicians are corrupt and immoral. He recognized sin in high places, but he expected sin in low places as well. Furthermore, he assumed that crime could never be completely eliminated from either low or high places and that we would have to struggle to make the world livable despite the impurity of even the best causes. When Niebuhr was struggling against sentimentality in the 1940s, the cause was democracy, and the danger was Nazism. At that time, idealists and pacifists advocated purifying America of racism and poverty before attempting to rid the world of Nazi totalitarianism. Niebuhr's answer was to insist that perfect causes cannot be found, that we must support the *better* cause lest the *worse* prevail, and that our own imperfections were no excuse for inaction (Niebuhr, 1946: 26).

Today the same kind of sentimentality that made some liberals unwilling to fight the Nazis makes some criminologists unwilling to acknowledge any moral blemish in convicted felons. I am not talking about convicted felons in South Africa, the Soviet Union, or Taiwan. I am talking about convicted felons in England or the United States, where it seems reasonable to assume that viciousness is more prevalent in prison populations than in the remainder of society. As one criminologist put it, the worst thing about prison is the other prisoners. Organized society should not give up on convicted offenders, but it should not idealize them either. Given the likelihood that many prison inmates are committed to an antisocial way of life, it does not require callousness on the part of correctional administrators to explain high rates of recidivism. It is to be expected in a population containing large numbers of antisocial personalities.

There are those who point to the moral blemishes among respectable people—police and judicial corruption or, to take a spectacular example, Richard Nixon and his ill-chosen subordinates—as an argument against punishment in general and imprisonment in particular. It is a form of sentimentality to require the police and the judiciary to be perfect before societal defense can be undertaken. To put it another way, the struggle to achieve a tolerable level of moral behavior in a society must be ongoing; it cannot be abandoned because a judge is bribed or a president violates the law. This is not to say that the moral and legal transgressions of respectable people are unimportant. When President Nixon abused the prerogatives of his office, he undermined by *his* example the will of the ordinary citizen to remain law-abiding just as the rapist and the robber do by *their* examples. Since he had respect and power in American society, the damage to the moral fabric was probably worse. But it would be "throwing the baby out with the bath water" to abandon all attempts to distinguish deviant from acceptable behavior. Without this distinction, society becomes a social jungle: a war of all against all, as Hobbes put it.

Crime in high places does not legitimate crime in low places. Although not a world-shaking conclusion, this appears to need restatement. It is not possible to operate a humane criminal justice system unless persons at every level of the system—from police to jurors to correction officers—are trying to "do right." If they give way to the cynical conclusion that organized society is a jungle where justice is only the will of the stronger, their conclusion becomes a self-fulfilling prophecy. They cannot put forth the moral effort that makes society less of a jungle. Paraphrasing Reinhold Niebuhr, any criminal justice system is a proximate solution to an insoluble problem. Thus, prisons are unsatisfactory solutions to the problem of discouraging violent and predatory behavior, and we must continue to use imprisonment only as a last resort. But it is either sentimental or cynical (or both) to encourage murderers and rapists to regard themselves as the political victims of an oppressive society. Such feelings contributed to recent disturbances in American prisons—for example, in California. It would be far better for prisoners as well as for the rest of society to encourage a realistic recognition (1) that no social level has a monopoly on crime and that no system of criminal justice can sort out the virtuous from the reprehensible with perfect efficiency; but (2) that most prisoners are paying the price of being caught for serious misbehavior; and (3) that rehabilitation occurs rarely in prison, not because prison administrators are disinterested in rehabilitation, but because rehabilitation is a result of new commitments made by the individual, and they cannot be *forced* upon him by methods short of brainwashing.

In short, some criminologists are too ready to discount sin in low places and unduly prone to exaggerate the incidence of sin in high places. Criminality and immorality occur on every social level, but the likelihood is that the *relatively* disadvantaged contribute disproportionately to the crime rate. The New Criminology, far from being new, is the explicit assertion of a relativism and a sentimentality that is as old as sympathy for members of the oldest profession.

NOTE

1. Only July 13, 1977, New York City suffered a general electrical failure starting at 9:34 pm and continuing until the next day. Widespread looting occurred, and sympathetic note was taken of the fact that the looting occurred mainly in ghetto communities, presumably by the most deprived New Yorkers. However, appliance, furniture, and jewelry stores suffered as much as food stores. And a statistical profile of a sample of those arrested for looting showed that looters were more likely to be

employed and less likely to be welfare cases than a cross section of persons arraigned between June 6 and June 12, 1977 for other reasons. See the New York *Times*, August 14, 1977, p. 32.

REFERENCES

CLARK, J. P. and L. A. TIFFT (1966) "Polygraph and interview validation of self-reported deviant behavior." American Sociological Review 3 (August): 516-523.

CHRISTIE, N., J. ANDENAES, and S. SKIRBEKK (1965) "A study of self-reported crime." Scandinavian Studies in Criminology 1: 86-116.

CLEAVER, E. (1968) Soul on Ice. New York: Dell.

HUGO, V. (1862) Les Misérables. Paris: Maison Quantin.

KITSUSE, J. I. (1975) "The new conception of deviance and its critics," pp. 273-284 in W. P. Gove (ed.) The Labelling of Deviance. New York: Halstead (a Sage Publications book).

NIEBUHR, R. (1946) Discerning the Signs of the Times: Sermons for Today and Tomorrow. New York: Scribner.

NYE, F. I., J. F. SHORT, Jr., and V. J. OLSON (1958) "Socio-economic status and delinquent behavior." American Journal of Sociology 63 (January): 381-388.

REISS, A. J., Jr. (1971) The Police and the Public. New Haven, CT: Yale University Press.

SCHUR, E. M. (1975) "Comments," pp. 285-294 in W. R. Gove (ed.) The Labelling of Deviance. New York: Halstead (a Sage Publications book).

SUTHERLAND, E. (1949) White-Collar Crime. New York: Dryden.

TAYLOR, I., P. WALTON, and J. YOUNG (1973) The New Criminology: For a Social Theory of Deviance. London: Routledge & Kegan Paul.

TOBY, J. (1974) "The socialization and control of deviant motivation," pp. 85-100 in D. Glaser (ed.) Handbook of Criminology. Chicago: Rand McNally.

--- (1971) Contemporary Society. New York: John Wiley.

7

FURTHER CRITICAL THOUGHTS ON MARXIST CRIMINOLOGY: COMMENTS ON TURK, TOBY, AND KLOCKARS

Ronald L. Akers

My primary task in my role of invited commentator is to remark on the essays by Austin Turk, Jackson Toby, and Carl Klockars. Since Turk's essay is in part and the other two essays are wholly critiques of what is variously called radical, new, critical, or Marxist criminology, there is not much in the essays in the way of substantive theory or analysis to which I may respond. Therefore, I want to comment mainly on the central issue to which all the essays refer—the adequacy of American-style Marxist criminology as both a theory of crime and criminal justice and an ideology or political philosophy.

The editor of this volume, James Inciardi, has given me great flexibility and freedom in the content, style, and tone of what I want to write about these essays. I shall avail myself of that freedom by indulging in a very informal discussion rather than presenting scholarly argumentation and analysis. Also, the relevant literature is ably and amply cited in the essays presented in this volume, and I have not felt the need to add space with footnoting, referencing, and documentation. I shall also take advantage of the flexibility to state personal beliefs and commitments.

I have written elsewhere about the central questions which theories of crime and deviance must answer. The first major question is how behavior gets defined as deviant and how society responds to it. As far as criminology is concerned, this is the question of the formation of law and operation of the criminal justice system. The second question has to do with explaining the development of deviant behavior and its distribution in society, which in criminology is the question of correlates and causes of criminal behavior. Except for early writings on culture and group conflict, conflict theorists seldom have attempted to explain criminal behavior. They have, as Klockars notes, concentrated on the first question of the formation and enforcement of law. This is seen in Turk's essay which does not say anything about causation of criminal behavior. There is, of course, no single conflict or radical view. Encompassed within this are views ranging from varieties of pluralistic conflict, to radical, non-Marxist, to Marxist and neo-Marxist perspectives. Turk's position is closer to pluralistic conflict than to Marxist criminology, but his is still basically a framework for analyzing labeling and reaction to criminal behavior, applied especially to "political criminality," not a theory of crime. Ideologically or politically motivated crime may in part be accounted for by these conflict perspectives, and class-based, politically motivated crime might be accounted for by the Marxist versions, but there is no uniquely radical-conflict theory of the etiology of criminal behavior.

I suppose that it is at least implicit in the Marxist view that class position explains most if not all behavior including criminal, and this may be why both Klockars and Toby analyze problems with the assumptions radical criminology makes about class causation of criminal behavior. Klockars cites Chambliss as supporting the view that class differences generate crime, the Schwendingers as seeing class producing war, racism, and sexism, and Quinney as finding the capitalistic class system productive of bad art. Toby argues that radical criminology continues traditional criminology's "overidentification with the underdog" which leads to an explanation of crime among the poor as compelled by their misery. I am not sure that radical criminologists are united in their view of class as "bad", but the use of class as an explanation of crime is not unique to Marxist criminology. For instance, in his essay, Toby argues that there is good theoretical reason to expect that lower-class persons would commit more crimes than middle- or upper-class persons. Does this make Toby a radical criminologist? It does not, and in fact Toby argues that his position is *contrary* to radical criminology. Reference to class position as a motivation to crime does not constitute a new theory departing from traditional criminology, and emphasis on class surely does not itself distinguish Marxian from other brands of conflict, radical, or traditional criminology. The distinguishing feature is an economic class analysis of a certain kind applied to capitalist society (but not to socialist society). Thus, not all findings of class or economic effects on crime support the Marxist view, and not all class analysis is Marxist analysis.

The important point is that radical theory basically does not offer an answer to the question of why people, even those in elite groups whose interests supposedly are particularly served by the law, commit crimes. Marxist criminology, thus far, seems little interested in delineating why people behave in ways defined as criminal. It is concerned, rather, with accounting for the definition and control of crime. Class, then, for conflict, radical, and Marxist criminology is important not so much as a cause of crime but as an explanation of why certain things are defined as crime and why crime is responded to in the way it is.

Turk's position then shares some commonality with Marxian theory, but his is obviously not a Marxist theory. Indeed, his essay is in large measure a critique of some central and ancillary positions taken by Marxists. He takes the classic Weberian stance of separating *studying* values from *making* value judgments and the separation of the citizen's role from the scientist's role. Contrary to the Marxist argument that objective science is not possible in capitalist society, this is a necessary and vital distinction to make in judging the merits of assertions about society. Theoretical assertions must be judged primarily by comparison with other theories and by empirical evidence on their validity. Value judgments about what is wrong with current society and how to achieve a better one are philosophical positions which must be judged primarily by comparison with other philosophies and how they have worked in practice. Turk views much of radical or Marxist writing to be "partisan ideological treatises," rather than theoretical conflict analysis. I agree with Turk that a nonpartisan conflict analysis is possible. That a value-free theory of crime is difficult to achieve does not mean the "ideal of objectively valid and reliable knowledge," is impossible to attain. While Turk's view that much of Marxist analysis is in fact political polemics asserting the evil of the capitalist system and the virtues of the socialist system is probably correct, much of Marxist or neo-Marxist analysis is not especially polemical. Surely, a nonpartisan, objective Marxian theory is possible just as other ideology-free criminological theory is possible.

Turk recognizes that whatever overlap there is between a theory explaining what is and judgments of what ought to be (and proposals to bring it about), the two are clearly different and separable enterprises. Turk recognizes that a Marxian theory of the structure of society and the enactment/enforcement of law can be constructed and tested for validity regardless of one's belief about the value of the Marxist vision of what society should be. It is quite possible to be persuaded by the facts that there is indeed an elite capitalist ruling class controlling the entire criminal justice system to its own ends, and still be vehemently opposed to the establishment of a dictatorship of the proletariat. Ideology cannot be judged as theory, but must be compared to rival social-political ideologies, a point which both Turk and Klockars make and one to which I shall return below.

As most conflict theorists do, Turk tends to dismiss as irrelevant the now voluminous body of research findings (some of which is cited in the Klockars essay) that there is considerable normative consensus in society cutting across class, sex, race, and age divisions on the undesirability and seriousness of certain criminal acts. The existence of such widespread consensus is not a trivial finding. Such research findings run directly counter to assertions made by all varieties of conflict-radical theory. They cannot be dismissed and must be accepted as either disconfirming conflict-radical assertions about lack of consensus in society or affirming some modified conflict model which recognizes consensus on some issues.

Toby need not go back as far as he does to find the old sentimentality contained in the "new" criminology. The underdog ideology of labeling theory has been taken on by some radical criminologists even while being critical of labeling theory. But I do not agree with Toby that emphasizing crime in high places and excusing or rationalizing the crimes of lower-class members is the keystone of the "new" criminology. A much more central assertion is that the higher levels, indeed a single elite group, controls the lower levels of societies and that crime and injustice are woven into the very fabric of capitalist society. Therefore, radical criminology is not so much the old sentimentality as it is the old structural-functionalism. It is the most recent embodiment of the old sociological adage that if something is wrong it is the system that needs to be changed. The new criminology's version of this is the capitalist system which needs structural overhaul. The "capitalist system" is to Marxist theory what "the unconscious" is to Freudian theory, and what "structure" is to sociological theory.

Toby rightly notes that there is little evidence in more recent studies to support the notion that there is class discrimination in the criminal justice system. This is not only contrary to "new" criminology. The preponderance of research showing little discrimination by social characteristics and the great importance of legalistic variables in criminal justice processing has not been satisfactorily explained by any variety of new criminology—Marxist, conflict, or labeling. However, we should not forget that these findings also go against much of what was taught in the "old" criminology, and indeed even much of popular belief.

Klockars's point about objective and subjective interest is not enhanced by his review of the changing perspective of some leading Marxist theorists. Most recent radical or Marxist theories have developed out of the pluralistic conflict perspective. Some have deliberately and self-consciously repudiated their earlier stances. In giving up pluralistic conflict theory for Marxist theory, some criminologists have moved toward a two-class model of society. Nevertheless, not all have moved entirely to that position and this is not an illogical direction to take. Moreover, I am not sure what is proven by detailing the change or by showing that Chambliss, who has moved less in that direction, changed some sentences in his vagrancy article in its latest reprint. Certainly change is allowable, and I do not believe that Chambliss made the changes to correspond with his latest stance to mislead the reader. More to the point, this says nothing about the validity or value of the new stance. The question is, did the change take place because of new evidence or lack of empirical validity of the old perspective? In this light Klockars can be seen to misread Turk. Turk's is not an attempt to "rescue some portion of the radical perspective before its total bankruptcy is declared." Rather he is maintaining fidelity to conflict theory as a theory capable of and intended for testing free of its ideological freight. Other conflict theorists may have, in greater or lesser degree, pretty much given up this attempt. Turk has not, but he has no interest in salvaging a radical ideological perspective.

I find myself in basic agreement with Klockars's critique of Marxist criminology in this country. I believe he overstates the case, however, for not all of Marxist criminology is as wedded to the class dogma or trying to escape its own history as Klockars charges. Also, he needs to qualify his characterizations in more places than he does and to spend more time pointing to some of the recognized differences between the major figures. I make no claim to being a scholar of Marxist writings and am unable to evaluate properly all that Klockars contends. However, I believe Klockars is correct in the essential and major points he makes about Marxist criminology. Indeed, I think it is a devastating critique which will be widely cited in the future and which Marxist criminologists will find difficult to answer.

Toby makes the important point that radical critiques of American society sometimes make it appear as if democratic societies have the same repressive characteristics of such societies as South Africa or Nazi Germany. As Toby says, we live in an imperfect world with imperfect justice. Therefore, to be meaningful the type of comparison of social-political ideology referred to above should be one real, imperfect system with another real, imperfect system. Compared to a socialist ideal system, the real American system looks unjust, repressive, and controlled by a tiny capitalist elite. Compared to the Soviet Union, China, Vietnam, North Korea, East Germany, or Cambodia, to name some socialist alternatives, or to Iran, South Korea, or Chile, to name some nonsocialist alternatives, American society looks pretty good.

In neither communist nor democratic societies is the ideal achieved, but when comparisons are made, the real and historic societies based on Marxist doctrine invariably look worse than the real and historic societies based on democratic ideals. This is true on whatever ground the comparison is made; quality of life of the people, freedom and human rights, political control by the people, economic well-being, economic disparity and inequity, imperialism and control of puppet states, encroachment on other nations' sovereignty, repression of liberation movements around the world, and so on. This is the point of the telling comparisons which Klockars makes of the American system with Cuba, China, the Soviet Union, and other communist states. This comparison need not be complex, profound, or esoteric, or made by experts. It need not involve mystification and glorification of our system. Any informed citizen can make it, and it has been made in the popular press.

Klockars claims such a comparison is not made by Marxists because it would discredit the promise of a nonrepressive, crime-free society and bring up the issue of the cost of achieving it. The fact is that some radical criminologists, including Chambliss, have made comparative reference to Marxist societies and to the fact that some things which are defined as crime there would not be crime here. As a blueprint for the good society, the Marxist ideal has not proven to be reliable. Socialist societies have been unable to deliver on the promise of classlessness and economic equality. Instead, they have been characterized by self-serving, privileged party elites and ruling cabals or dictatorships which very closely resemble the tight-knit, self-perpetuating ruling class controlling the criminal justice system which some Marxists claim is true for capatalist society.

8

A TOWER OF BABEL: MARXIST CRIMINOLOGISTS AND THEIR CRITICS

Milton Mankoff

The heated polemical exchanges that have passed for intellectual debate between Marxist and anti-Marxist criminologists in the United States resemble the confusion of a tower of Babel, except for the fact that those on each side are not seriously interested in communicating with their adversaries. Rather, there is simply a desire to impress one's ideological and intellectual allies by scoring debating points.

The articles in this section which I have been asked to comment upon, with the exception of Austin Turk's effort, represent an unfortunate continuation of the substitution of pure ideology for reasoned analysis. To be sure, a number of charges leveled against some prominent Marxist or radical criminologists have validity. I have been very sympathetic to attempts to incorporate Marxist ideas into criminological theory and research. Yet this has not prevented me from being highly critical of anti-intellectualism and posturing in the work of Richard Quinney, one of the primary targets of anti-Marxist criminologists (Mankoff, 1978).

MARXIST CRIMINOLOGY'S GROWING PAINS

The problem of anti-intellectual Marxism has affected criminology perhaps far more than any other branch of Marxist scholarship.[1] The reasons for this are undoubtedly complex, but a few seem of particular importance. First, Marx himself paid little systematic attention to the creation of law and the causes of crime, and made no substantial contributions to knowledge in this area. A sophisticated tradition of Marxist criminology never fully developed in the same sense that, for example, Marxist economics did (Hirst, 1975; Taylor et al., 1973: 209-236).

Second, despite the charge that mainstream criminology has always tended to side with the law rather than the offender, adopting a correctional approach to criminality, it is also true that sociologists of crime have, far more than the typical middle-class citizen, been sensitive to the social deprivations that contribute to property and violent crime by the poor. The relatively liberal mainstream approach to the "crime problem" has made it more difficult for those who want self-consciously to develop a Marxist criminology to differentiate it from the standard paradigm. I would suggest that one consequence of this has been the publication of exaggerated intellectual positions. Marxist economists, by contrast, were less likely to substitute polemics for analysis because mainstream economics' dominant paradigm was so devoid of historical and sociological understanding that Marxists did not have to go very far to divorce themselves from that tradition. Marxist economics, because it was concerned with such distinctive intellectual matters, could evolve somewhat autonomously. There was no necessity to combat mainstream approaches on every point.

Finally, the virtual absence of Marxist criminology combined with extreme political polarization in the academic community in the 1960s to add far too much fuel to the fire of intellectual debate. Had a mature Marxist criminological tradition existed, it is more likely that its followers would have avoided a great deal of the shallowness that has characterized an all too significant part of its development. Unfortunately, all new paradigms, like infants, have their irrational "impulses." They interpret the world with little humility. This is to be expected. Strong criticism is needed, but not criticism which both distorts the strong points in what is a creative impulse and substitutes nothing but the dead weight of tradition.

THE ANTI-MARXIST POLEMICISTS:
TOBY AND KLOCKARS

In initially commenting on the articles by the anti-Marxists, Jackson Toby and Carl B. Klockars, I had hoped to adopt a more dispassionate tone in order to bridge the chasm between them and Marxists working in the area of criminology. Unfortunately, the character of their contributions would appear to preclude any rapprochement.

If intellectual shoddiness has characterized some criminology purporting to be informed by Marxist theory,[2] neither Toby nor Klockars provides an appealing alternative. Both critics seem so emotionally driven to exorcise what they believe to be Marxist criminology that they present barely coherent attacks on ideas that either have no significant bearing on Marxist criminological theory or only represent criticisms of the more absurd intimations of some who claim to speak for it. A more challenging task, and one not taken up by either author, would be to criticize some of the more sophisticated spokesmen for Marxist criminology such as Mark Kennedy (1976) and David Greenberg (1977), who may not be as prolific as others, but deserve more attention.

Jackson Toby's article, "The New Criminology Is the Old Baloney," appears concerned with an issue that has *not* been a major concern of radical criminology, namely, whether the lower social classes have a higher incidence of criminal behavior than the middle or upper class. For some unexplained reason Toby seems to feel that the "new criminologists" are deeply committed to the view that there is no relationship between class and criminality. Actually, it was *conventional* sociologists not radicals who first made such a claim and it has been, as he notes, widely and inconclusively debated ever since. To the extent that Marx himself has served as a guide to the new criminologists it is unlikely they would deny excessive criminality among the downtrodden, for as Hirst (1975) and Taylor et al. (1973: 209-236) note, Marx had a conventional view of crime as being rooted in the life-style of a segment of the *lumpenproletariat*. Moreover, far from romanticizing criminality in this stratum, Marx had some sympathy, but primarily contempt for, and fear of, those who responded to oppressive social conditions by preying upon others.

Even if one ignores Marx's own scattered comments on the class incidence of crime, it hardly makes sense for radical critics of society to believe that the most disadvantaged social strata are not driven to violate certain laws more than those who enjoy material and psychic comfort. Yet it should also be obvious that a given social order creates, in *all* strata,

distinctive strains and opportunities to relieve them. The wealthy capitalist, if living beyond his or her means, may be tempted to engage in stock
fraud, drink to excess, or even commit suicide. The poor can respond to a
similar situation by engaging in the latter two activities, but have no
opportunity to consider the first. Crime and deviance are a reflection of
strains and opportunities, and one should expect them at all levels of
society, albeit in different forms and quantities. Changes in economic,
political, and cultural forces naturally should affect the incidence of crime
and deviance. All this seems so obvious that it is unclear why any radical,
liberal, or conservative cares about the debate in the abstract form in
which Toby expresses it.

The second thrust of Toby's attack on the radical criminologists involves his belief that they are opposed to all criminal sanctions. In this case
Toby is, once again, setting up a straw man. His quotation from *The New
Criminology* and reference to Eldridge Cleaver hardly constitute evidence
that either the authors of the book or Cleaver are opposed to punishing
any criminal acts. The new criminologists may be naive in saying it is
possible to have a truly crime-free society in which only harmless deviance
(i.e., idiosyncrasies) will flourish, and it is true that they often make few
distinctions between advanced Western capitalist parliamentary systems
and fascist states. These are embarrassing errors when they occur, but it is
unlikely very many radical sociologists, perhaps not even those Toby refers
to, really believe in these notions. Rather, they represent a style of
presentation, an excess in the face of what they believe to be the repressiveness and cynicism toward radical social change in countries such as the
United States. It may well be that Toby's credo "imperfect justice in an
imperfect world" is a more practical approach to the social reality of our
times, but it also represents the world view of someone who is unlikely to
be suffering terribly from the imperfections.

Carl B. Klockars's "The Contemporary Crises of Marxist Criminology"
approaches Marxist criminology with a bludgeon instead of a scalpel. It is
as if he were told that the article must contain all of his collected thoughts
and pet peeves for he will never be permitted to write again. Some of his
barbs are on target. He is correct, for example, in accusing many Marxists
of comparing the imperfect social justice under capitalism with an idea-
lized model of a socialist society which has never been realized in practice.
Unfortunately, few Marxists, sadly including those living in socialist countries, have scrutinized existing socialist societies with the same intellectual
tools they apply to capitalist states.[3]

Klockars seems, however, to commit the opposite error. He presents a fanciful view of American society, one in which class relations have no role, the managerial revolution has triumphed over family capitalism, Common Cause has replaced class struggle, and there is no such thing as a sociology of politics. While celebrating American exceptionalism to the extreme, Klockars indicates that socialist countries (*always* defined as the Soviet Union, without recognizing considerable variations between it and some Eastern European and non-European socialist states) need not be dispassionately analyzed from the perspective of history and social science. Simply citing Solzhenitsyn and various authorities on repression and bureaucratization suffices.

Fortunately, not all mainstream social scientists are so blinded by ideology that they are incapable of recognizing the complexity that exists in all societies—capitalist, socialist, and even fascist. I would recommend, in particular, a fascinating attempt by a non-Marxist Soviet specialist, Jerry Hough (1977), to give the Soviet Union the status of a nontotalitarian society, one that is certainly not truly democratic, but has significant elements of pluralism, impressive citizen participation in many institutional spheres, and an increasing degree of public discussion of policy alternatives. This is not to suggest that the treatment of dissenters, official censorship, and other undemocratic practices should not be considered when appraising the Soviet Union, but that such phenomena are not the *only* reality there.

It is important for criminologists and other social scientists to engage in comparative studies, but neither the vulgar Marxist comparisons that Klockars rightly attacks or the vulgar mainstream approach which he champions is terribly useful for increasing knowledge. Probably the most valuable form of comparison is *within* a particular society when it changes its social structure in some fundamental way. Thus, comparing China before and after 1949, or Cuba before and after 1959 makes more sense than comparing either with the United States or Haiti or India. Too many confounding variables are brought into play when nations having different levels of economic development, and distinctive political and cultural traditions, are juxtaposed in order to determine the relative effects of capitalism or socialism on a social institution or problem.

Although it is not possible to begin to correct all of Klockars's theoretical and empirical errors in analyzing the character and dynamics of American society, I believe discussion of his "theory of social stratification" and "political sociology" will be sufficient to raise questions about his skill as an analyst of social structures.

One of Klockars's major points of contention with Quinney and other Marxists is their alleged reliance on class as an explanatory concept in understanding the development of law and patterns of criminality. Actually, Klockars runs into difficulty at the outset of his discussion when he fails to distinguish between the behavior of different classes and the social effects of capitalism as an economic and cultural *system*. Klockars has great difficulty divorcing institutional processes from the wishes of individual actors. While there are also Marxists such as Quinney who believe that contemporary history is a conspiracy of individuals consciously pursuing their class interests, there are far more sophisticated ones as well. These scholars emphasize the interaction between the imperatives of institutional arrangements operating within the context of a given mode of production and the elites and nonelites pursuing their perceived interests through sincerely believed ideologies.

Klockars is not content to criticize Marxists who substitute conspiracy theory for rigorous social analysis. Nor does he want to empirically refute Marxist theses. Rather, he only wishes to oppose the view that class is evil, which he ascribes to Marxists (again, Marx himself had far more complex views on this question), with its opposite: Class systems are responsible for high culture and progress. Both claims are, of course, absurd in their unwillingness to admit the unintended negative consequences of institutions which also have unintended positive ones.

Klockars, after giving the moral stamp of approval to class distinctions, proceeds to deny that such distinctions occur any longer in the United States. Even the most minimal perusal of literature on wealth distribution, trends in equality of opportunity, and other indices of class structure would naturally refute this wild claim, but it is possible that Klockars, though poor at expressing his ideas, is simply indicating that the *social* expression of economic class differences in the United States has diminished over time. This may possibly be true and serious students of stratification have noted that the American class structure is somewhat less socially rigid than the Western European ones.

A more open class system could have an effect upon law development and crime patterns in the United States, but Klockars fails to pursue the matter once he has used it for polemical purposes.

In my own view the lack of a deeply seated class *consciousness*, as distinct from the lack of a class *structure*, has channeled the frustrations of many members of the American underclass into prepolitical criminal acts of violence and theft which might otherwise find political expression. The absence of a mass-based political movement of the left in the United States creates an ideological vacuum for the disadvantaged and no institutional means of working for fundamental social change. Acting out against authority figures or targets of convenience becomes a substitute for political activity. Feelings of powerlessness are temporarily relieved, though no genuine alteration of powerlessness is achieved.

Class consciousness can reduce certain kinds of criminality even when there is no oppositional mass-based political movement. Under conditions, as in England, when an element of class *deference* exists, the underclass' frustrations are reduced because its members tacitly accept hierarchy and privilege. In the United States neither oppositional nor deferential class consciousness exists to the extent it does elsewhere, and this may increase anger among those on the bottom of the social order. These possible contributions to understanding America's crime pattern are offered as hypotheses only, but I think they illustrate how little critical reflection Klockars engages in after having his "insights."

A potentially fruitful proposition which Klockars once again leaves unexplored is his belief that repressive forms of social control primarily account for crime reduction in socialist countries. Assuming that crime reduction has occurred, can this be traced only to fear of punishment?

The 1979 revolution in Iran strongly suggests that repression, even torture, are not sufficient to make a population cower. The Shah's political police and mightily equipped armed force failed to produce political compliance. One also doubts that ordinary criminals ceased their activities because of police power. If crime rates have been reduced in socialist countries I am more likely to believe that economic security, increased mobility chances for the offspring of disadvantaged strata, strong community organizations, and *informal* group pressures to conform play the major role. It is also possible in places where revolutionary values have not been superseded by bureaucratization that even relatively disadvantaged citizens feel an identification with values which militate against predatory behavior. All this is purely speculative, and perhaps Klockars's view is correct. Unfortunately, Klockars provides the mirror image of those arrogant Marxist criminologists he criticizes for admitting no uncertainties. He offers only his assertions in place of theirs.

I would like to conclude my comments on Klockars's article by noting one last theoretical failing, one which deals with his discussion of "interests" and "false consciousness." Klockars seems unable to acknowledge the existence of stable social structures which have a specific character, require certain institutional supports, and create groups of people who identify their well-being and that of all people with particular policies. He ridicules Chambliss's use of the concepts "mobilization of bias" and "non-decisions" and the possibility of manipulated consensus, as if history never existed. In Klockars's view, power does not exist in the United States, only in the Soviet Union. In America every possible policy direction either has already been fully discussed, with all sides getting a fair share of time to present their points of view, or debate will soon be getting under way. Public opinion is formed *naturally* without any attempt by the more powerful to close off debate or demagogically attack opponents. Of course, in the Soviet Union everything is the reverse. If all have not revolted they are either afraid or brainwashed. No issues are ever discussed.

Obviously, no society can exist in the forms Klockars's approach implies. Simply comparing the content of party platforms of American political parties over the past century and actual policy enacted or not enacted should render absurd the notion that critical "non-decisions" do not occur. But without attacking the Marxian theory of interests and concepts such as "non-decisions" Klockars would have to leave the world of endless polemicizing and begin to examine to what extent the history of concrete societies have been shaped by the many, the few, or both in contention with each other. Then some of the theoretical issues developed by Marxist criminologists would have to be considered, even if the particular conclusions of Quinney and Chambliss were modified òr rejected.

NONPARTISAN CONFLICT THEORY

It is unfortunate that Austin Turk's "Analyzing Official Deviance: For Nonpartisan Conflict Analyses in Criminology" does not use the polemical style of the other authors in this volume. Those who employ the tactic generally do get more attention than they deserve. Turk is to be commended for writing soberly and intelligently, unlike Toby and Klockars. Nonpartisan conflict theory has many virtues, its nonpartisan stance being a particularly welcome relief after so much confusing of social science with ideology. Yet, in its very reasonableness, Turk's approach shows itself to be of limited intellectual utility.

The fundamental problem with all attempts at building *universal* theories of deviance, or any other social phenomenon, is that one must usually move to such a high level of abstraction to encompass *all* cases of the object of study that the result is often banal. Banality rarely sounds unreasonable, but it often fails us at critical moments when we wish to predict social outcomes.

I believe that it is far more useful to recognize that social laws of a nonbanal type are more likely to be developed when examining specific types of societies. Crime and conflict in preliterate societies, feudal societies, and socialist societies may exhibit certain distinctive features that can lead to valuable sociological generalizations. If one finds that Marxist categories are not helpful in organizing social patterns, one can try "industrial versus agrarian," or "Christian versus Moslem" societies for purposes of comparison. Since conflict is ubiquitous (as is cooperation), it is only such an approach that is capable of locating *specific* institutional contradictions in *types* of societies which are likely to generate *particular* kinds of conflicts and resolutions. Without doing this conflict theory is reduced to purely descriptive analysis and is incapable of predicting patterns of conflict before they emerge.

In concluding my review of Toby, Klockars, and Turk, I hope rather than increasing the confusions of a tower of Babel I have opened up a new space where Marxists and at least some of their critics can find the possibility of intellectual exchange and enrichment of criminology. Without this development the criminological enterprise and the cause of social justice will both suffer.

NOTES

1. Marxist academics have contributed mightily to the improvement of social scientific disciplines in the past decade or so. In history, they have revitalized the study of international relations, altering the sterility of Cold War diplomatic history and bringing needed revision of traditional versions of the Progressive and New Deal eras. In economics, they have made major critiques of existing theories of dependency between advanced and undeveloped economies as well as exposing the limitations of neo-classical and Keynesian theory in grappling with such nagging problems as proverty and urban blight. Marxist sociologists have made signal contributions to political sociology, stratification theory, the study of mass media, and even deviance and criminology. Important Marxist journals such as *Marxist Perspectives,* the *New Left Review,* and *Socialist Review* have contributed both to social science theory and political practice.

2. Not all those who claim to be Marxists should be taken as seriously working within that tradition. Nevertheless, I will refrain from passing on anyone's credentials and, for the sake of argument, simply call those criminologists Marxists who identify themselves as such.

3. One of the few efforts to provide this much-needed perspective on socialist societies is *Critique: A Journal of Soviet Studies and Socialist Theory.*

REFERENCES

GREENBERG, D. (1977) "Delinquency and the age structure of society." Contemporary Crises 1 (April): 189-233.

HIRST, P. Q. (1975) "Marx and Engels on law, crime and morality," pp. 203-244 in Walton et al. (eds.) Critical Criminology. London: Routledge & Kegan Paul.

HOUGH, J. (1977) The Soviet Union and Social Science Theory. Cambridge, MA: Harvard University Press.

KENNEDY, M. (1976) "Beyond incrimination," pp. 34-65 in W. Chambliss and M. Mankoff (eds.) Whose Law? What Order? New York: John Wiley.

MANKOFF, M. (1978) "On the responsibility of Marxist criminologists: a reply to Quinney." Contemporary Crises 2 (July): 293-301.

TAYLOR, I., P. WALTON, and J. YOUNG (1973) The New Criminology. London: Routledge & Kegan Paul.

9

CARL KLOCKARS VS. THE "HEAVY HITTERS": A PRELIMINARY CRITIQUE

David O. Friedrichs

The tendency to perceive the controversy regarding radical criminology in dichotomous terms (you are either for it or against it) is false and misleading. *Four* significant positions regarding radical criminology can be identified, analogous to the hard determinism, soft determinism, soft indeterminism, and hard indeterminism positions (Abelson, 1963: 491).

"Hard" radical criminology is the self-identified posture which subscribes to at least an interpretation of Marxist theory and applies a neo-Marxist analysis quite comprehensively to its understanding of crime and criminal justice. Proponents of this position have in some instances rejected the "simpleminded" criticisms of nonradicals as unworthy of response.

"Soft" radical criminology is the "fellow traveler" posture, taken by those who subscribe to the broad tenets and objectives of the radical position (e.g., that the structure of economic relations is the basic point of departure for understanding crime and criminal justice and that a funda-

AUTHOR'S NOTE: I wish to thank Professors Richard Quinney, Alfred McClung Lee, and Stuart Hills for their encouragement over the past year in connection with my recent papers on radical criminology. Needless to say, this acknowledgment does not imply approval by these individuals of the ideas advanced in the present essay.

mentally socialistic transformation is a precondition for substantial reduction of both criminality and criminal *in*justice). But this posture disavows a totalistic rejection of contemporary American society (and in fact wishes to preserve some of its democratic, due process features) and is subscribed to by an eclectic grouping of democratic socialists, various humanists, and left-leaning liberals. Proponents of this position do not unilaterally reject the value of mainstream criminological perspectives (especially of the interpretive form) nor are they committed to a "revolutionary"solution to the problems of contemporary capitalist society. In fact they tend to be somewhat skeptical about both the viability and, in any case, the ultimate outcome of such a revolution.

"Soft" mainstream criminology, essentially liberal and often interpretive, subscribes to a variety of theoretical positions—including those focusing upon economic deprivation—but does not adopt the Marxist framework. Those who identify with this position tend to be concerned with various forms of governmental abuse of criminal justice powers and with a persistence of inequitable and oppressive features of the justice system, but they also favor reform and "getting rid of rotten apples" over restructuring the system as such, and in any case are more likely to adopt a position that the criminologist's commitment should be toward enhancing the sophistication of his or her research, and to scientific "truth," rather than to ideological objectives per se. Commonly a proportion of those associated with this position are at least moderately interested in what radical criminologists have to say, and may not be averse to maintaining a dialogue with them and even to adopting aspects of their interpretive insights.

"Hard" mainstream criminology, in the present context, either maintains the pretext of a pure scientific commitment or unapologetically formulates research designed to win government grants and is directed toward enhancing the efficiency and effectiveness of the existing criminal justice system. Criminologists who might be identified with this position tend to either disregard or entirely ignore the emergence of radical criminology, dismissing its analysis out of hand.

In the present essay I am writing essentially from the second position outlined above, insofar as it is my observation that it is quite widely held but too little heard from. Little attempt will be made to represent substantively the present work and position of self-identified radical criminologists for several reasons: (1) I cannot put myself forth as representing the position, and given the present diversity of directions taken by leading radical criminologists, I would question whether any individual can presume to represent a significant group of adherents to this perspective; (2) the *recent* work of radical criminologists (largely ignored by Carl Klockars in his critique, the main focus of the present essay) is to be found in such readily accessible journals as *Crime & Social Justice* and *Contemporary Crises,* for example, and those authentically open to an understanding of this perspective should expose themselves directly to this work; (3) at several radical caucuses over the past year (1979) the prospect of radical criminologists advancing their own analysis in a special issue of *Criminology,* or a book, has been considered, and preliminary steps in this direction have been taken. We may expect in the not-too-distant future, then, to have available an up-to-date presentation of the substance of radical criminology. The purpose of the present essay is to at least suggest possible objections to Carl Klockars's controversial critique, "The Contemporary Crises of Marxist Criminology" (1979), and to acknowledge—quite individually, in this case—the seriousness with which some of Klockars's analysis should be taken by those interested in developing an externally persuasive and effective, as opposed to an internally pure and impotent, radical criminology.[1]

Klockars begins his critique by referring to Tony Platt's 1974 assertion that the most imaginative criminology has been written by "criminals" (e.g., Claude Brown and Eldridge Cleaver) (1979: 478). While this claim need not be regarded as a literal tenet of radical criminology, the fact is that radical criminology includes a phenomenological dimension and has recognized the validity of the actor's voice as heard directly, not through the screen of a formal research framework, but as experienced.[2] The *sense* of being a black ghetto juvenile delinquent, and such a delinquent's understanding of his world, is indeed captured by Claude Brown (1965) with an authenticity unavailable to the objective, outsider criminologist; the *depths* of black anger, and its projection through illegal predatory acts, is starkly conveyed by Eldridge Cleaver with potent impact (1968). "Imagination is one thing, criminology another," writes Klockars (1979: 478). In fact too much mainstream criminology is decidedly unimaginative; why should we not allow the imaginative insights of "nonprofessionals" who contribute a great deal to our understanding of crime and justice to be regarded quite simply as a valid form of criminology?

The perceived crisis of American Marxist criminology[3] is regarded by Klockars as theoretical (1979: 479). If there are indeed theoretical inadequacies in an emerging radical criminology it is worth noting that the formidable theoretical shortcomings of the much more enduring enterprise of mainstream criminology are also quite obvious, and conceded by those who are identified with it or have reflected seriously upon it (e.g., see Gibbons, 1979a, 1979b). Michalowski's characterization of radical analysis as in its adolescence (1979: 561) is quite reasonable; Klockars's claim that it cannot, in effect, mature theoretically beyond its present stage is open to challenge, with some elements of this challenge to be indicated further on.

That many criminologists "right, left, and center" find racism, brutality, corruption, and so on repulsive, and wish, as do the radicals, to see these social pathologies eliminated is true enough, no doubt (Klockars, 1979: 480), but the radical criminologist objects to the failure of mainstream criminologists to link these conditions to the structure of a capitalist economy or to commit themselves to the structural transformation of society which is a precondition to their elimination. In fact the radical posture holds that mainstream criminology consciously, or unwittingly, contributes to the perpetuation of unjust attributes of capitalist society through upholding the legitimacy of the legal order and by providing data utilized by a repressive criminal justice system for its own purposes.

Klockars moves on in his analysis to identify *class* as a central concept of radical criminological analysis (1979: 480). Undeniably a negative evaluation of the role of class is, and logically must be, a major dimension of radical criminological analysis. Klockars finds that "class" has had some beneficial effects on society, that the "lower class" is relatively well off in our contemporary class system, and that in any case "class" in the modern American context pertains to ideology more than to social reality (1979: 482-483). Without venturing into the turbulent waters which swirl through the formidable literature addressing these questions in some form it may still be pointed out that: *All* basic social phenomena, crime included (as Marx himself noted), have positive, productive, or functional effects; the *relative* economic well-being of the American lower classes should not divert us from the persistence of a great deal of real poverty, as Harrington (1962) and many others since have shown, and that such material well-being as does exist cannot compensate for the immense psychic damage of a system which, in the view of many astute observers, may still be validly described as a class system (see Terkel, 1975; Sennett and Cobb, 1972).[4]

If the work of any contemporary radical criminologist can indeed be read as arguing that crime, criminal law, and criminal behavior can be *comprehensively* and *exclusively* explained by reference to class, as Klockars suggests (1979: 483), the epithet "simpleminded" could justifiably be attributed to Marxist criminologists. Rather, class and the capitalist system, in radical criminology, are regarded as the basic point of departure, as providing the larger framework within which crime, criminal behavior, and criminal law must be understood. As Beirne (1979: 379) has recently pointed out, *structural* Marxist criminologists concede that many specific laws and legal acts do not favor the capitalist elite, but rather the underprivileged, and that the economic and governmental elite are not entirely united in their interests; but the *overriding* thrust and purpose of the criminal law and criminal justice system, in the radical criminological interpretation, is geared toward maintenance of the existing social order and capitalist economy.[5] We might venture to say, then, that within the context of a *structural* radical criminology it is possible to concede that Klockars is essentially correct in suggesting the existence of a multitude of overlapping interest groups and a problematic relationship between direct ownership and degrees of control in capitalist society, as well as the oppressive nature of bureaucratic management in existing socialistic countries (1979: 484-486). But the oft-noted dichotomy of owners and workers advanced in radical analysis can also be read as a *metaphor* focusing attention upon the dramatically disproportionate distribution of power and wealth in capitalist societies and as a *generalized* framework for understanding this distribution, rather than as an attempt to identify a clear-cut empirical reality. Such an analysis does not preclude the possibility of aberrant power relations developing in socialistic societies, a phenomenon which has to be analyzed independently of the critique of capitalist society. In certain respects it may be true, then, as Klockars suggests with reference to the evolving orientation of Platt, Chambliss, and Quinney (1979: 487), that these radical criminologists have carried their analysis, at least in some of their work, to its logical extreme point insofar as the operation of capitalist interests is concerned. Again we could argue that such analyses may be said to counter the dominant thrust of traditional American mainstream criminology, which for the most part has omitted or downplayed the role of a capitalist economy in generating both law and crime. Thus the radical criminological treatment of interests may be regarded as presenting a revealing counterimage which serves as a point of departure for a "critical" understanding of capitalist society, but which also requires significant qualification.

A careful reading of the radical criminological literature does not necessarily challenge the claim that there is a wide consensus on what acts should be defined as criminal, and direct approbation of predatory criminality can*not* be regarded as a tenet of radical criminology, as Klockars suggests (1979: 490-491). But several points are pertinent here. First, there are serious methodological difficulties with assessment of crime surveys, especially those of a cross-cultural nature (e.g., Newman, 1976) and we need not therefore accept the findings at face value. Second, even if there is considerable public consensus on crime and criminality this can at the very least be partially explained by reference to media manipulation (e.g., see Quinney, 1974: 151-153) and the impact of a conventional socialization process. Finally, if (as Jackson Toby notes) "Crime in high places does not legitimate crime in low places" (1979: 525), it remains true that in terms of public images and applied penal sanctions our society has a considerable way to go in achieving an equitable balance of response toward crimes of the rich and crimes of the poor; the radical posture suggests that the structure of a capitalist society ultimately precludes the possibility of achieving any such balance. In this context we may also recognize that radical criminologists have challenged the widely diffused, "taken-for-granted" assumption that the criminal law quite systematically identifies and proscribes objectively harmful acts. This type of assumption has, of course, been challenged from a number of criminological perspectives and in a variety of ways, but radical criminology has tended to emphasize the structural bases of this assumption and its implications, and two leading radicals in particular, the Schwendingers, have proposed replacing the legalistic definition of crime with an alternative, humanistic definition (1970, 1977).[6]

One need not believe that the civil liberties which American citizens enjoy are *solely* an instrument for the maintenance of dominant class interests, as Klockars's reads Quinney and Chambliss to be saying (1979: 493, 497), to appreciate the general thesis that many protective guarantees for ordinary citizens and actions taken or not taken by the state on their behalf *do* serve (whether or *not* it is their manifest function to do so) the broader interests of the capitalist legal order. Reiman (1979) has recently developed a "pyrrhic defeat" thesis which attributes the formidable failure of contemporary American criminal justice to reduce street crime to the usefulness of a persistent street crime problem in deflecting public attention from the larger crimes of the corporate and governmental elite. Klockars's point that Marx harshly repudiated the crimes of the "*lumpen* proletariat" (1979: 498) has in fact been generally conceded by radical criminologists (e.g., Platt, 1978: 32); furthermore, radical criminologists have not necessarily dismissed the need for certain practical strategies to deter or contain street crime (e.g., see Humphries, 1979: 237). That most of the victims of predatory street crime are other poor people is obvious, and it is also quite evident that countries like the Soviet Union have not eliminated street crime. But the *role* of a capitalist society in generating conditions bound to promote street crime (which, in addition to Reiman's "pyrrhic defeat" thesis noted above, include *relative* poverty and "false consciousness" regarding material needs, psychic brutalization of lower-status individuals, resulting frustration, anger, and hostility most easily misdirected toward one's fellow poor and, at least in *some* instances, the willful flaunting of a legal order which can be regarded as illegitimate) has been properly highlighted by radical criminology. The overriding thrust of mainstream criminological etiological theory has been to downplay or disregard entirely the contribution of capitalism qua capitalism (not simply in terms of its cultural values) as a primary force in the production of predatory crime.

Much work remains to be done in terms of empirical testing of radical propositions and accounting for the impact of noneconomic sources of crime and criminal law within the framework of a Marxist analysis. The radical criminological appreciation of the *complexity* of the phenomenon of crime and criminal law may not fully emerge in prominent work by its adherents, which sometimes veers toward the rhetorical (and prophetic); but the charge of orthodoxy and dogmatism which Klockars makes (1979: 502, 505) and attempts to document could be countered with the alternative interpretation that the work of the "heavy hitters" of radical criminology has been characterized by singular intellectual openmindedness, if one considers the evolution of this work as a whole.[7] Klockars contends further (1979: 501) that Marxist criminology differs from conventional criminology insofar as the former is dedicated to changing history and the latter to testing theory. Without even presuming to enter into another long-standing debate within the discipline, one can simply assert that the claim for the possibility of truly "objective" and nonideological theory-testing need not be conceded (one version of the radical thesis argues that Marxist theory simply states its ideological objectives more openly than does conventional theory-testing). If this position is quite commonly regarded as academic heresy it is not so clear that the contrary position need be regarded as an expression of eternal truth. From quite a different angle it can be argued that the *primary* task of radical criminology *to date* has been to provide us with an alternative *image* and *framework* for understanding crime and criminal justice; now radical criminology may take on the formidable task of systematically examining the empirical validity of its propositions. That some, or even many, of these propositions either fail to lend themselves to facile empirical verification, or are specifically rejected following the standard canons of empirical research, need not compromise the radical criminologist's commitment to a basic societal transformation.

Although cross-cultural comparisons present a variety of difficulties, I believe most radical criminologists would, and certainly ought to, concede that: (1) gross abominations committed in the name of Stalin and Mao, for example, cannot be justified; (2) that crime and justice system abuses have not been eliminated in existing socialistic countries; and (3) that insofar as crime and deviance have been contained or eradicated a considerable cost in terms of human liberty has been involved (Klockars, 1979: 502). But several points should be made here. The fact that no existing "communist" country approximates the original ideal does not necessarily invalidate the possibility of a dialectical transformation of existing societies into humane, essentially democratic, and noncapitalistic entities (which is *one* socialistic ideal). The skepticism of Klockars and others (e.g., Akers) with regard to "millenial promises" (1979: 507) of utopia is obviously not without foundation; many who would concede this point *also* find the radical analysis of the *structural* injustices of a capitalist society to be convincing. The resolution of this dilemma, such as it is, may be very difficult indeed, but it does not follow that pursuit of this resolution should be abandoned. Furthermore, many of the justice-related abuses of communist regimes may be viewed as an extension of *national* institutions rather than as authentic products of Marxist ideology (e.g., secret police and trials, oppressive labor camps, and the like were czarist creations rather than Bolshevik inventions). We still have much to learn about the existence of crime and the operation of criminal justice institutions in communist countries, but the *hypothesis* that "popular justice" is, on some levels and in some respects, more effective and "more just" than our form of bureaucratic justice cannot be dismissed out of hand. Radical scholars such as Harold Pepinsky (1976) have given us the beginnings of a deeper understanding of the meaning of crime and justice in socialist societies.

Is Marxist (or radical) criminology in the throes of a multifaceted crisis, as Klockars contends (1979: 501-508)? In the undeniable sense that it is characterized by considerable internal debate and some obviously unresolved issues, one could agree. I believe that many of those who identify in some way with the radical paradigm would concede that radical criminologists have been sporadically guilty of some of the "sins" with which Klockars charges them, including some distortions, mystifications, and evasions (e.g., regarding communist *in*justices). Even such vigorous adherents of radical criminology as the Schwendingers concede lapses and mistakes (1979: 3). I myself have elsewhere argued that radical criminology has focused on the alleged *inherent* illegitimacy of the capitalist state but has not as fully addressed itself to the problem of *perceptual* legitimacy, especially its own perceived legitimacy as a valid paradigm (Friedrichs, 1979c). I have also proposed, in still another essay, that radical criminology might enhance its own perceived legitimacy and effec-

tiveness by moving more consciously toward a synthesis with the specifically humanistic perspective within sociology and socialism, which has
been reemerging within criminology itself (Friedrichs, 1979b).[8] Such a
synthesis does not, incidentally, require the abandonment of quantitative
empirical inquiry.

It is possible, then, to be critical of certain features of radical criminology, and even to concede the seriousness of some of Klockars's objections, without conceding the validity of his assertion that "The real evils of
crime, discrimination, sexism, racism, corruption, and injustice are fully
visible within the concepts of conventional criminology" (1979: 506). Nor
is it necessary to concede Klockars's claim that radical criminology is
structurally irresponsible (1979: 506) and theoretically at a dead end
(1979: 502). We need not argue that radical criminology is in exclusive
possession of the "holy grail" of serious scholarly inquiry, "the truth."
But it has challenged in a fairly formidable way the traditional explicit and
implicit "truth claims" of mainstream criminology, especially insofar as
neglect of the structural impact of the economic order is concerned. That
the perspective of the "new criminology," a designation incorporating
radical criminology, has had an impact on the thinking of a significant
number of criminologists has been recently demonstrated (Pelfrey, 1979).
That most of these criminologists would not embrace the more extreme
formulations of radical criminology is also evident. In the present essay
some tentative objections to Carl Klockars's harsh critique of radical
criminology have been raised. More substantial and complete responses
will emerge in the increasingly subtle, sophisticated, and more broadly
based modes of analysis being adopted by radical criminologists. At the
same time the point of view advanced in this essay is that radical criminology must resolve its own contradictions, must respond positively and
substantially to its critics, and must move toward reconciling the "hard"
and "soft" liners—without surrendering to cooptation or compromising its
general line of analysis—if it is to become a persuasive, effective, and
enduring alternative to mainstream criminological paradigms.

NOTES

1. Two radical criminologists, Herman and Julia Schwendinger, contend that
Klockars's analysis is "demagogic," incompetent, and preposterous, and thereby
(presumably) does not warrant a serious substantive response (1979: 2-4). The
problem with this position, in my view, is that it fails to address itself to the fact that
Klockars's interpretation of radical criminology is probably consistent with that held
by most mainstream criminologists. Now whether this can be attributed to the biased
hostility of these criminologists to the radical perspective, or to the failure of radical

criminology to get its point of view across effectively, can be debated. But *if* radical criminology is to be effective in reaching and persuading other criminologists of the basic validity of its point of view—if it is to be something other than a cult-like enterprise of a small group of criminologists who only talk to each other—it *must* respond quite directly to these interpretations, however "preposterous" they may be, and respond in forums most likely to reach *non*radical criminologists.

2. This phenomenological dimension of radical criminological analysis is controversial within the paradigm itself (e.g., see Taylor et al., 1974: 191-199, 279-280).

3. Whether American Marxist criminology is more advanced than its European counterpart, as Klockars asserts (1979: 479), is open to possible challenge as an ethnocentric judgment; certainly significant contributions have been made by Taylor et al. (1973, 1974) and other English members of the National Deviancy Conference, and by various German scholars, for example Werkentin and his colleagues (1974).

4. For one "defense" of the contemporary relevance of the concept of class, contra Klockars's interpretation, see Giddons (1973).

5. Beirne objects, as have others, to the failure of critics of Marxist perspectives "to ignore the important differences in the theoretical finesse of competing versions of Marxism" (1979: 374). While the debate pertaining to which Marx is the "real" Marx continues, the most widely adopted posture by radical criminologists is that an openended interpretation of Marx is most appropriate, that Marxist thought develops dialectically, through time, and therefore the claim that only one interpretation is correct is generally false (e.g., see Melossi, 1976: 26-32; Quinney, 1973: 86; Rock, 1974: 597-598; Chambliss, 1975: 150-169; Anderson, 1974: 2-5). Furthermore, no serious person treats Marx's work as "holy writ," devoid of error, ignorance, and possibly (in places) bigotry (Klockars, 1979: 509-510; but see Greenberg's repudiation of this interpretation of Marx's bigotry, 1979). In fact all major radical theorists in and out of criminology are probably guilty of periodic excesses. There is a dimension to radical analysis which quite deliberately attempts to provoke, even to outrage, but ultimately to challenge our premises totally. While rejecting specific aspects of this challenge it is still possible to appreciate, and perhaps embrace, the larger framework of the analysis.

6. Although the Schwendingers are concerned with the larger "crimes" of imperialism, racism, sexism, and so on, one may ask whether, in a time of widespread inability to provide for basic needs (food, shelter, heat, and the like), we should reject out of hand the notion of regarding gross indulgence in luxury as criminal? (One recognizes, of course, that the mere suggestion of such a move is the sort of thing which outrages many mainstream criminologists!)

7. Klockars's indictment of Marxist criminologists for orthodoxy and dogmatism (1979: 502, 505) is not appropriately applied to "Heavy hitter" Richard Quinney, for example, if one considers his intellectual career as a whole. Jeffery (1979) recently remarked that he is quite convinced that there is a gene which prevents most people from learning anything after they leave graduate school! If Jeffery himself has moved away from his graduate training toward an emerging interest in biosocial explanations for crime, Quinney's career movement from an essentially mainstream orientation (with philosophical interests) through conflict, critical, neo-Marxist, and prophetic thought has been even more dramatic and remarkable (see Friedrichs, 1979b). Recently Quinney has undertaken the extraordinary challenge of reconciling sociological, Marxist, and theological thought and perspectives. As he writes: "My objective is that of integrating into a Marxist materialist analysis of the world a critical and prophetic theology" and "The project is to create a theonomous culture,

a sacramental community—'a more righteous social order, established in the prophetic spirit.' " (Quinney, 1979b: 207, 212; see also Quinney, 1979a). While most criminologists right, center, *and* left will probably not be prepared to follow Quinney down this path toward a deeper understanding of our social reality, his singular existential courage, treading "where angels dare not," is quite awesome and worthy of the humble admiration of his more timid professional colleagues. And who is to say, when all is said and done, that Quinney's perspective will not be vindicated at some future time, in some future place?

8. Different models for the further development of criminology and radical criminology have been proposed, of course, with recent examples being the dialectical (Ball, 1978) and the anarchistic (Tifft, 1979).

REFERENCES

ABELSON, R. (1963) Ethics and Metaethics—Readings in Ethical Philosophy. New York: St. Martin's.

ANDERSON, C. H. (1974) The Political Economy of Social Class. Englewood Cliffs, NJ: Prentice-Hall.

BALL, R. A. (1978) "Toward a dialectical criminology," pp. 11-26 in M. D. Krohn and R. L. Akers (eds.) Crime, Law, and Sanctions: Theoretical Perspectives. Beverly Hills, CA: Sage.

BEIRNE, P. (1979) "Empiricism and the critique of Marxism on law and crime." Social Problems 26 (April): 373-385.

BROWN, C. (1965) Manchild in a Promised Land. New York: Macmillan.

CHAMBLISS, W. J. (1975) "Toward a political economy of crime." Theory & Society 2 (Summer): 150-169.

CLEAVER, E. (1968) Soul on Ice. New York: McGraw-Hill.

FRIEDRICHS, D. O. (1979a) "The law and the legitimacy crisis: a critical issue for criminal justice," pp. 290-311 in R. G. Iacovetta and D. H. Chang (eds.) Critical Issues in Criminal Justice. Durham, NC: Carolina Academic Press.

——— (1979b) "Criminology: a radical-humanist perspective." Presented at the annual meeting of the Association for Humanist Sociology, University of Pittsburgh at Johnstown, October.

——— (1979c) "Inherent and perceptual legitimacy: a critique of the radical criminological perspective." Presented at the 31st Annual Meeting of the American Society of Criminology, Philadelphia, November.

GIBBONS, D. (1979a) The Criminological Enterprise. Englewood Cliffs, NJ: Prentice-Hall.

——— (1979b) "The criminological enterprise: where do we go from here?" Presented at the 31st Annual Meeting of the American Society of Criminology, Philadelphia, November.

GIDDONS, A. (1973) The Class Structure of the Advanced Societies. New York: Harper & Row.

GREENBERG, D. (1979) "Letter." Criminology 17 (November): 277-278.

HARRINGTON, M. (1962) The Other America. New York: MacMillan.

HUMPHRIES, D. (1979) "Crime and the state," pp. 224-241 in A. J. Szymanski & T. G. Goertzel, Sociology: Class, Consciousness & Contradictions. New York: Litton.

JEFFERY, C. R. (1979) "Sociobiology and criminology: the long lean years of the unthinkable and the unmentionable." Presented at the 31st Annual Meeting of the American Society of Criminology, Philadelphia, November.

KLOCKARS, C. (1979) "The contemporary crises of Marxist criminology." Criminology 16 (February): 477-515.

——— (1979) "Letter." Criminology 17 (November): 279-280.

MELOSSI, D. (1976) 'The penal question in capital." Crime & Social Justice 6 (Spring-Summer): 26-32.

MICHALOWSKI, R. (1979) "Crime and a theory of the state: the adolescence of radical analysis." Criminology 16 (February): 561-580.

NEWMAN, G. (1976) Comparative Deviance. New York: Elsevier North-Holland.

PELFREY, W. V. (1979) "Mainstream criminology: more new than old." Criminology 16 (November): 323-330.

PEPINSKY, H. (1978) "Anarchist communism as an alternative to the rule of law." Contemporary Crises 2: 315-334.

——— (1976) Crime and Conflict. New York: Academic.

PLATT, A. M. (1978) "'Street' crime: a view from the left." Crime & Social Justice 10 (Spring/Summer): 26-33.

QUINNEY, R. (1979a) Capitalist Society. Homewood, IL: Irwin.

——— (1979b) "The theology of culture: Marx, Tillich and the prophetic tradition in the reconstruction of social and moral order." Union Seminary Quarterly Review 34 (Summer): 203-214.

——— (1974) Critique of Legal Order. Boston: Little, Brown.

——— (1973) "Crime control in capitalist society: a critical philosophy of legal order." Issues in Criminology 8 (Spring): 75-99.

REIMAN, J. (1979) The Rich Get Richer and the Poor Get Prison. New York: John Wiley.

ROCK, P. (1974) "Comment on Mugford." Sociological Quarterly 15 (August): 597-598.

SCHWENDINGER, H. and J. SCHWENDINGER (1979) "On the American Society of Criminology: letter." Crime & Social Justice 11 (Spring/Summer): 2-4.

——— (1977) "Social justice and the definition of crime." Crime & Social Justice 9 (Spring/Summer).

——— (1970) "Defenders of order or guardians of human rights?" Issues in Criminology 5 (Summer): 123-157.

SENNETT, R. and J. COBB (1972) The Hidden Injuries of Class. New York: Random House.

TAYLOR, I., P. WALTON, and J. YOUNG (1975) Critical Criminology. London: Routledge & Kegan Paul.

——— (1973) The New Criminology. London: Routledge & Kegan Paul.

TERKEL, S. (1975) Working. New York: Random House.

TIFFT, L. (1979) "The coming redefinitions of crime: an anarchist perspective." Social Problems 26 (April): 392-401.

TOBY, J. (1979) "The new criminology is the old sentimentality." Criminology 16 (February): 516-526.

WERKENTIN, F., M. HUFFERBERT, and M. BAURMANN (1974) "Criminology as police science or: 'how old is the new criminology?' " Crime and Social Justice 2 (Fall-Winter): 24-41.

10

PRAXIS AND RADICAL CRIMINOLOGY
IN THE UNITED STATES

Elmer H. Johnson

A radical commitment to practice consists of "practical critical activity" and participation in ongoing political struggles. ... This is a difficult task because criminologists, like intellectuals generally in advanced capitalist societies, suffer from elitism and arrogance as a result of our socialization, specialized training and privilege which insulates us from working people [Platt, 1974: 7].

This able American radical criminologist refers to the Marxist concept of "praxis" which conveys the idea of a unity between theory and practice. This essay postulates that the relationship is problematic, first, for the development of a radical criminology and, second, for the expansion of its membership in the United States.

CRITICAL THEORY AND PRAXIS

As "critical theory" Marxism challenges positivism, or "traditional theory," which is described as dealing only with the world of appearance; "reality" is the representation of experiences (symbols) through linguistic communication dominated by the values and institutions of capitalism.

Scientific activity is carried on within a division of theoretical studies at a particular stage of the development of theories. Then, science addresses human life in only one isolated sphere in its historical evolution. Rather than coming to grips with the eternal human meanings, positivism expresses the social arrangements determined by the current mode of production—capitalism at this stage of history. Unlike this "bourgeois science," critical theory pierces (or "demystifies") the "false consciousness" of the bourgeois theorist by recognizing that what is perceived as reality is a product of human activity. Yet this search for truth, uncolored by time-bound norms and values, is neither neutral nor objective (scientifically value-free). Critical theory would reconstruct society so exploitation is replaced by giving a central position to self-conscious, self-managing persons (Horkheimer, 1972: 188-243).

Running through critical theory is the theme of a unity between theory and practice. Here "practice" is used in the sense of the act or process of executing or accomplishing; "practice" is distinguished from theory. But, for critical theory, "praxis" implies the two discrete phenomena (theory and practice) are interrelated. The practical questions encountered in criminology can be clarified by theory, but this clarification must proceed through communication among members of the general public which is not controlled and inhibited by the institutionalized patterns limited to the contemporary stage of human evolution. The proletariat are to be encouraged to see that the existing order controls them against their own interests through engendering a "false consciousness" of reality. Critical theory is an instrument for revealing how official myths maintain this false consciousness. Now "liberated," the proletariat are freed to develop a new consciousness. The task of critical theory is to anticipate and apprehend the future course of human evolution, but the validity of theory can be realized only through enlightenment which leads "to the acceptance of those concerned, free of any compulsion, of the theoretically derivable interpretations" (Habermas, 1973: 37).

"Real, living human beings struggling against the oppressive conditions of capitalism," Quinney says, are essential to the "socialist revolution" he believes to be necessary to overcome the crime problem. Theory and practice must be unified, he believes. "Theory without practice not only makes bad theory but also shuts off the possibility of actual political struggle." But practice without theory would produce action undermining prospects for a socialist revolution. Quinney calls for a unity of theory and practice in a style that would not manipulate people but rather would enlighten them so they see themselves and their social situation in a new way. A new consciousness would lead them to the decision to alter conditions they then would see as repressive. Theory would be a catalytic agent (Quinney, 1977: 159-161).

ENLIGHTENMENT VERSUS STRATEGIC ACTION

As careful, precise, and intellectually diligent evaluation, Marxian thought would be as subject to Marxist critique as would any other theory which can be properly understood only by viewing it as a historic product and subject to the contradictions stemming from opposing principles within it. "A critique, then, aims at making men's potency more fully manifest," Gouldner (1973: 429) says, "so that men might then make their own history—consciously rather than blindly. But Marx also saw critique in the sense of partisan radicalism. He wrote that critique "is not a lancet but a weapon. It's object is an *enemy* which it aims not to refute but to destroy.... Criticism is no longer an end in itself, but simply a means; *indignation* is its essential mode of feeling, and *denunciation* its principle task" (Bottomore, 1963: 46).

Habermas (1973: 38-40) identifies praxis with "making men's potency more fully manifest" and disavows the instrumental employment of the Marxist critique. Instrumental employment has characterized much of the literature produced by American radical criminologists. When expressing their rage against criminal justice, they have surrendered opportunities to apply critical theory for generation of an intellectual culture through discourse outside of their own ranks. Habermas (1973: 38-40) associates "enlightenment" with praxis and finds "strategic action" undermining critical theory:

> We see that a reflexive theory can only be applied without contradiction under the conditions of enlightenment and not those of strategic action. ... When and insofar as it is successful, the organization of enlightenment initiates processes of reflection. The theoretical interpretation in terms of which the subjects come to know themselves and their situations are retrospective: they bring to consciousness a process of formation. Thus the theory that creates consciousness can bring about the conditions under which the systematic distortions of communication are dissolved and a practical discourse can then be conducted; but it does not contain any information which prejudges the future action of those concerned.

That the strategic action of those who have decided to engage in struggle, and that means to take risks, can be interpreted hypothetically as a retrospection which is possible only in anticipation, but at the same time not *compellingly justified* on this level with the aid of a reflexive theory, has its good reason: the vindicating superiority of those who do the enlightening over those who are enlightened is theoretically unavoidable, but at the same time it is fictive and requires self-correction: in a process of enlightenment there can only be participants.

STRATEGIC ACTION AND CONFLICT

Praxis as strategic action is more likely to benefit a radical cause in the short run when a nonradical constituency perceives—not necessarily accurately—a power elite applying the suppressive tactics reaching beyond political legitimacy. An examination of Kent State students involved in the 1970 protest movement indicated radicalization was promoted by exposure to extreme social control violence, such as that employed by National Guardsmen on Kent's campus (Adamek and Lewis, 1975). A radical explanation of the closing of the School of Criminology at Berkeley identifies the appearance of the "student-supported people's criminology" with the many-faceted social protest of the 1960s. The explanation also refers to "the academic repression of the radical elements within the School" (Schauffler and Hannigan, 1974).

Radical ideology assumes the absence of universal consensus and the predominance of conflict. The concurrent existence of order and conflict is recognized by most social theorists although their relative emphasis varies. Liberal ideology lends itself to the conflict approach, refuting the claim of radicals that they monopolize the approach. As a change strategy, conflict is useful in shattering the image of consensus when the image is exploited by defenders of an unsatisfactory status quo as an insulation against needed change. The deliberate use of conflict has been defended as more likely than a cooperative policy to effect desired changes, more likely to gain influence for the otherwise powerless groups, more likely to shake up ossified bureaucracy, and more likely to rejuvenate organizations by redistributing power (Schaller, 1966: 76-86; also see Coser, 1956).

However, the central difficulty with conflict is its short life; rancor and temporary emotionalism are inferior foundations for persistent cooperation essential to orderly implementation of new arrangements. Unless officials identify with the changes, the realities of policy-making and administrative practices lend themselves to the sabotage of persistent change once the heat is off. Conflict is useful in winning concessions on specific issues but risks the destruction of broad plans appropriate for a complex social system. Exacerbated partisanship may shut the protesters off from the larger community and its long-term support (Wilson, 1966: 482-483; also see Riessman, 1969: 3-15). Finally, the conflict may be directed against the wrong "enemy," one who lacks the power to remedy the conditions being protested.

In departing from science-oriented praxis, American radical criminologists have sought to gain allies through strategic action based on "anticorrectionalism." Taylor et al. (1973: 232) define the "correctional perspective" as "understanding a social phenomenon only to the point of being able to rid society of the phenomenon in question." Anticorrectionalism opposes the claimed support of criminology to the "agents of social control" (prison administrators, judiciary, social workers, and the psychiatric professionals) under the view that "pathological" individuals, undermining the preferred social order, are the source of the crime problem (Taylor et al., 1975: 7).

Anticorrectionalism breaks the theory-praxis linkage, Ainlay (1975-1976) argues, by plunging radical criminology into the "swamp of subjectivism" through avoiding criminal action, by abstaining from rigorous inquiry into the concrete nature and meaning of crime, and by aborting the process of enlightenment whereby the "false consciousness" of correctionalism would be unhinged. "Thereby separated from and opposed to the criminal domain, the radical criminologist—*as a human being*—can glorify or deplore crime (e.g., rape), but can never intervene *qua* radical criminologist."

DIFFICULTIES OF RECRUITING FOR ENLIGHTENMENT

Radical criminologists face the difficulties of all "outsider" ideologues when they engage in partisanship without the benefit of a broad issue that enlists the commitment of a significant nonradical constituency and without the benefit of suppressive tactics by the defenders of a status quo widely resented and therefore ultimately counterproductive. Deprived of these benefits, radical criminologists face the difficulties of winning broadly based support that all advocates of profound change encounter in America.

Political ideologies are characteristic chiefly of elites of various moral persuasions and intellectual preferences. The ideologues confront each other in disagreements which are only a portion of the many ideas shaping the behaviors of the much larger group of ordinary people. The bulk of Americans are issue oriented rather than being moved by an elaborate ideology applied consistently to a series of public issues.

As occupants of alien statuses in general society either by choice or exile, radicals are "outsiders" who often are able to make objective criticisms of the conventional society from which they stand apart. But the alien status and their dedication to a radical cause color their relationships with the conventional social structure and with one another. Exclusive dedication to the cause tends to isolate radicals from more conventional persons and compels them to suppress private interests, other than radical activities, such as family concerns and development of a vocational career. The intensity of this commitment, so difficult to maintain in the long run when tangible success is not forthcoming, lends cohension to radical groups, but it exacts costs in recruiting a substantial number and variety of new members. Relatively few persons are willing to suppress private interests and accept penalties imposed by opponents in the long term. Recruiting a large membership dilutes the unity of belief lending discipline to hard-core members (Kornhauser, 1962).

Liberal groups, on the other hand, demand less personal sacrifice, less intense dedication to a given political goal, and draw their strength from the involvement of members in many interest groups in their daily activities. Reform liberalism is thereby more consistent with sharing a wide spectrum of the activities and interests found in diversified urban life. It conveys a theme of enjoying these benefits personally while assuming, usually, a more limited responsibility for making this a better world. The weaknesses of reform liberalism stem from these advantages. It tends toward elitism because participation tends to be avocational. The affluent are more likely to have sufficient leisure time for investing energies in voluntary movements, whereas low-income persons are absorbed more in the struggle for survival. Reform movements are more prone to diffusiveness, sporadicness, perversion of political pluralism to the service of privileged groups, and aborted outcomes because only a fraction of participants match most radicals in the major investment of time and energies to a cause.

CONCLUSIONS

When a genuine linkage between theory and practice exists, praxis holds promise for realizing the potential of scientific Marxism for further development of theoretical criminology. Although conceptually distinct from the usual liberal conception of the need to relate theory and practice, praxis invites a detached reexamination of "value-free" theory, the relevance of "enlightenment" in "new consciousness" in narrowing discrepancies between criminal justice and contemporary mores without the narrow purposes of "strategic action," and the intellectual merits of serious Marxist scholarship. Through instrumental employment of praxis, the American radicals have tended excessively to mere exposé criminology. They have also shown signs of elitism and arrogance. However, regardless of these departures from praxis, American radicals face formidable odds against being a significant force in either criminological theory or practice.

REFERENCES

ADAMEK, R. J. and J. M. LEWIS (1975) "Social control violence and radicalization: behavioral data." Social Problems 22 (June): 663-674.

AINLAY, J. (1975-76) Review of Taylor, Walton and Young, *The New Criminology* and *Critical Criminology*. Telos 26: 213-225.

BANKOWSKI, Z., G. MUNGHAM, and P. YOUNG (1977) "Radical criminology or radical criminologist?" Contemporary Crises 1 (January): 37-52.

BOTTOMORE, T. B. [ed.] (1963) Karl Marx: Early Writings. London: C. A. Watts.

COSER, L. A. (1956) The Functions of Social Conflict. New York: Macmillan.

GOULDNER, A. W. (1973) For Sociology: Renewal and Critique in Sociology Today. New York: Basic Books.

HABERMAS, J. (1973) Theory and Practice. Boston: Beacon.

HORKHEIMER, M. (1972) Critical Theory: Selected Essays. New York: Seabury.

KORNHAUSER, W. (1962) "Social bases of political commitment: a study of liberals and radicals," pp. 321-39 in A. Rose (ed.) Human Behavior and Social Process. Boston: Houghtin Mifflin.

PLATT, A. M. (1974) "Prospects for radical criminology in the United States." Crime and Social Justice 1 (Spring-Summer): 2-10.

QUINNEY, R. (1977) Class, State and Crime. New York: David McKay.

RIESSMAN, F. (1969) Strategies Against Poverty. New York: Random House.

SCHALLER, L. S. (1966) Community Organization: Conflict and Reconciliation. Nashville, TN: Abington.

SCHAUFFLER, R., and M. HANNIGAN (1974) "Criminology at Berkeley: resisting academic repression, Part 2." Crime and Social Justice 2 (Fall-Winter): 42-45.

TAYLOR, I., P. WALTON, and J. YOUNG [eds.] (1975) Critical Criminology. London: Routledge & Kegan Paul.

——— (1973) The New Criminology. New York: Harper & Row.

USEEM, M. (1972) "Ideological and interpersonal change in the radical protest movement." Social Problems 19 (Spring): 451-469.

WILSON, J. O. (1966) "Planning and politics. Citizen participation in urban renewal," in R. L. Warren (ed.) Perspectives on the American Community. Chicago: Rand McNally.

11

"LEFT-WING" CRIMINOLOGY—AN INFANTILE DISORDER?

Steven Spitzer

Criticism has plucked the imaginary flower from the chain not so that man will wear the chain without fantasy or consolation, but so that he will shake off the chain and cull the living flower.

—Karl Marx

Every cop's a criminal and all the sinners saints.

—The Rolling Stones

In the end, glorification of splendid underdogs is nothing other than glorification of the splendid system that makes them so.

—Theodor W. Adorno

On June 12, 1920 the book *'Left-Wing' Communism—An Infantile Disorder* was published. This work, inaugurating the Second Congress of the Communist International, represented one of Lenin's many attempts

AUTHOR'S NOTE: Some of the ideas contained in this essay were presented at the Third National Conference on Critical Legal Studies, November 1979.

to shape the direction and clarify the motives of revolutionary socialism. The major targets of Lenin's attack were the European, particularly German and British, opposition movements which sought to build social-ism without any compromises with or participation in existing structures of power (i.e., bourgeois parliaments, reactionary trade unions, and so on). In developing his criticism of the "childish" opponents of compromise, Lenin (1971: 552) argued that:

> One must be able to analyse the situation and the concrete condi-tions of each compromise, or of each variety of compromise. One must learn to distinguish between a man who has given up his money and fire-arms to bandits so as to lessen the evil they can do and to facilitate their capture and execution, and a man who gives his money and fire-arms to bandits so as to share in the loot.

I have not chosen the title of this essay to suggest that radical crimi-nology is seriously flawed by its unwillingness to compromise with the practical demands of political life under capitalism, although an argument of this sort has indeed been convincingly made by Mankoff (1978). I would like, rather, to raise the entire question of "left-wing" criminology's ability to *both* compromise with and provide an alternative to ideological, oppressive, and instrumentally defined varieties of criminological theory and research. Since I am raising this issue as a "friendly" critic, that is, one who wishes to strengthen rather than undermine the accomplishments of critical forms of criminological work, I shall avoid taking either of the two most popular, and I believe least fruitful, paths toward the condemnation of radical criminology. The first of these paths has been adopted by those who seek to defend the virtues, methods, and purposes of mainstream criminology from conservative, moderate, or liberal positions. Some of the scholars contributing to this volume have doubtless traveled down this path. The second critical direction which I wish to distinguish from my own is embodied in the objections of orthodox Marxists to the very concept and practice of a "Marxist" or "radical" criminology.

Since the points of attack adopted by those who defend the "honor" and scientific legitimacy of conventional criminology are relatively well known, I shall restrict my comments at this juncture to those intended to clarify what separates my vantage point from the dismissive tack taken by some other Marxist critics.

The dismissive forms of Marxist criticism are best exemplified by the work of two analysts operating outside the American context—Paul Q. Hirst and Stephen K. Mugford. In Hirst's view (1972: 29):

> There is no Marxist theory of deviance; either in existence, or which can be developed within orthodox Marxism. Crime and deviance vanish into the general theoretical concerns and the specific scientific object of Marxism. Crime and deviance are no more a scientific field for Marxism than education, the family, or sport. The objects of Marxist theory are specified by its own concepts: the mode of production, the class struggle, the state, ideology, etc. Any attempt to apply Marxism to this pre-given field of sociology is therefore a more or less 'revisionist" activity in respect of Marxism; it must modify and distort Marxist concepts to suit its own pre-Marxist purpose.

Mugford (1974: 595), following much the same reasoning, concludes:

> Although it may be possible in some senses to radicalize criminology by taking the side of the underdog, if as Marxists we wish to go further, to ask how the positions of ruler and ruled, overdog and underdog, are produced and relate to each other, then we will produce an analysis of power—both economic and political. Such a further step leads inevitably to moving beyond what is—including the existence of "laws" and of "crimes"—and thus must lead to the dissolution of the subject area. There thus can be no Marxist criminology. Criminologists who thus turn to Marxism are caught in a paradox which is probably insoluble. Marxists who turn to criminology are making a serious theoretical—and hence political—mistake.

The attitudes adopted in these attempts at "purification" are not unlike those of a religious fundamentalist who is horrified at the prospect of "deviations" from his reading of the sacred texts. To an extent, this orthodoxy is based on an Althusserian bifurcation between the early and mature (i.e., idealist and materialist) portions of Marx's work and a judgment that the former is somehow peripheral to the core of Marx's theoretical contribution. In addition it represents an attempt to decompose, through a type of theoretical *legerdemain,* all superstructural forms (i.e., religion, politics, law, family, art, and so on) into the economic nuclei from which they are assumed to directly spring-forth.[1] While few Marxists would argue against the importance of anchoring the analysis of superstructural forms in a consideration of the class structure and production relations of a society, the Hirst-Mugford position forces us to dissolve all noneconomic relations into "pure" economic categories. Not only does this perspective support a kind of "knee-jerk" economism which is acceptable to only the most vulgar of materialists, it also introduces a rigidity into Marxist theory which is both misleading and unnecessary. While there are clearly many ways, as we shall see, in which radical criminology has been limited and deformed by its habit of clinging to the agenda laid down by the predefined "field of criminology," it is also true that the substance of radical criminology cannot be discredited merely because it addresses topics which are somehow "extraeconomic" in their form or "ideological" in that they take as their starting point concepts (e.g., crime, deviance, and so on) which misrepresent the "true" relations between classes and the "real" laws of economic organization. What Marx opposed was not the study of bourgeois (i.e., ideological) forms, but the confusion of those forms with the underlying reality of capitalist life. We have no more right to expunge the study of crime from Marxist scholarship then we have to abolish critical investigations of music, art, religion, sports, the family, education, or politics. To dismiss all studies which begin at the level of superstructure as "revisionist" is to demand a type of intellectual lock-step which is neither true to Marx's own method nor likely to bring about an understanding of bourgeois society on which all efforts to achieve socialism must ultimately be based.

In evaluating the propriety of studying crime and its control as superstructural forms, much can be gained by examining exactly how Marx approached another superstructural phenomenon—religion. Marx defined religion as a "fantastic reality." Commenting on this reflection, Caudwell (1971: 17-18) pointed out that for Marx religion was:

> *Fantastic* because the statements it makes about existents are incorrect, because the ideas of outer reality incorporated in it do not correspond with outer reality. *Real* because these ideas are causally linked with material reality, and are not only determined but also determine in their turn exerting a causal influence on their matrix. Thus by acknowledging that religious ideas are not spontaneous but form part of active reality, Marxism is able to analyse more deeply the real causes which produced them. The analysis of religion becomes also an analysis of society.

If we substitute the word "crime" for "religion," it is clear that there can be a Marxist criminology insofar as "the analysis of crime becomes also an analysis of society."

What I intend to do in the analysis that follows is to delineate the specific ways that "left-wing" criminology can and cannot be considered an infantile disorder. I will begin by examining the major weaknesses of radical criminology with a constructive purpose in mind. To wit: rebuilding faulty foundations, redirecting theoretical energies, and disentangling questionable lines of inquiry and reasoning. Through this effort I hope to demonstrate that even though there are many features of Marxist-oriented criminology which were and continue to be hampered by "growing pains" and "errors of excess," this body of work cannot be rejected *tout court*. In order to demonstrate why I feel so little of the criticism which has been made is constructive, I shall also briefly consider some of the major points of misunderstanding surrounding the differences between Marxist and positivist methodologies as they have been applied to the study of crime and its control.

RADICAL CRIMINOLOGY RECONSIDERED

In 1874 Frederick Engels (cited in Lenin, 1971: 552) proclaimed: "What childish innocence it is to present one's own impatience as a theoretically convincing argument." Indeed, it is possible to suggest that most of the problems attending the birth and infancy of radical criminology have grown out of its profound impatience with the stagnation, narrowness, and self-righteousness of traditional criminological thought. Because it was so anxious to break free from the suffocating assumptions and methods of the "old criminology," the focus, shape, and theoretical directions taken by the new criminology were as much a product of what it was trying to leave behind as what it was looking toward. Considering the political events surrounding its birth, the hostility of the context within which it first breathed life, and the brevity of the period during which its theoretical and methodological groundwork was first laid, it is hardly surprising that the most important limitations, distortions, and excesses of the new criminology surfaced in precisely those areas where it was most intent on rejecting and leaving behind the old.[2] Like the new boy on the block who tries to prove his mettle by bloodying the noses and discrediting the boasts of the "toughest guys," the new criminology was sometimes more interested in rapidly destroying the old than in carefully identifying and demonstrating the virtues of the new. Assuming that bourgeois criminology could only see its subject ideologically, that is, through a camera obscura which projected the real character of crime in society "upside down,"[3] it was logical for the new criminologists to proceed through an inversion of what was most sacred in criminological thought. In consequence, the very definition of what was "new" in criminological theory came to be forged, in many instances, through an abstract and simplified reversal of the "worst" that the old criminology had to offer.[4]

In the eyes of the radical criminologists, the "diseased core" of conventional criminology consisted in its conception of society as consensual, its assumption that law was emergent rather than imposed (the social contract theory), its inattention to economic structure, and its commitment to or at least acquiescence in the view that "criminals" (legally defined) should be the essential target of all efforts at amelioration of or responses to "the crime problem." Each of these touchstones of bourgeois ideology, because of their long-standing role in legitimating the exploitation and oppressiveness of bourgeois society, became a *bête noire*—a collection of "false idols" which had to be pulled down before the seeds of the new criminological enterprise could take root in fresh intellectual soil. In their eagerness to "demystify" the conceptions of crime, law, and criminal justice and root out the hypocrisy of bourgeois criminological theory, the proponents of the new criminology followed the course of least resistance— the course which consisted in turning these core assumptions on their head. Thus, even before it had become a bona fide "tendency" in criminological thought, the new criminology was painting a portrait of capitalist society as hopelessly conflict-ridden, law as a tool of the ruling class, and existing criminological theory as nothing more than an apologia for the exploitation of the underdogs by a capitalist elite. Moreover, since the "criminal classes" were seen as victimized by the supercilious and/or "zookeeper" attitudes (Young, 1970) cultivated by bourgeois criminology, the vindication of these classes came to depend on a kind of "moral inversion": A redefinition of the underdogs as a progressive force in the struggle for human liberation and a castigation of the ruling (capitalist) class as the "real" criminals.

Whatever truth may have been contained in these "counter-images" of bourgeois society and its crimes, the important point is that these images were not developed and applied as part of an independent and ongoing critique of bourgeois society in general. They represented, rather, an *internal* form of rebellion from and opposition to the bourgeois study of crime. In this sense, the "antidote" that was concocted by the new criminology was integrally linked to the very "disease" it was intended to cure. Thus, because capitalist society was assumed to "need" social order, the radicals took pains to point out that it actually "needed" crime; because the law was assumed to be free-floating above classes and mediating innocuously between economic interests, the radicals emphasized the ways in which the law was no more than a cudgel in the hands of economic and political elites; and because the "criminals" were invariably defined as those at society's depths and margins, the radicals sought to demonstrate that the worst might really be the best and that capitalist society and its institutions should be the real target of criminology's investigative energies and moral scorn. In each case, the major excesses of radical criminology—its metafunctionalism, instrumentalism, and romanticism of illegality—grew out of attempts to defeat conventional criminological wisdom from within. In what follows we shall explore each of these weaknesses and try to understand how they have prevented radical criminology from taking a genuinely critical path.

METAFUNCTIONALISM

Among the major targets of those who have criticized the old criminology are the consensus assumptions upon which may of its explanations are based. The willingness of mainstream criminology to depict societies as holistic, unitary, organic phenomena whose institutional components (i.e., the family, polity, economy, law, and so on) are functionally integrated into a single interlocking unit has been frequently called into question by the new criminologists. These criticisms have been organized around objections to the functional paradigm (see Chambliss, 1976)—a perspective which interprets crime as either a cause or an effect of social disorganization and the breakdown of normative regulation and crime control as a necessary "corrective" which restores the system to equilibrium. The ideological and theoretical weaknesses of the functional view of social life and social problems are well known (see Mills, 1943; Gouldner, 1970; Liazos, 1972; Allen, 1975), but the specific contours of the theory of crime which is intended to take its place are not. These alternatives seem to suffer from one of two deficiencies: They are either inadequately developed and therefore "vulgar" or oversimplified in a way which recapitulates the errors of the very explanations which the new criminologists have tried to transcend. More specifically, it appears that in many instances the attack on the "holism" of the old criminology has been launched from the battlements of a new holism—an explanation based on a hypostatization of either capitalism as an international system, capitalist society, or "the capitalists" as a socially definitive group.

In their effort to persuade us that society is characterized by conflict rather than consensus and that the unity of bourgeois society is merely an illusion, the new criminologists have sometimes gone too far in the opposite direction. By giving capitalism a reality apart from the concrete conditions out of which it grows, these critics have unwittingly *reified* the forces which are organized within and through the workings of the capitalist system. The problem in linking capitalism to crime is not that capitalism is falsely accused, but that in their eagerness to assign greater responsibility to capitalism for its "crimes" the new criminologists have sometimes imputed a "phantom objectivity" (Lukacs, 1971) and rationality to their nemesis. Capitalism is thus seen as "needing" crime in order to justify its oppression of the masses in much the same way that "society" is conceived by the structural-functionalists as needing law and crime control to integrate and coordinate its increasingly differentiated parts (see Bredemeier, 1962). In those cases where the structure of crime or crime control is seen as arising from the "functions" that they perform for the capitalist system "as a whole," it is possible to sustain a sense of neatness and simplicity. But this streamlined conception of capitalist oppression is clearly at odds with both the Marxian perspective on dialectical development and the realities of conflict in capitalist life. As I have argued elsewhere (1977), it is only when we rip capitalist societies from their historical context and ignore the contradictory features of their organization that we can assume a functional unity or teleology in their development. To the extent that the new criminology has been willing to settle for schematic, formalized, and ahistorical assertions about the relationship between the whole of society and its many parts, it has easily degenerated into a mechanical form of metafunctionalism—a formula which explains all features of a society by their consequences for the "capitalist system." On the other hand, where historical context and dialectical relationships have been emphasized (see Hay, 1975; Spitzer and Scull, 1977; Spitzer, 1979; Hall et al., 1978) we can more easily appreciate how crime and its control are *both* functional and dysfunctional for capitalism at specific points in its historical development and within specific sociocultural environments. By recognizing that the relationships between capitalism and crime are always shaped by a particular configuration of historical and cultural conditions, we can remove many of the "automatic" features of the new criminology's conclusions, "loosen" the functional relationship between the whole and its parts (see Greenberg, 1976) and increase our sensitivity to the ways in which the parts also "determine" the whole.

INSTRUMENTALISM

The problems of metafunctionalism which we have just discussed are not only associated with the positing of a "capitalist system"; they also find expression in those explanations which emphasize the instrumental and conspiratorial dimension of crime control. As Rock (1974: 144-145) has argued in a somewhat different context:

> Although there are exceptions, it is most difficult to discover ... a description of legislation and rule-making which embodies more than an anthropomorphic conspiracy theory. There is little conception of history. If the social contract was not imposed today, it was certainly imposed in the recent past. The contract conceived by the deviancy theorist contains a pristine set of vested interests which have not lost their immediate connections with a dominating elite. The perspective offers no understanding of law as a complex and variegated rule-system whose origins were frequently mysterious to elites as to governed. It offers no vision of a legal system as a series of constraints upon law-giver and ruled alike. ... The law-giver is an Olympian figure endowed with a rationality, an innocence of unintended consequences, and a clear self-interestedness.

Much of the problem outlined by Rock would seem to be based on the new criminologists' uncritical acceptance of an instrumentalist theory of the state.[5] This theory defines the state "in terms of the instrumental exercise of power by people in strategic positions, either directly through the manipulation of state policies or indirectly through the exercise of pressure on the state" (Gold et al., 1975: 34). The problems with this perspective as formulated by Gold et al. (1975: 35) are that (1) "there is no systematic analysis of how the strategies and actions of ruling-class groups are limited by impersonal structural causes"; (2) it fails to take into account the significance of struggles and conflicts of interest both within the state itself and between the state and the class that it ostensibly represents; and (3) "there are important realms of state-related activity which are clearly not manipulated by specific capitalists or coalitions, such as culture, ideology and legitimacy" and these realms "possess a degree of autonomy which tends to place them outside the realm of simple manipulation." In fact, it might even be argued that the effectiveness of criminal justice functionaries as agents of class rule and as representatives of the capitalist legal order depends, at least in part, on the ability of the state to act with a certain degree of independence from the narrow interests of capitalist elites. In an important critique of "the conspiracy theory of criminal law"? Steinert (1977) has pointed out that for the state to truly serve the logic of capital accumulation and protect capitalist interests *as a whole,* it must "step out of the competition between capitalists" and "have a certain amount of independence from capital and its factions." In other words, because of its relative independence and autonomy "the State cannot be collapsed back into, and 'read' as if *directly* expressive of the narrow class interests of a particular ruling group. It is not, except in a mediated form, the 'executive committee of the ruling class' " (Hall et al., 1978: 205).

In stressing the "functional" contribution of crime control to the maintenance of capitalist rule and that this control is tightly tied to "the repressive needs of the system as a whole" (Center for Research on Criminal Justice, 1975: 11), the new criminologists sometimes attempt to understand the whole of society's reaction to crime in terms of its immediate functions for the ruling class. But this connection is developed at the cost of reducing all variations in the structure and organization of crime control to the competitive interests and activities of two specific groups: the capitalists and the working class. While it is certainly true that the intentions and actions of these groups will have an important impact on the form and content of crime control in capitalist societies, by ignoring the complex and changing structural context within which these relationships develop and unfold, the instrumentalists cannot move beyond an interest-group model of social order and social change. From their perspective, when expenditures in criminal justice increase, it is related to the "use-value" of criminal justice workers in maintaining domestic order, making society safe for capital accumulation, and protecting class relations (Quinney, 1977). And since it is assumed that "the instruments of force and coercion are on the side of the capitalist class," resulting in the fact that "much of the activity of the working class struggle is defined as criminal" (Quinney, 1977: 59), the analysis of crime and crime control is narrowed to the arena of class struggle.[6] By limiting their viewpoint in this way the instrumentalists have exaggerated the political side of the political-economic matrix. The problem with this orientation is not simply that it ignores underlying economic relationships and contradictions which bind the criminalizers more or less firmly to their repressive roles, but that it forces us to reconstruct an understanding of their behaviors and "functions" entirely through the prism of political interests and activities. A Marxist conception of criminalization in capitalist society cannot be developed by limiting our investigation to the relationships between the policies and procedures of criminal justice agencies on the one hand, and the interests and "needs" of the capitalist class on the other. To the contrary, it depends on our understanding that all coercive institutions in class societies are surrounded and shaped by a framework of material relationships, conditions and conflicts within which these political arrangements and interests emerge.

THE ROMANTICISM OF ILLEGALITY

As should be clear from the discussion thus far, radical criminology too often assumes that a theory of crime can be developed entirely from a more limited theory of control. Starting with the assumption that the criminal class is created because of its threat to the capitalist system, the new criminologists frequently lead us to believe that this threat is therefore revolutionary in nature. But according to Marx, the class which represents the most fundamental threat to capitalism is not the "criminal class," but the proletariat; and Marx is extremely careful to distinguish the two. The proletariat, because of its special relationship to the means of production, is the only class which is capable of challenging capitalism and engineering the transformation to socialism. Far from representing a proto-revolutionary vanguard, Marx and Engels viewed the criminal classes as "the natural enemies of any disciplined and principled workers movement" (Hirst, 1972: 41).

Instead of attempting to clarify the differences between the criminal and revolutionary classes in capitalist society, the new criminologists are sometimes willing to gloss over those differences because they equate the struggles around "criminalization" with class conflict. This perspective reflects what Lukacs (1971: 263) has called the *romanticism of illegality:*

> By surrounding illegal means and methods of struggle with a certain aura, by conferring upon them a special, revolutionary "authenticity," one endows the existing state with a certain legal validity, with a more than just empirical existence. For to rebel against the law *qua law,* to prefer certain actions *because* they are illegal, implies for anyone who so acts that the law has retained its binding validity.

The motives, perceptions, and activities of the underclass are more than forms of rebellion against oppression; just as the motives, perceptions, and activities of the ruling class are more than simply justifications, rationalizations, and self-serving strategies which support and extend oppression. Crime must be understood dialectically as *both* a protest against and an expression of the conditions of oppression. In other words, we need to appreciate the ways in which "crime" and "criminals" sustain, reproduce, and directly promote the very conditions of oppression and exploitation to which they are assumed to represent a "revolutionary" response. To endow ordinary crime with revolutionary "authenticity" is to both remove the criminal from the structural sources of his crime and confuse isolated acts of rebellion, "striking out," and "putschism" with purposive collective work. Without denying that under certain conditions crime may contain the germ of revolutionary consciousness,[7] we must also be aware of the ways in which it creates barriers to attaining any real consciousness of and reaction against the working class's collective plight.

One reason why the new criminology may shy away from a study of the sources of crime in favor of studying the sources of criminalization is that such a focus might give bourgeois criminology an ontological validity which it does not deserve. By giving serious attention to the causes of "ordinary crime," even if those causes are located in the structure of capitalist society, it is feared that the new criminology will slip into the habits and pitfalls of the old. But until we are willing to take the problem of crime causation in capitalist society seriously (see Greenberg, 1977), begin developing a social psychology of crime under capitalism, and realize that crime is much more than a mirror image of control, we have little hope of breaking through the antinomies that have plagued both conventional and Marxist efforts to understand crime.

FROM POSITIVISM TO MARXISM: A NOTE ON METHOD

One reason why new and old criminologists so frequently talk past one another is that they operate with widely different conceptions of what constitutes the "correct" way of studying crime and its control. Behind these methodological disagreements lie important points of divergence in the domain assumptions (Gouldner, 1970), epistemological positions, (Horkheimer, 1974), and philosophical traditions (Taylor, 1966) embraced by each group. By briefly exploring some of these differences in methodological perspective it will be possible to suggest not only why Marxist analysis is so widely misunderstood, but also why it seems to represent such an "unscientific" approach to the investigation of crime in capitalist society.[8]

Facts and Values. It is commonly assumed by many critics of Marxist criminology that it suffers from an unwarranted intrusion of values and "wishful thinking" into the study of the "facts" of crime in society. However, this criticism fails to recognize that for Marx and those who seek to follow his method it is impossible to achieve a watertight separation between "facts" and "values." While most positivists operate within a philosophical universe in which values may be parsed from facts and held in abeyance while "scientific" investigation proceeds, for Marx all knowledge which we generate about the world must bear some relationship to our needs and purposes. Thus, it is impossible to separate judgments and evaluations from what we know, and any attempt to do so inevitably involves some form of self-deception. In Ollman's (1971: 48) words:

> It is not simply that the "facts" affect our "values," and our "values" affect what we take to be the "facts"—both respectable common sense positions—but that, in any given case, each includes the other and is part of what is meant by the other's concept. In these circumstances, to try to split their union into logically distinct halves is to distort their real character.

A number of conclusions about the study of crime seem to flow from these assumptions about the relationship between facts and values. First, there is no way we can "factor out" values from facts. The facts we generate about crime are directly conditioned by and derive their meanings from the values which we carry into our pursuit of "the facts." To assume that facts about crime can be "cleansed" of their evaluative features is to forget that crime is an endemically social phenomenon and that all such phenomena can only be understood as "facts" through the prism of our attitudes, interests, and motives.

Second, we must be aware that what we choose, therefore, to study as "the facts of criminology" will invariably predispose us to express and support certain interests and ignore, suppress, or condemn others. To place the study of crime on an Olympian peak of "science" and to decry all deviations from "scientific" procedures, language, and technique is to ignore the necessary connection between the immediate technical purposes of our inquiry and the larger social context within which that inquiry takes place. By proceeding as if it were possible to identify a set of "facts" which criminology can objectify, isolate, and manipulate to find the "truth" about crime, positivism only succeeds in severing the study of crime from the very relationships which enable us to understand it sociologically. The "facts" about crime which are discovered by positivist empiricism are thus the product of a false concreteness—"a concreteness isolated from the conditions which constitute its reality" (Marcuse, 1964: 107).

Finally, in studying crime in a way which we take to be "useful" we are far from engaged in a "value-neutral" process. Because of the connection between information about and power over our social environment (Lehman and Young, 1972), whenever we generate "useful" rather than "idealistic" or "utopian" facts we are necessarily contributing to the maintenance of some existing structure of power and beliefs.[9] And as long as the criteria defining "usefulness" are subject to the control of those who provide resources and encouragement to study crime "as it is," we can be sure that the "facts" we produce will be selected and distributed *within* rather than outside of the dominant structure of ideas and values about and "solutions" to the crime problem. Because it recognizes the interpenetration of facts and values, the Marxist perspective forces us to be sensitive to the ways in which the very facts we study have been prepackaged, predigested, and preselected, as well as the differing implications of studying certain sets of "facts" rather than others.

The Meaning of Objectivity. As Moore (1966: 522-523) has pointed out:

> There is a strong tendency to assume that mild-mannered statements in favor of the *status quo* are "objective" and that anything else is a form of "rhetoric." This type of bias, this misinterpretation of objectivity, is the one most common in the West today. It confuses objectivity with triviality and meaninglessness. ... Any simple straightforward truth about political institutions or events is bound to have polemical consequences. It will damage some group interests. In any society the dominant groups are the ones with the most to hide about the way society works. Very often therefore truthful analyses are bound to have a critical ring, to seem like exposures rather than objective statements, as the term is conventionally used.

If, as Moore suggests, we assume that what we know is not available to us as a freely circulating commodity in a marketplace of facts and concepts, but that it is structured, distorted, and sanitized to protect certain structures of interest and forms of privilege, then "objectivity" clearly requires a concentrated and persistent effort to get behind what we normally take to be "the facts." From this perspective, a study can only be objective and therefore scientific if it is able to *penetrate* the appearance of social phenomena and discover their essence. As Marx (1958: 797) argues, "All science would be superfluous if the outward appearance and the essence of things directly coincided." It is this lack of coincidence which forces the Marxist investigator to doubt the "objectivity" of the obvious and search for the truth by burrowing beneath the "hard facts."

In contrast to the prevailing view in empiricist positivism, this position sees science as the work of uncovering essences, as "primarily concerned with those major relations which are not open to direct observation; it is a matter of extending the ties between entitites, conceived of as internally related to one another, further than we do in ordinary life" (Ollman, 1971: 65).

Because of this attitude toward "objectivity," much of Marxist analysis is easily perceived to be tendentious and polemical rather than cautious and balanced. But it is precisely this lack of caution and balance—as distinguished from hollow rhetoric and sloppy reasoning (see Stinert, 1978)—which is necessary to the success of the Marxist enterprise. This does not mean, of course, that simply because an interpretation is disputatious it is necessarily correct. What it does mean is that before we either accept or reject the truth claims of any statement or conclusion we must examine the precise way in which those claims are related to the distribution of power and privilege in the society in which they are put forth.

Furthermore, because of their binary perception of facts and values, positivists are likely to confuse objectivity with detachment. In addition to its other defining characteristics, objectivity requires that one maintain intellectual honesty in the face of disturbing or contradictory evidence (see Gouldner, 1975). To be detached, however, is to abdicate one's responsibility to assess, interpret, and place that evidence in its social and political context. For a Marxist scholar there is no way one can be objective while remaining disengaged from the phenomenon under scrutiny.

Plausibility Versus Proof. The positivist method tries to provide a way of choosing between alternative interpretations by establishing a hierarchy of exclusions; its objective is to arrive at a "proof" by excluding incorrect interpretations. This kind of pinning-down strategy inevitably leads to a miniaturization of focus and a freezing of social process. From the point of view of Marxian method, this approach is more likely to obfuscate than reveal what is really going on.

As the study of crime has become more "scientific" it has involved a greater and greater reliance on utilizing "controls" to remove the effects of "extraneous" variables and "purify" the search for truth. These controls have been of two sorts—*explicit* and *implicit*. Explicit controls are used when a researcher tries to control or "hold constant" background factors which he feels may contaminate his ability to identify the salient causal relationships. He may therefore try to control such factors as age, sex, race, and social class. But in trying to hold these factors constant the researcher inadvertently diverts attention from the structural features of the society which may be far more important than the lower-level relationships he chooses to explore. However, insofar as this type of exclusionary procedure is explicit, it is potentially capable of correction. A far more subtle, and therefore more difficult to correct form of "tightening down" or "cleaning up" a study involves implicit controls. Thus, when studies are done within a single police or judicial district, among a single "class" of criminals, or at a single point in time, not only is the researcher limiting his or her ability to generalize about other organizational systems, classes of criminals, points in time, and societies, but he or she is actually removing what may be the decisive explanatory factor from consideration. This exclusion is implicit whenever the researcher proceeds as if the truth can only be grasped by studying the specific parts or moments of social structure and social process without attention to the larger whole. In these cases variables become "extraneous" without conscious or purposive manipulation by the researcher, but they are effectively removed nonetheless.

Instead of trying to "prove" a given theory by trying to progressively eliminate confounding variables, and in the process giving more and more attention to detail and less and less to the whole, most Marxist investigations seek *empirical plausibility*: being able to demonstrate the logical connections among phenomena and over time which can be described concretely. While the search for plausibility rather than proof by no means guarantees the discovery of "truth," the ability to understand social phenomena like crime "relationally" rather than atomistically enables Marxist critics to appreciate the reality of crime in a way which avoids the pitfalls of searching for a definitive positivist proof.

The Dialectical Method and Its Limits. One of the central features of Marxist methodology is its commitment to the logic of dialectical inquiry. A dialectical analysis of crime and its control focuses on the internal tendencies and contradictions of class society which give rise to the "crime problem," societal reactions to crime, and the interaction between the two. The major advantage of the dialectical perspective over other approaches to crime and social change is that it encourages us to understand crime as growing out of the *simultaneous* operation of stabilizing and destabilizing elements at a specific historical juncture. By approaching the study of crime dialectically, the Marxist investigator is able to understand why "specific institutions serve progressive roles in some situations and regressive roles in others," and why we must always study "stable social structures ... with reference to the elements which undermine them, and social change with reference to its constraints" (Johnson, 1976: 90).

The problem with applying the dialectical method in criminological investigations is not that it is inherently biased or limited, but that it is incorrectly viewed as a basis for "scientific" predictions and control. As Ollman (1971: 60) points out:

> When used for predictions, the dialectic can never be shown wrong, only foolish and worthless. If the synthesis predicted does not occur, it is easy to change to another synthesis—what is to stop one?—or to talk of a time lag. Like a balloon, when hit in one place, it bulges out in another. The real fault lies in harnessing the dialectic for predictive purposes in the first place. The same kind of difficulty arises when the dialectic is used to prove something. There is no way of getting agreement on what constitutes the thesis, the anti-thesis and the synthesis in any given problem, even among people who claim to view the world dialectically. Marx himself does not share in this guilt. He never rests a proof on the grounds that an entity is the "negation of the negation," or says some particular event must happen because "spiral development" requires it.

If, when viewed through positivist lenses (see Chiricos and Waldo, 1977; Horwitz, 1977), the dialectic is forced to represent itself as a precise scientific instrument rather than a useful sensitizing device, it is hardly surprising that forms of dialectical analysis can be accused of tautology, teleology, and theoretical sloppiness. While positivist critics are concerned that Marxists have used the dialectic to stand on both sides of the theoretical fence and avoid the implications of their own "predictions," these same critics fail to recognize that for those who understand these problems dialectically "the fence does not exist" (Ollman, 1971: 26). As long as opponents of Marxists criminology continue to endow its methods with content and purposes they do not have, it will be extremely difficult to move beyond the pattern of "scientific" one-upsmanship from which all intellectual progress and communication in criminology currently suffers.

Quantiphobia. The Marxist approach rejects the notion that the only phenomena that are worth studying are those subject to precise quantification. This does not mean that all Marxists are quantiphobic; only that "the so-called facts ascertained by quantitative methods, which positivists are inclined to regard as the only scientific facts, are often surface phenomena that obscure rather than disclose the underlying reality" (Horkheimer, 1974: 82). Moreover, by confusing observability and operationalizability with "validity" and forgetting that the very concept of "fact" is a product of social alienation, the positivists glorify "the facts" in a way which denies the penetrative (critic) function of scientific inquiry. To dismiss the

Marxists who have studied crime as "idealists" and "millenarians" (Klockars, 1979), is, ironically, to idealize the "real world" and to flatten out the dynamic tension between the "is" and the "ought to be." In practice, while Marxists who study crime and crime control are willing to quantify when necessary (see Greenberg, 1979b), they are continually wary of the "fetishism of measurement" and the abuses that can be committed in the name of doing "scientific" as opposed to other types of research. It is not quantiphobia, but rather the pretensions of positivism which have turned radical criminology away from what has become an article of faith of empiricist sociology—the facile equation of measurement and symbolic manipulation with scientific truth.

EPILOGUE

For all except those who continue to mindlessly finger the positivist rosary, there can be little doubt that traditional criminology, in both its liberal and conservative forms, is theoretically moribund. The stunning supernovas that first appeared on the criminological horizon have long since suffered one of two fates: They have either exploded into fragmentary and self-contained solar systems of "social reinforcement," "interactionist," "dramaturgical," "deterrence," and "conflict" theory or imploded into enormous "black holes," extracting both creative energy and public resources from those who remain prepared to believe in the "correctional" capacity of an uncorrectable system. Just as light and matter seem to vanish when they venture beyond the black hole's point of no return, many of the most important insights, discoveries, and critical directions in understanding crime and its control have been neutralized, sanitized, or even completely obliterated as they continued to be absorbed into the ever-growing void of theory-free criminology. If, as the most popular explanation has it, captive stars which are caught in black holes can reappear in another part of the universe or in a different cosmos, then we have reason for hope. But this hope cannot be turned into a genuine source of political resistance and theoretical vitality by slogans and criticism alone. It must depend, in the final analysis, on the willingness and the capacity of "critical" criminology to provide a grounded, sophisticated, and accessible body of research findings—findings which will give substance to the claim that criminology can go beyond the limitations of its origins; that it can become, in other words, one of the forces operating *against* the "technology of subjection" (Foucault, 1977) which has become such an integral feature of the attempts to solve the problems and contain the contradictions of modern capitalist life. The way in which radical criminology responds to this challenge will determine whether it will break out of the integument of its infantile origins or simply become yet another symptom of the very disorder which it seeks to cure.

NOTES

1. One possible source of this type of economic reductionism, at least for readers of the Moore and Aveling English translation of *Capital,* is the incorrect rendering of the German *sich widerspiegelt* as "reflex." For example, as Wood (1972) points out, Moore and Aveling translate the phrase "this juridical relation [of exchange] . . . is a relation of wills in which the economic relation is mirrored [*sich widerspiegelt*]" as "this juridical relation . . . is a relation of two wills, and is but the reflex of the real economic relation between the two." Wood (1972: 252) notes that "this translation suggests that the juridical relation is like a knee-jerk produced by an economic hammer-tap, or the mechanism of a Pavlovian dog emitting juridical saliva in response to economic stimuli. Such an impression is entirely the result of mistranslation, and has nothing to do with Marx's view of the matter."

2. For a brief discussion of some of the contextual factors surrounding the emergence of radical criminology at Berkeley see Platt (1974). I realize, of course, that this argument applies with much more force to the United States than to other areas (e.g., Britain) where a tradition of Marxist scholarship was far more firmly entrenched.

3. The "camera obscura" model of ideology which appeared in Marx's early writings was later abandoned in favor of a more sophisticated view. For a discussion of Marx's maturing conception of ideology from the 1844 manuscripts to *Capital* see Lichtman (1975).

4. For a discussion of some of the differences between the English and American varieties of "inversion" and "antithetical" logic, see Ainlay (1975-1976).

5. This section is based on a more focused discussion of policing in Spitzer (1980).

6. For a more complete discussion of some of the problems in Quinney's *Class, State and Crime,* see Greenberg (1979a).

7. The problem of understanding the relationship between crime and class consciousness is put into its proper social-psychological perspective by Wilhelm Reich (1972: 294):

> If two human beings, A and B, are starving, one of them may accept his fate, refuse to steal, and take to begging or die of hunger, while the other may take the law into his own hands in order to obtain food. A large part of the proletariat, called *Lumpenproletariat,* live according to the principles of B. We must be clear about this, although we certainly do not share the romantic admiration of the criminal underworld. Which of the two types has more elements of class consciousness in him? Stealing is *not yet* a sign of class consciousness; but a brief moment of reflections show despite our inner moral resistance, that the man who refuses to submit to law and steals when he is

hungry, that is to say, the man who manifests a will to live, has more energy and fight in him than the one who lies down unprotesting on the butcher's slab. We persist in believing that the fundamental problem of a correct psychological doctrine is not why a hungry man steals but the exact opposite: Why doesn't he steal?

Two additional questions need to be posed by Marxist criminology: Under what conditions is a crime an impediment as well as a basis for class consciousness? Why does the criminal steal rather thn engage in other forms of aggressive rebellion against his conditions of oppression?

8. The following discussion is greatly indebted to the arguments presented by Ollman (1971), Moore (1966), and Lehman and Young (1972).

9. The positivist attack on "utopian" perspectives in Marxist criminology is itself on shaky ground. As Horkheimer (1974: 91) has noted, "the positivist command to conform to facts and common sense instead of to utopian ideas is not so different from the call to obey reality as interpreted by religious institutions, which after all are facts too."

REFERENCES

AINLAY, J. (1975-1976) "Review of *The New Criminology* and *Critical Criminology.*" Telos 26 (Winter): 213-225.

ALLEN, V. L. (1975) Social Analysis: A Marxist Critique and Alternative. London: Longman Group.

BREDEMEIER, J. J. (1962) "Law as an integrative mechanism," pp. 73-88 in W. Evan (ed.) Law and Sociology. New York: Macmillan.

CAUDWELL, C. (1971) Studies and Further Studies in a Dying Culture. New York: Monthly Review.

Center for Research on Criminal Justice (1975) The Iron Fist and the Velvet Glove: An Analysis of the U.S. Police. Berkeley, CA: Center for Research on Criminal Justice.

CHAMBLISS, W. J. (1976) "Functional and conflict theories of crime: the heritage of Emile Durkheim and Karl Marx," pp. 1-28 in J. J. Chambliss and M. Mankoff (eds.) Whose Law, What Order? New York: John Wiley.

CHIRICOS, T. G. and G. P. WALDO (1977) "Reply to Greenberg, Hopkins and Reasons." American Sociological Review 42 (February): 181-185.

FOUCAULT, M. (1977) Discipline and Punish: The Birth of the Prison. New York: Pantheon.

GOLD, D. A., C.Y.H. LO, and E. O. WRIGHT (1975) "Recent developments in Marxist theories of the capitalist state." Monthly Review 27 (October/November): 23-43/36-51.

GOULDNER, A. W. (1975) "The dark side of the dialectic: toward a new objectivity." Sociological Inquiry 46: 3-15.

––– (1970) The Coming Crisis of Western Sociology. New York: Avon.

GREENBERG, D. F. (1979a) "Review of *Class, State and Crime: On the Theory and Practice of Criminal Justice.*" Crime and Delinquency 25 (January): 110-113.

––– (1979b) Mathematical Criminology. New Brunswick, NJ: Rutgers University Press.

——— (1977) "Delinquency and the age structure of society." Contemporary Crises 1 (April): 189-223.

——— (1976) "On one-dimensional Marxist criminology." Theory and Society, 3: 610-621.

HALL, S., C. CRITCHER, T. JEFFERSON, J. CLARKE, and B. ROBERTS (1978) Policing the Crisis: Mugging, the State, and Law and Order. London: The Macmillan Press.

HAY, D. (1975) "Property, authority and the criminal law," pp. 17-63 in D. Hay et al. (eds.) Albion's Fatal Tree: Crime and Society in Eighteenth Century England. New York: Pantheon.

HIRST, P. Q. (1972) "Marx and Engels on law, crime and morality." Economy and Society 1 (February): 28-56.

HORKHEIMER, M. (1974) Eclipse of Reason. New York: Seabury.

HORWITZ, A. (1977) "Marxist theories of deviance and teleology: a critique of Spitzer." Social Problems 24 (February): 362-363.

JOHNSON, B. (1976) "Taking care of labor: the police in American politics." Theory and Society 3: 89-117.

KLOCKARS, C. B. (1979) "The contemporary crises of Marxist criminology." Criminology 16 (February): 477-515.

LEHMAN, T. and T. R. YOUNG (1972) "From conflict theory to conflict method-ology." Presented at the 67th Annual Meeting of the American Sociological Association.

LENIN, V. I. (1971) Selected Works. New York: International Publishers.

LIAZOS, A. (1972) 'The poverty of the sociology of deviance: nuts, sluts and preverts." Social Problems 20 (Summer): 103-120.

LICHTMAN, R. (1975) "Marx's theory of ideology." Socialist Revolution 23 (April): 45-76.

LUKACS, G. (1971) History and Class Consciousness. Cambridge, MA: MIT Press.

MANKOFF, M. (1978) "On the responsibility of Marxist criminologists." Con-temporary Crises 2 (July): 293-302.

MARCUSE, H. (1964) One Dimensional Man. Boston: Beacon.

MARX, K. (1958) Capital (3 vol.) S. Moore and E. Aveling (trans.) Moscow: Progress Publishers.

MILLS, C. W. (1943) "The professional ideology of social pathologists." American Journal of Sociology 49: 165-180.

MOORE, B., Jr. (1966) Social Origins of Dictatorship and Democracy. Boston: Beacon.

MUGFORD, S. K. (1974) "Marxism and criminology: a comment on the symposium review of 'The New Criminology.'" Sociological Quarterly 15 (Autumn): 591-596.

OLLMAN, B. (1971) Alienation: Marx's Conception of Man in Capitalist Society. New York: Cambridge University Press.

PLATT, A. M. (1974) "Prospects for radical criminology in the United States." Crime and Social Justice 1 (Spring-Summer): 2-10.

QUINNEY, R. (1977) Class, State and Crime: On the Theory and Practice of Criminal Justice. New York: David McKay.

REICH, W. (1972) Sex-Pol: Essays, 1929-1934. Lee Baxandall (ed.). New York: Vintage.

ROCK, P. (1974) "The sociology of deviancy and conceptions of moral order." British Journal of Criminology 14: 139-149.

SPITZER, S. (1980) "The political economy of policing," in D. F. Greenberg (ed.) Crime and Class: Essays in Marxian Criminology. Palo Alto, CA: Mayfield.

――― (1979) "The rationalization of crime control in capitalist society." Contemporary Crises.

――― (1977) "On the Marxian theory of social control: a reply to Horwitz." Social Problems 24 (February): 364-366.

――― and A. T. SCULL (1977) "Social control in historical perspective: from private to public responses to crime," pp. 281-302 in D. F. Greenberg (ed.) Corrections and Punishment. Beverly Hills, CA: Sage.

STEINERT, H. (1978) "Can socialism be advanced by radical rhetoric and sloppy data? Some remarks on Richard Quinney's latest output." Contemporary Crises 2 (July): 303-313.

――― (1977) "Against a conspiracy theory of criminal law a propos Hepburn's 'social control and the legal order.' " Contemporary Crises 1 (October): 437-440.

TAYLOR, C. (1966) "Marxism and empiricism," in B. Williams and A. Montefiore (eds.) British Analytical Philosophy. London: Routledge & Kegan Paul.

WOOD, A. W. (1972) 'The Marxian critique of justice." Philosophy and Public Affairs 1 (Spring): 244-282.

YOUNG, J. (1970) "The zookeepers of deviancy." Catalyst 5: 38-46.

12

SOME PROBLEMS OF CREDIBILITY IN RADICAL CRIMINOLOGY

David Shichor

INTRODUCTION

Writing about broad-scale intellectual trends always poses the problem of generalization and the blurring of differences among ideas presented by various proponents of a certain viewpoint. No doubt this is the case also with regard to radical criminology.[1] As Klockars (1979) points out there is not only one version of Marxism or neo-Marxism, and obviously this diversity is reflected in the criminological theories based on these ideological viewpoints. This chapter deals with some issues that radical criminologists are focusing on, and with some theoretical and empirical problems that may raise doubts about the credibility of their claims.

There is a growing trend in the field of criminology to focus on the analysis of social control and the nature of crime in Western capitalist societies. This trend, which is reflected in radical criminology, shifted the attention of many social scientists from the search for causes of criminal behavior to a concern with definitions of crime and the processes of

AUTHOR'S NOTE: I would like to thank Solomon Kobrin for his remarks on an earlier version of this chapter.

criminalization (Nettler, 1978). This changed focus on the methods of social control and particularly on the criminal law and criminal justice agencies contrasts with the emphasis of "mainstream" criminology on the behavior of criminals and on factors leading to criminal involvement. Radical criminologists also place criminological study forthrightly into the political spectrum by emphasizing the political and socioeconomic context of social control. While it has considered the social structural defects as having a major role in crime causation, mainstream liberal criminology has maintained that they can be corrected by social reform (Gibbons, 1978). Radical criminologists criticize this view on the grounds that it is basically a conservative stance since it does not challenge seriously the status quo, but indirectly supports it.

Whether this is in fact the case deserves analysis.

THE NATURE OF THE LAW

Radical criminology, according to some of its adherents is

founded on the Marxist approach to social reality, understanding social life in relation to the underlying mode of production and class struggle. This criminology mainly focuses on the relation of the economic system to the production of crime [Quinney, 1979: 26].

Radical criminologists define crime differently than mainstream criminologists. The widely accepted legal definitions are rejected by them since they claim that the law is not objective but is designed to protect the interest of the ruling class which controls the means of production, and to maintain the existing social order.

Radicals see as a starting point the notion of human rights to self-determination, dignity, food and shelter, and freedom from exploitation, or crimogenic systems, such as imperialism, racism, capitalism and sexism, because they promote inherently repressive relationships and social injury [Klein and Kress, 1976: 36].

Others include among these rights also the right to employment, "safe working conditions, child care, education, housing, medical care" (Schwendinger and Schwendinger, 1976: 10). Michalowski (1976: 38) contends that criminologists should focus their study on social harms. He holds that criminology should be "a science of social harms . . . concerned with the adequacy of social systems in meeting human needs." This focus would bring into the scope of criminological study socially harmful forms of behavior, such as capitalist exploitation, imperialist relations, and violation of human rights. It is notable that the human rights mentioned by radical criminologists are quite different from those considered as basic in Western capitalist societies, such as freedom of religion, speech, and the press, search and seizure, habeas corpus, due process, and so on. In other words, the concept of human rights espoused by radical criminologists differs from those accepted by large segments of American society. This statement may well elicit a counterclaim by radical criminologists. The idea of the existence of a consensus regarding basic values in capitalist society is widely challenged by radical criminologists. The challenge is particularly strong with respect to their view of the function of law. The major contention of radical criminologists is that law is legislated by the ruling class or its representatives to maintain and protect their interests.

For example, Chambliss (1975: 152) states: "Acts are defined as criminal because it is in the interests of the ruling class to so define them." Therefore,

> critical criminology examines the enactment and enforcement of law as an oppressive force utilized in a capitalist society to promote and stabilize the existing economic-class relations. The law maintains order, but it is an order imposed upon the powerless by the powerful [Hepburn, 1977: 77].

Similarly, Quinney talks about the "demystification of the criminal law" which is, according to him "used by the state and the ruling class to secure the survival of the capitalist system" (Quinney, 1973: 95).

The problematic nature of these contentions has been pointed out by several scholars, and has been widely criticized.

One problem concerns the concept of the "ruling class." In Marxist theory a social class is not only an "aggregate of people who are merely situated identically" in terms of economic or power relations, they also must, beyond the "identity of interest," participate "in political conflicts as organized groups" (Dahrendorf, 1957: 24-25).

Consequently, one line of criticism is leveled against the oversimplification of the character and function of law presented by the radical view. The critics claim that the power structure is much more complex in capitalist societies than it is described by radical criminologists (Gibbons, 1978). The emergence of criminal law in complex societies is portrayed as a compromise among powerful interest groups (Carson, 1974). This view is stated succinctly in the following:

> Powerful groups are generally portrayed as operating virtually without constraint, never as being forced to make concessions to chal-

lenging groups or as being forced to act contrary to short-run interests so as to maintain legitimacy by responding to the expectation of a public. The role of law in regulating conflicts among members of the propertied classes has been ignored just as completely as the problem of crime within the working class [Greenberg, 1976: 612].

A similar view is voiced by Hagan and Leon (1977), who point out that conflicts often occur between government bureaucracies and private industries, although both are considered to be a part of the ruling class. Radical criminologists using a monolithic model of "ruling class" do not attempt to specify the various situations and conditions under which one interest group prevails and becomes the major representative of the "ruling class."

The problematic nature of the radical class-oriented approach is pointed out also by some Marxist criminologists.

It is not necessarily true, however, that all forms of crime originate directly in the problems confronting a particular class, even if class is defined in the flexible manner I propose. The dynamic functioning of a class society leads to social differentiation along many lines other than class and the resulting differences in experiences, opportunities and costs may have great relevance for criminal involvement. The contribution of Marxism is to view such differentiation as the product of relations of production and reproduction, rather than as an a priori given [Greenberg, 1977: 216].

Another related issue which raises some questions is whether criminal law protects only the interests of the ruling class or the powerful? Critics of radical criminology point out that the

general assumption underlying the whole argument seems to be that a capitalist social formation is distinguished by the fact that all and everything that goes on in it is in the immediate interest of the ruling "capitalist elite" [Steinert, 1977: 439].

However, several scholars (Gibbons and Garabedian, 1973; Gilham, 1978; Klockars, 1979) point out that there seems to be an overwhelming consensus on the relative seriousness of most common crimes in the United States. This consensus seems to exist also in cross-cultural perspective among quite diverse societies such as India, Indonesia, Iran, Sardinia, Yugoslavia, and the United States, as found in Newman's (1976) study.

The standard answer to this claim offered by radical criminologists is that the consensus which considers "street" crimes to be the most serious ones is an outcome of the false consciousness of the socially and economically powerless, who do not recognize their real enemy. This argument is difficult to refute. It is used as a ready answer to diverse problems, and as an "explanatory factor" concerning a wide range of issues.

There is also a lack of sensitivity to the fact that there are differences among various capitalist societies (see, for example, Mankoff, 1978). Taking the United States as the embodiment of capitalist society does not contribute to the understanding of the crime problem either. It does not explain why in countries like England, France, Sweden, Norway, or New Zealand violent crimes are not as frequent as in the United States. Indeed, in some they probably do not exceed the crime level of socialist regimes.

The use of such a "catchall" explanatory concept may raise doubts about the credibility of the radical approach.

CRIME CAUSATION

A related issue which opens radical criminology to criticism and raises problems of credibility is their unicausal perception of crime. They claim that crime is clearly attributable to the capitalist socioeconomic system in which the means of production are concentrated in relatively few private hands, which inevitably results in exploitation.

Buchholz et al. (1974: 29) point out that according to the Marxist approach:

Criminality is explained as a social phenomenon by the limited state of productivity of human society and the resultant form of production in the shape of man's exploitation of man, as reflected in the private ownership of the means of production. This private ownership produces selfishness and individualism as the basic pattern of social behavior in man. From private ownership inevitably springs alienation, conflict between individuals and an antagonism between individual and society.

This explanation assumes that the abolition of the capitalist socioeconomic system would result in the abolition of crime. It is clearly stated by Quinney (1973: 16) that "only with the collapse of capitalist society and the creation of a new society, based on socialist principles, will there be a solution to the crime problem."

Accordingly, "socialism presumably is to be accompanied by the decline and eventual disappearance of social malformations" (Mankoff,

1978: 297). Would this mean that in countries which have a socialist socioeconomic system there will not be murders, rapes, thefts, embezzlements, and a host of other crimes? But so far in socialist countries the abolition of crime has not become a reality. This fact is obviously a disturbing one for radical criminologists since, as Hollander (1969) points out, while in capitalist countries crime can be explained relatively easily, explaining criminal behavior in socialist countries is not a simple undertaking. Interestingly, these societies use "bourgeois" explanatory concepts such as faulty socialization (Shichor, 1979) "to solve their crime and deviance problems, because such approaches never seriously question basic political and economic institutions" (Mankoff, 1978: 297).

Ample use is made of this explanation in socialist regimes for example:

> Soviet theorists propose that the ultimate course of deviance is rooted in the inability of the character education system to prevent individuals from falling into the clutches of a capitalist mentality. . . . This "inability" is due to the presence of defects in the major socialization agencies and in the failure of these agencies to coordinate their efforts [Cullen and Cullen, 1977: 404].

Similarly, in the explanation of juvenile delinquency in Cuba the major etiological factors mentioned are: broken homes, poverty, unemployment, lack of schooling, and faulty socialization (Loney, 1973). In China, according to Brady (1977) there are two major trends in viewing crime; the conservative bureaucratic approach views criminality as

> caused by individual character disorders, or by the influence of "counter-revolutionary elements" remaining from the "old society."

On the other hand, the progressive "popular justice" model regards most crimes

> as extreme expression of broad social contradictions which extend to the non-criminal public. The offender, then, is not usually "sick" or "counter-revolutionary"; but he/she offends because of "backward social attitudes" [Brady, 1977: 137].

In order to become more knowledgeable about the problems of criminality in socialist societies, there would be a need for a radical analysis "using the same concepts to uncover the contradictions of socialism that have been so artfully utilized in discovering those of capitalism" (Mankoff, 1978: 297). Bottomore (1972) points out that there are historical examples of failures of socialist social arrangements in the twentieth century, and the analysis of "what can go wrong with the efforts to create a more equal, less coercive type of society" (Bottomore, 1972: 4) could be an important one for radical criminologists. But while these suggestions seem to be logically sound, they are not followed by radical criminologists because of their heavy ideological commitment to the criticism and abolition of the capitalist social system and the idealization of the Marxist social alternative. Their failure to conduct this kind of analysis is one of the strongest criticisms against radical social scientists, and it raises serious questions regarding their credibility.

THE ROLE OF THE CRIMINOLOGIST

Related to the previous discussion is the radicals' criticism and their negation of liberal reform attempts. These attempts, according to radical criminologists, lead to "correctionalism," are a plot of "liberal practicality," (Taylor et al., 1973), and are basically supportive of the existing capitalist social system.

> Piecemeal reform efforts, when applied to social issues such as crime, racism, poverty, or mental illness, support the myth that progress and improvement can occur without major restructuring of the social order. . . . The standards of practicality are always taken from those who rule and who wish to preserve their status quo [Krisberg, 1975: 18].

As has been seen, radical criminologists believe that only a revolutionary change can alter the capitalist socioeconomic and political system. This position categorically excludes gradual or small-scale change; compromises by definition are eliminated. Compromise is the hallmark of liberalism.

Since reforms do not solve the real problems, they serve only to make life more palatable under the capitalist system. They therefore pacify the exploited masses and strengthen the capitalist system. This contention points to a serious dilemma which cannot be dismissed easily. Even if this argument has some merit, should it deter criminologists from trying to improve the lot of the socially, politically, and economically less powerful? Would not this radical doctrine imply the increased victimization of the "underdogs" in the short run for the abolition of their (or their descendents') oppressed status in the long run?[2]

Connected with this issue is the self-image of the radical criminologists as political activists which corresponds with the "praxis" concept of Marxist ideology. "Praxis" is conceived as revolutionary action necessary for the transformation of society through the growing class awareness of the proletariat (Giddens, 1971). It also means that there is a need of unity between theory and practice for the successful abolition of the capitalist system. "Marxist criminology," according to Quinney (1977: 162) is "allied to the popular struggle against capitalist oppression and for the creation of a socialist society." Habermas (1973: 2) points out that it is a "political praxis which consciously aims at overthrowing the existing system of institutions." Following this line, the role of the criminologist should be similar to that of a political activist, putting into practice the theoretical principles of radical criminology (Meier, 1976). The "radical commitment to practice consists of 'practical critical activity' and participation in ongoing political struggles" (Platt, 1975: 105). This implies that political action becomes the major function of the criminologist.

The strong political commitment of radical criminologists precludes tolerance toward alternate types of theorizing or intellectual endeavors. Tolerance is regarded as the hallmark of liberalism; it is said to be a conservative concept and supports the status quo (Wolff, 1965; Marcuse, 1965). In capitalist regimes tolerance "is turned from an active into a passive state, from practice to non-practice: laissez-faire the constituted authorities" (Marcuse, 1965: 82). The radical negation of tolerance is "a kind of epistemological imperialism" (Rock, 1973: 595) and rejects the concept of "academic freedom." It also might reveal a lack of confidence in one's ideas, on the one hand, or a superiority complex in knowing the "absolute truth," on the other. In this vein, Bankowski et al. (1977: 44-45) point out that

> the final arbiter and guarantor of knowledge for radical criminology is to be the individual theorist: in effect the theorist can never be wrong. It is he or she who is to evangelically pursue the notion of socialist diversity and it is he or she who will define the criteria of the acceptability of claims to knowledge. The unity of theory and praxis will be both defined by, and depend for validity on, the enlightened morality of the individual radical criminologist as he lays down the nature of freedom and justice for the working-class. It is indeed a strange conception of radicalism that conceives of the possibility of knowledge only in the souls of liberated criminologists!

Interestingly, the negative and even hostile attitude toward tolerance does not prevent radical criminologists from complaining against "academic repression" in American universities (Platt, 1975). Others claim that the research funding agencies and the publishing industry impede empirical research and the publication of the work of radical criminologists. Regarding publications, if we try to judge from the volume of published professional literature by radical criminologists, this claim seems to be less than well founded. Regarding research, as seen, the virtual absence of empirical work among radical social scientists can be traced mainly to their extremely strong emphasis on ideology:

> As Marxism already contains some fundamental propositions about the character of modern capitalism, the revolutionary role of the working class, the more or less necessary transition to a socialist society, it may well appear, from an extreme ideological and dogmatic Marxist perspective, that research into such matters is otiose [Bottomore, 1972: 3].

Another factor which also weighs heavily in the empirical orientation or the lack of it on the part of radical social scientists is their strong future orientation. A radical social scientist

> must try to discern those trends and movements, in the present, which seem likely to bring about a future social transformation, and he has to be concerned, in part, at least, with sketching the characteristics of institutions which do not yet exist. Thus, radical thought has, inevitably, a more speculative character, and it is less easy to embody in programs of research [Bottomore, 1972: 4].

As seen earlier, Bottomore points out that these considerations cannot satisfactorily justify the neglect of empirical research. Another strong reason for the lack of empirical research is the deep "contrapositivism" characterizing radical criminologists. This tendency is seen mainly in their opposition to quantitative research. Giddens (1975: 3-4) talks about "positivistic attitude" in sociology which includes the following connected assumptions:

> (1) That methodological procedures of natural science may be directly adapted to sociology. . . . (2) That the outcome or end-result of sociological investigations can be formulated in terms parallel to those of natural science. . . . (3) That sociology has a technical character, providing knowledge which is purely "instrumental" in form.

Radical criminologists not only question these premises but like the phenomologists (e.g., Schutz, 1963), or the students of the sociology of knowledge (e.g., Mannheim, 1936), actively join the attack on them mounted by Gouldner (1962) and others (e.g., Hoult, 1968). Their attack is directed especially against the "value-free" assumption of "science" because, according to them, it is conservative and supports the capitalist status quo, since it inhibits criticism by professionals who study social problems and have the intellect and tools to understand them. Taylor et al. (1975: 28-29) admit that in the near future empirical radical research very likely will be minimal since there is a debate among radical criminologists concerning "the appropriate and correct departure points for research (away from liberalism and into praxis)."

They criticize "radical empirical research" on the "propertied nature of crime in propertied societies," on the grounds that this kind of research ends up in an empirical analysis of the same official records which are deemed to be biased by the capitalist ruling class. Thus, the right way to conduct radical empirical research is materialist criminology. This is based on Marx's method according to which "one should understand legal relations as originating in the material production of society" (Taylor et al., 1975: 48). But while they go into a lengthy analysis to prove the appropriateness of this method for radical empirical research, they claim that this kind of research will not be conducted in the foreseeable future. Another reason for this negative attitude toward empirical research might be due to the fact that "there is no absolute standard of rightness/wrongness which can be articulated and applied at the empirical level" (Turk, 1979: 466). However, radical criminologists tend to claim absolute rightness of their approach and opinion. This claim immediately raises questions about radical criminology or radical criminologists: Are they incompetent empirically? Are they afraid of the possible findings? Or, is it simply easier and more "profitable" to write ideological treatises than to get involved in painstaking research?

"RELIGIOUS" DEVOTION AND "LIBERATION"

Radical criminologists exhibit a religious devotion to the Marxist ideology and an almost total belief in the "goodness" of socialist society which eventually as seen will be a crimeless society and will lead to the liberation of mankind.

In this spirit, the Schwendingers claim that since violent crimes (including rape) were produced by capitalism, it can be alleviated only by changing "the class system of oppression in America today to a socialist political economy and a relatively crime-free tomorrow" (Schwendinger and Schwendinger, 1974: 25). Similarly the East German criminologists Buchholz et al. (1974) make the point that

> by establishing a socialist society we have made a start on abolishing the barriers created against humanity in man-to-man relations by private ownership, so that individuals can now gradually lose the habit of unproductive destructive conflict between themselves, as manifest in criminality.

As Turk (1969: 12) succinctly summarizes Bonger's contentions: "Capitalism causes crime; socialism will ultimately eliminate it."

This approach thus reveals a deterministic belief in the crime-producing nature of capitalist society, and an almost exclusive attribution of crime causation to the institution of private ownership.

Again there are some issues of credibility which arise. First, by claiming that the removal of economic exploitation will eliminate the main cause of crime, this approach is reductionist and simplistic. It is the monolithic doctrine of social etiology of crime (see Radzinowicz, 1966). It demands that people believe in the doctrine because it is a matter of faith in a utopian future. Since it is not proposed as a theory, which would suggest refutable propositions (probably this would indicate "conservative" positivism), the only possibility of acceptance of this claim remains in the domain of a belief system. It demands a religious devotion to the belief that the abolition of the capitalist state and the creation of a social system based on Marxist principles will lead to a crime-free society. This may be a plausible assertion for some, just as would be the alternative assertion that if people follow God's ways there would be no crime. While religion according to Marx "is the opium of people" in capitalist society, Marxism can be conceived of as a form of religious faith among people in socialist societies. Second, radical criminologists also base their criticism of capitalist society on the comparison of that system with an "ideal type" of socialist system (Akers, 1979). They promise "a new and better world" (Nettler, 1978: 211). Their contention is that socialist revolution will secure the basic human rights (see their concept of these rights earlier in this chapter) for everyone and "there will be no reason for the coercive state to exist" (Nettler, 1978: 211). Some of the radical statements in this respect are quite illuminating. For example, Taylor et al. (1973: 282) in the concluding sentence of their book state that the task of radical criminology, is "to create a society in which the facts of human diversity, whether personal, organic or social, are not subject to the power to criminalize."[3]

Young (1975: 90) talks about the socialist goal as creating

a socialist culture which is diverse and expressive—that is, a culture
which takes up the progressive components in pluralism, whilst
rejecting those activities which are directly the product of the
brutalizations of existing society. . . . This involves a fight on two
fronts: first, against the existing class society; and, secondly, against
those tendencies within the socialist movement and the working
class which would gravitate towards a strictly economistic interpretation of the socialist revolution. . . . Capitalism is successful in creating a rubric of personal repression to which individuals do adapt:
and hence it is clear that great resistance will occur against the
achievement of a diversive and expressive society. There will, indeed,
be a "fear of freedom."

Unfortunately, it is not very clear how this socialist culture would become
diverse in reality. So far, one of the major characteristics of societies which
have espoused socialist ideology is their monolithic character. They repress
vigorously tendencies toward cultural diversity which, by definition, is
based on tolerance and is "liberal" in nature.

Quinney promises a global society where the "state," which has the
power to criminalize, will cease to exist and in which will prevail "the true
socialist values of cooperation, equality, participatory democracy, and
freedom" (Quinney, 1973: 188). He also states that the "socialist vision is
one of human liberation" (1973: 189). In comparison with the "ideal"
socialist system, capitalist society appears unjust, and oppressive. However,
a more realistic comparison would be between the actual social arrangements as they presently exist. When this comparison is made, the picture is
quite different. Societies which have embraced the Marxist ideology as a
model for establishing a social system tend to be totalitarian, ruled by a
much smaller and more closed elite than capitalist societies. The criminal
law and its enforcement in these regimes seem much more strikingly than
in capitalist societies to serve the ruling group in its effort to sustain its
power. The definition of crime remains in the hands of this small closed
ruling elite which has an exclusive grip on political power. For instance, in
the Soviet Union

Marxism-Leninism legitimates a view of elite and masses as unequal
in the clarity of their perception of social reality. The leadership,
with a monopoly over the interpretation of the ideology, has typically seen itself as the guide, the instructor, the educator of the
masses [Connor, 1972: 253].

There exists in such societies a phenomenon of "overcriminalization" of
dissident political activity which is controlled by the criminal law and its

enforcement machinery (Berman, 1972). A rigid control of dissidence is accompanied by an "overpoliticization" of crime in the sense that "conventional" criminal activity (mugging, stealing, and so on) is often defined as subversion since it endangers the stability of the political system (Shichor, 1978).

The claim here is not that every political regime based on Marxist ideological premises will necessarily become a totalitarian one, but that so far this has tended to be the case. Radical criminologists do point out that these societies are only in the process of building a truly socialist system and they have not arrived at that stage of development as yet. Therefore, the criticism of their accomplishments on this account is not fair. This situation seems to contribute to the fact that very few references are made by radical criminologists to the character of social control in socialist societies. For example, only China and Cuba are mentioned briefly in this vein. Quinney extols the use of popular justice in these countries since the state as the primary source of social control is fated to be abolished (Quinney, 1977).

> These institutions protect and solidify the working class against internal and external class enemies, as well as against elitist bureaucratic tendencies in the state apparatus.

But he and others neglect to mention possible excesses of these kinds of institutions, such as those which occurred during the "cultural revolution" in China.

In a recent review of Quinney's *Class, State and Crime: On the Theory and Practice of Criminal Justice,* Greenberg (1979: 112-113) states succinctly:

> It is evident that Quinney neglects crime and repression in societies he considers—on what basis is unclear—as socialist. This omission permits him to avoid the embarrassing questions their existence poses for someone who urges socialist revolution as an instant cure for both crime and repression. Thus the author who advocates a critical approach to crime and legal order appears as insufficiently critical of his own received orthodoxy.

The features of religious belief, missionary zeal ("praxis") the striving for and the promise of socialist liberation are highly apocalyptic, resulting in a gross neglect of the faults and blemishes in the social control systems of existing socialist regimes. These create a strong credibility gap between the claims, premises, and promises of radical criminology on the one hand, and the possible outcome of their real application on the other.

CRIME AND REVOLUTION

An additional problem area which creates controversy and confusion is related to the view of those radicals who see crime as an expression of revolutionary activity against the capitalist socioeconomic system (for example, Werkentin et al., 1974; Davis, 1971).

This mode of reasoning can be traced to the tautologous conclusion that criminal law is political, therefore the violation of it is a political act.[4] However, this simplistic view (a matter of doctrine in the socialist countries)[5] has been revised and given a more sophisticated version. It became obvious that to claim that every mugging in capitalist societies is a political protest, does not promote radical claims, particularly when the principal victims of those acts are poor lower-class people. One of the major claims advanced by some radical criminologists as seen before is that the socioeconomic conditions created by the capitalist system have a dehumanizing effect on people and that therefore they commit these kind of crimes. This reasoning is in line with "selective determinism" which implies that

> only the behavior of "underdogs" is socially determined that only people assigned to such groups are not in full control of their lives and behavior [Hollander, 1973: 148].

Interestingly, there are some radical criminologists who attack "mainstream" explanations on the ground that they are deterministic in nature. For instance, Taylor et al. (1973: 128) in their criticism of the "differential association" theory point out that according to that approach

> the individual does not choose a type of behavior because it has meaning to him—he is merely "templated" with the meanings prevalent in his social environment.

This explanation in a sense takes away from the ability of the individual to choose consciously to violate the laws of the capitalist system. As seen, radical criminologists use similar reasoning in their explanations of lawbreaking by lower-class people. In other words, deterministic explanation is acceptable when it serves the radical argument.

One attempt to break out of this bind is to adopt the Marxist distinction between two types of lower-class people in capitalist societies: the proletariat—the industrial working class; and the *lumpenproletariat*—the surplus population who do not work. (One of the contradictions of capitalist society is that it cannot provide work for everyone.)

According to the Marxist ideology, the proletariat, the exploited productive industrial working class, is the bearer of the socialist revolution.

This social class has the potential of developing a class consciousness based on their real interests, and the political and organizational power to mobilize (Giddens, 1975: 37). On the other hand, there exists the *lumpenproletariat,* a mass of socially and economically powerless people who have no legitimate position in the capitalist system vis-à-vis the system of production (Anderson, 1974: 129-130). These people have no real "class consciousness." As is known, Marx and Engels (1947) saw them as the scum of the earth. They are a

> parasitic class living off productive labor by theft, extortion and beggary, or by providing "services" such as prostitution and gambling, their class interests are diametrically opposed to those of the workers. They make their living by picking up the crumbs of capitalist relations of exchange, and, under socialism they would be outlawed or forced to work.... They are open to the bribes, blandishments of the reactionary elements of the ruling classes and the state; they can be recruited as police informers and the armed elements of reactionary bands and "special" state forces [Hirst, 1972: 41].

The members of this class commit most of the street crimes, victimizing mainly other lower-class people. Street crime is

> an important aspect of demoralizing social relations and individualistic ideology that characterize[s] the capitalist mode of production at its highest stage of development [Platt, 1975: 33].

Lumpenproletariat is a segment of the population whose "principal means of support is the labor of the productive class, and its relationship to the proletariat is therefore inherently parasitic" (Franklin, 1970: 14). While this surplus population is a necessary product of the capitalist economic system, it is found to be dangerous and tightly controlled by the agencies of social control (Spitzer, 1975; Bonomo and Wenger, 1978).

Marxist ideology claims that the social revolution leading to the socialist system will be carried on by the proletariat, the industrial working class. However, as Bonomo and Wenger (1978: 9) point out, there are some radical thinkers who believe that the *lumpenproletariat's* false consciousness, "characterized by egoism and an apolitical nature," can be inherently progressive since basically it weakens the capitalist system. They also believe that the *lumpenproletariat* can be revolutionized by the alteration of their false consciousness. One of the goals of the praxis propagated by radical criminologists is to achieve this effect. So far they show little success in this endeavor.

The question to be raised is how it may be determined which crimes under what circumstances are "progressive," supporting the desired social change inducing class struggle, and under what categories of crimes what conditions are antiprogressive.

Currie (1974: 112) states that

> a main task of Marxian theory of deviance is to uncover the conditions in which "deviance" becomes politically progressive and those in which it doesn't; the conditions in which deviance represents the beginnings of conscious political action, and those in which it is simply the action of people ground down by a system they neither understand nor challenge.

It is suggested by radical criminologists that this definition can be made on the basis of "consciousness" since that is what gives the purpose to human action.

> If criminally defined behavior becomes a conscious activity in the organization of workers, including the organization of those who are unemployed (in the surplus population), then crime attains a political and revolutionary character [Quinney, 1977: 99-100].

This approach raises a number of problems. How is political class consciousness determined? For example, if Eldridge Cleaver (1968), after reading Marx, Lenin, and others, arrived at the conclusion that fighting white supremacy (ruling class) is best done on his part by raping white women (he first practiced on black girls in order to refine his technique), would these actions be considered *lumpen* deviance or working-class revolutionary protest? If they would qualify for revolutionary status, then the problem is that since Cleaver at the height of his rapist career was a member of the surplus population, would his revolutionary rhetoric qualify him for a designation as a member of the "revolutionary proletariat" (how about a "honorary" membership?)? If his activities are considered as a reflection of *lumpen* involvement, what is the justification for that? He supposedly had a strong class consciousness.

Other concerns can be raised regarding this issue. It is known that in many Western capitalist societies, particularly in the United States, members of the working class are among the most conservative segments of society. They have seemingly absorbed capitalist norms and values probably more than other strata. This situation is clearly seen as a matter of "false consciousness" by radical criminologists. Since their successful cooptation by the capitalist system, they are most concerned with law and order, perhaps because their vulnerability to criminal victimization. There seems to be a much higher propensity for fascist and racist responses to social problems from this class than for radical class struggle. They seem to prefer their condition of "relative deprivation" coupled with the promise of potential upward mobility of capitalist society rather than the lower living standards and lack of personal freedom offered by the countries which are in the socialist transformation stage. In fact, it seems to be that many people from the "classless" socialist countries would be ready to choose that option also if they would be permitted to. In fact, this is an indication that "flase consciousness" pervades the working classes not only in capitalist systems, but also in societies which embraced socialist ideology.

The tendency of the late sixties and early seventies of certain prisoner groups composed particularly from minorities, to declare themselves as political prisoners, made the issue of the revolutionary nature of crime even murkier. The members of these groups were clearly from the surplus population, but in the prison (and seldom before that) they adopted a revolutionary stance, or a "political consciousness." The question still remains to be answered: To what degree is this transformation a "permanent" politicization rather than a temporary rationalization motivated at least partially by gaining "respectability" and political support among middle-class radicals (e.g., students, the "lawyers guild," and so on).[6]

This kind of "politicization" can be seen also as a rationalization or prisoner's self-justification (Emery, 1970), an attempt to support a "positive" self-esteem, rather than participating in a basically revolutionary action. Even the demands of these movements can hardly be perceived as revolutionary. In his analysis of the Attica riots Hawkins (1976: 77) points out:

> When one looks at the riots in American prisons in recent years their most surprising feature is that the prisoners have exercised appreciable restraint in their revolts. . . . Indeed it could be said that the real tragedy of Attica is that at issue in that confrontation, in which forty-three men died . . . was really the simple request that we implement promises over a century old that have not been kept.

These considerations seem to indicate that the issue of the revolutionary nature of criminal activity by working-class people and the reactionary nature of criminal activity of the *lumpenproletariat* is speculative at best, and far from being convincing, the claims of some radical criminologists respecting the revolutionary thrust of criminal activity raise serious questions of credibility.

CONCLUSION

This chapter was aimed at analyzing some issues concerning the credibility of claims put forward by radical criminologists. The analysis pointed out several controversial issues:

(1) *The Nature of the Law.* There is a basic difference in the theoretical concept of human rights held by radical criminologists and as viewed by most Western "capitalist" societies. The role of law in the control of deviant behavior differs according to the differing concepts.

Radical criminologists perceive the law in capitalist societies as a control mechanism serving the interest of the ruling class. They present a simplistic picture of social classes in Western industrial societies. At the same time, they tend to overlook the existence of any real consensus regarding laws among various segments of the population. They refer to these expressions of consensus as "false consciousness" of the working class. This leads more to rhetoric than to any real understanding.

(2) *Crime Causation.* Radical criminologists attribute crime to the socioeconomic arrangements of capitalist society. They neglect the problems of explanations of crime in "socialist" societies, which in reality tend to use "conservative" explanatory concepts.

(3) *The Role of the Criminologists.* The role of the criminologists, with the adaptation of the Marxist principle of "praxis," is conceived as political activism by radical criminologists. They also reject reform movements ("correctionalism") as a liberal "plot" to reinforce the status quo. Because of their strong ideological commitment, they are intolerant of ideas other than their own. They regard competing explanations as superfluous, since they know the "truth." Consequently, there is a neglect of empirical research among radical criminologists, because the answers to research questions are already known.

(4) *Religious Devotion and Liberation.* Radical criminologists, as "true" religious believers, put their faith in the liberating nature of Marxist ideology. They believe that the change from a capitalist to a socialist social system will ultimately eliminate crime, and will result in human liberation. However, social control policies of political regimes based on socialist principles do not bear out these beliefs. The claim of radical criminologists that these societies have not yet reached the complete socialist stage, and their refusal to deal with the repressive control practices of these societies, further undermines their arguments. They cannot remain oblivious to negative consequences of the Marxist ideology when it is put into practice.

(5) *Crime and Revolution.* Another controversial issue concerns the "problem" of the definition of crime by lower-class people as a revolutionary act, as propounded by some radical criminologists and refuted by others. Radicals try to distinguish between revolutionary action of working-class people, motivated by the true class consciousness, and the crimes

of the *lumpenproletariat* who possess false consciousness and support the capitalist system.

There are problems in determining which acts of lawbreaking belong to the category of revolutionary action and which are ordinary crimes. Can the class position be the only main defining element? How can true or false consciousness be attributed with reliability?

These issues, and others raised by many criminologists (e.g., Nettler, 1978; Gibbons, 1978; Klockars, 1979; Akers, 1979; Greenberg, 1979; Hagan and Leon, 1977), bring the credibility of the claims of radical criminologists into serious question.

The mere raising of these questions and the controversies about the pros and cons of radical criminology by themselves have contributed to criminological knowledge and enhanced professional scholarship. To a large extent these represent at best the inadvertent contributions of radical criminologists to the field of criminology.

NOTES

1. This broad explanatory approach to crime is often called the new criminology, critical criminology, or conflict criminology.

2. In a personal communication David F. Greenberg points out that not many radical criminologists would agree that it is bad to work for immediate reforms now. Similar opinions are expressed also by Garofalo (1978). If that is the case, then this constitutes quite a contradiction to the stance of the advocates of "anticorrectionalism." See, for example, Young (1975) regarding decriminalization, and Scull (1977) concerning decarceration.

3. Regarding this statement Currie (1974: 141 points out that

it would be more reasonable to argue that what has happened in contemporary revolutionary societies and ought to happen in future ones, is not that the power to criminalize disappears, but that the definition of crime loses its class character.

4. This claim is tautologous, since by definition an enactment of law is a political activity regardless of the nature of the political regime.

5. For example, see the social control of "loafing" in Cuba (Loney, 1973).

6. Some of the prison gangs which have networks also on the outside and which created a new form of organized crime were also politicized and revolutionary before they blended into the "illegitimate opportunity structure" of the American capitalist system.

REFERENCES

AKERS, R. L. (1979) "Theory and ideology in Marxist criminology: comments on Turk, Quinney, Toby, and Klockars." Criminology 16 (February): 527-544.

ANDERSON, C. H. (1974) The Political Economy of Social Class. Englewood Cliffs, NJ: Prentice-Hall.

BALBUS, I. D. (1971) "The concept of interest in pluralist and Marxian analysis." Politics and Society 1 (February): 151-177.

BANKOWSKI, Z., G. MUNGHAM, and P. YOUNG (1977) "Radical criminology and radical criminologist?" Contemporary Crises 1: 37-52.

BERMAN, H. J. (1972) Soviet Criminal Law and Procedure. Cambridge, MA: Harvard University Press.

BONOMO, T. A. and M. G. WENGER (1978) "A critique of radical criminology on surplus population: an examination of Quinney's thesis." Presented at the annual meeting of the American Society of Criminology, Dallas.

BOTTOMORE, T. B. (1972) "Introduction," pp. 1-8 in Varieties of Political Expression in Sociology. Chicago: University of Chicago Press.

BRADY, J. F. (1977) "Political contradictions and justice policy in people's China." Contemporary Crises 1, 2: 127-162.

BUCHHOLZ, E., R. HARTMAN, J. LEKSHAS, and G. STILLER (1974) Socialist Criminology: Theory and Methodology. Westmead, Farnborough, Hants: Saxon House.

CARSON, W. G. (1974) "The sociology of crime and the emergence of criminal laws," in P. Rock and M. McIntosh (eds.) Deviance and Social Control. London: Tavistock.

CHAMBLISS, W. J. (1975) "Toward a political economy of crime." Theory and Society 2 (Summer): 149-170.

CLEAVER, E. (1968) Soul on Ice. New York: McGraw-Hill.

CONNOR, W. D. (1972) Deviance in Soviet Society. New York: Columbia University Press.

CULLEN, F. T., Jr. and J. B. CULLEN (1977) "The Soviet model of Soviet deviance." Pacific Sociological Review 20 (July): 389-410.

CURRIE, E. (1974) "Review of Taylor, Walton and Young's *The New Criminology*. Crime and Social Justice 2 (Fall-Winter): 1.

DAHRENDORF, R. (1957) Class and Class Conflict in Industrial Society. Palo Alto, CA: Stanford University Press.

DAVIS, A. Y. (1971) If They Come in the Morning. New York: New American Library.

EMERY, F. E. (1970) Freedom and Justice Within Walls. London: Tavistock.

FRANKLIN, B. (1970) "The lumpenproletariat and the revolutionary youth movement." Monthly Review (January): 10-25.

GAROFALO, J. (1978) "Radical criminology and criminal justice: points of divergence and contact." Social Justice (Fall-Winter): 17-27.

GIBBONS, D. C. (1979) The Criminological Enterprise: Theories and Perspectives. Englewood Cliffs, NJ: Prentice-Hall.

——— (1978) "Radical criminology revisited: social interests, social change, and the criminal justice system." Presented at the annual meeting of the Pacific Sociological Association, Spokane.

——— and P. GARABEDIAN (1974) "Conservative, liberal and radical criminology: some trends and observations," in C. E. Reasons The Criminologist: Crime and the Criminal. Santa Monica, CA: Goodyear.

GIDDENS, A. (1975) The Class Structure of the Advanced Societies. New York: Harper & Row.

――― (1971) Capitalism and Modern Social Theory: An Analysis of the Writings of Marx, Durkheim and Max Weber. New York: Cambridge University Press.

GILHAM, S. A. (1978) "State, law, and ruling class interests." Presented at the annual meeting of the American Society of Criminology, Dallas.

GOULDNER, A. W. (1962) "Antiminotaur: the myth of a value-free sociology." Social Problems 9 (Winter): 199-213.

GREENBERG, E. F. (1979) "Class, state and crime: on the theory and practice of criminal justice by Richard Quinney." Crime and Delinquency 25 (January): 110-113.

――― (1977) "Delinquency and the age structure of society." Contemporary Crises 1: 189-223.

――― (1976) "On one-dimensional 'Marxist Criminology.'" Theory and Society 3: 610-621

HABERMAS, Y. (1973) Theory and Practice. Boston: Beacon.

HAGAN, J. and J. LEON (1977) "Rediscovering delinquency: social history, political ideology and the sociology of law." American Sociological Review 42 (August): 587-598.

HAWKINS, G. (1976) The Prison: Policy and Practice. Chicago: University of Chicago Press.

HEPBURN, J. R. (1977) "Social control and the legal order: legitimated repression in a capitalist state." Contemporary Crises 1: 77-90.

HIRST, P. Q. (1972) "Marx and Engels on law, crime and morality." Economy and Society 1, 1: 28-56.

HOLLANDER, P. (1973) "Sociology, selective determinism, and the rise of expectations." American Sociologist 8 (November): 147-153.

――― (1969) "A converging social problem: juvenile delinquency in the Soviet Union and the United States." British Journal of Criminology 1 (April): 148-166.

HOULT, T. F. (1968) "Who shall prepare himself to the battle?" American Sociologist 3 (February): 39-41.

KLEIN, D. and J. KRESS (1976) "Any woman's blues: a critical overview of women, crime and the criminal justice system." Crime and Social Justice 5 (Spring-Summer): 37-49.

KLOCKARS, C. B. (1979) "The contemporary crises of Marxist criminology." Criminology 16 (February): 477-515.

KRISBERG, B. (1975) Crime and Privilege: Toward a New Criminology. Englewood Cliffs, NJ: Prentice-Hall.

LONEY, M. (1973) "Social control in Cuba," in T. Taylor and L. Taylor (eds.) Politics and Deviance. New York: Viking.

MANNHEIM, K. (1936) Ideology and Utopia. New York: International Library of Psychology, Philosophy and Scientific Method.

MANKOFF, M. (1978) "On the responsibility of Marxist criminologists: a reply to Quinney." Contemporary Crises 2: 293-301.

MARCUSE, H. (1965) "Repressive tolerance," in R. P. Wolff et al., A Critique of Pure Tolerance. Boston: Beacon.

MARX, K. and F. ENGELS (1947) The German Ideology. New York: International Publishers.

MEIER, R. F. (1976) "The new criminology: continuity in criminological theory." Journal of Criminal Law and Criminology 67, 4: 461-469.

MICHALOWSKI, R. J. (1976) "Emic vs. etic: toward a science of social harms." Presented at the annual meeting of the American Society of Criminology, Tucson.

NETTLER, G. (1978) Explaining Crime. New York: McGraw-Hill.

NEWMAN, G. (1976) Comparative Deviance. New York: Elsevier North-Holland.

PLATT, A. M. (1975) "Prospects for a radical criminology in the U.S." in T. Taylor et al. (eds.) Critical Criminology. London: Routledge & Kegan Paul.

QUINNEY, R. (1979) Criminology. Boston: Little, Brown.

——— (1977) Class, State, and Crime: On the Theory of Practice of Criminal Justice. New York: David McKay.

——— (1973) Critique of Legal Order: Crime Control in Capitalist Society. Boston: Little, Brown.

RADZINOWICZ, L. (1966) Ideology and Crime. New York: Columbia University Press.

ROCK, P. (1973) "Symposium review on 'The New Criminology.' " Sociological Quarterly 14 (Autumn): 594-596.

SCHUTZ, A. (1963) "Concept and theory formation in the social sciences," in M. Natanson (ed.) Philosophy of the Social Sciences. New York: Random House.

SCHWENDINGER, H. and J. SCHWENDINGER (1976) "The collective varieties of youth." Crime and Social Justice 5 (Spring/Summer): 7-25.

——— (1974) "Rape myths: in legal, theoretical and everyday practice". Crime and Social Justice 1 (Spring/Summer): 18-26.

SCULL, A. T. (1977) Decarceration: Community Treatment and the Deviant–A Radical View. Englewood Cliffs, NJ: Prentice-Hall.

SHICHOR, D. (1979) " 'Socialization'–the political aspects of an explanatory concept in delinquency causation." Presented at the annual meeting of the Society for the Study of Social Problems, Boston.

——— (1978) "The new criminology: some critical issues". Presented at the annual meeting of the Society for the Study of Social Problems, San Francisco.

SPITZER, S. (1975) "Toward a Marxian theory of deviance". Social Problems 22 (June): 638-651.

STEINERT, H. (1977) "Against a conspiracy theory of criminal law a propos Hepburn's 'Social control and the legal order.' " Contemporary Crises 1: 437-440.

TAYLOR, I., P. WALTON, and J. YOUNG (1975) "Critical criminology in Britain: review and prospects," in I. Taylor et al. (eds.) Critical Criminology. London: Routledge & Kegan Paul.

TURK, A. T. (1979) "Analyzing official deviance: for nonpartisan conflict analysis in criminology." Criminology 16 (February): 459-476.

——— (1969) "Introduction," in W. Bonger, Criminality and Economic Conditions. Bloomington: Indiana University Press.

WERKENTIN, F., M. HOFFERBERT, and M. BAUERMAN (1974) "Criminology as policy science or: how old is the new criminology?" Crime and Social Justice 2: 24-41.

WOLFF, R. P. (1965) "Beyond tolerance", in R. P. Wolff et al., A Critique of Pure Tolerance. Boston: Beacon.

YOUNG, J. (1975) "Working-class criminology", in I. Taylor et al. (eds.) Critical Criminology. London: Routledge & Kegan Paul.

13

CONFLICT THEORY AND DIFFERENTIAL PROCESSING: AN ANALYSIS OF THE RESEARCH LITERATURE

Franklin P. Williams III

At present there are several theoretical positions available to criminologists, of which one of the most popular has been conflict theory. Even though the conflict approach had been in existence for some time, it was not until a concern with criminal law had been voiced by the societal reaction perspective in the early 1960s that conflict gained attention and began a resurgence. Its relatively rapid growth and growing support has even been characterized as a revolution within criminology (Chambliss, 1973: 1).

The basic concerns of conflict theory spring from the general outline presented by Marx and Engels but are perhaps equally characterized in the field of criminology through the Simmel-like adaptations of Dahrendorf (1958, 1959). Until recently, criminological conflict theorists have been less concerned with the concept of class in the strict Marxian sense than with the concept of conflicting groups and power elites. In the main, this may be attributed to the initial reemergence of conflict theory not as an

AUTHOR'S Note: This is a revised version of a paper presented at the 1977 Annual Meeting of the American Society of Criminology.

application of Marxist perspectives but more as a concern with the possibility of criminogenic societal control mechanisms. This orientation has, of course, been changing with the emergence of the "New Criminology."

This very change, and the divergent positions of the two major orientations (conflicting groups/class interest), has the result of rendering empirical examination of conflict theory problematic. At one level, all seem to agree that powerless members of society are the nominal fare of the criminal justice system; yet methods of defining differential processing differ by the two basic positions. Those of the conflicting-groups orientation (Turk, 1966, 1969, 1976; Chambliss and Seidman, 1971) might well suggest that the varying degrees of power held by members of the various competing societal groups allow for some consideration of differential processing within the criminal justice system. On the other hand, the expanded population group inherent in the class-interest orientation (Quinney, 1974a, 1974b, 1977b; Taylor et al., 1973; Gordon, 1973) may very well suggest that any examination of differentials in criminal justice processing is merely a within-class examination (Reasons, 1977) and that the major evidence lies in the disproportionate class arrest rates. Even the question of amenability to empirical test arises if conflict is to be considered a perspective (Chambliss, 1973; Reasons, 1977), with some doubt being expressed that positivistic empiricist methodology can be applied to the conflict perspective. It is perhaps of note that the class-interest conflict theorists tend to reject empirical tests of their position even though the major impetus of modern criminological conflict positions sprang from the discoveries of a decidedly empiricist group of self-report studies initiated by the work of Short and Nye (1958). Further, Scheff (1974: 445) in a response to Gibbs's (1972) criticism of labeling theory has suggested that even perspectives are amenable to empirical evidence: "The proper question to ask is not . . . whether [a perspective] is literally true, but whether the relevant studies are more consistent with [the perspective] . . . than with its competitor." Lastly, even class-interest conflict theorists have quoted empirical evidence of processing differentials as support for their positions.[1] Thus it would appear that at least *some* of the conflict position is amenable to empirical test.

If conflict theory bears examination, then, it would be instructive to provide a generalized conception of the basic position. In light of the discussion above, a basic outline of conflict theory is provided with an emphasis which more closely approximates the conflicting-groups orientation; yet little is presented that is totally alien to the class-interest version. A simplified version of the basic approach yields the following:

(1) Society is best represented by conflict and the existence of conflicting groups.

(2) Control of society is gained by those societal groups who wield the most power and resources.

(3) Societal groups exhibit differential normative patterns and behaviors.

(4) Once a group achieves dominance over others it seeks to use the available societal mechanisms to its advantage in order to maintain that dominance.

(5) Law is a societal mechanism that provides the group in power with strong means of control over other, less powerful groups.

(6) Laws are formulated in the interest of the dominant group so that those behaviors common to the less-powerful groups are restricted.

(7) The dominant group provides for enforcement of the law through the establishment of social control agencies.

(8) The law enforcement and control system will operate to disproportionately process the less-powerful members of society.

(9) Each point in the law enforcement and control system will process clientele such that the more severe disposition will accrue to members of the less-powerful group while the more lenient disposition will accrue to members of the more powerful group.

There would appear to be two basic points of evaluation: (1) that of law formulation in the interests of those in power; and (2) that of differential processing by the criminal justice system. The first point is reflected in examination of vagrancy laws (Chambliss, 1964), the Marijuana Tax Act (Becker, 1963; Lindesmith, 1959, 1965; Dickson, 1968), theft (Hall, 1952), and prohibition (Sinclair, 1964). Generally, findings would appear to support the conflict notion that laws are, in fact, formulated to benefit power groups. The interpretative nature of historical methodology, however, leaves room for doubt. Fortunately, a recent and methodologically different approach by Berk et al. (1977) on the laws in California shows promise of eliminating some of the subjectivity inherent in previous analyses.

The second point, differential processing, has indeed been conducive to empirical examination for some time, although much of that work probably rests with a pervasive disciplinary interest in racial and social inequality and discrimination. A focus on race and socioeconomic variables as measures of power has characterized this research. As with any accumulation of research on a given subject, there are differences in operational definitions, areas of examination, general methodology, and most of all, differences in findings. The usual technique of making sense of these differences is to briefly review and "tally up" those studies which come to one's attention through some definition of "adequacy." In the event of a large number of such studies, the probability of making a selectively biased sample of those studies increases, thus resulting in a particular group which may ultimately become defined as standard references. One method of overcoming the problem of a biased group of "standard" studies is that of nonselectively reviewing and evaluating the available research in the area. For all the interest and activity in the area of racial and socioeconomic differentials in criminal justice processing, there has been, to date, only one systematic review and evaluation of applicable research (Hagan, 1974b). That particular review, however, was limited to studies on sentencing. The field is lacking similar assessment of evidence regarding differential disposition by racial and socioeconomic correlates throughout the criminal justice system.

The present article is partially an attempt to rectify this situation and partially an effort at introducing the field to a concept of rigorous evaluation of its existing research literature. As noted, too often the tendency is to arrive at an evaluation of the evidence for a particular position by enumerating the familiar studies, both pro and con, and assessing the tally. Such methods at best produce a haphazard accounting of knowledge and at worst invalidate criminologists' claims to membership in a rigorous and progressive discipline.

THE RESEARCH LITERATURE

Previous literature has noted that differences in analytical methods, types of samples, geographical locations, processing areas examined, and operationalization of variables serve to confound whatever trends might appear in the accumulated research (Hagan, 1974b; Chiricos and Waldo,

1975; Hindelang, 1969). Generally, literature reviews have consisted of an examination of the more popular research articles (the "standard references") and a conclusion that there is either general support or lack of a definitive viewpoint. Indeed, in a previous paper (Williams, 1977) which focused on 61 research studies largely published prior to 1975, a simple tally found an almost perfectly even split between those studies which supported the existence of both racial and socioeconomic differentials and those which did not.

Some work exists which moves beyond this quandary. Hagan (1974b), in a review of 20 sentencing studies, noted that (1) the type of analysis and (2) the presence of controlling legal variables such as prior record and offense seriousness greatly affected findings. Moreover, in applying a measure of association to the data found in those studies, Hagan found only one case (Wolfgang and Riedel, 1973) in which the relationship between race and sentence justified a finding of support for conflict propositions. No support for socioeconomic differentials was found in the reanalysis. It would therefore appear that presumption of racial and socioeconomic differentials in the area of sentencing is rather questionable.

Hindelang, in an earlier review of eight pre-1965 empirical studies (1969: 312-313), commented that findings of racial bias seemed to be concentrated among those studies which: (1) used older data; (2) collected data in the South; (3) concerned themselves primarily with capital offenses; and (4) were less rigorous in their use of relevant control variables. This particular review does not provide much more rigorous *analysis* of the research than the "obligatory" review found in any one of the myriad articles on discrimination research. Nonetheless, Hindelang at the very least contributed to the organization of racial research evidence. At present there has been no similar attempt to organize conflicting evidence from the socioeconomic research. Given the subjective, or non-existent, interpretations of the research literature beyond the area of sentencing, it would appear to be instructive to examine that literature with somewhat more diligence.

In an effort to adequately assess the evidence bearing upon the point of differential processing of less powerful societal groups, a search of the literature was conducted which located some 89 studies investigating variables associated with racial or socioeconomic characteristics. These 89 empirical studies were further split for each area of the criminal justice system which each examined. This was done in an effort to compensate for potential problems arising from a comparison of some studies which examine more than one area and other studies which concentrate on a single stage of the processing system. Failure to compensate for such research differentials has the effect of clouding empirical evidence and has, perhaps, contributed to some of the uncertainty surrounding the conflict issue thus far. Once these areas were separated, 123 different examinations of racial or socioeconomic variables at different stages of the criminal justice system were available for review and evaluation. In addition, these 123 "studies" provide 115 cases in which racial characteristics were examined and 68 cases in which socioeconomic correlates were examined.

In order to begin the analysis it was necessary to determine which studies had findings of support for hypotheses of differential processing and which ones did not. Such a seemingly simple task did not, in fact, present itself in that manner. Some authors attributed importance to doubtful findings; others, firmly ingrained in the art of sociological writing, managed to take both sides of the issue; yet others ignored the presence of data and took a concluding position contrary to their reported evidence. The final outcome was to rely on the original author's reportage of his own findings unless the reported data was blatantly contradictory. This led to the establishment of three categories: support for differential processing, no support for differential processing, and neutral.

The inclusion of the neutral category was made necessary by those studies which reported contradictory findings or purposefully refused to interpret their findings in a support/no-support framework. The neutral category also serves another purpose; contrary to normal scientific reportage, the flavor of conflict theory often leads to an ideological attack on those who use a conservative, null-hypothesis framework because they *fail to lean toward the existence of differentials*. Therefore, those studies remaining in the support/no-support categories are those that are least questionable in their findings. This does not preclude one from assuming that findings which are not firm enough to indicate support also fail to meet the criteria of substantiality demanded by the conflict position and as a result are nonsupportive.

Based on the observations by Hagan (1974b) and Hindelang (1969), the literature was examined through the use of six variables: (1) the processing area of the criminal justice system (arrest/referral, arraignment through conviction, sentencing, postsentencing); (2) whether the sample popula-

TABLE 13.1 Characteristics of the Research Literature

	Race Research (N = 115)			SES Research (N = 68)		
	Support	Neutral	No Support	Support	Neutral	No Support
Area of Criminal Justice System						
Arrest/Referral	4	3	14	4	3	7
Court Process/Conviction	7	4	19	6	2	14
Sentencing	19	4	29	6	4	17
Postsentencing	7	3	2	1	2	2
Juvenile/Adult System						
Juvenile	8	3	22	5	4	12
Adult	29	11	42	12	7	28
Capital Studies						
Capital Offenses	12	4	3	4	4	1
Noncapital Offenses	25	10	61	3	7	39
Region of Study						
Northeast	9	6	19	4	4	8
Other North	5	—	11	1	1	11
South	16	2	7	4	3	5
West	1	3	15	1	2	10
National	5	2	5	5	—	3
Non-U.S.	1	1	7	2	1	3
Median Year of Sample						
Prior to 1961	27	6	13	8	6	7
1961 and after	10	8	51	9	5	33
Method of Analysis						
Tabular	18	2	16	4	3	1
Measure of Significance	10	5	6	2	5	2
Measure of Association	9	7	42	11	3	37
Total	37	14	64	17	11	40

tion was composed of juveniles or adults; (3) whether or not the study population was primarily charged with capital offenses; (4) the geographical location of the sample (Northeast, other North, South, West, national, and non-U.S.); (5) the median year of the sample data; and (6) the method of data analysis used in the study (tabular analysis, measure of significance, measure of association). There was no attempt to provide a further analysis of individual studies as was done by Hagan (1974b).[2]

Table 1 contains the distribution of study findings by their characteristics. First, it should be noted that of 115 instances in which racial differentials were examined, the majority offered no support. The totals for the socioeconomic studies indicate similar results. Thus, even if one were to "tally" the results of a review of a large number of these studies, it is obvious that a conclusion of "contradictory" findings becomes questionable.

Upon examination of the study characteristics, some consistencies emerge. It seems that those studies which find racial differentials in processing are more likely to be: at later stages in the system (sentencing and postsentencing); of adult populations; of capital offenses; from southern jurisdictions; older, with at least half the data coming from populations prior to 1961; and more simplistic in their data analysis. As a cautionary note, however, these characteristics should not be taken as exclusive. Studies with the same characteristics can, and do, produce opposite findings.

On the other hand, of those studies which do not produce findings of racial processing differentials, characteristics tend to be almost the opposite of those above: earlier stages in the system; juvenile populations; noncapital offenses: western or non-U.S. jurisdictions; samples with median years of 1961 or after; and more rigorous analyses. Socioeconomic studies lacking support for the existence of processing differentials are of a similar nature but the area of the system and juvenile/adult populations provide little distinction.

Just as failing to control for variables in the data base may provide erroneous conclusions in the studies reviewed, so might the simple bivariate analysis reported thus far. A stepwise multiple discriminant analysis, not reported in detail here, revealed the same general characteristics referred to above and suggested that the median year of the sample data was the main predictor of the study findings. It appears that recent sample populations show little evidence of either racial or socioeconomic differen-

TABLE 13.2 Characteristics of Rigorous Multivariate Studies

	Race Research (N = 37)			SES Research (N = 32)		
	Support	Neutral	No Support	Support	Neutral	No Support
Area of Criminal Justice System						
Arrest	—	—	2	1	—	1
Court Process/Conviction	—	3	11	2	—	11
Sentencing	1	1	15	1	1	13
Postsentencing	1	1	2	—	—	2
Juvenile/Adult System						
Juvenile	1	—	7	1	—	5
Adult	1	5	23	2	1	22
Capital Studies						
Capital Offenses	—	—	3	2	0	1
Noncapital Offenses	2	5	27	2	1	26
Region of Study						
Northeast	1	2	6	1	—	7
Other North	—	—	3	—	—	3
South	1	—	5	—	1	3
West	—	1	10	1	—	9
National	—	1	2	—	—	2
Non-U.S.	—	1	4	2	—	3
Median Year of Sample						
Prior to 1961	—	—	—	—	—	—
1961 and after	2	5	30	4	1	27
Total	2	5	30	4	1	27

tials. Method of analysis and capital offenses also were important dis-
criminators. Juvenile/adult samples, however, had virtually no impact on
the ability to discriminate between support/no-support studies.

The importance of the sample time period also illuminated a problem
with the categorization of the method of analysis variable. The category
"measure of association" tends to produce information loss since the most
rigorous analytical methods are equated with nominal bivariate measures.
Hagan's (1974b) work shows the importance of rigorous analysis in delineating whether evidence is forthcoming for differential processing hypotheses. Further, the rigor of criminological research has certainly improved
over time and the effect of the sample period may well be an artifact of
that circumstance. In order to approach this important question as well as
to provide close examination of the "best" criminological research, all
studies using rigorous multivariate analyses (stepwise multiple regression,
path analysis, stepwise multiple discriminant analysis, and Goodman's
log-linear analysis) were combined and examined as a separate category.[3]

Table 2 presents the characteristics of the multivariate studies. The
striking results of the findings of this group immediately become apparent.
*Over 80 percent of both racial and socioeconomic studies fail to support
differential processing hypotheses.* To the extent that one is justified in
considering this particular portion of the research literature as the best
available evidence, it becomes difficult to accept either statements of
contradictory findings or suggestions of the existence of racial and socioeconomic processing differentials within the criminal justice system. The
sole exception appears to lie in those instances in which capital offenses
are considered. The scarcity of rigorous studies within this category creates
problems of interpretation; but for socioeconomic characteristics a potential differential exists. Suggestions that the effect of race is due largely to
socioeconomic factors (Swigert and Farrell, 1975; Clarke and Koch, 1976)
may very well have some degree of merit as an interpretation of the lack of
racial effect in capital offense areas.

The previous prediction (Hindelang, 1969) that southern studies produce evidence of differential processing is not borne out, but certainly
predictions of relationships with older data and less rigor in analyses are
supported. Given the fact that no rigorous multivariate analyses were
found in the literature prior to 1961, the age of the data is probably less
important than methodology. In sum, then, the available evidence suggests
that, with the possible exception of capital offenses, pervasive and systematic processing differentials do not exist within the criminal justice system.

POSSIBLE ALTERNATIVE EXPLANATIONS

Considering the importance of suggesting that the presence of pro-cessing differentials due to power structures is largely nonexistent and far from pervasive, alternative explanations are deserving of exploration. Since the age of the data surfaces as a major separating characteristic, there is a possibility that society has undergone major change and, where previously prevalent, differentials have now become negligible. First, granting that this may have happened, conflict theory is still not relieved of the responsibility of modification so that a true representation of societal mechanisms becomes available (conflict theorists certainly do not seem to be ready to concede that theirs is only a historical perspective). Second, after examining the relationship between methodological rigor and age, it appears likely that the relationship between age and supportive evidence is little more than an artifact of analytical method. Studies with less than rigorous analyses have generally found evidence of processing differentials regardless of age.

As a second concern, even though subject to empirical evaluation, the conflict position of processing differentials ordered by power is not without problems of application. A question arises as to the amount of differential processing that must exist in order to provide evidence for conflict propositions. The point must be made that discrimination hypoth-eses are not, of necessity, conflict hypotheses. Evidence of *some* discrimi-nation does not justify a theoretical stance based on pervasive, system-wide, differential processing; thus conflict theory demands the criteria of substantiality. Even minute discrimination is still discrimination, but is *not* sufficient to predict that such inequalities constitute predetermined social order. Moreover, individual prejudices of decision makers at various pro-cessing stages may produce discriminatory actions, yet unless they can be shown to be attributable to social structure, there is no necessary support beyond that of directional tendency. Insofar as the general issue of discrimination is concerned, it should be noted that many studies which failed to support the existence of significant processing differentials did not question the existence of some small degree of discrimination. Yet, given the relationship between sample size, correlation, and significance (Blalock, 1972: 384), it becomes very difficult to substantiate minor discrimination.

Another alternative explanation might be found within the initial process of filing charges and plea bargaining for lesser offenses. Since it is difficult to gain data on the early stages of arrest and charge determination, it might be that the original behavior bears no necessary resemblance to the officially charged offense. If this process is applied differentially, then further differential processing would not be necessary and research at those stages would produce results indicative of nonsupport. Similarly, differentials in the plea bargaining process would serve to obviate conviction and sentencing data. At this point the few studies which have managed to allow for these factors do not seem to lend credence to this explanation of the findings (Terry, 1967a, 1967b; Cohn, 1976; Sumner, 1970; Hagan, 1974a; Bernstein et al., 1977a, 1977b).

Wellford (1975) has noted an additional possibility as an explanation of the general lack of evidence supporting processing differentials. Much of the research literature examines the processing system as if it were a piecemeal operation; there may, then, be a cumulative effect which is not detectable by such research. Recent investigations have included prior decisions in their analyses, however, and do not support such a position (Hagan, 1974a; Swigert and Farrell, 1975; Williams, 1976; Bernstein et al., 1977a, 1977b). The small amount of discrimination found in most studies may have a more important effect outside of a present case and provide legal justification for more severe sanctions in future criminal justice appearances. This has not as yet been examined.

A final alternative concerns methodological problems. The main characteristic of rigorous multivariate techniques of data analysis is that of controlling for the effects of other independent (or control) variables on the relationship between the variable of interest and the dependent variable. The process of statistical equality rests on the assumption that such controlling can in fact take place in reality. When one introduces such variables as prior record or offense seriousness as controls, reality may be denied if powerless groups simply do not have those factors present in the same form as power groups. Thus if laws are designed to disproportionately process some group members, then those group members ultimately will be legally processed in a differential manner. It may be possible that, in statistically controlling for certain legal variables which have intrinsic interrelationships with racial or socioeconomic variables, the resulting equation adjusts evidence of differential processing at the same time. Nonetheless, since even the simple process of bivariate analysis is associated with decreased support for processing differentials, the evidence presented in this literature analysis would seem to stand.

IMPLICATIONS FOR THEORY AND RESEARCH

Certain implications arise for conflict theory generally as a result of the analysis. The evidence presented here does not, of course, treat the whole of the theory. That portion of the theory which deals with the construction of criminal law is untouched by the present review and remains a viable conception of the structure of society. If that conception represents reality, then the presence of laws created to restrict and control less-powerful members of society are, by themselves, sufficient to account for the disproportionate representation of those members in the criminal justice system. Further differential treatment by the system itself is both unnecessary and potentially problematic since it could very well engender violations of the original intent of the law. In sum, predictions of differential processing by some power hierarchy are superfluous to the main body of conflict theory. Conflict theorists might better expend their efforts (as the class-interest orientation already has done) along lines which focus on the structure and promulgation of law.

Implications for future research in this area are manifold. Increased rigor of both data collection and analysis are obvious, but additional factors demand attention. First, rigorous multivatiate analytical techniques are a necessity; yet some attention needs to be paid to the effects of statistical controls on "real-world" situations. Second, the research analyzed uniformly indicated a general lack of explanatory power in the traditional variables. Other potential explanatory variables must be sought out and included in future analyses of processing differentials. Certainly factors such as individual system actors and demeanor of the defendant have *some* explanatory power but have been ignored in the vast majority of research efforts due to the difficulty of incorporating them into the research design. Other factors of more traditional importance should also be examined (i.e., sex, the defendant's release status, dismissal of cases, and the actual behavior on which the charge is based). Third, research which explicitly focuses on the cumulative nature of the processing system should be undertaken. As a consequent, longitudinal research examining the effect of minute discriminatory decisions on subsequent court appearances is called for. Finally, discrimination research (not conflict research) should address itself to the design of data collection instruments and methods of analysis which provide the sensitivity needed to isolate discriminatory handling from "chance" outcomes.

As a closing comment, it must be noted that this review of the literature was not designed to be a survey but, rather, an analysis. Divested of the analytical design, the conclusion would have been that evidence concerning processing differentials in the criminal justice system is contradictory; and that was the exact state of past knowledge. More rigorous reviews, within some form of analytical framework, may benefit other areas where accumulated evidence is presently seen as contradictory.

NOTES

1. See, for example, Quinney's *Criminal Justice in America*, pp. 11-20; Quinney's *The Problem of Crime* (1977a), pp. 107-108; and Krisberg's *Crime and Privilege*, pp. 60-62.

2. An earlier version (Williams, 1977) incorporated Hagan's reanalysis and found a substantial reduction in the number of studies supporting both racial differentials (from a total of 34 to a new total of 17) and SES differentials (from a total of 16 to a new total of 9).

3. Those studies in this category are: Arnold (1971), Baab and Ferguson (1967), Bernstein et al. (1977a, 1977b), Burke and Turk (1975), Carroll and Mondrick (1976), Chiricos and Waldo (1975) Clarke and Koch (1976), Cohen (1975a, 1975b, 1975c, 1975d), Cohn (1976), Hagan (1974a, 1975a, 1975b), Hall and Simkus (1975), Hartnagel (1975), Hewitt (1975), Hogarth (1971), Jacob and Eisenstein (1975), Jarvis and Messinger (1974), Judson et al. (1969), Kelly (1976), Landes (1974), Scott (1974), Sumner (1970), Swigert and Farrell (1975), Tiffany et al. (1975), and Williams (1976).

REFERENCES

ARNOLD, W. R. (1971) "Race and ethnicity relative to factors in juvenile court dispositions." American Journal of Sociology 77: 211-227.

AXELRAD, S. (1952) "Negro and white institutionalized delinquents." American Sociological Review 57: 569-574.

BAAB, G. W. and W. R. FERGUSON (1967) "Texas sentencing practices: a statistical study." Texas Law Review 45: 471-503.

BECKER, H. (1963) Outsiders. New York: Macmillan.

BEDAU, H. A. (1965) "Capital punishment in Oregon: 1903-64." Oregon Law Review 45: 1-37.

——— (1964) "Death sentences in New Jersey: 1907-1960." Rutgers Law Review 19: 1-55.

BENSING, R. C. and O. SCHROEDER, Jr. (1960) Homicide in an Urban Community. Springfield, IL: Charles C Thomas.

BERK, R. A., H. BRACKMAN, and S. L. LESSER (1977) A Measure of Justice. New York: Academic.

BERNSTEIN, I. N., W. R. KELLEY, and P. A. DOYLE (1977a) "Societal reaction to deviants: the case of criminal defendants." American Sociological Review 42: 743-755.

BERNSTEIN, I., E. KICK, J. T. LEUNG, and B. SCHULTZ (1977b) "Charge reduction: an intermediary stage in the process of labelling criminal defendants." Social Forces 56: 362-384.

BIENVENUE, R. M., and A. H. LATIF (1974) "Arrests, disposition and recidivism: a comparison of Indians and whites." Canadian Journal of Criminology and Corrections 16: 105-116.

BLACK, D. J. (1970) "Production of crime rates." American Sociological Review 35: 733-748.

——— and A. J. REISS, Jr. (1970) "Police control of juveniles." American Sociological Review 35: 63-77.

BLALOCK, H. M. (1972) Social Statistics. New York: McGraw-Hill.

BLANSHARD, P. (1942) "Negro delinquency in New York." Journal of Educational Sociology 16: 115-123.

BOCK, E. W. and C. E. FRAZIER (1977) "Official standards versus actual criteria in bond dispositions." Journal of Criminal Justice 5: 321-328.

BULLOCK, H. A. (1961) "Significance of the racial factor in the length of prison sentences." Journal of Criminal Law, Criminology and Police Science 52: 411-417.

BURKE, P. J. and A. T. TURK (1975) "Factors affecting post-arrest dispositions: a model for analysis." Social Problems 22: 313-331.

CAMERON, M. O. (1964) The Booster and the Snitch. New York: Macmillan.

CARROLL, L. and M. E. MONDRICK (1976) "Racial bias in the decision to grant parole." Law and Society Review 11: 93-107.

CHAMBLISS, W. J. (1973) "Functional and conflict theories of crime." MSS Modular Publications, Module 17: 1-23.

——— (1964) "A sociological analysis of the law of vagrancy." Social Problems 12: 67-77.

——— and R. B. SEIDMAN (1971) Law, Order and Power. Reading, MA: Addison-Wesley.

CHIRICOS, T. G., P. D. JACKSON and G. P. WALDO (1972) "Inequality in the imposition of a criminal label." Social Problems 19: 553-572.

CHIRICOS, T. G. and G. P. WALDO (1975) "Socio-economic status and criminal sentencing: an empirical assessment of a conflict proposition." American Sociological Review 40: 753-772.

——— and C. M. MARSTON (1974) "Race, crime and sentence length." Presented at the annual meetings of the American Sociological Association.

CLARKE, S. H. and G. G. KOCH (1976) "The influence of income and other factors on whether criminal defendants go to prison." Law and Society Review 11: 57-92.

COHEN, L. E. (1975a) "Who gets detained?: an empirical analysis of the pre-adjudicatory detention of juveniles in Denver." Washington, DC: Government Printing Office.

——— (1975b) "Juvenile dispositions: social and legal factors related to the processing of Denver delinquency cases." Washington, DC: Government Printing Office.

——— (1975c) "Pre-adjudicatory detention in three juvenile courts: an empirical analysis of the factors related to detention decision outcomes." Washington, DC: Government Printing Office.

——— (1975d) "Delinquency disposition: an empirical analysis of processing decisions in three juvenile courts." Washington, DC: Government Printing Office.

COHN, Y. (1976) "Court and probation—two interacting systems." Probation and Parole 8: 15-30.

DAHRENDORF, R. (1959) Class and Class Conflict in an Industrial Society. London: Routledge & Kegan Paul.

——— (1958) "Toward a theory of social conflict." Journal of Conflict Resolution 2: 170-183.

DICKSON, D. T. (1968) "Bureaucracy and morality: an organizational perspective on a moral crusade." Social Problems 16: 143-156.

FERDINAND, T. N. and E. G. LUCHTERHAND (1970) "Inner-city youth, the police, the juvenile court and justice." Social Problems 17: 510-527.

FORSLUND, M. A. (1969) "Age, occupation and conviction rates of white and Negro males: a case study." Rocky Mountain Social Science Journal 6: 141-146.

GARFINKEL, H. (1949) "Research note on inter- and intra-racial homicides." Social Forces 27: 369-381.

GIARDINI, G. I. and R. G. FARROW (1952) "The paroling of capital offenders." Annals 284: 85-94.

GIBBS, J. (1972) "Issues in defining deviant behavior," pp. 39-68 in R. A. Scott and J. D. Douglas (eds.) Theoretical Perspectives on Deviance. New York: Basic Books.

GOLDMAN, N. (1969) "The differential selection of juvenile offenders for court appearance," pp. 264-290 in W. J. Chambliss (ed.) Crime and the Legal Process. New York: McGraw-Hill.

GORDON, D. M. (1973) "Capitalism, class, and crime in America." Crime and Delinquency 19: 163-185.

GREEN, E. (1970) "Race, social status, and criminal arrest." American Sociological Review 35: 476-490.

——— (1964) "Inter- and intra-racial crime relative to sentencing." Journal of Criminal Law, Criminology and Police Science 55: 348-358.

——— (1961) Judicial Attitudes in Sentencing. London: MacMillian.

——— (1960) "Sentencing practices of criminal court judges." American Journal of Correction 3: 32-35.

HAGAN, J. (1975a) "Law, order and sentencing: a study of attitude in action." Sociometry 38: 374-384.

——— (1975b) "The social and legal construction of criminal justice: a study of the pre-sentencing process." Presented at the annual meetings of the Americn Sociological Association.

——— (1974a) "Parameters of criminal prosecution: an application of path analysis to a problem of criminal justice." Journal of Criminal Law and Criminology 65: 536-544.

——— (1974b) "Extra-legal attributes and criminal sentencing: an assessment of a sociological viewpoint." Law and Society Review 8: 357-383.

HALL, E. L. and A. A. SIMKUS (1975) "Inequality in the types of sentences received by native Americans and whites." Criminology 13: 199-222.

HALL, J. (1952) Theft, Law and Society. Indianapolis: Bobbs-Merrill.

HARTNAGEL, T. H. (1975) "Plea negotiation in Canada." Canadian Journal of Criminology and Corrections 17: 45-56.

HARTUNG, F. E. (1952) "Trends in the use of capital punishment." Annals 284: 8-19.

HEWITT, J. D. (1975) "The effects of individual resources in judicial sentencing." Presented at the annual meetings of the American Sociological Association.

HINDELANG, M. J. (1974) "Decision of shoplifting victims to invoke the criminal justice process." Social Problems 21: 580-593.

——— (1969) "Equality under the law." Journal of Criminal Law, Criminology and Police Science 60: 306-313.

HOHENSTEIN, W. (1969) "Factors influencing the police disposition of juvenile offenders," pp. 138-149 in M. D. Wolfgang and T. Sellin (eds.) Delinquency: Selected Studies. New York: John Wiley.

HOGARTH, J. (1971) Sentencing as a Human Process. Toronto: University of Toronto Press.

JACOB, H. (1962) "Politics and criminal prosecution in New Orleans." Tulane Studies in Political Science 8: 77-98.

——— and J. EISENSTEIN (1975) "Sentences and other sanctions in the criminal courts of Baltimore, Chicago, and Detroit." Political Science Quarterly 90: 617-635.

JARVIS, G. K. and H. B. MESSINGER (1974) "Social and economic correlates of juvenile delinquency rates: a Canadian case." Canadian Journal of Criminology and Corrections 16: 361-372.

JOHNSON, E. H. (1957) "Selective factors in capital punishment." Social Forces 36: 165-169.

JOHNSON, G. B. (1941) "The Negro and crime." Annals 217: 93-104.

JUDSON, C. J., J. J. PANDELL, J. B. OWENS, J. L. McINTOSH, and D. L. MATSHULLAT (1969) "A study of the California penalty jury in first degree murder cases." Stanford Law Review 21: 1297-1431.

KELLY, H. E. (1976) "A comparison of defense strategy and race as influences in differential sentencing." Criminology 2: 241-249.

LANDES, W. M. (1974) "Legality and reality: some evidence on criminal procedure." Journal of Legal Studies 32: 287-337.

LEMERT, E. M. and J. ROSEBERG (1948) "The administration of justice to minority groups in Los Angeles County." University of California Publications in Culture and Society 2: 1-28.

LINDESMITH, A. R. (1965) The Addict and the Law. Terre Haute: Indiana University Press.

——— (1959) "Federal law and drug addiction." Social Problems 7: 48-57.

LUNDMAN, R. J. (1974) "Routine police arrest practices: a commonwealth perspective." Social Problems 22: 127-141.

MARTIN, R. (1934) "The defendant and criminal justice." Bulletin No. 3437. University of Texas: Bureau of Research in the Social Sciences.

McEACHERN, A. W. and R. BAUZER (1967) "Factors related to disposition in juvenile police contacts," pp. 148-172 in M. Klein and B. Myerhoff (eds.) Juvenile Gangs in Context. Englewood Cliffs, NJ: Prentice-Hall.

McKEOWN, J. E. (1948) "Poverty, race and crime." Journal of Criminal Law and Criminology 39: 480-484.

MILESKI, M. (1971) "Courtroom encounters: an observation study of a lower criminal court." Law and Society Review 5: 473-538.

NAGEL, S. S. (1975) Improving the Legal Process. Lexington, MA: D.C. Heath.

——— (1969) The Legal Process from a Behavioral Perspective. Homewood, IL: Irwin.

PARTINGTON, D. H. (1965) "The incidence of the death penalty for rape in Virginia." Washington and Lee Law Review 22: 43-75.

PAWAL, E. J. (1977) "Differential selection of juveniles for detention." Journal of Research in Crime and Delinquency 14: 152-165.

PERRY, R. W. (1977) "The justice system and sentencing: the importance of race in the military." Criminology 15: 225-234.

PETERSEN, D. M. and P. C. FRIDAY (1975) "Early release from incarceration: race as a factor in the use of 'shock probation.' " Journal of Criminal Law and Criminology 66: 79-87.

PILIAVIN, I. and S. BRIAR (1964) "Police encounters with juveniles." American Journal of Sociology 70: 206-214.

POPE, C. E. (1977) "Crime-specific analysis: an empirical examination of burglary offender characteristics." Washington, DC: Government Printing Office.

——— (1976) "The influences of social and legal factors on sentence dispositions: a preliminary analysis of offender-based transaction statistics." Journal of Criminal Justice 4: 203-221.

——— (1975) "The judicial processing of assault and burglary offenders in selected California counties." Washington, DC: Government Printing Office.

QUINNEY, R. (1977a) The Problem of Crime. New York: Harper & Row.

——— (1977b) Class, State and Crime. New York: David McKay.

——— (1974a) Critique of Legal Order: Crime Control in a Capitalist Society. Boston: Little, Brown.

——— (1974b) Criminal Justice in America. Boston: Little, Brown.

REASONS, C. E. (1977) "On methodology, theory, and ideology." American Sociological Review 42: 177-181.

SCHEFF, T. J. (1974) "The labelling theory of mental illness." American Sociological Review 39: 444-452.

SCOTT, J. (1974) "The use of discretion in determining the severity of punishment for incarcerated offenders." Journal of Criminal Law and Criminology 65: 214-224.

SELLIN, T. (1935) "Race prejudice in the administration of justice." American Journal of Sociology 16: 212-217.

——— (1928) "The Negro criminal: a statistical note." Annals 140: 52-64.

SHANNON, L. W. (1963) "Types and patterns of delinquency referral in a middle-sized city." British Journal of Criminology 4: 24-36.

SHORT, J. F. and F. I. NYE (1958) "Extent of unrecorded juvenile delinquency: tentative conclusions." Journal of Criminal Law, Criminology and Police Science 49: 296-302.

SINCLAIR, A. (1964) Era of Excess: A Social History of the Prohibition Movement. New York: Harper & Row.

Southern Regional Council (1969) Race Makes the Difference. Atlanta: Author.

SPAETH, H. J., D. B. MELTZ, G. J. RATHJEN, and M. V. HAFELWERDT (1973) "Is justice blind: an empirical investigation of a normative ideal." Law and Society Review 7: 119-137.

SUMNER, H. (1970) Locking Them Up. Western Region: National Council on Crime and Delinquency.

SWIGERT, V. L. and R. A. FARRELL (1975) "Normal homicides and the law." American Sociological Review 40: 16-32.

TAYLOR, I., P. WALTON, and J. YOUNG (1973) The New Criminology: For a Social Theory of Deviance. London: Routledge & Kegan Paul.

TERRY, R. M. (1967a) "Discrimination in the handling of juvenile offenders." Journal of Research in Crime and Delinquency 4: 218-230.

——— (1967b) "The screening of juvenile offenders." Journal of Criminal Law, Criminology and Police Science 58: 173-181.

THOMAS, C. W. and R. J. CAGE (1977) "The effect of social characteristics on juvenile court dispositions." Sociological Quarterly 18: 237-252.

——— and C. SIEVERDES (1975) "Juvenile court intake: an analysis of discretionary decision-making." Criminology 12: 413-432.

THORNBERRY, T. P. (1973) "Race, socio-economic status and sentencing in the juvenile justice system." Journal of Criminal Law and Criminology 64: 90-98.

TIFFANY, L. P., Y. AVICHAI, and G. W. PETERS (1975) "A statistical analysis of sentencing in federal courts: defendants convicted after trial, 1967-1968." Journal of Legal Studies 4: 469-390.

TURK, A. T. (1976) "Law as a weapon in social conflict." Social Problems 23: 276-291.

——— (1969) Criminality and Legal Order. Chicago: Rand McNally.

——— (1966) "Conflict and criminality." American Sociological Review 31: 338-352.

WEINER, N. L. and C. V. WILLIE (1971) "Decisions by juvenile officers." American Journal of Sociology 77: 199-210.

WELLFORD, C. F. (1975) "Labeling theory and criminology: an assessment." Social Problems 13: 332-345.

WILLIAMS, F. P. (1977) "A review of the evidence on class and racial differentials in criminal justice processing." Presented at the annual meetings of the American Society of Criminology.

——— (1976) "On the question of differential justice: a look at a criminal justice system." Ph.D. dissertation, Florida State University.

WILLIAMS, J. R. and M. GOLD (1972) "From delinquent behavior to official delinquency." Social Problems 20: 209-229.

WILLICK, D. H., G. GEHLKER, and A. M. WATTS (1975) "Social class as a factor affecting judicial disposition: defendants charged with criminal homosexual acts." Criminology 13: 57-77.

WOLF, E. D. (1964) "Abstract of analysis of jury sentencing in capital cases: New Jersey: 1937-1961." Rutgers Law Review 19: 56-64.

WOLFGANG, M. E. and M. RIEDEL (1973) "Race, judicial discretion and the death penalty." Annals 407: 119-133.

WOOD, A. L. (1942) "Social organization and crime in small Wisconsin communities." American Sociological Review 7: 40-46.

14

THE NEW CRIMINOLOGY:
ACCEPTANCE WITHIN ACADEME

William V. Pelfrey

Criminology is a dynamic discipline. It is constantly in a state of evolving from one perspective to another and even from one discipline to another. The substantive area of criminology, beginning with Beccaria's *Of Crimes and Punishments* (1764), has been clothed in reform movements and even radicalism. "Radical" implies a considerable departure from the usual or traditional. New paradigms have always arisen to challenge the old. This seems to be just as true today as it has been in the past.

The crises, revolutions, and revelations of the last two decades have produced reverberations in many public and private structures. The academic area of social and behavioral sciences was one of the structures shaken by those crises. Gouldner stated in 1970 that academic sociology was "in the early stages of continuing crises" (1970: 341). Chambliss (1973: 1) used stronger terminology observing that "sociology is in the

AUTHOR'S NOTE: The material in this project was prepared under Grant No. 78-NI-AX-0050 from the Law Enforcement Assistance Administration, U.S. Department of Justice. Researchers undertaking such projects under government sponsorship are encouraged to express freely their professional judgment. Therefore, points of view or opinions stated in this document do not necessarily represent the official position or policy of the U.S. Department of Justice.

throes of what Thomas Kuhn has called a period of 'paradigm revolution'—there is intensified criticism of the dominant theoretical paradigm and formulation of an alternative." This is not to imply that there would be a demise of sociology as a result of the crisis or revolution, but that it would "become something quite different than it has been" (Gouldner, 1970: 342). This change was predicted to be in the direction of a radical or conflict perspective based on Marxism. In other words, academic sociology, synonymous with traditional-functional-consensus theory, was in the midst of a crisis which could result in the loss of dominance of that paradigm.

This crisis became exceedingly evident during the American Sociological Association Convention in 1968 when Martin Nicolaus delivered a speech which attacked the "sanctimonious sociological concepts of objective value-free science" (1970: 154). His speech followed the address of the Secretary of Health, Education, and Welfare whom Nicolaus characterized as the "Secretary of Disease, Propaganda, and Scabbing" (1970: 154).

> The department of which the man is head is more accurately described as the agency that watches over the inequitable distribution of preventable disease, over the funding of domestic propaganda and indoctrination, over the preservation of a cheap and docile reserve labor force to keep everybody else's wages down [1970: 155].

He assailed sociologists by saying that their research and scientific study was focused on the "down people" and the "professional palm of the sociologist is stretched toward the up people" (Nicolaus, 1970: 155).

Just as criminology gleaned its very existence from sociology (Gibbons, 1966: 3), it appears that it may also have contracted the coming "crisis" to which Gouldner referred. One writer even sees criminology as "both a reflection of and a force behind this revolution" (Chambliss, 1973: 1). "In the United States we are presently witnessing and practicing a radical criminology which has been developing in its latest form since the early 1960s and has begun to challenge the hegemonic domination of the field of liberal scholars" (Platt, 1974: 2). Annual increases in serious crime, overburdened prisons, and the apparent inability of corrections to correct, have caused many to question the ability of traditional criminology to effectively deal with the problem of crime. The result of this anomaly has been the awakening of the "era of radical writings" calling for a replacement of existing paradigms (Reasons, 1975: 332). Gibbons noted in 1974 that even though radical criminology at that time was immature and unsophisticated as a theory, it was certainly worthy of attention and should not be ignored. It is time to closely inspect the new criminology in light of the old criminology in order to better identify that which may represent the impetus of a "paradigm revolution" (Kuhn, 1970).

Just as a "sociology of sociology" strives to "dissect, examine, and in other ways both analyze and criticize the discipline, profession, and science of sociology" (Reynolds and Reynolds, 1970: v), the "sociology of new criminology" presented here is an attempt to identify, delineate, and evaluate this new perspective. The apparent growth of "new criminology" as a paradigm in the discipline requires close inspection using various research methods intended to expose or demystify all the perspective has to offer. In 1978, a study was undertaken which was to determine the validity of the contention that criminology is in the throes of a paradigm revolution, and that "the prevailing consensus that has characterized the past 30 years of sociological and criminological inquiry in theoretical models has been shattered" (Chambliss, 1973: 1).

METHODOLOGY

In attempting to formulate an instrument to measure the respondent's perception of a perspective so ideologically bound as the new criminology, a panel of experts was utilized to assist in the design of the questionnaire as well as to assist in evaluating some of the results. This panel consisted of William Chambliss, Don Gibbons, Richard Quinney, Austin Turk, Charles Wellford, and Marvin Wolfgang. During visits with each of the panel members the various points of the questionnaire were developed.

One of the first areas to be addressed with this questionnaire, as with any research instrument, was how to ensure that the respondent is directed toward the object of the study. Because the terms "radical criminology" (Gibbons, 1974: 57), "critical criminology" (Quinney, 1977: 6), "power/ conflict criminology" (Reasons, 1975: 345), "conflict criminology" (Turk, 1976: 276), and "Marxian theory of criminality" (Quinney, 1975: 108) all include terminology which may key inherent biases quite apart from criminological theory, the term "new criminology" was used to indicate that perspective which subsumes all of the specific perspectives mentioned above. This makes the "new criminology" an extraordinarily broad perspective with many diverse ingredients. The term was not copied from the book which is intended to be a critical survey of criminological theory (Taylor et al., 1973), but was selected because it seemed to be the least "offensive" term to indicate the perspective being studied. Rather than attempt to establish a threshold definition of the "new criminology" to further focus the respondents' attention on the perspective, it was decided that a "definition by association" would be used. Some of the prominent works which would serve as a collective example of the perspective were suggested by the panel of experts and included. Additionally, a "traditional" definition of the new criminology (Sykes, 1978: 14-16) was included so that respondents who were not familiar with the literature could still conceptualize the perspective.

The questions asked of the respondents focused on issues concerning the unique qualities of the perspective. The statements, followed by a Likert scale of strongly agree to strongly disagree, were aimed at the general ideological stance of the respondent concerning traditional criminology versus the new criminology. Statements concerning the power, potential, validity, and ability of the new perspective to replace the old or traditional criminology were used to establish the respondents' evaluation of the new criminology.

Another area upon which the questionnaire focused was a determination of the definition of the new perspective by establishing its most acceptable elements. Elements used in various definitions of perspectives subsumed by the new criminology were presented in an effort to determine which ones were acceptable to the respondents as representative of the new criminology.

The population from which the sample was drawn was comprised of academicians who were within the crime-related discipline or who had expressed an interest in criminology or criminal justice. It was expected that if the new perspective is considered viable, its viability would first be recognized within academe and, if embraced by academicians, it would be perpetuated through courses dealing with the new criminology. The population included members of the Academy of Criminal Justice Sciences, the American Society of Criminology, the Criminology Section of the American Sociological Association, and the Criminal Justice Section of the American Society of Public Administration. The population composition was determined by the 1977 membership directories or membership lists as of December 1977, depending upon the format of the organization. Student members were omitted from the population because the questionnaire relates to perceptions of the *academic* community and this would not be as developed or accurately defined by students as by faculty.

The population size was 2284 persons. This total number does not equal the sum of the full membership of the organizations and sections used because of the numerous duplications of membership. The sample used in the questionnaire was composed of a systematic random sample of 761 members.

RESULTS OF THE STUDY

Of the 761 questionnaires mailed to the sample, 384 or 50 percent of the sample replied. Since it was assumed that the concepts and propositions contained within the new criminology were familiar only to a relatively small audience of theoreticians, a portion of the questionnaire was provided which allowed the respondents to indicate that they were not familiar with "new criminology" and did not want to participate. Of all respondents, 18 percent elected this option and the remaining 82 percent provided the bulk of the data for analysis.

The first three statements of the questionnaire were aimed at determining the respondents' general impressions and tendencies concerning "new criminology." The statements which followed attempted to determine the specific strong or weak points of the perspective. If the respondents indicated that they were undecided in many of the specifics of the new perspective, it would indicate that they have been less than convinced of its viability.

The first statement to which the respondent was to indicate his or her agreement or disagreement was, "The 'new criminology' is a viable alternative to traditional criminology." This statement is much stronger than simply classifying "new criminology" as an addition to or a part of traditional or "mainstream" criminology. The concepts within "new criminology" often are in direct opposition to and engage in criticism of traditional criminology. Table 1 indicates the degree to which respondents expressed their preferences for the new or the traditional. The data indicate that a majority (57 percent) prefer new criminology to traditional criminology by either agreeing or strongly agreeing that it is a viable alternative to traditional criminology. The undecided category is relatively small and the results would not be disturbed if the entire undecided category opted for the traditional criminology.

The next element of the questionnaire stated, "The 'new criminology,' as a perspective, has definite potential." This statement is less ideologically assaulting than the first. Since it was unknown what the consensus was concerning "new criminology," statements were constructed of varying crassness in the hope that if academe was ambivalent in its acceptance of

TABLE 14.1   New Criminology Is a Viable
Alternative

Response	Frequency	Percentage
Strongly agree	43	13.9
Agree	135	43.5
Undecided	44	14.2
Disagree	62	20.0
Strongly Disagree	26	8.4

the perspective, the present state of ideology could be determined through gradual changes in the "radicalness" of the statements. The response to this statement is indicated in Table 2. In this statement no reference is made to the direction of potential or the specific areas which hold potential. The intent was simply to determine whether academicians are cynical or encouraged as to the future acceptability of the new criminology. Over 80 percent of the respondents indicated agreement on the potential of the perspective. Even many who were not willing to agree to the statement that "new criminology" is a viable alternative to traditional criminology agreed that the perspective has definite potential.

The next statement sought to determine the etiological propensity of new criminology. This element stated, " 'New criminology' currently explains criminality better or more adequately than traditional criminology." The results of the responses to this statement (see Table 3) indicate that the academicians are not willing to accept "new criminology" on its ability to explain criminal or deviant behavior. Over half of the respondents (53 percent) selected "disagree" or "undecided" as their response. This result may be linked to specific deficiencies, such as the lack of research, to be discussed later.

The next two statements were intended to determine if "new criminology" has reached its peak, as some contend (Gibbons, 1977), or whether much attention will be paid to the perspective in the future. This can only be done by contrasting the past attention and the future attention. The results of these statements are shown in Table 4. Over 50 percent agreed that much attention had been given the new criminology and much would be given in the future. An important response, however, is the 26 percent who responded that they were undecided concerning attention to be given the perspective in the future.

Other statements in the questionnaire sought to determine the respondents' impressions of the amount of research which has been done in the

TABLE 14.2   New Criminology Has Definite
Potential

Response	Frequency	Percentage
Strongly agree	66	21.3
Agree	183	59.0
Undecided	19	6.1
Disagree	32	10.3
Strongly Disagree	10	3.2

area of the new criminology and the name as well as the elements of the new criminology. One interesting area concerned the amount of research in the past which tested the new criminology. The respondents overwhelmingly agreed (81 percent) that there has been a dearth of research testing the propositions of the new criminology. This almost seems to be a contradiction in the data when considering the agreement that the new criminology is a viable alternative to traditional; yet there has been little research in the perspective. Kuhn (1970) indicated that a paradigm revolution will not occur unless and until the new paradigm has shown, through research, that it is more capable as a puzzle solver. A cross-tabulation of the first statement concerning the viability of the new criminology as a paradigm and the statement concerning the amount of research indicates that 83 percent of those who did not agree that the new criminology is a viable alternative to traditional also stated that there has been little research testing the new criminology. The obvious implication is that those who did not agree with the new criminology's viability as an alternative did so because of the lack of convincing research.

The respondents indicated that there is no overwhelming consensus as to the name of the perspective referred to as "new criminology." The response which received most agreement was "conflict criminology" (29 percent), followed by "critical criminology" (21 percent), "new criminology" (17 percent), "radical criminology" (16 percent), and "Marxian criminology" (14 percent).

The questionnaire included numerous "elements" of conflict and critical criminology theories as well as more traditional theories such as labeling. The respondents were asked to grade the elements as: (1) essential to a definition of the new criminology, (2) to be included in a definition of the new criminology, or (3) should not be included in a definition of the perspective. The results allow us to specify the elements

TABLE 14.3   New Criminology Explains
             Criminality Better Than
             Traditional

Response	Frequency	Percentage
Strongly agree	30	9.7
Agree	67	21.6
Undecided	83	26.8
Disagree	83	26.8
Strongly Disagree	47	15.2

approved by academicians as the accepted elements of the new criminology. Those elements are listed below, with the two elements which were considered essential listed first.

The state is organized to serve the interests of the dominant economic class.

Criminal justice decision-making is loaded heavily with class and status considerations.

The criminal justice system is the tool of the powerful and functions to suppress opposition to the ruling-class interests.

The political process of lawmaking, lawbreaking, and law enforcement is a reflection of the conflict between groups and their struggle for control of the state's police power.

Members of the powerful or ruling class are able to violate the law with impunity.

Crime is largely a product of social ills such as poverty, unemployment, poor education, and unequal opportunities.

Society enhances crime by maintaining segregation—race from race, the poor from the affluent, and the deviant from the conventional.

Due to the fact that everyone conforms and deviates, people should not be dichotomized into criminal and noncriminal categories.

The act of "getting caught" begins the process of identification as a criminal.

CONCLUSION

It appears that the "early stages of continuing crisis" (Gouldner, 1970: 341) have indeed progressed to a paradigm revolution. The contention that

TABLE 14.4   Attention to New Criminology

	Academe Will Give Much Attention to New Criminology	
Response	Frequency	Percentage
Strongly agree	26	8.3
Agree	135	43.3
Undecided	81	26.0
Disagree	65	20.8
Strongly disagree	5	1.6
	Much Attention Has Been Given to New Criminology in the Past	
Strongly agree	36	11.6
Agree	146	46.0
Undecided	31	9.9
Disagree	93	29.9
Strongly disagree	5	1.6

radicalism, as opposed to traditional or mainstream criminology, has peaked (Gibbons, 1977: 1) is invalid in light of the data collected in this study. The statement by Chambliss (1973: 1) that "the prevailing consensus that has characterized the past 30 years of sociological and criminological inquiry in theoretical models has been shattered" is supported by the fact that over 57 percent of the respondents in this study indicated that "new criminology" is a viable alternative to traditional criminology. The study has presented the first empirical picture of where criminology stands in respect to conflict-critical-radical-new criminology.

The respondents were inclined toward the new criminology as a perspective with definite potential and one which is seen to be capable of transposing traditional criminology. The academicians felt that while much attention has been given "new criminology" in the past, much will also be given in the future. The study indicated that the crime-related discipline does not feel "new criminology" explains criminality better than traditional, but that a great deal more research needs to be done in that area. Many academicians are undecided as to the future of "new criminology" and feel that much more research is necessary before they can lend their support to the perspective. Further, most of those who do not agree as to the viability of the new criminology stated that there has been little research testing the propositions of the perspective. A vast majority of the academicians feel that more research needs to be done on the propositions of "new criminology," but it needs to be a different kind of research than has been done in the past. The respondents indicated that research has not been clearly tied to the propositions. If the proponents of "new criminology" are to convince those who are undecided that the perspective is a viable one, the research of the future must be methodologically more closely related to the perspectives. For this to occur, the theoretical propositions must be more tightly formulated so as to provide an arena for testing through research.

The results indicate that the largest percentage of the respondents prefer the label of "conflict criminology" for the perspective. This perspective is the most traditional of the nontraditional; therefore, it could well be that the paradigm is at the critical moment of acceptance.

Traditional criminology is severely threatened by the new criminology. Often the result of a scientific revolution is the displacement of an old paradigm by a new one (Kuhn, 1970). An indication of the presence of the threat is the fact that in the study by Geis and Meier (1978: 275-280), 40 percent of the "most heavily cited [scholars] in the criminological literature during the period 1945 through 1972" believed that the new criminology trend is the most unhealthy element in the discipline. Donald R. Cressey, one of the foremost "traditional" criminologists, noted that the new criminology calls for "an abolition of criminology . . . to replace traditional criminology, not to supplement it. [This] approach is antiscientific" (1978: 185-187). The concerns of the prominent traditional criminologists may be explained by vested interests in the traditional theories or their suspected decline in prominence, but regardless of their concerns, the discipline is shifting or has shifted to *include* some of the new criminology based on this study. The fact that 57 percent of criminologists view the new criminology (generally defined as conflict criminology) as a viable alternative to traditional criminology indicates that "mainstream criminology" now includes traditional criminology *and* conflict criminology represented by Turk and Chambliss. Further, it appears, based on the definitional elements of this study and the high degree of agreement with the concepts and propositions of the new criminology, that the discipline, synonymous with mainstream criminology, could easily accept most of the propositions and elements of critical criminology. This is possible because of volumes such as the one published by Reasons and Rich (1978) which include research into the conflict perspective by Chambliss, Turk, Diamond, Pepinsky, Petras, and others.

It is not expected that traditional criminology will be abandoned, but should the research into the new criminology continue and validate its propositions, mainstream criminology may be composed of another "new criminology" which finds acceptable such concepts as conflict, labeling, and certain traditional sociological perspectives. This would allow the new criminology to represent a viable contribution to the discipline without requiring that one criminology displace the other. Many would find this compromise unsavory; yet, based on this research, many more would find it agreeable.

This suggested direction of the discipline is not pure speculation but is supported by contributions to the literature, particularly those which are critiques of the new criminology. Meier stated (1976: 469): "The stuff on the new criminology is deeply rooted in criminological theory. This is neither praiseworthy nor an indictment, since the utility of criminological theory is founded on other criteria." Another comment focused on the proposition that crime exists in high places as well as low places and it is inappropriate to discount or exaggerate criminality at either level (Toby, 1980).

To speculate that future criminology will contain both the traditional views as well as the new is not to forsake Kuhn's view of scientific revolutions (1970). It is not contradictory to propose that both perspectives can coexist. Coexistence would be highly unlikely if the discussion involved two "theories," but the case in point concerns "perspectives" or points of view; therefore, while there are inherent differences and similarities, one complements the other and neither is seen as exclusively etiological. Future criminology may not be the "old" criminology or the "new" criminology, but it appears that it will be a *revised* criminology.

REFERENCES

BECCARIA, C. (1963) Of Crimes and Punishments (H. Paolluci, trans.). Indianapolis: Bobbs-Merrill.

CHAMBLISS, W. (1973) "Functional and conflict theories of crime." MSS Modular Publications 17: 1-21.

CRESSEY, D. R. (1978) "Criminological theory, social science, and the repression of crime." Criminology 16, 2: 171-191.

GEIS, G. and R. F. MEIER (1978) "Looking behind and forward: criminologists and criminology as a career." Criminology 16, 2: 273-288.

GIBBONS, D. C. (1977) Society, Crime and Criminal Careers. Englewood Cliffs, NJ: Prentice-Hall.

––– (1966) Society, Crime and Criminal Careers. Englewood Cliffs, NJ: Prentice-Hall.

––– and P. GARABEDIAN (1974) "Conservative, liberal and radical criminology: some trends and observations," pp. 51-65 in C. Reasons (ed.) The Criminologist: Crime and the Criminal. Santa Monica, CA: Goodyear.

GOULDNER, A. W. (1970) The Coming Crisis of Western Sociology. New York: Avon.

KUHN, T. S. (1970) The Structure of Scientific Revolutions. Chicago: University of Chicago Press.

MEIER, R. F. (1976) "The new criminology: continuity in criminological theory." Journal of Criminal Law and Criminology 61, 4: 461-469.

NICOLAUS, M. (1970) "Text of a speech delivered at the American Sociological Association convention, August 1968," in L. T. Reynolds and J. M. Reynolds (eds.) The Sociology of Sociology. New York: David McKay.

PLATT, T. (1974) "Prospects for a radical criminology in the United States." Crime and Social Justice 1: 2-10.

QUINNEY, R. (1977) Class, State and Crime. New York: David McKay.

——— (1975) Criminology: Analysis and Critique of Crime in America. Boston: Little, Brown.

REASONS, C. W. (1975) "Social thought and social structure." Criminology 13: 332-365.

——— and R. M. RICH (1978) The Sociology of Law: A Conflict Perspective. Toronto: Butterworth.

REYNOLDS, L. T. and J. M. REYNOLDS [eds.] (1970) The Sociology of Sociology. New York: David McKay.

SYKES, G. (1978) Criminology. New York: Harcourt Brace Jovanovich.

TAYLOR, I., P. WALTON, and J. YOUNG (1973) The New Criminology. London: Routledge & Kegan Paul.

TOBY, J. (1980) "The new criminology is the old baloney. This volume.

TURK, A. T. (1976) "Law as a weapon in social conflict." Social Problems 23: 276-291.

15

TEACHING CRITICAL CRIMINOLOGY:
THE ETHICAL ISSUES

Stephen J. Pfohl

A critical theory is one that is radically critical. It is a theory that goes to the roots of our lives, to the foundation and the fundamentals, to the essentials of consciousness. In the rooting out of presuppositions we are able to assess every actual and possible experience. ... Without critical thought we are bound to the only form of social life we know—that which currently exists.

—Richard Quinney (1974a)

To teach criminology is to teach about the construction of criminal law, the development of criminal behavior, and the organization and application of criminal control measures. To teach a critical criminology is to subject each of these topics to the test of social justice. Does the criminal law contribute to the protection of human rights, human dignity,

AUTHOR'S NOTE: I wish to thank Sandra Joshel, Mary Tarling, Dick Batten, Ron Kramer, Ron Huff, and Michael Rustad for specific comments and helpful criticisms of this essay and Richard Quinney for the numerous conversations on this and many topics. A previous version of this paper was presented at the 1979 meetings of the American Society of Criminology.

human possibility? Or is the law guided more by the interests and influence of some more than others? To what degree does the law protect the prerogatives of the privileged while infringing the rights, denigrating the dignity, or destroying the possibilities of the dispossessed? What about criminal behavior? It is by definition a political statement, a statement of trespass or disregard or disavowal of the rules of the legally sanctioned game of life. Does it also reveal a story of inequity or socially structured impotence? Do the structures of social life make obedience a less likely or less meaningful option for some more than others? Who benefits by the organization of criminal controls? In their effort to maintain order do criminal control agencies also contribute to the oppression of those who benefit little by the order of things as presently structured? These are the questions raised by a critical criminology.

If raised successfully and answered in the affirmative, the above questions present a moral dilemma for the criminology student. The student is provided with more than a simple knowledge about criminal law, the criminal, and criminal controls. One is also confronted with the awareness that each either contributes to or reflects the presence of social injustice. One is confronted with the awareness of socially structured evil. How should one respond? How should one act in light of this awareness?

The successful teaching of a critical criminology engages the student with these ethical questions. This poses a difficult problem for many students. Many may be taking the criminology course in hopes of later becoming an actor in the criminal justice system. All, at least in some indirect fashion, are citizens who pay for and are supposedly represented by this system. How can one contribute to a solution to this dilemma, to a reduction or elimination of structured inequality in the name of us all? Is it possible to act within the system without being coopted? Is meaningful change possible without destroying the system as a whole? These are ethical questions which the critical criminology instructor raises among her or his students. What are the instructor's responsibilities or ethical mandates in this regard? These are the issues to be pursued in the following pages.

THE SCOPE OF CRITICAL CRIMINOLOGY

A critical criminology is one that employs a "conflict model" of social life to explore the relationship between social, economic, or political power differentials and the production of criminal law, the emergence of criminal behaviors, and the application of criminal controls. There are several subtraditions within the critical framework.

Three of the most prominent subtraditions include the pluralistic, universalistic, and Marxist models of conflict. Each differs somewhat in its theoretical and empirical focus. Yet each shares a vision of criminal law, crime, and criminal controls as processes caught in the struggles of people aligned in accordance with conflicting cultural, political, and/or economic interests.

The pluralistic subtradition finds its conceptual grounding in the writings of George Vold. It is later revived in Richard Quinney's propositions regarding "the social reality of crime." The pluralistic model emphasizes the dominance of certain groups or segments of society in using the criminalizing power of the state to advance and protect their own interests. According to the revised edition of Vold's classic 1958 text, *Theoretical Criminology*, "As one political group lines up against another, both seek the assistance of the organized state to help them defend their rights and protect their interests" (1979: 287). To the winner goes the protection of the state; to the loser, often the burden of criminality. In the words of Vold (1979: 292):

> Many kinds of criminal acts must be recognized as representing primarily behavior on the front-line fringes of direct contact between groups struggling for the control of power in the political and cultural organization of society. On the surface, the offenses may seem to be the ordinary common-law ones involving persons and property, but on closer examination they often are revealed as the acts of good soldiers fighting for a cause and against the threat of enemy encroachment.

In his 1970 *The Social Reality of Crime,* Richard Quinney expanded Vold's notion of crime as group conflict to include the struggles between a variety of competing societal "segments." Each segment—political, economic, religious, ethnic, or whatever—is said to be in a state of conflict with other segments with greater or lesser social power. The likelihood that the criminal law will be defined and applied in the interests of the more powerful is said to vary "according to the extent to which the behaviors of the powerless conflict with the interests of the power segments" (Quinney, 1970: 18). A similar model of conflict is presented by Chambliss and Seidman in their analysis of the criminal justice system. In *Law, Order and Power* Chambliss and Seidman contend that "the higher a group's political or economic position, the greater is the probability that its views will be reflected in the [creation and application of criminal] laws" (1971: 474).

A second subtradition of critical criminology involves a universalistic model of conflict. Conflict is understood, not in terms of a multiplicity of competing interests, but as the outgrowth of the inherently unstable nature of authority-subject relations. Austin Turk's analysis of the con- flictual nature of crime and criminalization exemplifies the concerns of this universalistic conflict tradition. Drawing upon the theoretical imagery of sociologist Ralf Dahrendorf, Turk views conflict as a universal or omnipresent feature of all societies. His "theory of criminalization" repre- sents an attempt to specify "the conditions under which cultural and social differences between authorities and subjects will probably result in conflict, the conditions under which criminalization will probably occur in the course of conflict, and the conditions under which the degree of deprivation associated with becoming a criminal will probably be greater or lesser" (Turk, 1969: 63).

The Marxist subtradition of critical criminology views the repressive contradictions of the capitalist political economy as responsible for the alignment of criminal law and criminal controls with interests of the dominant capitalist class. The Marxist model views both crime and crime control as manifestations of society's material conditions. A contemporary understanding of crime and crime control thus demands an understanding of the development and consequences of the capitalist economic mode. According to Quinney, whose 1970s' writings contributed greatly to the formulation of a Marxist criminology in the United States, "The basic question in Marxist analysis of crime is this: What is the meaning of crime in the development of capitalism?" (1979b: 399). Quinney's Marxist model calls for detailed consideration of (1) the development of the capitalist political economy; (2) the structures of criminal justice domina- tion or repression that emerge to preserve the privileged position of the capitalist class; and (3) the various forms of accommodation and resistance (including criminal or criminalized accommodations and resistance) devel- oped by oppressed peoples in response to capitalist structures.[1]

While the pluralistic, universalistic, and Marxist models may be most prominent, these are not the only formulations associated with a critical criminology. Indeed, such works as Sellin's theory of "culture conflict" (1938), Taylor et al.'s "new criminology" (1973), and Quinney's recent efforts (1979a) to synthesize the insights of a Marxian analysis with the liberating concerns of "prophetic theology,"[2] all stand within the critical tradition. Moreover, recent efforts to combine the essential elements of the critical model with the concerns of interpretive or phenomenological sociology (Pfohl, 1978, 1979) are evidence of the expanding base of critical criminology. Each of these developments is concerned with socially structured power differentials and their relationship to crime and criminalization. Regardless of its specific subtradition, this theoretical concern with the development and criminological consequences of structured social inequality is a central feature of critical criminology as a whole. Empirically, critical criminologists have employed a diversity of research methods and have drawn data from numerous disciplines (history, sociology, economics, anthropology, and political science) to support their theses regarding the role of differentiated power in giving historical shape to criminal acts, legislation, and containment activities.

THE ETHICAL DILEMMA OF A "SUCCESSFULLY" TAUGHT CRITICAL CRIMINOLOGY

While I am convinced by the essential thrust of the critical criminological thesis, its theoretical and empirical adequacy is not the focus of this essay. That, I am sure, is the focus for other discussions and debates throughout this book and throughout the discipline. What is at issue here is the successful teaching of this thesis to students. When this occurs a student's analytic and ethical framework may be significantly altered.

If one becomes convinced by the critical criminology thesis one can no longer, at least no longer with ease or comfort, talk about or act toward crime or criminals without addressing a wider social landscape of inequality or oppression. The initial fruits of critical criminology are uneasiness and discomfort. The student may have come to class simply with curiosity or within a concern for helping criminals and/or their victims. But now the issue is more complicated. The student may come to "recognize" that helping can only be effected meaningfully by actively opposing the structures through which criminal justice services are presently provided. What passes for "help" may become viewed as but a repressive continuance of the structures which produce the need for help in the first place. If one tries to help in this more traditional sense, is one really furthering the historical generation of hurt?

The same questions may come to plague one's concern for better securing individual justice. Is this seemingly humanistic goal really a centrifuge for the continuation of social injustice. By channeling one's time and effort in this direction is one really only draining some tension from a repressive system that might better explode by the force of its own contradictions? If so, then how should one act?

How can one practically apply a critical criminology and ethically align one's practical actions with one's theoretical convictions? Seemingly one's instructor has promoted more questions than answers. A commitment to overall structural change is important in theory, but where within the historical confines of American society in 1980 does it take one in "praxis." Must one actively resist and oppose the state and the interests which control it to truly accept the ethical demands of a critical criminology? Must one step outside the system?" Is becoming the critical criminal the most logical response to a critical criminology?

To a greater or lesser extent each of the preceding questions is prompted by the "successful" instruction of a critical criminological perspective. They have been and still are the questions of my students. I assume that I am not alone in this regard; that these are the questions of any students bit by the troubling awareness that the study of crime is first and foremost the study of the way people struggle to gain, maintain, or resist the "authorized" or "legalized" domination of others. What are the instructor's responsibilities toward students for whom she or he facilitates this troubling awareness? What can the instructor offer as conceptual and/practical life tools for living with and acting upon this awareness? Without such offerings an instruction in critical criminology may produce nothing more than cynicism. It may disillusion rather than generate a commitment to structural social change. As Davis (1975: 195) suggests:

> The debunking tradition, adopted by recent theorists, demystifies authority but fails to provide guidelines for reorganizing regressive social structures. Unmasking the frailty of legitimate authority provides catharsis for debunkers, but when divorced from moral and political commitments, it can contribute to a high degree of moral incoherence, social fragmentation, and political privatism.

CONCEPTUAL AND PRACTICAL TOOLS OF "CRITICAL CRIMINOLOGY" INSTRUCTION

In order to assist students to live with and responsibly act upon the troubling awarenesses and ethical dilemmas engendered by a critical criminology, an instructor needs to attend to particular stylistic and content areas in her or his own teaching. Six such areas are briefly outlined below. This list is neither inclusive nor exclusive of all that an instructor might or must do. Nor is it intended as some specification of ethical requirements on the instructor's part. It is offered as a partial list of suggestions and recommendations. It is offered in response to the ethical dilemma that instructors may face in responding to the ethical dilemma they may promote among their students.

TEACHING "CRITICAL THOUGHT"; NOT PREACHING "CRITICAL BELIEFS"

Critical criminology raises serious ethical issues about justice and injustice, right and wrong. It is tempting for the instructor involved with such issues to become more of a preacher than teacher. This is a disservice to students. It is also a violation of one of the fundamental themes in the critical perspective. Preachers are spokespersons for "the truth." They try to engender belief in and action in accordance with "the truth." "The truth" is a statement of "objective" fact independent of the historically bound, interest-filtered vision of the criminologist. From the critical perspective "the truth" does not exist. For the critical criminologist the truth about crime and its control involves a reflexive search process rather than a set of beliefs. In this process the criminologist finds theoretical ideas and empirical findings about crime to be intrinsically bound to the practical social, political, and economic contexts in which they are produced. As one comes to understand the diverse ways that these contexts shape what is "known" about crime, the "knowledge" of the critical criminologist included, one begins to approximate an "objective" understanding of the truth about crime.

To study crime is to enter into a certain relationship with regard to the power struggle between criminal lawmakers and enforcers on the one hand, and law challengers and breakers on the other. To recognize one's place in that struggle is to be somewhat freer to stand back and appreciate the role of others. This recognition is a step toward objectivity. It contributes to clarifying one's vision by clarifying its limitations and biases. We come to recognize parts of ourselves in the criminal and in the criminal controller. Each is recognized as known only by the names that we have given to them. To recognize this is to recognize the historically based reflexivity of criminological work to recognize its practical affinity with certain arrangements of power. For to name something (in this or that fashion) is to partially control it, to establish a kind of power relationship with regard to it. Certainly this is the case with our use of names in criminological theory and research.

No criminologist can avoid this. However, the critical criminologist can partially overcome this problem of impaired vision, this problem of historically filtered objectivity, by (1) subjecting all truth claims about crime and the criminal to the rigorous test of empirical scrutiny by a community of fellow namers or fellow scholars; and (2) scrutinizing all truth claims for what they say about the historical affinities of the researcher with a particular alignment of power. The former commitment to empirical rigor is said to be shared by criminologists of all orientations. The latter commitment to a reflexive understanding of theory within the context of practical action is a distinctive feature of critical criminology.

A critical criminology engages in a process of truthful search by rejecting all claims about "the truth," while seeking to partially clear one's vision of how crime and its control exists for people struggling with each other in the world. To be true to this commitment the critical criminology instructor must avoid all preaching about "the truth." She or he must attempt, instead, to provide students with the empirical and reflexive tools of critical scholarship. With these tools students will have the opportunity to recognize for themselves the filtered truths about crime within history. In doing so students may also come to recognize themselves and how their affinities with particular arrangements of power have biographically shaped their particular understandings of the crime problem. This recognition cannot be achieved through preaching about "the truth." If critical criminology instructors are to prepare their students for critical thought and action, they must then avoid the powerful seductions of becoming "the preacher."

PROVIDING KNOWLEDGE OF OTHER PERSPECTIVES AND FINDINGS

In order to react thoughtfully to the theories, research findings, and action proposals derived from other criminological perspectives, critical criminology students need to have an in-depth knowledge of a wide range of traditional criminological issues. Students should be exposed to the diverse ways that the classical, pathological, social disorganizational, functionalist, anomie, social learning, and social reaction perspectives have defined, studied, and proposed solutions for crime. It is not enough to know only the theory and research derived from the critical tradition.

In order to adequately critique the limitations and/or repressive potential of something like the current sociobiological framework, one must seriously study the research and writing that constitute this tradition. One must also understand the intellectual appeal and practical attraction of other perspectives within their appropriate sociohistorical context. This provides insight both into the other perspectives and into the affinity between thought and action regarding crime. A detailed knowledge and evaluative comprehension of the field of criminology as a whole should thus be an essential component of any education in critical criminology.

PROVIDING DIRECT EXPERIENCE WITH CRIMINAL JUSTICE

Another tool that can be offered by the critical criminology instructor is the opportunity for firsthand observation and/or experience within the present criminal justice system. Such experiences, if paired with a reflective in-class discussion and assessment, can contribute several valuable things to the student concerned with social change. First, it can provide a lesson in how to act in a world of criminal justice actors. This is unfortunately not part of most academic educational programs. Students learn *about* but not *how* to intereact with people draped with the stigma of being criminal or the shield of being a law enforcer or lawmaker. If the student is to later act as an agent of change she or he will someday have to cross the social distance established by such stereotypical roles and role management. Getting out into the fields of criminology and criminal justice activity, while still in a supportive and reflective academic environment, is a useful way to disabuse oneself of such stereotypes. Field placements or field research experiences which are tied to critical criminology coursework are particularly helpful in this regard.

Field placements serve two additional purposes as well. By being in the field and yet being an outsider the student is provided with the freedom and opportunity to notice things that "full-time actors" may miss. In particular, students may be presented with the awareness of how routine pressures and subtle organizational regularities appear to structure participants' activities, catching them in a work or life process that does little to challenge or alter existing oppressive relationships. Such structures are frequently more noticeable to outsiders than insiders. In another sense the field placement may instill a confidence that allows the student to speak out articulately in a critical fashion. Without direct experience the critic can always be silenced by invoking the question, "What do you know of the 'real world' "? The student knows and has confidence in her or his knowledge because she or he has been in the field of "real" criminal justice activity.

SUPPORT FOR AND CRITIQUE OF REFORM

What posture should the critical criminology instructor take toward reform within the criminal justice system? From the perspective of critical criminology, reform (as distinguished from holistic or radical social change) is to bandage the broken parts of a system which should in its entirety be abandoned. Attempts to humanize or secure justice for parts within such a system is often viewed as (1) either prolonging the life of the repressive system as a whole, or (2) distracting attention from the larger structural roots of dehumanization and injustice. Reformist efforts are critiqued more than they are endorsed by a critical criminology. This may represent a concrete problem for the student who abstractly accepts the critical model, but who concretely is moved by compassion for people made to suffer injustice by one changeable or modifiable aspect of the larger system.

I believe that the critical criminologist should both support and provide a constructive critique of the reform efforts of such students. Support should be given for several reasons. First, any concrete opposition to unnecessary human suffering should be supported. Second, by engaging in concrete reform activity the student can experientially learn the structural resistances inherent in the system. The frustrations of coopted reform efforts are often better lessons in a critical criminology than any available in the classroom. Third, in line with the observations of Trotsky, it appears that reform can indeed stress or stretch the unjust system by both exaggerating and exposing contradictions to which it cannot structurally respond. On the other hand, by offering a consistent and constructive critique of reform programs, the critical instructor can remind students of the cooptive dangers of being absorbed by the parts and thus losing sight of the large structural terrain within which one acts.

EXPOSURE TO AND CRITICAL ASSESSMENT OF ALTERNATIVE STRUCTURES

In order to realistically address structural changes that impact on crime and criminal control processes the student needs a concrete and critical exposure to alternative social, political, and economic structures. It is not enough to say something like the elimination of capitalism will eliminate crime and an unjust criminal control system. Students should be provided with the opportunity of critically reviewing the problems of crime in alternatively structured societies, past and present, as well as debating the alternative avenues of structural change available to our own future. As Quinney (1974b: 13) points out, "In order to reject something, we must have some idea of what things could be like."

PROVIDING A COMMUNITY OF SHARED CONCERN

This is perhaps the most crucial gift of the critical criminology instructor. Yet it is the least tangible. When it occurs it provides a sense of purpose and hope among students. Students come to recognize that they are preparing for something that will not be realized in a moment but only in their collective work within history. They come to recognize that they are preparing for a process of major structural change. They come to share a commitment to this vision of change with others. They come to feel that they are not alone. This provides hope that change is possible. In the course of the critical criminology class they may have experienced changes in themselves and in their classmates. Despite this change they sadly recognize that much, even most, remains too much the same. By itself this sadness can become demoralizing and disillusioning. But in combination with a communal vision of another way, a vision of a more just arrangement of structures, this sadness can be accepted and transcended.

From the vantage point of a community of vision, students can find the support to say no to those things that subtly bind us to the present structures of injustice and yes to those that prepare the way for more just alternatives. They can become less committed to this order and more to another order, the realization of which awaits the growth of a human community which breaks open the doors to a more justly structured future. No instruction in critical criminology will mobilize such a community or dramatically contribute to such a future. Yet, if taught with care and sensibility, critical criminology can contribute in some small but concrete way to the formation of a critical community of persons whose present lives will contribute to the nucleus of major structural change in the future.

CONCLUSION

In the preceding pages I have argued that the successful teaching of a critical criminology poses certain ethical dilemmas for the concerned student. The presentation of such a dilemma promotes, in turn, a sense of ethical responsibility on the part of the critical criminology instructor. In outlining ways in which the instructor might address this responsibility, I have attempted to suggest avenues by which a critical criminology can combine a serious program of theory and research with an equally serious commitment to build a knowledgeable community of persons accepting the historical responsibilities of present structural arrangements and future structural change. It is only through the creation of such a community that a critical criminology can hope to realize its own vision of unified theory and action, of thoughtful social criticism and concrete societal reconstruction.

NOTES

1. In addition to Quinney's work, an increasing number of alternative Marxist formulations have appeared in recent years. Many are to be found in the pages of the journal, *Crime and Social Justice,* edited by Tony Platt and Paul Takagi. One of the most succinctly stated positions is found in Spitzer's "Toward a Marxian Theory of Deviance" (1975). According to Spitzer, "The formulation of a Marxist perspective on deviance (or crime) requires the interpretation of the process through which the contradictions of capitalism are expressed. In particular, the theory must illustrate the relationship between specific contradictions, the problems of capitalist development and the production of a deviant class" (1975: 642).

2. Quinney suggests the interconnection between liberating socialist and religious concerns. In Quinney's words, "A socialism without the sacred would become a system as materialist and alienating as that of capitalism. What is emerging in the transition to socialism is a new religious concern, a concern which not only repudiates the essential secularity of capitalism, but one that makes socialism whole by integration of the sacred" (1979a: 127).

REFERENCES

CHAMBLISS, W. J. and R. B. SEIDMAN (1971) Law, Order and Power. Reading, MA: Addison-Wesley.

DAVIS, N. J. (1975) Sociological Construction of Deviance: Perspectives and Issues in the Field. Dubuque, IA: Wm. C. Brown.

PFOHL, S. J. (1979) "Deciding on dangerousness: predictions of violence as social control." Crime and Social Justice 11 (Spring-Summer): 28-40.

——— (1978) Predicting Dangerousness: The Social Construction of Psychiatric Reality. Lexington, MA: D.C. Heath.

QUINNEY, R. (1979a) A Capitalist Society. Homewood, IL: Irwin.

——— (1979b) Criminology. Boston: Little, Brown.

——— (1974a) Criminal Justice in America: A Critical Understanding. Boston: Little, Brown.

——— (1974b) Critique of the Legal Order: Crime Control in Capitalist Society. Boston: Little, Brown.

——— (1970) The Social Reality of Crime. Boston: Little, Brown.

SELLIN, T. (1938) Culture Conflict and Crime. New York: Social Science Research Council.

SPITZER, S. (1975) "Toward a Marxian theory of deviance." Social Problems 22 (June): 641-651.

TAYLOR, I., P. WALTON, and J. YOUNG (1973) The New Criminology: For a Social Theory of Deviance. London: Routledge & Kegan Paul.

TURK, A. (1969) Criminality and the Legal Order. Chicago: Rand McNally.

VOLD, G. B. (1979) Theoretical Criminology (prepared by T. J. Bernard). New York: Oxford University Press.

16

RADICAL CRIMINOLOGY AS FUNCTIONALIST THEORY: THE NATURE AND IMPLICATIONS OF AN UNACKNOWLEDGED IDENTITY

Anne E. Pottieger

The argument presented in this essay is that the future development of radical criminology could be enhanced by recognition that, in terms of theoretical structure, radical criminology *is* structural-functionalism. Thus the thesis here is a very specific variation on the general theme of strong commonalities between structural-functionalism and radical, or Marxist, sociology—an idea which has been debated many times, in many ways, for many purposes. The variations in this debate are so extensive that perhaps the only conclusion derivable from them is that the idea tends, on the whole, to be more palatable to mainstream theorists (e.g., Merton, 1957; van den Berghe, 1963; Stinchcombe, 1968; Lipset, 1975) than to their more radical colleagues (e.g., Frank, 1966; Gouldner, 1970; Flacks and Turkel, 1978). Even so, some Marxists (e.g., Bandyopadhyay, 1971), other radicals (e.g., Atkinson, 1972), and analysts sympathetic to them (e.g., Friedrichs, 1970) do argue that congruencies exist between Marxism and functionalism, while some mainstream writers are so sweepingly hostile toward radical sociology that they would consider the suggestion ludicrous were they not also at best indifferent to specifically structural-functionalist analysis.

Although several of these discussions will be used later in this essay, it should be noted that the argument here is considerably more limited in scope than are most other analyses of radical versus functionalist theory. First, the present argument is more limited in subject matter, in that it deals only with radical *criminology*. In the interests of space, no attempt is made to extend the argument to other topics. (On the other hand, unlike most comparative analyses of radical criminology per se, the point of comparison used here is specifically structural-functionalist explanations, rather than "mainstream criminology" as a whole or some nonfunctionalist variation of it.) Further, while most other examinations of the radical-functionalist linkage are concerned with some sort of overall understanding of the relationship between the two perspectives, this essay has the much more limited purpose of commentary on the future development of radical criminology through analysis of its present nature. For this purpose, structural-functionalism is discussed only as a form of theoretical logic; the use made of this logic by conventional functionalist theorists is of only secondary interest. Finally, the present argument also rests on a very limited analytical base—namely, the theoretical structure, in and of itself, of radical criminology as it currently exists.

The last-mentioned limitation requires a few additional introductory remarks. The term "theoretical structure" is used here to mean the logic by which propositions are fitted together into a theory. The primary referent, therefore, is the *logical form* of explanations, but this should not be interpreted as implying a strict differentiation between "structure" and "content." At least in practice, the logical form of an argument places limitations on the types of variables which can be used in that argument— and the concern here is specifically the current theoretical *practice* of radical criminology. A strict differentiation *is* implied, however, between "theoretical" concerns—explanation per se—and such "metatheoretical" concerns as definitions of the ultimate goals of criminological inquiry, criteria for assessing the adequacy of explanations, or prescriptions regarding the proper subject matter for criminology. Because such matters necessarily play a role in theory construction, their impact on the main argument will be examined. But the main argument itself concerns theory in the strict sense of logically interrelated propositions which form an explanation, and the words "theory" and "theoretical" are used in only this sense throughout the essay.

The discussion which follows is organized into three main sections. The first defines the theoretical structure of functionalist analysis, argues that this structure is displayed in even the defining theoretical characteristics of radical criminology, and demonstrates the use of this structure throughout the range of topics studied by radical criminologists. The second section traces the implications of this theoretical identity for the future development of radical criminology. Finally, the third section is a reconsideration of the preceding arguments in the light of radical criminology's metatheory, emphasizing the special consequences of the radical position on value neutrality for the use of specifically structural-functionalist logic.

THE THEORETICAL STRUCTURE OF RADICAL CRIMINOLOGY

Of all sociological strategies, structural-functionalist analysis is quite possibly the most widely practiced, least acknowledged, and most dimly understood. Its essential form is very simple: The social phenomenon being studied is explained on the basis of its consequences for—its function in—the surrounding sociocultural structure. As both Davis (1959) and Merton (1957) note, the same basic strategy is commonly found in all the sciences: Data are interpreted in terms of their consequences for a larger structure of which they are a part. The widespread use of structural-functionalist explanations in sociology is thus easily understood, since the sociocultural environment is the major concern of both uniquely sociological analysis and specifically structural-functionalist sociological theory.

In its most elementary form, then, a structural-functionalist argument is a logical-analytical structure involving only three basic elements: the phenomenon to be explained, the consequences resulting from the existence of that phenomenon, and the larger arrangement of which the phenomenon and its consequences are a part. But, as Stinchcombe (1968: 80-93) points out, the phenomenon to be explained in a functionalist argument is "caused" only indirectly by its consequences. The more direct cause is some aspect of the larger, surrounding arrangement.[1] That is, the maintenance of certain consequences by a particular social phenomenon implies the existence of some problematic tension tending to upset or prevent those consequences. If there were no such tensions coming from the surrounding arrangements, then there would be no reason for the existence of a special phenomenon to maintain those consequences. In Stinchcombe's words (1968: 88): "Clean-air committees do not grow up in farm areas."

Stinchcombe's complete formulation is of course more complex (and useful) than the brief summary provided here. In addition, this three-variable skeleton argument can be elaborated in a number of ways Stinchcombe does not discuss, most notably by specifying who benefits from the consequences of the phenomenon to be explained or, in alternative phrasing, by specifying the persons or groups for whom the "problematic tension" is in fact problematic.[2] This matter of whose problem/who benefits will be discussed shortly. First, however, let us examine the logic of radical criminology in relation to the basic three-factor structural-functionalist argument.

Radical criminology has three defining characteristics—features which, when all present in the same work, identify it as "radical" criminology. One of these characteristics is *meta*theoretical: the rejection of the idea of a value-free science. This characteristic represents a strong contradiction to traditional functionalist metatheory and therefore has potentially serious consequences for any argument that the two perspectives are otherwise similar, let alone identical. For this reason, a rather lengthy consideration of the nature and implications of such metatheoretical issues is undertaken in the final section of this essay. But the immediate concern of the argument in progress, which is the central point of this essay, has to do with the logical-analytical structure of explanations. Before discussing metatheory, we therefore turn first to the other two defining characteristics of radical criminology, since they are the elements which *directly* describe its theoretical logic. The argument which follows is that, taken together, these two theoretical characteristics include an implicit structural-functionalist argument. That is, the *theoretical structure* of radical criminology can be *defined* as a form of structural-functionalist analysis.

Specifically, the two theoretical characteristics of radical criminology are the arguments that (1) crime and criminal justice problems have a logically inherent relationship to the fundamental sociocultural structure of the society in which they occur and, (2) therefore, they are problems which can be solved only by fundamental (i.e., "radical") changes in that basic structure. "Reform" of the system is necessarily inadequate; the very nature of the system itself must be changed because as it is now constituted, crime and criminal justice problems are an inseparable part of its continuing operation. The translation of this argument into explicitly structural-functionalist terms is straightforward. The basic sociocultural structure of a society in which crime and criminal justice problems occur is a structure which requires the existence of these problems in order for it to be maintained as a sociocultural system. That is, the fundamental structure of the society has characteristics which would subvert its own existence as a system were it not for the system-supporting consequences of crime and criminal justice problems.

The logic of this argument, and its clearly structural-functionalist form, is perhaps easiest to see in specifically Marxist radical criminology. Although explanations provided in any variety of radical criminology display this theoretical structure, Marxist explanations generally employ a common label to summarize the problem-tension variables in their arguments: "the contradictions of capitalism." For example, Quinney explains crimes against subordinate classes committed by those in positions of power as the result of a basic contradiction in the necessary legal underpinnings of a capitalist economy. Laws protecting subordinate classes must be strict enough to legitimate the capitalist order, and yet if such laws were obeyed, continued accumulation of capital would be strangled (Quinney, 1979: 397). As a result, these laws must be violated by members of the capitalist class and their agents, in order for the capitalist economy to be sustained. That is, "It is one of the contradictions of capitalism that some of its own laws must be violated to secure the system" (Quinney, 1979: 164). Both "the crimes of domination" (crimes committed by the state, the capitalist class, and agents of the capitalist system) and the criminal justice problems which permit and sustain these crimes are, Quinney argues, social patterns which have system-supporting consequences for capitalist political economies. Were it not for these crimes and criminal justice problems, the capitalist system would be destroyed by its own required legal framework.

Before looking at other examples, the further significance of one of the initial limitations of this essay should be spelled out. It was stated in the introduction that the present discussion has a very limited analytical base—namely, the theoretical structure, in and of itself, of radical criminology as it currently exists. The nature of that theoretical structure is specifically the logic of structural-functionalism. But in addition, and very likely relatedly, the limitation to radical criminology as it currently exists is a limitation to radical criminology as a critique of capitalism. Radical criminologists themselves have commented on this aspect of their writings, although they do not agree on its significance. Some argue that a true socialist economy would mean little or no crime. Quinney (1977: 125-126), for example, calls the argument that crime is inevitable in any society "absurd," since it does not apply to socialism; the Schwendingers (1974: 25) refer to a "relatively crime free" future under socialism. Other radical criminologists (e.g., Gordon, 1973: 174, n34) do allow for the possibility of crime even in an economically ideal communist economy, but argue that it would be a different kind of crime from that produced by capitalism and would thus need to be explained by reference to a different set of forces. These as yet nonexistent explanations might well take some form other than structural-functionalist logic. But existing radical criminology deals with crime only in relation to capitalism, consistently traces the origins of crime to inherent problems in the capitalist order for which crime provides a system-supporting solution, and, accordingly, uses a structural-functionalist theoretical structure.[3]

This is not to say that radical criminology necessarily involves either Marxist terminology or systemwide analysis of capitalist societies. Chambliss's (1973) study of "Rainfall West," for example, deals with organized crime and its relation to political and economic structures in one city. Chambliss discusses everyday operational difficulties experienced by respected community members, such as fund-raising problems for politicians, financial insecurities for local businessmen, and conflicting demands on law enforcement officials to both permit access to the services offered by organized crime but also at least appear to be controlling it. His analysis indicates these operational difficulties to be inherent problems in the political and economic structure of American cities, problems which in instances like "Rainfall West," have been successfully resolved by the operation of crime syndicates. Thus, although Chambliss's argument uses neither the systemwide focus nor the explicit Marxism of Quinney's argument, both demonstrate the same basic theoretical logic in explaining crime.

Nor is the radical argument confined to crimes committed by the powerful, or at least the comfortable, and those who conspire with them. At least three other foci of radical criminology can be identified, one of which serves to make its range of concerns even wider than that of conventional criminology. This is its focus on what might be called the comfortable who do not consciously conspire with the powerful but end up serving their ends anyway. Most particularly, this is exemplified by radical concern with the consequences of mainstream social science, especially mainstream criminology. The Schwendingers' (1970) argument, among others, is essentially an argument that mainstream criminology, with its restriction to conventional legal definitions of crime and its primary focus on individual offenders, fits into the economic and political concerns of the powerful in strictly analogous ways to those in which organized crime is shown by Chambliss's argument to fit in; however different the motivation patterns may be, the consequences—support of an inegalitarian status quo—are the same.

The second additional focus of radical criminology is its analysis of the criminal justice system. This is sometimes handled as part of an examination of a particular type of crime (as in the explanations by Quinney and Chambliss just discussed). Where treated separately, the argument follows the same logic as the radical argument about mainstream criminology. It should perhaps be noted that analyses of criminology and criminal justice are the radical explanations most easily identifiable as structural-functionalist, because their explicit concern is with the sociocultural consequences of criminological and criminal justice activities, regardless of the motivation of the actors involved.

Finally, the third additional focus is on crimes of the powerless. Radical criminologists argue that a major reason for conventional criminological inquiry being supportive of capitalist law and order is its degree and manner of focus on these crimes. That is, the mainstream focus on crimes of the powerless is both too exclusive and too confined to the acts of individual offenders rather than their relationship to the sociocultural system in which they act. Radical analysis of these crimes therefore tends to emphasize their relationship to both other types of crime and the sociocultural context in which crime occurs. The specifics of these relationships are handled somewhat differently by different authors, particularly in the degree to which structural conditions are explicitly connected to the psychological conditions of individual actors. For example, Gordon (1973) begins his "radical economic analysis" of crime by arguing that ghetto, organized, and corporate crime are strikingly similar in motivation in that they all represent rational responses to the structured economic inequality and insecurity of life in capitalist society. Explicitly Marxist arguments, on the other hand, more frequently express the relationships in terms of class position and class conflict, tracing crimes of both the powerful and the powerless to the societal system and conditions of production. In showing the effect of these conditions specifically on criminality among the powerless, particular Marxist analyses vary widely in their emphases, ranging from Bonger's (1916) rather primitive reasoning about economic deprivation, to Quinney's (1977) more direct use of Marx's work such as tracing the implications of capitalism's reliance on an "industrial reserve army," to the more contemporary concern with similar class rates of criminality but differential law enforcement patterns (e.g., Chambliss, 1975). Radical criminology encompasses many other variations, both Marxist and non-Marxist, in specifying the relationships between ordinary property and personal crimes, other forms of crime, and their common sociocultural context. But these variations are all complementary specifications of the same basic structural-functionalist argument: Capitalist societies have certain structural and cultural characteristics which are required for a capitalist economy but also necessarily motivate people to steal and commit violent acts. To eliminate the sociocultural causes of ordinary property and personal crime, that is, would require elimination of the distinctive social and cultural characteristics of capitalism itself.

This argument is a modified version of the radical argument concerning crime generally, but it should be noted that it is still a clearly structural-functionalist theoretical structure. With other crime and criminal justice problems, the argument is made that the consequences of these problems are system supporting. The same argument is occasionally extended to ordinary property and personal crimes (see, e.g., Chambliss, 1975: 8), but such direct applications are rare. The more common argument begins not with garden-variety crimes themselves but with the sociocultural conditions which even mainstream criminologists agree are responsible for them: cultural emphasis on money and achievement, chronic poverty, and so forth. However, while mainstream criminologists argue that these conditions can be at least ameliorated by reform efforts, radical criminologists argue that the major consequences of these conditions—and hence the conditions themselves—are absolutely necessary for the operation of a capitalist economy. Thus, the radical argument concerning the ordinary crimes of the powerless is somewhat more indirect than the logic used with other forms of crime: The main emphasis is on criminogenic conditions rather than the crimes as such. Nonetheless, the logic—the theoretical structure—of the argument is identical, and distinctively structural-functionalist, in both cases: The crime-related phenomenon in question has system-supporting consequences and thus cannot be eliminated without changing the nature of the system itself.

Finally, the matter of whose problem/who benefits raised earlier can be addressed at this point. The argument thus far is that *in terms of theoretical structure,* radical criminology *is* structural-functionalism, because its logic is that of the three-variable skeleton theory outlined by Stinchcombe in describing functionalist explanations. It is obvious, however, that radical criminology also maintains a theoretical concern with a fourth element: identification of those persons or groups who benefit from crime because they are the people for whom the "problematic tension" solved by crime is in fact problematic. But Chambliss (1975), for one, argues that functionalist explanations of crime ignore this element of conflicting interests, maintaining instead a theoretical interest in identifying the ways in which crime and criminal justice phenomena reflect value consensus, collective sentiments, and unifying themes for the society. At first glance, the whose-problem/who-benefits question does indeed seem to differentiate the theoretical structures of radical versus functionalist explanations of crime.

A full discussion of this issue is beyond the scope of this essay since it would require, at a minimum, discussion of (1) the attention functionalists have in fact given to social change and conflict (see Lipset, 1975; Coser, 1956, 1967); (2) the nature of "consensus" as a logically gratuitous postulate for functionalist theory (see van den Berghe, 1963); (3) problems involved in the concept of "interest" in both Marxist and conventional social theory (see Balbus, 1971; Kockars, 1979); and (4) the similarities in the questions, methods, and answers employed by Marx and various functionalists, particularly if somewhat astoundingly, Parsons (see Atkinson, 1972). Let it suffice for present purposes to note that Chambliss himself freely admits (1975: 3) that his analysis concerns functionalism as derived from the work of Durkheim and therefore only a limited view of functionalism, although it is arguably an appropriate one for his purpose of comparative commentary on the heritage of Marx. But the concern of the present discussion is with the theoretical structure of contemporary radical criminology, whether Marxist or not, and hence the appropriate point of comparison *here* would seem to be contemporary structural-functionalism. Stinchcombe's (1968) analysis has already been presented as one such reference point. Although the specification of whose problem/who benefits does not appear as an explicit element in his formulation, it should be noted that, first, neither are consensus assumptions included, even implicitly, and, second, the whose-problem question does follow quite directly, albeit implicitly, from what Stinchcombe does include. But Stinchcombe was aiming for a brief description, from the viewpoint of a theoretical pragmatist. Merton's (1957) paradigm for functionalist analysis, in contrast, is the work of a theorist who is himself a contemporary functionalist, and his formulation has been treated as the definitive explication of contemporary functionalism in sociology by adherents and critics alike. It can therefore be taken as significant that Merton's work includes several explicit discussions of the whose-problem/who-benefits question. His paradigm as such specifies eleven sets of concepts as minimal for adequate functionalist analysis, the fourth of which is "concepts of the unit subserved by the function"—i.e., specification of the individuals and subgroups for whom the phenomenon being analyzed has the designated consequences. In his application of the paradigm to the case of urban political machines, Merton says the same thing less abstractly. He states that understanding the political machine requires that we look at two types of sociological variables: the sociocultural context making it difficult for other (legitimate) structures to fulfill the functions being provided by the machine, and the subgroups whose needs would go unserved were it not for the machine. These instructions are followed by a page of specifics on the sociocultural context and then seven pages discussing the subgroups who benefit from machine activities.[4] In short, there are at least reasonable grounds for arguing that while the whose-problem/who-benefits question is a significant concern for radical criminology, it is an equally significant question for (other) functionalist analyses of crime.

The argument presented thus far is that *in terms of theoretical structure,* radical criminology is a structural-functionalist analysis of crime, criminal justice, and criminology itself. It has been noted, however, that the value stance of radical criminology represents a metatheoretical dimension which is quite different from that of structural-functionalism; discussion of this dimension and its significance is undertaken in the final section of the essay. But first the implications of the argument made thus far—the identity of radical criminology as structural-functionalist theory—are explored briefly in the next section.

IMPLICATIONS

Perhaps the most important implication of the preceding argument is that radical criminology is in danger of producing bad criminology because of the ease with which bad functionalism can be constructed even when the analyst is deliberately engaged in it. The many ways in which this can occur have been widely discussed in the form of commentaries on functionalism (e.g., besides Merton and Stinchcombe: Hempel, 1959; Nagel, 1957; Martindale, 1965), so that an even partial inventory of the perils of functionalist analysis seems inappropriate here. Rather, only two of the most common errors in functionalist analysis will be discussed in order to illustrate the point that these commentaries are indeed applicable to radical criminology in ways which reflect upon both its explanatory power and its comprehensibility to mainstream criminologists.

One such problem is what Merton (1957) calls confusing objective observable consequences (functions) with subjective dispositions (aims, motives, purposes). For radical analyses, this confusion is most likely to occur in discussions of crimes committed by persons in positions of economic or legal power—"capitalists and their agents." In the sporadic but not infrequent analyses displaying this problem (the best known of which is probably Quinney's [1974] *Critique of Legal Order*), the result is, at best, a loss in clarity. At worst, the study becomes a simplistic conspiracy theory that does precisely what radical theorists cite as the cardinal sin of mainstream criminology: focusing on attributes of the criminal to the exclusion of all else. This is not to say that motives are irrelevant to functionalist analysis. On the contrary, they are not only legitimate but even central concerns, so much so that Merton (1957) gives them equal status with objective consequences in his functionalist paradigm. The point, rather, is that motives must be distinguished theoretically and empirically from consequences because they are separate phenomena which vary independently and may or may not coincide. Matza (1969) goes so far as to conclude that one of the outstanding contributions of functionalist theories of deviance is their repeated demonstration of the evil consequences of virtuous motives and, alternatively, the beneficent results of intended malevolence. *To the extent that* particular radical criminologists limit themselves to connecting the ravages of capitalism to only the greed of its power holders and servants, their analyses are in turn limited to kinds-of-people theories—theories which radical criminology as a whole has shown to be a naive diversion of attention from the real problem of structural arrangements in capitalist societies. That government officials and corporate leaders are self-interested may still be a point which needs making. But the main thrust of radical analysis must, to avoid conceptual confusion, be on (1) the institutional arrangements which enable the self-interest of the powerful to be served at the expense of the self-interest of others in the society, and (2) the empirical and historical evidence substantiating the assertion that any given social arrangement actually is more beneficial to one class than others. (For the same two arguments in Marxist terms, see Bierne, 1979, especially 379-382.)

A second major theoretical problem common in functionalist analysis to which radical criminology can easily fall prey is what Merton (1957) calls "the postulate of indispensability." This is the assumption that certain cultural or social forms are indispensable for achieving certain consequences. While the motive/function confusion is an error which appears sporadically in individual radical analyses, the indispensability postulate can be imputed to radical criminology as a whole—and the entire foregoing description of radical criminology implies exactly this imputation. That is, it was argued in the preceding section that *any* analysis of crime which is properly labeled "*radical* criminology" asserts that the structure of capitalist societies is such that crime is *required* for their continued existence. Certainly, the range of variation in items able to fulfill designated functions in a social structure is a limited one. But at the same time, structural indispensability of a single social pattern is at best exceedingly rare and hence cannot be asserted without careful defense. Thus, the point here is that the radical argument would be much more theoretically adequate were it accompanied by explicit attention to the possibility of *functional alternatives* to crime. Radical theory does frequently mention alternatives to "crime in industrial society," in the form of advocating socialism as an alternative to capitalism. But in terms of theoretical logic, this is too simple an answer: The concern of radical criminology is not industrial society in general but capitalism in particular. The more adequate although more difficult procedure would be for radical criminologists to consider alternative structures within capitalism itself, providing logical, historical, and contemporary empirical evidence to support the indispensability postulate. This seems all the more critical in recent years, given the many sociocultural innovations—ranging from nontraditional living arrangements to explicitly economic experiments such as consumer cooperatives and participatory management—which have arisen *within* capitalist societies since the 1960s. Further, this is not simply a matter of adequate *functional* analysis. An established canon of scientific procedure states that a good theory permits a "crucial experiment"— simultaneous empirical testing of contradictory hypotheses. For radical criminology, such studies require explicit theoretical attention to functional alternatives to crime, and hence recognition of the theoretic difficulties involved in a postulate of indispensability.

Thus far this discussion has dealt primarily with explanatory power. It has been emphasized that a major implication of the theoretical identity of radical criminology as structural-functionalism is that radical criminologists are in a position to profit from what is known about difficulties in functionalist analysis, simply for the sake of better theory. But a related implication is that these kinds of improvements might well make a difference in the ability of radical criminologists to communicate with their mainstream counterparts. The latter most often balk at two particular points in the radical argument: overtones of conspiracy theory, and the need for radical reconstruction of American society if we want to eliminate crime. Both areas contain theoretical problems which mainstream criminologists accuse radicals of "solving" by value fiat. But the preceding discussion implies that these are problem areas which can be at least attacked, if not actually resolved, in strictly theoretical terms. Motives for behavior can be analyzed independently of behavioral consequences; structural constraints on viable alternatives to crime and criminal justice problems can be addressed with explicit logic and empirical evidence. In short, radical criminology's functionalist theoretical structure means that existing guides to avoiding the theoretical confusions peculiar to functionalism can provide radical criminologists with the opportunity to demonstrate that controversial aspects of radical theory are a matter not simply of value preference but of logical and empirical evidence.

METATHEORETICAL CONSIDERATIONS

At this point the matter of the third, and metatheoretical, characteristic of radical criminology can be brought into the argument. This is the value neutrality issue. For radical criminology, as for radical analysis in general, values are considered inseparable from any form of thought itself, including science. Accordingly, radical analysts argue that aiming for a value-free science is not only futile but a reprehensible exercise in self-deception. This position carries two further implications, both of which bear directly on theory. First, there is a moral directive to concern oneself as a criminologist, and not merely as a citizen, with moral questions—particularly the question of "whose side we are on." Theory is affected in that the goal of criminological inquiry itself becomes defined as the achievement of a humane, egalitarian society, and this goal is set forth as a prescription regarding the appropriate subject matter for criminological study. Second, the view that values are inseparable from any form of thought has the more direct implication for theory that value-related positions are particularly significant factors in human behavior. Radical theory thus has an extra, metatheoretical impetus for placing special explanatory emphasis on value-related phenomena—economic interests, culturally defined goals, ideological systems, individual motives, or whatever other forms they might take.

The radical value commitment contrasts strongly to the premise of structural-functionalism, as for mainstream social science generally, that the *effort* to separate values from scientific procedure is imperative. However involved as a citizen, the structural-functionalist is enjoined to be *positionless* as a social scientist. Thus, the consequences of any value system may be investigated, but—contrary to the radical position—moral values cannot be incorporated into science as science, and no greater theoretical concern is attached to values, interests, ideologies, and so forth than to any other subject of sociological inquiry.

This metatheoretical clash has several consequences relevant to the preceding arguments about theory. The most noticeable of these consequences is itself metatheoretical in that it pertains to politics and communication patterns in theory construction. Inspired by metatheoretical visions, many radical and mainstream criminologists alike have in essence substituted rhetoric for analysis when discussing radical criminology. Mainstream theorists decry radical "dogma," "soothsaying," and "sentimentality" as if there were no relationship worth mentioning between radical criminology and their own theoretical traditions. The same image is projected by those radical analysts who regard structural-functionalism as irrelevant to their own analyses and thus happily throw out the theoretical baby with the metatheoretical bathwater. In short, one consequence of the value-neutrality dispute has been to divert the attention of both mainstream and radical analysts from strictly theoretical issues of the type discussed in this essay. As a result, the identity of radical criminology as structural-functionalist theory has gone generally unrecognized, as have its implications for future strategy in the radical analysis of crime.

But what about the possibility that these metatheoretical issues in some way negate the entire foregoing argument that radical criminology *is* structural-functionalist theory? It has been noted that the value stance of radical criminology does have direct implications for theory as such. This in turn implies that the value issue may be the source of some underlying theoretical incompatibility between radical criminology and structural-functionalism, reducing the thesis of this essay to an academic exercise with little relevance for the future development of radical criminology.

This essay itself, its announced thesis notwithstanding, can be taken as evidence that such an incompatibility exists. The preceding section includes references to some specific difficulties with structural-functionalist analysis which appear in radical criminology: (1) confusing consequences of and motives for behavior, particularly by emphasizing the importance of actors' value positions; and (2) assuming a postulate of the indispensability of crime for the operation of capitalist societies. Both of these theoretic problems stem in part from specifically theoretical motives easily identified in the analytical legacy of Marx himself. But, more significantly for the context of the present discussion, both problems can also be linked to the radical value stance. Specifically, they can be interpreted as resulting from the two theory-relevant implications of the radical value position traced in the beginning of this section of the essay: respectively, (1) a commitment to regarding value-related positions as being particularly significant factors in human behavior; and (2) the commitment to concern oneself, as a criminologist, with moral questions and hence a commitment to the critique of inhumane, inegalitarian social conditions. In short, it appears that the value stance of radical criminology is at least in part responsible for some *theoretical* difficulties in the use of structural-functionalist analysis—indicating that the two kinds of theory may, after all, be basically incompatible.

But this would be an erroneous conclusion, for several reasons. In the first place, traditional functionalist theorists themselves have precisely the same difficulties with functionalist theory construction. The reasons for the problems were different, but the problems were the same. Merton's (1957) paradigm is in fact based on a critique of errors made by these theorists, as are most other guides to good functionalist analysis. Thus, while the problems radical criminologists display in the use of structural-functionalist logic may stem from the radical value position, such errors are not unique to radical analysts and hence cannot be taken by themselves as evidence of logical incompatibility between functionalist arguments and radical criminology.

Further, regardless of their source, the theory problems radical criminologists have with structural-functionalist analysis are neither inevitable nor irresolvable. Most of the preceding section of this essay is devoted to demonstrating that existing commentaries on traditional functionalist analysis are directly pertinent to radical criminology; it was emphasized that this body of work is of great potential value to the future development of radical criminology for purposes of both improved theory and better communication with mainstream criminologists. The relevance of this argument for the present discussion of possible incompatibility should be specifically noted: What it says is that "*value*-imbued" problems encountered in *radical* criminology may well be resolvable through the *theoretical* tools of *structural-functionalist* analysis. This situation is the exact opposite of incompatibility. Moreover, it implies not only theoretical compatibility but also the possibility that explicit attention to the theoretical congruencies between radical criminology and structural-functionalism would obviate the need for at least the vociferousness of the debates about their metatheoretical differences.

Thus far it has been argued that the value commitments of radical criminologists may have disadvantageous results for radical use of structural-functionalist theoretical logic, but that these theoretical problems are also found in more conventional functionalist arguments, are not inevitable, and are resolvable by specifically theoretical means. However, it is possible to go even further and consider the ways in which the value stance of radical criminology may actually represent an *advantage* in the use of structural-functionalist theory. The ethical neutrality stance of traditional structural-functionalist analysis has had, after all, some undesirable consequences in terms of theory as well as morality. For theory, it has served to put functionalism in danger of abstracting to the point of losing contact with anything readily identifiable as actual human life. Psychologism has thereby been avoided. But the price has often been explanations in which intervening psychological variables enter the theory only through unexamined premises—an omission by abstraction which has been a major source of simplism, if not outright error, in conventional functionalist theorizing. The moral consequences have been similar, in that functionalist analysis of crime has tended to emphasize the irony of social benefits provided by crime while neglecting the more prosaic topic of the social and personal damages it causes. The latter are left out of the picture because they are too obvious to be of theoretical interest—and there is no other justification for analytic effort in conventional functionalism (see Matza, 1969). It might also be noted that the combination of sociologistic abstractness and lack of justification for taking value-related interest in a subject has had the further consequence of making many functionalist theories irrelevant to practical affairs. The value commitment of radical criminology, in contrast, is a major force in putting its theorists under much more of an imperative to relate their concerns to concrete empirical situations, actual human lives, and the need for workable solutions. This is not to deny the previously discussed dangers of the radical value stance. It is, however, to say that the value position of radical criminology does put it in a better position to provide comprehensive explanations of real problems than traditional structural-functionalism ever was, if—as discussed in these last two sections—its practitioners can use the analytic tools available to them as functionalist theorists.

Finally, it is even possible to argue that there are advantages for theory construction in the specific commitment of radical criminologists, as criminologists, to criticism of inhumane, inegalitarian social arrangements. In its mildest form, such an argument would simply emphasize the need for social scientists to think in terms of alternatives to whatever social arrangements they are investigating, preferably to the point that comparative analysis becomes an automatic part of their conceptualization of any social phenomenon. The radical commitment to moral criticism provides an impetus for precisely this kind of thinking, since the idea of preferable alternatives is basic to the radical critique. The mainstream objection to this argument is, of course, that the radical commitment to moral critique is itself a form of bias which will operate even if the more usual cultural biases of the scientist are overcome. The beginning of an answer to this charge is provided by Homans (1967: 71), commenting on the problem of social scientists letting emotions get in the way of objectivity:

> I do not believe the danger to be as great as asserted. No doubt their emotions will lead them to study certain phenomena and not others.

> There are social scientists who prefer to study things in society they
> like, and others who are positively compelled to study things they
> don't. But no great harm is done: the evidence is that either group
> gets great pleasure from pointing out to the other what it has
> deliberately left out, so that no trifle remains forever unconsidered.

But Homans's contention is comforting only so long as social science
analysis is actually being done from multiple perspectives. This limitation
leads directly to the strongest variation on the argument that the radical
commitment to egalitarian values provides a theoretic advantage, a variation spelled out at some length by Harding (1977, 1978). She argues that
there is epistemological and not simply moral reason for the social scientist, as a scientist, to work toward an egalitarian society. That is, only in a
society in which many different perspectives on social phenomena can be
represented will there be sufficient dialogue between perspectives to
ensure scientific objectivity through value-based cross-criticism. Moreover,
she emphasizes that the problem of increasing the representativeness of
perspectives is particular acute with regard to certain social locations:

> For instance the poor seldom express their "true interests" through
> theories with which they study how to make the rich happier with
> less profit; blacks rarely have been in a position to use their values
> systematically to draw conclusions about the family life of racists;
> the normative standards of factory workers are rarely used to com-
> mission studies of how to improve the performance of factory
> owners; until recently, housewives had not developed theories to
> explain the bizarre behavior of psychoanalysts [Harding, 1978:
> 207].

Since it is precisely these kinds of perspectives which are most often left
out of the scientific dialogue, Harding argues that those scientists who, as
scientists, are committed to working for political egalitarianism are in a
better position than their value-neutral colleagues to contribute to a more
objective and comprehensive social science. For purposes of the present
discussion, then, this kind of argument implies that even the radical
incorporation of morality into scientific procedure is not inherently anti-
science and hence incompatible with the theoretic aims of structural-
functionalism. Further, the radical commitment to egalitarianism can be
viewed as *particularly* helpful in the construction of functionalist theory.
The special concerns of functionalism such as functional alternatives,
latent functions, and differential consequences for distinct subgroups are
all topics which require special attention to alternatives to the accepted
cultural assumptions about how things work in a society.

Again, none of this is to deny the potential dangers of the radical values
stance, particularly the ease with which the commitment to moral

criticism can lead to what Klockars (1979), in discussing the radical critique of class, calls "the passionate assumption of evil." The same assumption can be seen underlying the postulate of the indispensability of crime for capitalist societies. The point is not that these dangers can be ignored, but that there are analytical and empirical means of overcoming them, that guides to these means exist in the form of standard commentaries on functionalist analysis, and that—given the effort to make use of this guidance—radical criminologists are in a better potential position, precisely because of and not merely in spite of their value commitments, to provide more adequate functionalist explanations of crime than the value-neutral traditional structural-functionalists ever were.

Wright (1978: 10), in the methodological introduction to his recent essays on Marxist social theory, argues that Marxist social scientists should avoid both ideological and strictly positivistic empirical responses to the mainstream attack on the values issue and, instead, develop "empirical agendas firmly rooted within not only the categories but the logic of Marxist theory." This strategy, Wright argues, would enable Marxists to "simultaneously engage in debate with mainstream social theory and to develop a style of empirical research which advances Marxist theory." The argument presented in this essay is a strictly analogous one. The nature of radical criminology as structural-functionalist *theory* means that its development into a mature analytic scheme, as well as its response to the mainstream value-related attack, can be assisted by attention to the *logic* of its own arguments. The theoretic difficulties peculiar to structural-functionalism have resulted in a rich literature for the guidance of future functionalist analysis. It has been the contention of this essay that the end product of radical criminological use of this guidance would be both greater theoretical sophistication and improved communications with mainstream criminologists. The issue is not future paradigmatic "synthesis" but an already existing identity of theoretical structures and future strategy based on recognition of this identity. The very real metatheoretical differences between radical criminology and structural-functionalism prohibit synthesis, but they need not stand in the way of the strategy proposed and, moreover, they may even contribute to its effective employment.

NOTES

1. It might be noted that the inclusion of this third variable means, among other things, that functionalism need not be defined as either inherently tautological (since the third variable is outside the logical circle otherwise formed by the phenomenon-

consequence-phenomenon relationship) or inherently teleological (since even where desire for the consequences of X inspire the origination of X, such motives themselves are explained in terms of this third variable); on the latter point, also see Stinchcombe (1968: 85-87) concerning functionalist explanations which do not involve purposive behavior at all.

2. However, one of the elaborations Stinchcombe does include is a kind of theoretical linkage between functionalist and Marxist explanations which is different from that discussed here.

3. Note that "criminology" is used throughout this essay in the narrow sense of theories of crime and directly related criminal justice problems. Were study of the law explicitly included, it would involve a further complication at this point in the argument. While the study of law done by many of the radical theorists who discuss both law and crime (e.g., Chambliss, Quinney, the Schwendingers) would still fit the argument that current radical criminology is a critique of capitalism, a vast literature exists in which other radical theorists have analyzed law as such in both capitalist and other societies in ways which are *not* structural-functionalist. While radical criminologists work with law as related to crime (and only secondarily to the state), these other theorists deal with law as related to the state and the economy (and only secondarily—and a remote second at that—with issues of crime). To include this literature in the present discussion would require a far longer and somewhat different essay.

4. It is of interest that among the subgroups Merton designates as benefiting from the urban political machine are both legitimate and illegitimate businesses, so that he discusses the connections between local politics, legitimate businesses, and the activities provided by organized crime in a very similar manner to that found in Chambliss's (1973) discussion of urban crime syndicates.

REFERENCES

ATKINSON, D. (1972) Orthodox Consensus and Radical Alternative. New York: Basis Books.

BALBUS, I. D. (1971) "The concept of interest in pluralist and Marxian analysis." Politics and Society 1 (February): 151-177.

BANDYOPADHYAY, P. (1971) "One sociology or many: some issues in radical sociology." Science & Society 35 (Spring): 1-26.

BIERNE, P. (1979) "Empiricism and the critique of Marxism in law and crime." Social Problems 26 (April): 373-385.

BONGER, W. (1916) Criminality and Economic Conditions. Boston: Little, Brown.

CHAMBLISS, W. J. (1975) "Functional and conflict theories of crime: the heritage of Emile Durkheim and Karl Marx," pp. 1-28 in W. J. Chambliss and M. Mankoff (eds.) Whose Law What Order? A Conflict Approach to Criminology. New York: John Wiley.

––– (1973) "Vice, corruption, bureaucracy and power," pp. 353-379 in W. J. Chambliss (ed.) Sociological Readings in the Conflict Perspective. Reading, MA: Addison-Wesley.

COSER, L. A. (1967) Continuities in the Study of Social Conflict. New York: Macmillan.

––– (1956) The Functions of Social Conflict. New York: Macmillan.

DAVIS, K. (1959) "The myths of functional analysis as a special method in sociology and anthropology." American Sociological Review 24: 757-773.

FLACKS, R. and G. TURKEL (1978) "Radical sociology: the emergence of neo-Marxian perspectives in U.S. sociology." Annual Review of Sociology 4: 193-238.

FRANK, A. G. (1966) "Functionalism, dialectics, and synthetics." Science & Society 30 (Spring). Reprinted, pp. 62-73, in W. J. Chambliss (ed.) Sociological Readings in the Conflict Perspective. Reading, MA: Addison-Wesley.

FRIEDRICHS, R. W. (1970) A Sociology of Sociology. New York: Macmillan.

GORDON, D. M. (1973) "Capitalism, class and crime in America." Crime and Delinquency 19 (April): 163-186.

GOULDNER, A. W. (1970) The Coming Crisis of Western Sociology. New York: Basic Books.

HARDING, S. G. (1978) "Four contributions values can make to the objectivity of social science," pp. 199-209 in Philosophy of Science Association, 1978 Proceedings, Vol. 1. East Lansing, MI: Philosophy of Science Association.

——— (1977) "Does objectivity in social science require value-neutrality?" Soundings: An International Journal 60 (Winter): 351-366.

HEMPEL, C. G. (1959) "The logic of functional analysis," pp. 271-310 in L. Gross (ed.) Symposium on Sociological Theory. New York: Harper & Row.

HOMANS, G. C. (1967) The Nature of Social Science. New York: Harcourt Brace Jovanovich.

KLOCKARS, C. B. (1979) "The contemporary crises of Marxist criminology." Criminology 16 (February): 477-515.

LIPSET, S. M. (1975) "Social structure and social change," pp. 172-209 in P. M. Blau (ed.) Approaches to the Study of Social Structure. New York: Macmillan.

MARTINDALE, D. [ed.] (1965) Functionalism in the Social Sciences. (Monograph 5). Philadelphia: American Academy of Political and Social Science.

MATZA, D. (1969) Becoming Deviant. Englewood Cliffs, NJ: Prentice-Hall.

MERTON, R. K. (1957) "Manifest and latent functions," pp. 19-84 in Social Theory and Social Structure. New York: Macmillan.

NAGEL, E. (1957) "A formalization of functionalism," pp. 247-283 in Logic Without Metaphysics. New York: Macmillan.

QUINNEY, R. (1979) Criminology. Boston: Little, Brown.

——— (1977) Class, State and Crime. New York: David McKay.

——— (1974) Critique of Legal Order. Boston: Little, Brown.

SCHWENDINGER, H. and J. SCHWENDINGER (1974) "Rape myths in legal, theoretical and everyday practice." Crime and Criminal Justice 1 (Spring/Summer): 18-26.

——— (1970) "Defenders of order or guardians of human rights?" Issues in Criminology 5 (Summer): 123-157.

STINCHCOMBE, A. L. (1968) Constructing Social Theories. New York: Harcourt Brace Jovanovich.

van den BERGHE, P. L. (1963) "Dialectic and functionalism: toward a theoretical synthesis." American Sociological Review 28 (October): 695-705.

WRIGHT, E. O. (1978) Class, Crisis, and the State. London: New Left Books.

17

CAN THE "OLD" AND "NEW" CRIMINOLOGIES BE RECONCILED?

Edwin M. Schur

INTRODUCTION

I would like to suggest that within the past few decades, perhaps at an accelerated pace during the past few years, the sociology of crime has for the most part been moving in "healthy" directions. We have seen and are seeing the growing acceptance by sociologists of perspectives and focal points for research that increase the promise of a comprehensive and insightful understanding of crime and crime-related forces and processes, and that may even work to promote—if sometimes rather slowly and indirectly—a more humane and equitable social system. (I want to emphasize my reference to "sociologists" and to the "sociology of crime," because for certain purposes it becomes important to distinguish between, on the one hand, what sociologists of crime are doing and, on the other hand, features of the criminal justice system itself or the activities of

AUTHOR'S NOTE: This paper was originally presented as part of a panel discussion on the topic, "Criminology and Criminal Justice: The Emergence of a New Criminology?" at the annual meeting of the American Sociological Association, San Francisco, September 1978.

nonsociologist crime and corrections specialists—in which sociologists may themselves be only slightly implicated.)

The recent radicalism in sociology has been an important factor in promoting those general trends that I see as desirable, and which I will mention shortly. It has, however, been only one such factor, and indeed we might do well to keep in mind that at least some of the impetus for the very emergence of this radicalism may have derived from work that some declared radicals now seem prepared to dismiss peremptorily as "conventional" or "traditional." Furthermore, it may well be the case that there are considerably more points and lines of agreement on significant matters between avowedly radical criminologists and most of their present-day sociological colleagues working in this area than many of the former appear willing to admit. In considering this possibility, it may be useful to think in terms of three general domains of agreement-disagreement. There is, I would submit, a narrow range of concerns and involvements revealed in the work of some conventional criminologists today that radicals quite properly deplore or condemn. There is, however, also a narrow range of assertions made by certain avowed radicals that many sociologists of crime with at least equal warrant will not be prepared to accept. In between, there is a broad range of common concerns and mutually acceptable propositions—which are far from being trivial and which, I would insist, can usefully be developed along a number of different but often converging or complementary lines, as well as from a variety of ideological and methodological points of departure.

THE DANGER OF COOPTATION

With respect to the first of these domains, the radical critique has great value in warning us of the ever-present danger of cooptation and in providing documentation of specific instances in which sociologists clearly become "agents of the establishment" or otherwise actively and directly contribute to or foster social oppression. Criminologists who advocate blatantly racist or sexist policies, who condemn poor people for the very conditions by which they are victimized, who lend themselves directly to the implementation of repressive control—be it behavior modification, political surveillance, or prisoner pacification—or who publicly "whitewash" genocidal militarism, corporate crime, or official corruption, deserve our opprobrium. Certainly they cannot be permitted to hide behind a claim of supposed value neutrality. However, I have yet to see convincing evidence that large numbers of sociologists of crime are doing these things. The radical critique of criminal justice policies is most cogent, but the attempt to tie it to a critique of developments in the recent sociology of crime is not fully persuasive. These critics perform a public service, again, in exposing distorted government funding priorities—yet I remain unpersuaded that, insofar as *sociological* research is concerned, this kind of distortion has had great significance. The fact that government agencies are willing and eager to provide police with armanents and surveillance equipment, while exceedingly deplorable, is accounted for by a great many factors—including, perhaps, the public timidity of some sociologists—but any link to recent sociological theories of crime seems tenuous indeed.

In short, I believe that relatively few sociologists of crime have been directly or substantially coopted by the state. To the extent this line of radical criticism is directed against current sociological work, it may represent a questionable and counterproductive attack on a "straw"-person. How we should identify and react to more subtle and indirect forms of cooptation remains a thorny issue. After all, apart from a few who may divest themselves of worldly goods and substantially refuse cooperation with the established "system," *none* of us can claim to have totally avoided participating in and reinforcing processes and structures that, overall, we may view as oppressive.

THE DOMAIN OF CORE AGREEMENT

Let me now turn to what I see as a broad domain of sociological agreement regarding crime, returning to the evident disagreements later on. Notwithstanding undoubted variations in emphasis, the following important points are probably now acceptable to most sociologists of crime—whether they be "functionalists," "labeling" enthusiasts, Marxists, "critical theorists," or whatever. These common understandings, moreover, may well have greater current significance than the standard array of differences between "conflict" and "consensus" approaches that is still often cited (Chambliss, 1976).

Decompartmentalizing of Crime. Very few sociologists today subscribe to a simplistic view that crime is nothing but the behavior of so-called "criminals." There has been a gradual "decompartmentalizing" of crime (Schur, 1969)—a recognition that crime can never be fully understood apart from sociocultural context. The earlier "assumption of differentiation" (Matza, 1964), at least insofar as it purported to provide the basis for some complete explanation of crime, has been heavily discredited. This is so, despite both the continuing interest of some sociologists in studying individual offenders, and the ominous reversion within limited neoconservative circles to "correctional" or "pathology" perspectives.

Conflict and the Social Production of Crime. In this decompartmentalized view, a society's crime picture is seen to reflect the *dominance* of certain value priorities, socioeconomic arrangements, and cultural preoccupations and fears. Furthermore, particularly at the societal level but also in the selection and processing of individual "offenders," crime is recognized to be an outcome—a sociolegal construction or production. This has been emphasized both in the early work of Quinney (1970) and in various "labeling" analyses of deviance (Becker, 1963; Erikson, 1962; Kitsuse, 1962; and see also discussion in Schur, 1971; Hawkins and Tiedeman, 1975). I believe that most sociologists today are alert to the central role of power and conflict in shaping these outcomes, a role that has vital significance even within such general categories of consensus as some "seriousness of crimes" studies (e.g., Rossi et al., 1974) seem to indicate may exist. With respect to this now widespread recognition of conflict elements, we should continue to appreciate the very significant contributions of Sutherland (see Schuessler, 1973), Taft and England (1964), Vold (1958), Merton (1938), Cohen (1955), and Cloward and Ohlin (1960), among others, who—in writings on crime and delinquency now viewed as "traditional"—all emphasized the criminogenic features of our social stratification system. Also contributing to this recognition have been the supposedly conventional conflict theories of crime, such as those of Turk (1969) and Quinney (1970), as well as the inevitable conflict focus developed by labeling-oriented theorists (e.g., Lofland, 1966).

A Broadened Conception of Crime Statistics. It follows, too, from this contextual and sociolegal construction view of crime, that overall official crime rates and trends as well as crime-distribution statistics have come to be viewed in a new light. This is a development to which the now traditional "self-reported behavior" studies contributed, even if they did not settle definitively the debates over the meaning of recorded crime data. Most sociologists today realize that, whatever else they may represent, crime statistics necessarily reflect the nature and extent of the criminal justice system, and the allocation as well as inevitably selective application of enforcement resources (see Erikson, 1966; Kitsuse and Cicourel, 1963).

Research on Criminal Justice Agencies. A related trend of considerable importance has been the expanded focus on analyzing organizations that deal with, and to an extent "produce," crime. Among the major themes now commonly developed in this work are: the significance of ambiguous, contradictory, or untenable organizational goals and mandates; the on-the-job problems and role-set influences of the individual control agent; the operation and influence of interorganizational networks; the role of organizational imperatives of various kinds in shaping enforcement policies and practices; and the possibility that criminal justice agencies may themselves have vested interests in particular policies and practices.

Renewed Interest in the Criminal Law. Another major aspect of decompartmentalization has been the renewed interest in the sociology of criminal law. Sutherland, it will be recalled, cited the making and applying of crime laws as key objects for research and analysis in criminology (Sutherland and Cressey, 1955). Commenting on the state of crime studies almost 35 years ago, Mannheim (1946: 1) noted that "we have made considerable efforts to discover what sort of person the offender is and why he has broken the law, and we rack our brains to find out what to do with him. . . . Hardly ever do we pause for a moment to examine critically the contents of that very law the existence of which alone makes it possible for the individual to offend against it." This is much less true today, thanks not only to some of Sutherland's work but also to a variety of sociohistorical analyses (e.g., Chambliss, 1964; Erikson, 1966; Platt, 1969) and to the general influence of various social constructionist and labeling formulations. The conflicts that produce or prevent legislation, the latent as well as the apparent meanings and functions of crime laws, and the unintended consequences as well as the ostensible goals of criminalizing, are all key focal points in much present-day research. Although some critics consider the recent concern with the so-called victimless crime areas to represent an unwise preoccupation with "expressive deviance" (e.g., Young, 1975: 68), such work can equally well be seen as part of a more general concern with the impact of legislation, and also as part of a broad movement within sociology and without to redefine the legitimate scope and functions of the criminal law (Schur, 1965; Packer, 1968; American Friends Service Committee, 1971).

The other side of this task of studying criminalization, to which essentially the same kind of substantive factors are relevant, is the study of noncriminalization: The failure to effectively criminalize behaviors that many would consider to be socially harmful. This is a theme properly emphasized by recent radical criminologists, but obviously it is one that again is grounded in much traditional work. In particular, it was central to Sutherland's analysis (1949) of white-collar crime, and to subsequent "conventional" studies in that area. Recent interest in political dissent and civil disobedience, and also the renewed attention in the wake of Watergate to "official deviance" (Douglas and Johnson, 1977), suggest that attention to noncriminalization—in a number of substantive areas—may be growing even among crime specialists who do not describe themselves as political radicals.

The Schwendingers' argument (1975) for a "human rights" rather than a legal or legalistic definition of crime has undoubted appeal. Yet it is not necessarily a moral evasion for the sociologist to distinguish between what "is" criminal—that is, what has in fact been criminalized in a society—and what he or she believes "ought to be" criminalized. Indeed, the very question as to why and how some behaviors have been treated as criminal whereas others have not, has emerged as a central one for criminological analysis. Furthermore, insisting that acts we deplore but which have not been criminalized "are" criminal in the literal and not just figurative sense has the dysfunction that the approach can easily be turned around by those who support overtly punitive and repressive policies, enabling them similarly to assert that the acts they personally deplore "are" criminal. I believe that many sociologists of crime are quite prepared to strongly state their beliefs and preferences regarding substantive crime policies and related social issues, and that in fact they often do so—even if often they adopt the more modest or cautious "ought to be" and "I believe" terminology.

The Political Nature of Crime. At any rate, I am convinced that for a variety of reasons sociological recognition of the essentially political nature of crime issues has grown substantially in recent years. Sociologists are more and more alert to the conflicts that shape crime policies, to the influence of interest groups and organized campaigns, and to the range of vested interests that may affect developments relating to crime. Consciousness of the politics of crime has been gradually emerging for some time and reflects a variety of influences. These include, along with the new radicalism the previously cited "conventional" conflict theories, the labeling and social constructionist approaches, the value-conflict approach to social problems more generally, and even the work of some "functionalists"—who often were quite explicit, for example, about the role of vested interests in determining preferred solutions to perceived social problems.

PERSISTING DISAGREEMENTS

The points I have mentioned probably represent only part of the common ground that exists between conventional and radical criminologies. Let me turn now to a few key matters on which there is likely to be persisting disagreement. The radical criminologist's conviction that this body of common understandings is inadequate—that it is too "tame," that it does not go "far enough," that it is insufficiently geared to a "dialectical" analysis—may lead him or her in one or all of several directions that will continue to cause many sociologists to balk. Some radical criminologists may succumb to what Greenberg (1976) has called "one-dimensional Marxist criminology," rigidly insisting on a "mechanical economic determinism" as the exclusive and exhaustive explanation of all aspects of every crime situation. Others, though again by no means all, may engage in what might be termed "millenarian criminology," asserting the eventual "withering away" of crime along with the state and law, and viewing the crime-free society as the basic goal toward which criminologists should be orienting their work. I believe that most sociologists are convinced our present socioeconomic order is in many respects inequitable, oppressive, and criminogenic, and that a radical reordering of this system could greatly alter our crime picture. Yet in the light of the overwhelming evidence regarding all types of existing societies, the complete elimination of crime is going to continue to seem an unreal goal except to those who can accept it as an article of faith.

Perhaps the most basic divergence between radical and "conventional" perspectives concerns the nature of the sociological enterprise itself. Although traditional and narrow empiricists may see in such notions as praxis and "normative" or "critical" criminology an attempt to combine incompatible purposes and activities, these terms reflect a commendable desire to avoid the quietism that an extreme "value neutrality" may seem to imply. If there is any danger in this for sociology in my opinion it lies not in the new activism itself—but rather in the suggestion made by some professed radicals that such activism is the *only* legitimate path for sociologists to follow. In this connection, I would like to urge a greater mutual tolerance of task pluralism among sociological criminologists, a tolerance which need not be "repressive" in its consequences or implications. As we all know, the work and orientations of sociologists exhibit great variation both in style and substance. Some incline to active involvement in social change, others are disposed to attempt more indirect contributions through their research, writing, and teaching. Some are quantitatively oriented, some qualitatively oriented. Some are primarily interested in macrosociological problems, some in microsociological ones. Some criminologists want to study the situations and problems of rule-violating or "labeled" individuals, others want to study the administration of criminal justice, and still others choose to concentrate on the creation of crime categories. All these, and other specific modes of inquiry and substantive topics, are legitimately adopted and pursued by criminologists. Indeed, as Taylor et al. (1973) have shown, any comprehensive understanding of deviance or crime requires consideration of many diverse dimensions. What those authors have not, to my mind, provided any more than any other authors have done, is a single unified mode of inquiry that will enable us to treat adequately all these diverse facets or elements in one fell swoop.

CONCLUSION

If a diversity of styles and approaches continues to have value, as I believe it must, then it should be possible for at least most of those adopting different criminological orientations to work in their respectable ways without getting bogged down in intramural acrimony—while at the same time avoiding a mindless eclecticism and preserving a spirit of critical debate. In this connection, a moratorium on name-calling might well be in order. No doubt all of us at times give in to this tendency in the heat of sociological controversy. Yet certain of the recent avowed radicals seem to have succumbed to a kind of fetishism of rhetoric—according to which only those writings couched in the approved rhetoric are deemed worthy of favorable comment, and in which negative code words (such as "technocratic," "managerial," "pluralist," "bourgeois," and "careerist") are glibly used to characterize any work with which they do not fully agree, sometimes without much evident regard for its specific substance or probable implications.

As I have already suggested, I do not find much good reason for current radicals to be as greatly exercised over the work of their sociological colleagues who study crime as they often appear to be. In considerable measure, this vitriolic infighting may be a waste of time and energy. It remains to be seen who, in the long run, will have made a greater or more valuable impact on society or even our understanding of it: those criminologists who, in their lives as well as in their work, actively assert what they see as an all-embracing radicalism; or those who address smaller-scale issues and who promote what radicals describe, often quite accurately, as piecemeal reform. In the meantime, we should not ignore the possibility that *both* radical and more traditional criminologists, while working in what may have to be considered a state of uneasy coexistence, can nonetheless contribute usefully to the sociology of crime.

REFERENCES

American Friends Service Committee (1971) Struggle for Justice. New York: Hill & Wang.

BECKER, H. S. (1963) Outsiders. New York: Macmillan.

CHAMBLISS, W. J. (1976) "Functional and conflict theories of crime," pp. 1-28 in W. J. Chambliss and M. Mankoff (eds.) Whose Law? What Order? New York: John Wiley.

——— (1964) "A sociological analysis of the law of vagrancy." Social Problems 12 (Summer): 67-77.

CLOWARD, R. A. and L. E. OHLIN (1960) Delinquence and Opportunity. New York: Macmillan.

COHEN, A. K. (1955) Delinquent Boys. New York: Macmillan.

DOUGLAS, L. D. and J. M. JOHNSON [eds.] (1977) Official Deviance. Philadelphia: J.B. Lippincott.

——— (1962) "Notes on the sociology of deviance." Social Problems 9 (Spring): 307-314.

ERIKSON, K. T. (1966) Wayward Puritans. New York: John Wiley.

——— (1962) "Notes on the sociology of deviance." Social Problems 9 (Spring): 307-314.

GREENBERG, D. F. (1976) "On one-dimensional Marxist criminology." Theory and Society 3: 610-621.

HAWKINS, R. and G. TIEDEMAN (1975) The Creation of Deviance. Columbus, OH: Charles E. Merrill.

KITSUSE, J. I. (1962) "Societal reaction to deviant behavior." Social Problems 9 (Winter): 247-256.

KITSUSE, J. I. and A. V. CICOUREL (1963) "A note on the use of official statistics." Social Problems 11 (Fall): 131-139.

LOFLAND, J. (1966) Deviance and Identity. Englewood Cliffs, NJ: Prentice-Hall.

MANNHEIM, H. (1946) Criminal Justice and Social Reconstruction. New York: Oxford University Press.

MATZA, D. (1964) Delinquency and Drift. New York: John Wiley.

MERTON, R. K. (1938) "Social structure and anomie." American Sociological Review 3 (October): 672-682.

PACKER, H. L. (1968) The Limits of the Criminal Sanction. Palo Alto, CA: Stanford University Press.

PLATT, A. M. (1969) The Child Savers. Chicago: University of Chicago Press.

QUINNEY, R. (1970) The Social Reality of Crime. Boston: Little, Brown.

ROSSI, P., E. WAITE, C. E. BOSE, and R. E. BERK (1974) "The seriousness of crimes." American Sociological Review 39 (April): 224-237.

SCHUESSLER, K. [ed.] (1973) Edwin H. Sutherland on Analyzing Crime. Chicago: University of Chicago Press.

SCHUR, E. M. (1971) Labeling Deviant Behavior. New York: Harper & Row.

——— (1965) Crimes Without Victims. Englewood Cliffs, NJ: Prentice-Hall.

SCHWENDINGER, H. and J. SCHWENDINGER (1975) "Defenders of order or guardians of human rights?" pp. 113-146 in I. Taylor et al. (eds.) Critical Criminology. London: Routledge & Kegan Paul.

SUTHERLAND, E. H. (1949) White Collar Crime. New York: Holt, Rinehart & Winston.

——— and D. R. CRESSEY (1955) Principles of Criminology. Philadelphia: J.B. Lippincott.

TAFT, D. R. and R. W. ENGLAND, Jr. (1964) Criminology. New York: Macmillan.

TAYLOR, I., P. WALTON, and J. YOUNG (1973) The New Criminology. London: Routledge & Kegan Paul.

TURK, A. T. (1969) Criminality and Legal Order. Chicago: Rand McNally.

VOLD, G. B. (1958) Theoretical Criminology. New York: Oxford University Press.

YOUNG, J. (1975) "Working-class criminology," pp. 63-91 in I. Taylor et al. (eds.) Critical Criminology. London: Routledge & Kegan Paul.

18

AFTER LABELING AND CONFLICT:
AN ASPECT OF CRIMINOLOGY'S NEXT CHAPTER

Laurin A. Wollan, Jr.

The question of what comes after labeling and conflict suggests yet another theory, as if criminology marches onward in chapters, like the chronicles of Davis (1975) and Taylor et al. (1973), promising successive editions, each extended by a chapter on the new theory as the older theories move toward the beginning, much as class notes in the alumni magazine move relentlessly toward the front until, one day, Quinney, Turk, and Platt are pictured at the head of the alumni parade, bent and feeble under an ancient banner, as the class of 2008 applauds in wonder. Theories in criminology do seem to come—and maybe go—that way, as indeed they do in science generally, as Pareto observed: "The logico-experimental sciences are made up of the sum of theories that are like living creatures, in that they are born, live, and die, the young replacing the old." (quoted in Inkeles, 1964: 105). So there probably will be a grand successor to the theories of labeling and conflict. But I leave it to others to identify the leading theories of tomorrow's criminology. Instead, I suggest here something less than that: not a theory in the fullness implied by the

AUTHOR'S NOTE: This essay previously appeared in *Criminology: An Inter-disciplinary Journal* Vol. 16, No. 4, February 1979, pp. 545-560.

unfolding of criminology, but an aspect of what comes tomorrow, a tendency or a tilt in a direction that has been unfamiliar, certainly unfashionable, in criminology.

Tomorrow's criminology will very likely be more open than in the past to inquiry into certain matters, mainly of values, which have traditionally been deemed to be outside the domain of scientists, natural and social alike, and instead within the realms exclusively of theologicans and philosophers. These considerations and modes of normative inquiry associated with them promise—or threaten—to enter criminology in response to several developments of recent years. First, the crises in criminal justice and in criminology, the latter derived from "the coming crisis of Western sociology," will drive criminologists *as criminologists* into questions of values. Second, the critical criminologists would—and will somewhat—have our study shift to the normative aspects of crime and punishment. Third, changes in social science generally are opening up the field "officially" to such study. Fourth, and finally, broader circumstantial changes are working toward heightened concern for moral and ethical aspects of the study of crime and punishment.

THE CRISES OF CRIMINAL JUSTICE
AND CRIMINOLOGY

Criminologists are carried into the clutches of a good many moral and ethical questions by the nature and implications of things they study, such as environmental design, community crime prevention, preventive patrol, selective enforcement, pretrial detention, fixed sentences, behavior modification, psychosurgery, postsentence detention, intensive patrol supervision, decriminalization, community control, professionalism, departmental policy-making, and information exchange, to mention some. The issues arising out of knowledge about such things come heavily freighted with value conflicts. But the "ought" and "should" sides of the coins of "is" and "can" tend to be viewed as legal and especially as constitutional matters within the official purview of lawyers and judges. But informal gatherings of criminologists, be they students or practitioners or theoreticians, typically erupt sooner or later into argument over the moral and ethical issues. In other words, the criminologist-in-his-cups (a subject, incidentally, which warrants study, doubtless done best by participant observation) and the criminologist-as-citizen (questionnaires will do here) devote a fair amount of time and energy to the ventilation of opinions on those issues—about which, of course, they are laymen: "I don't know anything about ethics, but I know what I don't like!"

The increasing urgency of resolving these issues will surely cause a few more criminologists than in the past to gain some literacy in moral philosophy, just as many have gone about the study of biology not to become biologists but to become conversant with their works, if for no other reason than not to leave liberty and justice to lawyers and judges, or genetics to politicians. Other criminologists will invite axiologists to collaborate, lest the resolution of the moral issues go by default to others. Thus, the whole of criminology will shift slightly toward engagement of philosophical aspects of crime and punishment.

In addition to this effect of the crises of criminal justice, there is a crisis in criminology which is part of a broader crisis in the social sciences, which Gouldner said was "coming" when he wrote nearly a decade ago. His argument is that structural functionalism, the dominant sociology, is conservative—conservative of social order, the system it sustains, and the elite it supports; that it is coming apart under the force of technical criticism; that the younger generation, especially the younger sociologist, is drawing away from it—in reaction to its dependence on and its service to the state. The upshot, in criminology, too, it would seem, is what Gouldner calls "Reflexive Sociology":

> concerned with what sociologists want to do and with what, in fact, they actually do in the world . . . to *transform* the sociologist . . . to transcend sociology as it now exists . . . [to] surrender the assumption, as wrongheaded as it is human, that others believe out of need while we [sociologists] believe—only or primarily—because of the dictates of logic and evidence. . . . A Reflexive Sociology would be a moral sociology. . . . A Reflexive Sociology is not a bundle of technical skills; it is a conception of how to live and a total praxis. . . . In truth, a Reflexive Sociology is concerned more with the creativity than the reliability of an intellectual performance [1970: 489-491, 504; italics his].

Criminology reflects this in the views of a minority, vocal and active (and probably growing, to judge by the sentiments of graduate students). It is likely to have the sort of effect on the rest of criminology that feminism has had on men: It has liberated some a great deal, most to some extent, and therefore all on the whole—and that is important, albeit not revolutionary. Even if only a few go as far as Gouldner to argue, of the work of reflexive sociologists, that "their originating motives and terminating consequences would embody and advance certain specific *values*" (1970: 491), it would sensitize the discipline somewhat more to the moral and ethical dimensions of crime and punishment.

THE CALL OF THE CRITICAL CRIMINOLOGISTS

A leading contender for top spot in tomorrow's criminology, the "new" or "radical" or "critical" criminology, promises to draw criminology into an engagement with moral and ethical questions. Taylor et al. urge "a normative theory: it must hold out the possibilities of a resolution to the fundamental questions." (1973: 280). It is possible that "normative," for them, means only the empirical study of norms and values, which of course is well within the conventional scope of sociology. But the tenor of critical criminology is clearly of the usual sense of normative; it even entails an early, absolute, and dogmatic commitment:

> It should be clear that a criminology which is not normatively committed to the abolition of inequalities of wealth and power, and in particular of inequalities in property and life-chances, is inevitably bound to fall into correctionalism. And all correctionalism is irreducibly bound up with the identification of deviance with pathology. A fully social theory of deviance must, by its nature, break entirely with correctionalism ... precisely because ... the causes of crime must be intimately bound up with the form assumed by the social arrangements of the time.

> The task is to create a society in which the facts of human diversity, whether personal, organic or social, are not subject to the power to criminalize [1973: 281-282].

In any event, the ordinary meaning of normative suggests that criminology would pay more attention *officially* to the sort of thing one finds, for instance, in Feinberg's *Social Philosophy* (1973), which begins with "the concept of freedom" and ends with "social justice," or Schwartz's *Freedom and Authority: An Introduction to Social and Political Philosophy,* which begins, "The fundamental problem of social and political philosophy is that of *institutional justification.*" (1973: 3; italics his).

Critical criminology leads into normative matters for another reason, as well. Taylor et al. (1973: 278) urge a "criminology ... which will be able to bring politics back into the discussion of what were previously technical issues." Specifically, they aim "for a political economy of criminal action, and of the reaction it excites, and for a politically informed social psychology of these ongoing social "dynamics" (1973: 279)—that is, for a criminology which would deal with "man's relationship to structures of power, domination and authority" (1973: 268). If carried very far, and one assumes they would have it carried quite far, their political inquiry would increase attention to philosophical aspects of the subject because the study of the politics of crime and punishment would probably come to resemble the study of politics generally, as in "political science," where it divides between scientific or empirical on the one hand, and philosophical or normative on the other (Waldo, 1975). Sociology, in contrast to political science, can be fairly defined as it has been by Bierstedt (1957: 16): "A social, a categorical, a pure, an abstract, a generalizing, both a rational and an empirical, and general science," but significantly not as a normative science, which political science is in part.

Some of the difference on this score originates in the history of the discipline, which has had both the empirical and philosophical students of politics sharing the discipline, the journals, the university departments, the annual meetings, and so forth. This has made philosophy, or at least the philosopher, an inescapable presence even for the most behavioristic of political scientists. Hence, for them, too, the very discipline begins with Plato and Aristotle, not Ferguson. By contrast, most sociologists, notwithstanding Gouldner's *Enter Plato* (1965), would say their discipline began with Comte or perhaps Spencer or even Saint-Simon, if not Ferguson; in any case, well into the scientific age.

The affinity of political science for political philosophy is in part historical, but also in part circumstantial, a result of the proximity of political students to the levers of political power and influence, vicariously for most but nonetheless *virtually* (in its older sense), which has yielded for political science a faith described by Ranney (1976: 147):

> The main articles of that faith still hold that for every problem there is a solution. That is is better to do something about a problem than to do nothing even though the something may be less than perfect. That, above all, if we can figure out and establish the right *institutions,* the right policies are bound to follow [italics his].

The revolutionism of the new criminologists—"for crime to be abolished, then, those social arrangements themselves must also be subject to fundamental social change" (Taylor et al., 1973: 28)—differs in some considerable degree from the reformism of political science. Nevertheless, criminologists grasping those levers of policy (or igniting the torch of revolution) and asking, "Why one way and not another?" may ask further if there is not something more than interest or ideology to justify the choice.

Perhaps the very nature of politics, which has to do with aspirations and intentions for the public things of the *polis,* accounts for the affinity of political science for political philosophy. If the criminologist turns to the study of the politics of crime and punishment, an engagement of these concerns is likely to follow. Taylor et al. (1973: 270-278) have called for such a study by implication of a theory following their agenda of points to be dealt with: "the wider origins of the deviant act," "immediate origins of the deviant act," "the actual act," "immediate origins of social reaction," "wider origins of deviant reaction," "the outcome of the social reaction on deviant's further action," and "the nature of the deviant process as a whole." Broader political aspects may be included in that last item, but symmetry suggests an additional item for the agenda: "the wider origins of the social reaction." There one would find the values of interest and ideology, to be sure, but also those of morals and ethics. These account for some of the policies manifested in criminal law and its administration and the myriad programs and measures employed by the state in response to the threat and commission of criminal acts. How much of policy is shaped by interest and ideology and how much by philo-sophical principle I would not begin to say at this point, but some portion owes directly to it and some—probably greater—portion owes indirectly to it just as surely as "ideas have consequences" (Weaver, 1948).

The extension of labeling analysis, too, beyond the effect of the label on the labelee into "the wider origins of the social reaction" would similarly force an engagement of the interests, ideologies, values, and also the philosophies of the labelers. The result would be a more richly textured and arguably more realistic account of the sort suggested by Dean Allen in his Holmes' Lectures at Harvard a few years ago:

> The ultimate resolution involves an intricate vectoring of a great
> variety of forces, a complexity hardly hinted at by the assertion that
> the criminal law is the tool of the politically dominant [1974: 21].

Among those forces are the principles, persuasions, and indeed—if para-doxically—the powers of moral and ethical "politics."

Finally, the same division of labor that one finds in political study generally, between the empirical and the normative approaches, would very probably occur in the study of the politics of crime and punishment, not only because the normative is so vital a part of the *polis* but because the student of politics cannot help participating in it. The rural, industrial, and family sociologist can study those institutions disinterestedly, while caring passionately that *his* family, *his* factory, *his* farm be run right. But the *polis*: that is inescapably *ours* and can scarcely be contemplated without causing some to be greatly (if others only somewhat) concerned for its aims and actions. This may be the most basic reason for the division of labor in political study, hence in the study of the politics of crime and punishment, and so in criminology's next chapter.

The critical aspect of the new criminology is derived from early writings of Marx, certain themes of which have been elaborated in the "critical philosophy" of the Frankfurt School. As I understand it in the writings of its leading figures Habermas (1971), Horkheimer and Adorno (1972), Marcuse (1964), and the interpretations of them in Gouldner (1970), for instance, this approach aims to expose the interests and ideologies borne and served by the conventional scholar, unwittingly for the most part, and then to analyze society in a way that is as free as possible of such predispositions. In so doing, they do not eliminate values but come to grips with them, raising to a higher level the kind of values which ought (in their estimation) to influence the scholar's diagnosis and prescription. That some critical criminologists have elected a revisionist or neo-Marxist alternative does not seem to be inevitable. But the force of their approach, Marxist or otherwise, promises to deepen the question of what *really* "is" and what *really* "ought to be" (Dallmayr, 1976). And this must be, however "critical" or highly reasoned, a profoundly value-oriented enterprise.

CHANGES IN THE SOCIAL SCIENCES

Changes in the social sciences are making for more accommodation of value-oriented considerations in criminology. These changes include the demise of "value-free" social science, the movement toward humanism in social science, the weakening of its positivism, and its outreach toward the humanities. Each of these developments promises to heighten the moral and ethical sensibilities of social scientists and shift their studies, hence their discipline, somewhat (if only slightly) toward the philosophical end of the spectrum.

The illusions of "value-free" social science have dissipated and a value-sensitive social science is emerging. The Weberian aim is, of course, far from dead (Rudner, 1966), but it is clearer now than two generations ago that it is only partly possible (Becker, 1967) and not entirely desirable (Mills, 1959). The social scientist who would be "engaged" has today a more sophisticated understanding of the engagement (Gouldner, 1968). As a result, no thoughtful criminologist can be unconcerned about the values that involve themselves in his or her work—in its origins, its purposes, its

consequences—and this is a significant change in the "doing" of criminology. Not incidentally, the fact/value distinction continues to be both
troublesome—Hancock arguing that it is an "untenable dualism" (1974:
197-212)—and vital—the Foundations of Political Theory Group devoting
no less than thirty papers in eleven sessions to the fact/value dichotomy in
its 1978 meeting.

Related to this is a movement toward humanism in sociology. It is not a
new movement (Berger, 1973), but it is growing. In part, this is a
theoretical matter stemming from "the oversocialized conception of man"
(Wrong, 1961). In larger part, however, it is a reaction to the technological
threats to man, some of which are fed by the findings of social science
(Matson, 1976). The upshot is a concern for the "human" values of
autonomy, integrity, and dignity, among others—indeed, of mind and free
will. A humanistic sociology is not necessarily normative, but considerations of such values and of value-commitments seem to "come with the
territory." The criminologist, too, is likely to be more engaged, as time
goes on, with the constellation of values involved in becoming, and
remaining, human in the fullness of that attainment.

The weakening or epistemological loosening or opening of "hypothetico-deductive" science has not only eroded the influence of positivism
(Bernstein, 1976) but has admitted into science itself propositions that are
falsifiable, not merely verifiable, thereby redeeming nonempirical propositions from the status of "nonsense", to which they had been relegated by
the logical positivism of the Vienna circle. The highly personal element
Polanyi has observed in science (1958) is the vehicle that carries into its
operations the insights and imaginings that are rooted in values.

Flowing from all this is a reaching toward the humanities in sociology.
Sociology has long had a place among the humanities (Redfield, 1966) and
some have been doing sociology in the manner of humanities (Geertz,
1973). But the advent of ethnomethodology (and to some extent existen-
tialism) has carried some of sociology quite far toward the interpretive
methods of the humanities. The highly subjective, imaginative, empathetic
quality that has gained legitimacy adds credibility to Nisbet's thesis of
"sociology as an art form" (1976).

The limitations, as well as the strengths, of positivism have led to
synthesis at various levels with the resurgent "nonscientific" approaches.
At an epistemological level, synthesis is occurring in terms of "meaning" in
the works of Polanyi (1975). At the methodological level, Brown (1977)
has attempted to synthesize the science-imitative and the humanistic
modes of sociology by means of "cognitive aesthetics" or a "critical

poetic," while Moon (1975) has made a different synthesis of the "hypothetico-deductive" and hermeneutic or interpretive modes of inquiry. The cumulative effect of attempts such as these in establishing a union of the best of the positivistic and humanistic approaches must be some accommodation of the normative in social science, especially as collaboration develops with proponents and practitioners of the approaches heretofore peripheral to criminology but no less well suited to its already interdisciplinary constitution.

CHANGES BEYOND SOCIAL SCIENCE

Outside of the social sciences are several developments which, like those within, appear likely to open up criminology to more systematic consideration of the normative. One of these developments is the broader aspect of the crisis of criminal justice; namely the host of crises of our time—Vietnam and Watergate obscured for a time the crises of population, privacy, resources, family, bigness, energy, sex, bureaucracy, technology, violence, and others—all of them crises largely because of the moral dilemmas they force us into. The value-based crises of our time have given rise not only to an "ethical imperative" (Means, 1969) but to the involvement of increasing numbers of intellectuals from far-flung fields, such as Chomsky (1967) a decade ago, who moved from the unlikely base of linguistics to deep involvement in the resistance to the Vietnam war. His argument for the responsibility, for the involvement, of the intellectual sustained many academicians in their position on that issue; it has doubtless caused others to have misgivings over earlier work which was less informed by value considerations than it might have been (Paige, 1977). It can be expected that engaged intellectuals like Mitford (1973) will penetrate the field of criminal justice on the scent of moral outrages—and find them they will!

More critical than the accumulation of what might be called policy crises, but less dramatic and newsworthy, is the decline of the liberal state. Its troubles pose for the first time in a generation or so the need to contemplate alternatives to the liberal democratic state as we have accepted it in the West for so many generations. We fought a world war "to make the world safe for democracy," which would be extended around the globe (but was not), then another world war to protect remaining democracies from annihilation (which it did not), only to face now a political retreat from liberal democracy itself in its very homeland of Western Europe and America (Parkinson, 1958: ch. 19). This crisis is raising some intense value conflicts of the most profound sort (the nature and extent of freedom and equality, for instance), which reach into the realm of criminal justice and shake its value foundations as well.

Beyond this, and unsettling to sociologists who, as Hughes said, "[by] predilection rather than by logic . . . work on the here and now" (in White, 1956: 82), is the special problem of the future (Ferkiss, 1974): It forces the identification of resources and practices that accord with what is feasible (what can be) and what is desirable (what ought to be). Wilkins, for example, found it necessary to deal with values in his account of "Crime and Criminal Justice at the Turn of the Century" (1973). Scientists especially are sensing acutely the urgency of these crises because, as Snow once said, "Scientists have it within them to know what a future-directed society feels like, for science itself, in its human aspects, is just that" (1961: 82-83). The future increasingly troubles scientists as they contemplate the implications of their work—so much that some would halt the implementation of certain scientific findings (which a few scientists in the past have been willing to do) and some would even halt the research itself (which scientists have almost never countenanced). Thus, scientists, even in physics and chemistry, are in quest of the values by which they might judge such issues as recombinant DNA, test-tube babies, and so forth (Rosenfeld, 1977). So acute is this concern that the National Science Foundation's Office of Science and Society has created a program, "Ethics and Values in Science and Technology," to deal with emerging dilemmas.

The resurgence of moral philosophy promises to draw attention to normative matters in many fields. The notable books in philosophy recently have dealt with morals. Rawls's *Theory of Justice* (1971) is *the* philosophy book of the decade, followed at Harvard alone by Nozick's *Anarchy, State and Utopia* (1974), Unger's *Knowledge and Politics* (1975) and *Law in Modern Society* (1976), Fried's *Right and Wrong* (1978), and Bok's *Lying* (1978). After a decade of dominance in jurisprudence, the legal positivists are endangered by the arguments of Dworkin (1977), Benditt (1978), and Richards (1977), the last at least in the special context of American constitutionalism. Even in literature one finds Gardner's *On Moral Fiction* (1978).

Finally, the market, the bottom line for criminology and criminologists, suggests some tilt in the direction of a command of the normative aspects of crime and punishment. That is to say, if the foregoing developments are generally true, the contribution of criminology, hence its activities, must be responsible to the community's heightened concern for values. (This, of course, opens the question of whether—and if so, how far—criminology now does and should serve the community and its criminal justice agencies of policy and administration. It surely does in some degree and should, as most would agree.) In any event, this kind of value-oriented service can be of a higher sort than a primitive sabotage (or worship) or technological innovations. Providing this service will require criminology to be somewhat more attentive to matters of morals and ethics.

REFERENCES

ALLEN, F. (1974) The Crimes of Politics. Cambridge, MA: Harvard University Press.

BECKER, H. (1967) "Whose side are we on?" Social Problems 14: 239-247.

BENDITT, T. (1978) Law as Rule and Principle. Palo Alto, CA: Stanford University Press.

BERGER, P. (1973) Invitation to Sociology. Woodstock, NY: Overlook.

BERNSTEIN, R. (1976) The Restructuring of Social and Political Theory. New York: Harcourt Brace Jovanovich.

BIERSTEDT, R. (1957) The Social Order. New York: McGraw-Hill.

BOK, S. (1978) Lying. New York: Pantheon.

BROWN, R. (1977) A Poetic for Sociology. Cambridge, MA: Cambridge University Press.

CHOMSKY, N. (1967) "Responsibility of the intellectuals." New York Review of Books (February 23).

DALLMAYR, F. (1976) "Beyond dogma and despair: toward a critical theory of politics." American Political Science Review (March): 64-79.

DAVIS, N. (1975) Sociological Constructions of Deviance. Dubuque, IA: Wm. C. Brown.

DWORKIN, R. (1977) Taking Rights Seriously. Cambridge, MA: Harvard University Press.

FEINBERG, J. (1973) Social Philosophy. Englewood Cliffs, NJ: Prentice-Hall.

FERKISS, V. (1974) The Future of Technological Civilization. New York: George Braziller.

FRIED, C. (1978) Right and Wrong. Cambridge, MA: Harvard University Press.

GARDNER, J. (1978) On Moral Fiction. New York: Basic Books.

GEERTZ, C. (1973) The Interpretation of Culture. New York: Basic Books.

GOULDNER, A. (1970) The Coming Crisis in Western Sociology. New York: Basic Books.

——— (1968) "The sociologist as partisan: sociology and the welfare state." American Sociologist 3 (May): 103-116.

——— (1965) Enter Plato. New York: Basic Books.

HABERMAS, J. (1971) Knowledge and Human Interests. Boston: Beacon.

HANCOCK, R. (1974) Twentieth Century Ethics. New York: Columbia University Press.

HORKHEIMER, M. and T. ADORNO (1972) Dialectic of Enlightenment. New York: Herder & Herder.

INKELES, A. (1964) What Is Sociology? Englewood Cliffs, NJ: Prentice-Hall.

MARCUSE, H. (1964) One-Dimensional Man. Boston: Beacon.

MATSON, F. (1976) The Idea of Man. New York: Dell.

MEANS, R. (1969) The Ethical Imperative. Garden City, NY: Doubleday.

MILLS, C. (1959) The Sociological Imagination. New York: Oxford University Press.

MITFORD, J. (1973) Kind and Usual Punishment. New York: Knopf.

MOON, J. (1975) "The logic of political inquiry: a synthesis of opposing perspectives," pp. 131-228 in F. Greenstein and N. Polsby (eds.) Political Science: Scope and Theory, Vol. I. Reading, MA: Addison-Wesley.

NISBET, R. (1976) Sociology as an Art Form. New York: Oxford University Press.

NOZICK, R. (1974) Anarchy, State and Utopia. New York: Basic Books.

PAIGE, G. (1977) "On values and science: the Korean decision reconsidered." American Political Science Review (December): 1603-1609.

PARKINSON, C. (1958) The Evolution of Political Thought. New York: Viking.

POLANYI, M. (1958) Personal Knowledge. Chicago: University of Chicago.

——— and H. PROSCH (1975) Meaning. Chicago: University of Chicago.

RANNEY, A. (1976) " 'The divine science': political engineering in American culture." American Political Science Review (March): 140-148.

RAWLS, J. (1971) A Theory of Justice. Cambridge, MA: Harvard University Press.

REDFIELD, R. (1966) "Social science among the humanities," pp. 36-39 in A. Inkeles [ed.] Readings on Modern Sociology. Englewood Cliffs, NJ: Prentice-Hall.

RICHARDS, D. (1977) The Moral Criticism of Law. Encino, CA: Dickenson.

ROSENFELD, A. [ed.] (1977) "God and science: new allies in the search for values." Special Report in Saturday Review (December 10): 13-43.

RUDNER, R. (1966) Philosophy of Social Science. Englewood Cliffs, NJ: Prentice-Hall.

SCHWARTZ, T. (1973) Freedom and Authority. Encino, CA: Dickenson.

SNOW, C. (1961) Science and Government. Cambridge, MA: Harvard University Press.

TAYLOR, I., P. WALTON, and J. YOUNG (1973) The New Criminology. London: Routledge & Kegan Paul.

UNGER, R. (1976) Law in Modern Society. New York: Macmillan.

——— (1975) Knowledge and Politics. New York: Macmillan.

WALDO, D. (1975) "Political science: tradition, discipline, profession, science, enterprise," pp. 1-130 in F. Greenstein and N. Polsby (eds.) Political Science: Scope and Theory, Vol. I. Reading, MA: Addison-Wesley.

WEAVER, R. (1948) Ideas Have Consequences. Chicago: University of Chicago Press.

WHITE, L. (1956) Frontiers of Knowledge in the Study of Man. New York: Harper & Row.

WILKINS, L. (1973) "Crime and criminal justice at the turn of the century," pp. 13-29 in Annals of the American Academy of Political and Social Science (July).

WRONG, D. (1961) "The oversocialized conception of man in modern sociology." American Sociological Review 26 (April): 183-193.

19

A RADICAL ALTERNATIVE TO "RADICAL" CRIMINOLOGY

Harold E. Pepinsky

INTRODUCTION

In the minds of most criminologists today, "radical" criminology is equated with Marxist criminology. The equation is misleading. It is true that in the United States at least, Marxist criminologists are vastly outnumbered by liberal criminologists. It is also true that it is a political liability—both in and out of academia—for criminologists to espouse Marxist views. Conventionally, too, being "radical" is confused with being leftist, and advocacy of Marxist views is about as far to the left as most Americans, criminologists included, can imagine. But the essential feature of holding radical views is that one's ideas depart from convention in the extreme, and Marxist criminology does not meet this criterion. Rather, Marxist criminology falls within the conventional bounds of assuming that true criminals differ from most other members of a social system, and that crime and criminality can best be controlled by giving the true offenders special treatment.

The basic difference between liberal and Marxist criminologists is that the former equate criminality with poverty, while the latter equate criminality with wealth. One group would resocialize, or even liquidate, the poor, while the other would resocialize, or even liquidate, the rich. Without denigrating the important role Marxism has played in sensitizing criminologists to class oppression's being implicit in liberal criminology, the point has been made and is no longer new. On the other hand, radical criminology has joined liberal criminology in a synthesis representing the assumption that the primary task of criminology is to identify the true offenders and pinpoint their vulnerability to neutralization or change. As we shall see, it is above all this assumption that current analysis draws into question, pointing to a new radical alternative for today: a social systems perspective on the production and control of crime.

The history of Western criminology since the eighteenth century can be modeled as a Hegelian dialectical process. Although dialectics whose time has passed have continued to have spokespersons in succeeding generations of criminologists, the emergence of radical criminological thought has been an immanent result of the unfolding of syntheses of criminological ideas at the leading edge of the field. This Hegelian process is depicted in Figure 1. Within the Hegelian model, radical criminology for any period is the latest antithesis in criminological thinking. Let us review the model stage by stage.

CLASSICAL CRIMINOLOGY VERSUS RETRIBUTION

As the Enlightenment dawned on European thought, it shone upon a world of thought that assumed power and wealth to be a birthright. The sovereign derived his authority from God, and in turn the sovereign delegated authority to a nobility. For the most part, crime was perceived as a threat to this natural order of things; crime itself was tantamount to treason, and the punishment for crime a matter of asserting sovereign authority over those whose behavior reflected defiance of the natural order. If inordinate pain and suffering were inflicted upon offenders by the sovereign, it only reflected the power of the sovereign and further served to justify his hegemony.

The Reformation provided a spiritual basis upon which to question the divine right of kings, and the political theory of such Englightenment thinkers as Rousseau and Montesqieu—a statement of political implications of the idea that no human intermediary was needed to link each citizen to God. From this new perspective, the sovereign merited popular fealty only so long as he maintained his end of a social contract—by

FIGURE 19.1 Hegelian Progress of Criminological Thought

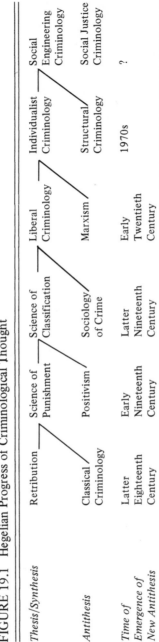

Thesis/Synthesis	Retribution	Science of Punishment	Science of Classification	Liberal Criminology	Individualist Criminology	Social Engineering Criminology
Antithesis	Classical Criminology	Positivism	Sociology of Crime	Marxism	Structural Criminology	Social Justice Criminology
Time of Emergence of New Antithesis	Latter Eighteenth Century	Early Nineteenth Century	Latter Nineteenth Century	Early Twentieth Century	1970s	?

promoting the greatest good for the greatest number. And if the sovereign of the Enlightenment met the terms of his contract, citizens would in rational self-interest obey his law and the need for government by force would be minimal.

In criminology, Enlightenment assumptions implied that the level of punishment inflicted by officials of state should be reduced to a level minimally necessary to keep the cost of criminality higher than the selfish gain the offender would derive from unpunished crime. Thus, for instance, to Beccaria (1968, originally published in 1764), a leading spokesperson for Enlightenment criminology, the severity of capital punishment was unwarranted. Efforts should instead be directed to making less severe punishment for crime swift, sure, and uniform, so that rational citizens would barely be deterred from breaking the social contract.

This utilitarian antithesis to retributive theories of criminology became the legitimation for punishment in the new, avowedly democratic political orders, notably those that followed revolutions in France and in the United States. But it is not fair to conclude that Beccarian or Benthamite principles of setting levels of punishment were carefully followed. Certainly, for example, the death penalty was not eliminated. What emerged instead was a synthesis of use of punishment as an expression of fear and moral outrage over crime on the one hand, and with an objective of deterring crime in rational social defense on the other. In criminology, the science of punishment had come of age. (See Duesterberg, 1979, for an excellent review of the progress of developing criminological thought from the Enlightenment until the end of the nineteenth century.)

POSITIVISM VERSUS THE SCIENCE OF PUNISHMENT

The classically endowed science of punishment assumed social equality before the law. In theory, the sovereign who upheld the social contract would need to punish members of one class no more than those of another. All citizens were presumed rational, and with siolated exceptions the poor, like the rich, should seldom provide a pretext for criminal sanction.

In practice, however, it was overwhelmingly the poor who were found guilty of crime, in increasing—not decreasing—numbers in the early nineteenth century. Although to a few isolated thinkers like Godwin (1971, originally written in 1793) this phenomenon drew into question the very premises of democratic revolutions, it was too much to expect that criminologists would so readily discard such a newly emergent political ideology. Instead of questioning the role of the political order in producing crime, the newly emerging school of criminological thought questioned the capacity of poor citizens to live up to utilitarian assumptions. The positivist antithesis to the science of punishment blamed the bulk of the crime problem on biological and moral developmental defects among the poor. The positivists set out to identify the defects of the poor, and to make institutional arrangements for the isolation or treatment of the unfortunate members of the dangerous class.

It is revealing to see, not only in Duesterberg's (1979) account of French criminological thought, but in Rothman's (1971) corresponding account of developments in the United States as well, that the terms of much contemporary criminological debate had already been articulated by the middle of the nineteenth century. Modern data bases may have changed, but modern inferences from the data remain largely unchanged. Thus, Van den Haag's (1975) conclusions might well have been stated prior to the Enlightenment, Wilson's (1975) conclusions on deterrence by Beccaria, and Wolfgang and Ferracuti's (1967) description of a subculture of violence less than a century thereafter. By 1850, the terms of debate over treatment versus punishment versus incapacitation had been fully elaborated. At this point, a synthesis was created in which a primary task of criminology was to classify offenders according to which theory of sanction fitted the circumstances of each.

THE SOCIOLOGY OF CRIME VERSUS THE SCIENCE OF CLASSIFICATION

Despite the application of the science of treatment, incapacitation, and punishment, crime rates continued to rise, notably for the growth of criminological theory, in France. Given continued political turmoil in France which led ultimately to the founding of the Third Republic in 1870, criminologists grew ready to question the sanctity of the political and social order that had followed the earliest democratic revolutions. Joly (1889), Tarde (1912, originally published in 1890), and Durkheim (1951, originally published in 1897) became leading exponents of the view that the poor were pressed to commit crime by the strains of functioning in the political economy of industrialization and modernization. If crime were to be prevented, the social plight of the poor had to be redressed through improved working conditions and compensatory moral education (shades of Lyndon Johnson's call for a Great Society!). In the differing emphases among Joly, Tarde, and Durkheim on emergence of conflict versus need for consensus, the basis for ongoing debate between conflict and consensus theorists was laid.

A compromise was reached in the early days of the Third Republic. Hard core recidivists would still be firmly dealt with by the criminal justice system, but justice for lesser offenders required that they be diverted into new social welfare programs. Liberal criminology had been synthesized, the idea of diversionary programs established. As criminal justice officials concentrated their efforts on incapacitating the most serious offenders, arrests and prosecutions dropped and so did the population of those imprisoned. The insights of what we know today as traditional criminology, not surprisingly considered a specialty in the field of sociology, had been articulated in full. To read the latest conventional American criminology text, scattered references to so-called "radical" criminology aside, is tantamount to reading a review of the latest findings of criminologists of the turn of the century. All that changes within this synthesis are details of allocation of turf to proponents of retribution, deterrence, incapacitation, biologism, developmental inadequacy, and social disorganization. The boundaries of rival explanations within the overall picture shift to and fro, while the overall picture of the criminal as a poor social misfit remains the same. Everyone agrees on who the real offenders are and that crime control entails taking special measures against them; the fights are over whether to beat, kill, cage, cut, educate, or train them.

MARXISM VERSUS LIBERAL CRIMINOLOGY

The unfolding of the dialectic between liberal criminology and Marxism has been subtle. Marx himself had begun writing by the middle of the nineteenth century even before sociological criminology rose to prominence. But among criminologists, whose historical role has been mainly that of being apologists for confinement and punishment of citizens by state officials, it was difficult to give legitimacy to Marxist analyses. Indeed, even today in the United States, it is hard for the few Marxist criminologists among us to gain and hold professional employment. Twenty-five years after the McCarthy era, academics are still wary of having Marxists in their midst, and the other major employer of criminologists, the government, is more loath still to hire even the few Marxists who might be willing to work there.

While it is small wonder that criminologists have been slow to entertain overthrowing the state in favor of proletarian control as a solution to the crime problem, it is scarcely surprising that the idea occurred to some analysts who saw the poor bearing the brunt of criminal justice sanctions under the guise of liberal democracy. If Marxist critiques of the social order were more extreme than those of the sociologists of crime, they were also more parsimonious and hence true to the logic of science born of the Enlightenment. If the social order were as messy as Durkheim, Joly, and Tarde found it to be, it was more straightforward to infer a need for revolutionary change than to become bogged down in details of evolutionary change. Marxists have had a strong point in criticizing liberal criminologists for obfuscating clear issues. Gradually, the point has been made. But given the political liability of assuming a Marxist stance as a criminologist, Marxist criminology was absorbed into a criminological synthesis before it had a chance to become firmly established in the field as an antithesis.

Bonger's (1969, originally published in 1916) work was the earliest hint of what the synthesis was to become. Bonger acknowledged that the role the poor played in criminality and crime control was a product of class oppression, but hedged his analysis by also concluding that as a result the poor really were more criminal than the rich and hence in need of special control.

Two sets of events made Marxist critiques more palatable to the criminological community. First, the Soviets demonstrated that a Marxist-based revolutionary movement could succeed in overthrowing the state in 1917. Second, in two world wars and in the Great Depression, the Western world was thrown into political turmoil that begged questions of whether liberal democratic orders were viable. In the 1930s, a number of criminologists began openly to wrestle with the idea that the association of criminality with poverty was a matter of political discrimination. Robison (1973, originally published in 1936) wrote that the police discriminated against children "from the wrong side of the tracks," and hence that class differences in delinquency rates were suspect. Sellin (1938) argued that much of crime in official eyes amounted to normative behavior in the eyes of offenders. Tannenbaum (1938) argued that official action creates career offenders who otherwise would be normal.

In his 1939 presidential address to the American Sociological Association, Sutherland (1940) took the final step in forging the synthesis between Marxist and liberal criminology. Sutherland argued that class differences in criminality were artifacts of criminal justice system bias, in which the law was written to make rich people's transgressions look like merely civil or administrative wrongs and in which officials further discriminated against the poor in applying the law. If, said Sutherland, we consider as crimes all acts which are ultimately punishable by fine or imprisonment (including wrongs defined in manifestly civil or administrative law provisions), and if we look behind official crime figures to discover who commits crimes without getting caught, we will find that the rich are just as likely to commit crimes as the poor.

This formulation was a stroke of genius in bridging the gap between the liberal view that criminals were predominantly poor and the Marxist view that the real wrongdoers were rich. It gave each side its due without sacrificing the assumption that there were really causal factors that predisposed some members of society as opposed to others to commit crime. Causes of criminality might still be isolated, and crime controlled by treating the culprits (or potential culprits) differently from law-abiding citizens, while recognizing that the identification of criminality with poverty was an artifact arranged to suit the interests of wealthier and more powerful members of society.

In ensuing years, with research developments notably including self-report research (Pepinsky, 1980: Ch. 9) and political developments nobably including Watergate, Sutherland's synthesis has become established as a focal point of criminology. Marxist criminologists (such as Quinney, 1977), of course, continue to argue that the rich and powerful are the real and only source of crime. And among the progeny of liberal criminology, the great debate is over whether the poor and the rich actually commit equally serious crimes equally often or whether the poor are slightly more prone to criminality (Tittle et al., 1978). Although proponents of each of these positions continue to find the distinctions among the positions vital, all perspectives are united in the view that (1) the relationship between class and criminality is problematic and (2) regardless of the role of class, a criminal subpopulation exists in any social system—a group of societal misfits on whom crime control efforts should be targeted. Marxist and liberal criminologists share a determination to strip away class bias to uncover the causes of true criminality. There is new debate on whether the true criminals are those revealed by dialectical analysis, those in trouble with the law, or those who confess error in questionnaires or in interviews, but the consensus remains that controlling crime entails beating, killing, caging, cutting (or now drugging), educating, or training the offenders. Their common error lies in their common objectives. By contrast, as we shall see, the radical criminologists of today are united in their opposition to trying to find the causes of true criminality.

STRUCTURAL CRIMINOLOGY VERSUS INDIVIDUALIST CRIMINOLOGY

The options of those who would control true criminality are limited. The criminals may be incapacitated (including being killed), punished for the sake of retribution or deterrence, or treated by training, psychotherapy, medically, or surgically. None of these approaches can conceivably succeed in sustained reduction of crime rates in a social system (Pepinsky, 1979, 1980). This applies even if one grants the Marxist premise that it is the rich and powerful who need to be incapacitated for the sake of crime control. Even Marx (1963, originally published in 1843) himself conceded that political revolution alone was insufficient to rid a social system of class oppression and its by-product, crime. Incapacitation of the rich and powerful cannot succeed in ending class oppression unless the revolutionaries themselves are disinclined to achieve wealth and power for themselves. Incapacitation of the rich and powerful itself implies a lust by some to gain power over others. It presages the rise to power of a "new class" (Djilas, 1957) of offenders, not an end to criminality. Conceding the injustice of some persons' profiting from the surplus value of others' labor, giving the profiteers their just deserts implies perpetuation, not control, of crime and criminality.

The common bond between Marxist and liberal criminology fits all too well within the bounds of American ethocentrism. Characteristically, Americans are individualists. If some good is achieved in the social order, Americans assume that some individuals deserve credit and reward for the accomplishment. On the other hand, existence of a social problem is assumed to imply that some persons must be individually to blame. If unemployment is to high, it must be the President's fault. If use of heroin proliferates, some organized crime boss must be responsible. If crime in general proliferates, it must be the doing of some perverse group of offenders. Curing or eliminating social problems is regarded as synonymous with curing or eliminating individual culprits. Identify the culprits, bring them to justice (or perhaps help them to overcome personal deficiencies), and the problem will be solved. This is the common preoccupation of Marxist and liberal criminologists of today. It is scarcely a "radical" perspective.

The antithesis of individualist criminology is a perspective that assumes the dynamics of a social structure to be the source of crime and its control. Of interest to the structural criminologist is what changes in social structure—having impact on the behavior of offenders and nonoffenders alike—affect rates of crime and criminality.

For the structural criminologist, crime and criminal justice are but one aspect of the larger phenomena of disputes and dispute management. When disputes or conflicts among members of a society arise, response varies. Parties to the dispute or conflict can simply *avoid* dealing with the problem—can act as though nothing has happened that calls for any response whatsoever. With or without the aid of third parties, disputants can attempt to *resolve* the dispute—as by mediation or negotiation—with the object of creating a framework for amicable, cooperative future relations through joint effort. Or a dispute can be treated as presenting a case of possible violation of law, in which officials of state are given jurisdiction for *adjudicating* blame or guilt according to law and deciding on an appropriate sanction for a blameworthy party. Administrative, civil, and criminal processes are the alternative adjudicatory processes available to disputants.

Felstiner (1974) has done a neat job of describing these responses and of using anthropology of law literature to begin to suggest the kinds of variation in social structure that might lead to more of one kind of response as opposed to the others. Felstiner draws on the literature to construct two ideal types—the technologically simple poor society (TSPS) and the technologically complex rich society (TCRS)—associating the former with dispute resolution and the latter with adjudication or avoidance. The structural literature, as reflected in Felstiner's work, suggests that crime and criminal justice processing of cases grow with technological complexity and some concomitants, including residential mobility, occupational mobility, attenuation of kinship ties, division of labor, and bureaucratic growth. Some theorists (e.g., Black, 1976; Black and Baumgartner, 1978; Pepinsky, 1976, 1980) disagree with Felstiner's premise that except by avoidance (or as Felstiner puts it, by "lumping it") the growth of crime and crime control cannot be retarded in the TCRS, but they share Felstiner's premise that structural elements other than technological complexity and material prosperity must be changed if crime and criminal justice processing of cases are to be contained.

Within this framework, proposals for change emerge from a social systems perspective, first outlined for criminologists by Wilkins (1964). As in systems analysis of plane crashes—considering, for instance, whether requisite changes in pilot training or in arrangement of instrumentation would be easier to effect—crime control proposals derived from a structural framework take the form of considering options as to which elements of a crime production system might most readily be disturbed. Thus, for instance, Black and Baumgartner (1978) propose depolicing, Danzig and Lowy (1975) establishment of Kpelle-style moots, and Pepinsky (1976) disincentives to occupational mobility. Implicit in each of these proposals is the premise that it is unnecessary and even counterproductive to identify criminals or potential criminals as a prelude to implementing crime control measures. The very enterprise of laying blame for crime at the feet of individuals is itself a force producing crime. From this perspective, the fundamental requisite of crime control is to provide citizens with alternatives to thinking of disputes as matters of someone's being at fault, or to thinking of resorting to state fault-finding apparatus for handling their problems with others (Kennedy, 1970).

At the present time, this perspective represents a radical departure from the ethos of American society in general and of criminology in particular. For the time being, structuralism has supplanted Marxism as criminology's antithesis.

WHAT NEXT?

From a Hegelian point of view, it is inevitable that structural criminology will be synthesized eventually into a criminological thesis, only to be supplanted by yet another radical antithesis. Let me venture a guess into the future. I foresee that class-free criminology and structural criminology will eventually merge into a social engineering perspective that treats class differences including offender/nonoffender differences as irrelevant to the study of crime and its control. One may suppose that in the process Americans and other citizens of industrialized nations will develop a body of applied knowledge with which substantial success in crime control is achieved. At that point, I foresee our discovery that success in crime control perpetuates and even exacerbates social injustice. As disputes are resolved within social groups, we will discover that the terms of resolution of disputes favor some over others, and that unresolved conflict among members of different groups looms larger as ties among group members requisite to dispute resolution strengthen, accentuating the difference between group members and strangers.

Criminological thinkers throughout history have assumed that success in crime control was both a necessary and sufficient condition for achieving social justice. To retributionists, proper crime control measures affirmed the morality of the political order, and hence promoted morality among members of the order. To classical criminologists, proper crime control minimized exercise of coercive power by officials of state and gained citizens' adherence to a social contract. To positivists, proper crime control helped, punished, and restrained those who unjustly hurt others in the social order. To sociological criminologists, proper crime control compensated for social inequities. To Marxist criminologists, incapacitation or liquidation of the bourgeoisie both removed the cause of crime and cured social injustice. By and large, structural criminologists are prone to assume that bureaucratic crime control efforts are unjust and that use of dispute resolution alternatives promotes just outcomes of conflict as it controls crime.

As a structural criminologist myself, I agree that criminal justice processing of cases is inherently unjust and hence that structural crime control is a necessary condition for promoting social justice. I fear, however, that successful crime control is not a sufficient condition for the establishment of social justice. The next radical breakthrough in criminology will come when effective crime control and promotion of social justice are distinguished, when it is recognized that promotion of social justice requires something beyond successful crime control. But before this idea can become empirically grounded, social engineers of crime control must begin to achieve results. The challenge for social justice criminologists of the future will be to conceive how to promote social justice without sacrificing gains in crime control.

THE PLACE OF THE RADICAL IN CRIMINOLOGY

Above all, criminologists are united in their concern for how people cope with fear of one another. Even criminal psychopaths, thought not to fear others where normals would, are a source of concern because of the fear and jeopardy they cause others (Hare, 1970). A broad range of criminologists infer that much crime or delinquency can be traced to fears with which offenders do indeed have to cope, as in Merton's (1957: 131-194) notions about outcomes of fear of social failure. The gamut of ideas about how to respond to crime and criminality, from retribution to structural change, implies responses to *fear* of crime and criminality. On the whole, the calling of criminology is to articulate fears of people in their societies and to analyze alternative responses to those fears. In the course of their studies, criminologists are themselves members of social orders trying to cope with their own fears of others.

In figuring out how to cope with fear of others, the other overriding concern of criminologists is with separating legitimate from illegitimate infliction of pain. To many criminologists, for instance, the state ought to have a monopoly over legitimate infliction of pain. Just as surely as the criminologist is concerned with defining boundaries beyond which infliction of pain is illegitimate, the criminologist is apt to develop an investment in defining boundaries within which infliction of pain is legitimate. Criminologists then carry the burden of reconciling legitimization of infliction of pain, or of social intolerance—implicit in their work—with their consciences. The mission of the criminologist is in part to be a party to hurting others by helping us understand how to do so properly, and that enterprise is hard to justify.

Justification takes two forms. One form, like that taken by most of Milgram's (1973) experimental subjects, is to defer to the authority of someone else's statement of how the hurting is to be done. The other is to oppose the range of existing rationalizations of how to do the hurting. The latter form entails a lot greater risk of social rejection than the former, and hence the pressure on criminologists to adhere to conventional or established ideology is tremendous. The establishment can be a school of thought or a person, or as is commonly the case today, a convention about choice of independent and dependent variables and choice of statistical models for finding a central tendency in a data set. In this regard, I was struck by an assertion that a noted Marxist criminologist made to me a little more than a year ago. I had criticized him for being so thoroughly accepting of all of Karl Marx's ideas, and he responded that every self-respecting criminologist needed an authoritative source of axioms to guide his or her work.

I doubt this assertion, and it strikes me that the defining characteristic of the radical criminologist is that she or he grounds axioms in questioning rather than in acceptance of authoritative premises. Even the radical criminologist cannot fail to fall into the trap of legitimizing some boundaries within which infliction of pain is assumed to be legitimate, but the starting point of the radical criminologist, at least, is to regard all time-honored definitions of boundaries as problematic. The social liability the radical criminologist faces is also her or his saving grace: that the radical criminologist's legitimation of infliction of pain carries no more than personal weight. To the extent that criminologists limit themselves to claims of purely personal responsibility or authority for their stands,

Milgram's (1973) findings suggest that they will be restrained and diffident about their ratification of or participation in infliction of pain or social intolerance.

In a larger sense, it behooves even those criminologists who are personally disinclined to take radical stands to provide support and encouragement to those who are so inclined. As a social fact, the capacity of criminologists collectively to contribute to infliction of pain or social intolerance will be more restrained the more substantial the role accorded to radical members of the field. Put another way, the more tolerant criminologists are of diversity in their midst, the more socially tolerant they are likely to be, period. Criminologists could do far worse than committing themselves to setting a cultural example of what form increasing social tolerance could take. This in itself would be a considerable academic and political achievement.

What makes a criminologist radical? Basically, radicalism is a state of mind—an unwillingness to accept what anyone else has said about crime and its control, or about how to study these phenomena, on faith, a determination to make personal experience and choice the explicit, final arbiter even of the presuppositions of one's own study. A result is that any radical criminologist is in substantial disagreement with every other criminologist, including other radical criminologists, at any given time. An important indicator to me that structural criminologists are radicals today is that as far as I can see, every structural criminologist departs in major ways from every other structural criminologist in choice of method, statement of theory, and in priorities for crime control policy. For instance, Felstiner (1974) is unique in formulating his ideal types upon which to ground his theory and in advocating avoidance as a prime mechanism for responding to disputes; Danzing and Lowy (1975) are unique in their advocacy of organizing Kpelle moots in the United States; Black (1976; and with Baumgartner, 1978) is unique in stressing the need for building theory on quantified measures and in recommending application of advanced communications technology to the task of strengthening community ties; Kennedy (1970) is unique in grounding his theory in an analysis of Anglo-American legal history and in the centrality of the role he gives the state in creating crime; Parnell (with Pepinsky, 1978) is unique in the emphasis he lays on the nature of kinship ties; Pepinsky (1976, 1978) is unique in the stress he lays on restricting geographical mobility and on giving social support to criminal justice officials; Wilkins (1977) lays stress on achieving structural change through the setting of procedural guidelines for criminal justice officials.

Some radical criminologists are far ahead of their time. They have gone beyond the issue of how community ties can be strengthened for the sake of crime control, to address the issue of how social justice can be achieved within the new communities. Parks (1977) wrestles with the problem of how respect for authority can be developed among community members without threatening the members with exercise of coercive power. Sullivan (1978) comes close to using poetry to depict how a community might develop a system of mutual aid that would make resort to punishment unnecessary. Tifft (1979) exhorts us to revolutionize our consciousness to define social justice in terms of meeting individual needs instead of thinking in terms of rights or of mutualism. These ideas have antecedents in anarchist literature, but never before has anyone tried to apply the ideas in the field of criminology. Each of these writers has had field experience in the criminal justice system and has done criminological research and teaching. It is particularly courageous of them to go even beyond radical issues of the moment to try to address radical issues of the future. The ground they tread is not empirically charted as it is for the structural criminologists of today. The task of conceptualization they have taken upon themselves is inordinately difficult. Yet they struggle to articulate their views, and serve as the conscience of other radical criminologists of today. They deserve special sympathy and support from other criminologists for daring an undertaking of such enormity.

Radicalism bears no necessary relationship to political extremism. Radicalism implies that one's views are independent of a political continuum. Any radical view is as likely to strike some observers as rightist as it is to strike others as leftist. Once a place on a political spectrum has been established for radical ideas, the ideas have by definition lost their radical nature and become a form of political convention. This is the fate that has befallen Marxist criminologists, and indeed it is ultimately the fate of any radical view that it dies from neglect or loses its radical nature. If the radicalism of a criminologist's views is precious, it is also mortal.

In his brilliant essay on "Science as a Vocation," Weber (1946, originally delivered as a lecture in 1918) declared it to be the fate of all scientific knowledge that it would become obsolete. Perhaps this should be so, but if we grant most criminological knowledge the dignity of calling it "scientific," then the bulk of scientific knowledge in the field survives attempts at empirical refutation. Two recent examples: The belief that offenders can and should be rehabilitated and the belief that criminality can and should in part be explained biologically survive and promise to return to criminological prominence despite the claims by a number of highly competent criminological researchers that the beliefs are empirically untenable.

The scientific fate of becoming obsolete is reserved to radical knowledge. Whether or not such knowledge survives at all, the radicals of a new age are bound to find empirical issues unaddressed and unaccounted for by the radical knowledge of old. To borrow from Kuhn (1962), the progress of criminology can be measured by paradigm shift, from one radical perspective to the next as the science of criminology evolves. The growth of criminological knowledge is not measured so much by what new data reveal is· known, but by what radical analyses of data reveal is *not* known that criminologists of the past had not even conceived of explaining.

Radicalism is vital to the growth of criminology. If radicalism is to have its place in the field, it is vital, too, that criminologists not decieve themselves by confusing radicalism with political extremism.

REFERENCES

BECCARIA, C. (1968) On Crimes and Punishments (trans. by H. Paolucci). Indianapolis: Bobbs-Merrill.

BLACK, D. (1976) The Behavior of Law. New York: Academic.

——— and M. P. BAUMGARTNER (1978) "Self-help in modern society." Yale University. (unpublished)

BONGER, W. (1969) Criminality and Economic Conditions (edited by A. T. Turk). Bloomington: Indiana University Press.

DANZIG, R. and M. LOWY (1975) "Everyday disputes and mediation in the United States: a reply to Professor Felstiner." Law and Society Review 9(Summer): 675-694.

DJILAS, M. (1957) The New Class: An Analysis of the Communist System. New York: Praeger.

DUESTERBERG, T. R. (1979) "The social origins of criminology in nineteenth-century France." Ph.D. dissertation, Indiana University.

DURKHEIM, E. (1951) Suicide: A Study in Sociology (trans. by J. A. Spaulding and G. Simpson). New York: Macmillan.

FELSTINER, W. F. (1974) "Influences of social organization on dispute processing." Law and Society Review 9 (Fall): 63-94.

GODWIN, W. (1971) "Enquiry concerning political justice," pp. 3-41 in S. Schatz (ed.) The Essential Works of Anarchism. New York: Bantam.

HARE, R. D. (1970) Psychopathy: Theory and Research. New York: John Wiley.

JOLY, H. (1889) La France Criminelle. Paris: Cerf.

KENNEDY, M. C. (1970) "Beyond incrimination: some neglected facets of the theory of punishment." Catalyst 1 (Summer): 1-37.

KUHN, T. S. (1962) The Structure of Scientific Revolutions. Chicago: University of Chicago Press.

MARX, K. (1963) Karl Marx: Early Writings (trans. and edited by T. B. Bottomore). New York: McGraw-Hill.

MERTON, R. K. (1957) Social Theory and Social Structure. New York: Macmillan.

MILGRAM, S. (1973) Obedience to Authority: An Experimental View. New York: Harper & Row.

PARKS, B. A. (1977) "Power without authority and authority without power: an essay on social control." Presented at the Society for the Study of Social Problems, Chicago, September.

PARNELL, P. and H. E. PEPINSKY (1978) "A case for treating violence and aggression socially rather than biologically." Presented at American Society of Criminology meeting, Dallas, November.

PEPINSKY, H. E. (1980) Crime Control Strategies: An Introduction to the Study of Crime. New York: Oxford University Press.

——— (1979) "The irresponsibility of explaining criminality." Presented at the Academy of Criminal Justice Sciences meeting, Cincinnati, March.

——— (1978) "Communist anarchism as an alternative to the rule of criminal law." Contemporary Crises 2 (July): 315-334.

——— (1976) Crime and Conflict: A Study of Law and Society. New York: Academic.

QUINNEY, R. (1977) Class, State, and Crime: On the Theory and Practice of Criminal Justice. New York: Longman.

ROBISON, S. M. (1973) Can Delinquency Be Measured? Millwood, NY: Kraus Reprint.

ROTHMAN, D. J. (1971) The Discovery of the Asylum: Social Order and Disorder in the New Republic. Boston: Little, Brown.

SELLIN, T. (1938) Culture Conflict and Crime. New York: Russell Sage.

SULLIVAN, D. C. (1980) Corrections in America: The Mask of Love. Toward a Mutual Aid Alternative. Port Washington, NY: Kennikat.

SUTHERLAND, E. H. (1940) "Is 'white-collar crime' crime?" American Sociological Review 5 (February): 1-12.

TANNENBAUM, F. (1938) Crime and the Community. Boston: Ginn.

TARDE, G. (1912) Penal Philosophy (trans. by R. Howell). Boston: Little, Brown.

TIFFT, L. (1979) "The coming redefinitions of crime: an anarchist perspective." Social Problems 26 (April): 392-402.

TITTLE, C. K., W. J. VILLEMEZ, and D. A. SMITH (1978) "The myth of social class in criminality: an empirical assessment of the empirical evidence." American Sociological Review 43 (October): 643-656.

Van Den HAAG, E. (1975) Punishing Criminals: Concerning a Very Old and Painful Question. New York: Basic Books.

WEBER, M. (1946) "Science as a vocation," pp. 129-156 in H. H. Gerth and C. W. Mills (ed. and trans.) From Max Weber: Essays in Sociology. New York: Oxford University Press.

WILKINS, L. T. (1977) "Keynote address." Presented at the Academy of Criminal Justice Sciences meeting, New Orleans, March.

——— (1964) Social Deviance: Social Policy, Action, and Research. Englewood Cliffs, NJ: Prentice-Hall.

WILSON, J. Q. (1975) Thinking About Crime. New York: Basic Books.

WOLFGANG, M. E. and F. FERRACUTI (1967) The Subculture of Violence: Towards an Integrated Theory of Criminology. London: Tavistock.

RONALD L. AKERS is Past President of the American Society of Criminology and Chairman of the Criminology Section of the American Sociological Association. He has held positions in Sociology at the University of Washington and in Criminology at Florida State University. He is currently Professor and Chair of the Department of Sociology at the University of Iowa. His published books include *Deviant Behavior: A Social Learning Approach* (Wadsworth, 1977) and (with Richard Hawkins) *Law and Control in Society* (Prentice-Hall, 1975). He is author and coauthor of numerous scientific and scholarly articles appearing in *Criminology, Journal of Criminal Law and Criminology, Social Problems, American Sociological Review, Social Forces, Law and Society Review,* and other journals. His current research activity is on adolescent drug and drinking behavior and evaluation of juvenile diversion and youth care facilities.

DAVID O. FRIEDRICHS is Assistant Professor of Sociology/Criminal Justice at the University of Scranton. His research interests include the problem of legitimacy as it applies to legal and criminological phenomena, paradigm controversies in criminology, the historical development of deviance and law reform, public perceptions of criminal justice decision-making, and higher education for the police. He has published or presented papers in all of these areas.

C. RONALD HUFF is Associate Professor of Public Administration and Sociology and Director of the Program for the Study of Crime and Delinquency at Ohio State University. He received his Ph.D. in Sociology from Ohio State University in 1974 and held faculty positions at the University of California (Irvine) and Purdue University prior to his current position. He is coauthor (with Ross F. Conner) of *Attorneys as Activists* (Sage, 1979) and is the editor of *Contemporary Corrections: Social Control and Conflict* (Sage, 1977). His research articles have been published in *Sociology and Social Research, Criminology, Urban Affairs Quarterly,* and other scholarly journals.

JAMES A. INCIARDI is Professor and Director, Division of Criminal Justice, University of Delaware. He received his Ph.D. in Sociology at New York University, and has extensive teaching, research, field, and clinical experiences in the areas of substance abuse and criminal justice. Dr. Inciardi was the director of the National Center for the Study of Acute Drug Reactions at the University of Miami School of Medicine, Vice President of Resource Planning Corporation, and Associate Director of Research at the New York State Narcotic Addiction Control Commission. He is currently editor of *Criminology: An Interdisciplinary Journal,* and has published more than seventy books and articles in the areas of substance abuse, medicine, criminology, and criminal justice.

ELMER H. JOHNSON has been a Professor of Criminal Justice and Sociology at the Center for the Study of Crime, Delinquency, and Corrections, Southern Illinois University at Carbondale since 1966. From 1949 to 1966 he was a member of the faculty of North Carolina State University at Raleigh. His doctorate in Sociology was earned at the University of North Carolina. While on academic leave (1958-1960) he served as Assistant Director of the then North Carolina Prison Department. Among his numerous publications are *Crime, Corrections, and Society: An Introduction of Criminology* (4th edition) *and Social Problems of Urban Man.*

CARL B. KLOCKARS is Associate Professor of Criminal Justice at the University of Delaware. He is the author of *The Professional Fence,* a life history of a large-scale dealer in stolen property; editor of *Deviance and Decency,* a collection of essays on the ethics of research with deviant subjects; and is currently working on an ethnographic study of detective-level policing for the Twentieth Century Fund. His other publications include scholarly works on probation and parole, research ethics, and criminological theory. Dr. Klockars has served as a consultant to Law Enforcement Assistance Administration projects on trade in stolen property, white-collar crime, and the management of criminal investigations. He is a graduate of the University of Rhode Island and the University of Pennsylvania.

MILTON MANKOFF is Associate Professor of Sociology at Queens College, City University of New York. He has written in the areas of political sociology, stratification, and deviance theory.

GEOFF MUNGHAM is Senior Lecturer in Sociology, University College, Cardiff. His research interests are primarily in the sociology of law, with particular reference to the study of lay participation in the legal process and the ideas "popular justice" and "socialist legality." He is the coauthor of *Images of Law* and the coeditor of *Working Class Youth Culture,* and *Essays on Law and Society.* He is also an Associate Editor of the *British Journal of Law and Society* and *Contemporary Crises.*

WILLIAM V. PELFREY received his B.A. degree from Auburn University in 1969, his M.S. in Criminal Justice from the University of Alabama in Birmingham in 1975, and his Ph.D. in Criminology from Florida State University in 1978. He has completed a book entitled *The Evolution of Criminology: From Old To New* to be released in 1980. He is presently an Assistant Professor in the Department of Criminal Justice at the University of Alabama in Birmingham.

HAROLD E. PEPINSKY is Associate Professor of Forensic Studies and East Asian Languages and Cultures at Indiana University. He is trained in Chinese language and literature, law, and sociology. In his first book, *Crime and Conflict: A Study of Law and Society* (Academic, 1976), he built a theory of the growth of crime in industrialized society on a comparison of law and social control in the U.S. and in modern China. His second book, *Crime Control Strategies: An Introduction to the Study of Crime* (Oxford University Press, 1980), is the first comprehensive response to the "So what?" question about criminological and criminal justice research. He has published a number of articles and chapters, some of them reprinted, in North America and Europe.

STEPHEN J. PFOHL received his Ph.D. in Sociology at Ohio State University in 1976. He is currently an Assistant Professor at Boston College, where he lectures on social deviance, social control, criminology, and sociological theory. His book *Predicting Dangerousness: The Social Construction of Psychiatric Reality* was published in 1978 by D.C. Heath. His is currently completing a second book, *Social Control and Social Deviance,* for publication with D. C. Heath. Other of his recent publications have focused on child abuse, criminal violence, ethnomethodology, predictions of dangerousness, critical criminology, and the implications of right to treatment litigation. He has also been involved in research on health service delivery for migrant farm workers, served as a full-time evaluation-research consultant for the Ohio Division of Mental Health, and participated in the 1976 court-ordered reclassification of all inmates in the

Alabama prison system. In 1979 he was appointed by the Governor of Massachusetts to chair the state's Juvenile Justice Advisory Committee.

ANNE E. POTTIEGER is Director of a research project on crime and drug use sponsored by the National Institute on Drug Abuse at the University of Delaware, Division of Criminal Justice. Dr. Pottieger is Managing Editor of *Criminology: An Interdisciplinary Journal* and has published in the areas of drug and alcohol abuse, suicide, and criminological theory.

EDWIN M. SCHUR is Professor of Sociology at New York University, and previously taught at Tufts University and Wellesley College. Among his best-known works on crime are *Crimes Without Victims, Our Criminal Society,* and *Radical Nonintervention.* During 1978-1979 he served as Chairperson of the Section on Criminology of the American Sociological Association.

DAVID SHICHOR received his B.A. at the Hebrew University in Jerusalem, his M.A. at California State University, Los Angeles, and his Ph.D. at the University of Southern California. He is currently Associate Professor of Sociology at California State College, San Bernardino. He has published articles, chapters in books, and presented papers at professional meetings mainly in the fields of juvenile delinquency, criminology, penology, and victimology.

STEVEN SPITZER is Associate Professor of Sociology at Suffolk University. He has researched and written in the areas of criminology, deviance, criminal justice, and the sociology of punishment and has edited Volumes 2 and 3 of *Research in Law and Sociology.* He will be spending 1979-1980 as a Fellow in Law and Sociology at Harvard Law School.

JACKSON TOBY is Professor of Sociology and Director of the Institute for Criminological Research at Rutgers College. He is particularly interested in cross-national studies of (1) the causes of criminality and (2) the differential effectiveness of societal responses to it.

AUSTIN T. TURK is Professor of Sociology and Criminology at the University of Toronto. He received his Ph.D. from the University of Wisconsin in 1962, has been chair of the criminology section of the American Sociological Association, is a past president of the North Central Sociological Association, and is currently on the editorial boards of *The*

American Sociologist and *Contemporary Crises*. In addition to articles in sociology and criminology journals, he has written *Criminality and Legal Order* (1969) and *Legal Sanctioning and Social Control* (1972). A book on political criminality and political policing is to be published soon, and another on the conflict perspective in sociology is nearing completion. Other major works in progress include a comparative analysis of legal control in America and South Africa, and a study of differential risks in the criminalization process.

FRANKLIN P. WILLIAMS III is an Assistant Professor of Criminal Justice at the Criminal Justice Center at Sam Houston University. Previously a member of the research faculty at the School of Criminology, Florida State University, and a professor at the Rochester Institute of Technology, he has a Ph.D. in Criminology. His experiences in the criminal justice system include a period as chief of law enforcement and corrections at a large military base and a year spent in research investigation of a West Coast criminal justice system. His major interests and writings include criminological theory, discretion in the criminal justice system, and the police.

LAURIN A. WOLLAN, JR., has degrees from Princeton (A.B.), University of Chicago (J.D.), and University of Illinois (M.A.P.A.), with further graduate study at Georgetown University; a nonacademic career of government and corporate work at various levels of policy analysis, including the Department of Justice's Office of Policy and Planning; and an academic career of teaching political science, business, and criminology. Recent articles include "Lawyers in Government—'The Most Serviceable Instruments of Authority' " in the March/April 1978 issue of *Public Administration Review*.